THE
BLACK CHURCH
IN
AMERICA

THE
BLACK CHURCH
IN
AMERICA

EDITED BY

HART M. NELSEN

RAYTHA L. YOKLEY

ANNE K. NELSEN

BASIC BOOKS, INC., PUBLISHERS

NEW YORK   LONDON

Contents

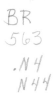

THE
BLACK CHURCH
IN
AMERICA

Introduction

The Black Church: An Overview

This book of readings has been designed for use in courses in sociology of religion. We would hope, however, that scholars and students in such related areas as black studies would find it of use as well. This volume is at least partially an outgrowth of the frustration we have experienced when trying to gather information on the black church, whether in working with students in directed studies or in preparing a research proposal to study the impact of religious attitudes and commitment on the political involvement of black people in the larger community. It is curious that though it has been argued that the Negro church antedates the Negro family (see, for example, Chapter 2 by W. E. Burghardt Du Bois) and that it is generally acknowledged to be, for better or worse, the center of the black community, the black church has received so little concentrated attention from sociologists. We have found that most texts on sociology of religion or on minority groups give the black church only cursory treatment at best. When the subject is covered at all, the author usually refers to a handful of older works[1] which, though useful, hardly reveal the extent of the partisan debate or the significant research that has centered on the black church. It is our hope that this selection of readings will provide the reader with the necessary background information and whetted appetite for further explorations in black religion.[2]

After countless orderings of this and other material, we have divided the material into four different areas. Because some of the selections refused to fit perfectly in any one of the divisions, we made the over-all continuity of the volume the final arbiter in decisions of placement. In Part I, Clifton Brown's profile, Chapter 1, "Black Religion—1968" should alert the reader to those elements of the early church that continue to plague or sustain institutionalized black religion today. W. E. B. Du Bois and Booker T. Washington in Chapters 2 and 3, respectively, offer conflicting estimates of the reality and potentiality of the church for a people in retreat before the forces of racism. In Chapter 4, "Africanisms in Religious Life," Melville J. Herskovits presents his much debated theory on Africanisms in the culture of black Americans. The origin and function of the black church in pre-Civil War days is covered in Chapters 5, 6, and 7, by the works of Winthrop D. Jordan, Kenneth M.

Stampp, and Richard C. Wade, respectively. The selection by James Cone on black theology and black power is one of those that eluded easy categorization, and the reader may want to see his remarks on the historical church.

In Part II we have tried to collect a variety of viewpoints on the traditional black Protestant church as it appears in different settings. W. E. B. Du Bois, Gunnar Myrdal, and Charles S. Johnson, in Chapters 8, 9, and 10, respectively, take a generally critical view of the church as a social and religious institution as it appears in a northern city at the turn of the century and in the cities and rural areas just prior to World War II. Chapter 11, Hylan Lewis's study of the church in a small southern milltown, provides an in-depth analysis of the religious and social functions of the post-World War II church that has seldom been equaled in black church studies. Chapter 12, by Vattel Daniel, suggests that the distinctions noted by Du Bois at the turn of the century had become highly elaborated class divisions within the metropolitan black churches by World War II. The last three Chapters in Part II examine the traditional church in modern American society. In Chapter 13 E. Franklin Frazier condemns the church as a conservative force in the integration of black Americans into the mainstream of American life; Kenneth B. Clark, in Chapter 14, expands Frazier's argument and suggests that the black people have given their allegiance to an institution that wields little power in American society. In Chapter 15 Gary T. Marx attacks the question latent throughout these works, namely: Does the "established" church promote or actually discourage social action for the good of the black community?

Since World War I, increasing numbers of black Americans (whether from the cities, country, or newly arrived from the West Indies) have rejected the traditional religion of the typical black Protestant church and have attempted to build more relevant alternatives. In Part III Arthur Fauset's discussion of the reform potential of the cult movements (Chapter 16) provides a theoretical backdrop for the following descriptions of specific cults and sects. In Chapter 17 Hadley Cantril and Muzafer Sherif's description of the Father Divine movement suggests important aspects of the millennial response. Chapter 18, Howard M. Brotz's study of the black Jews, reveals the beliefs of an early black nationalist cult, and C. Eric Lincoln, in Chapter 19, focuses on the protest aspect of the better known Black Muslim movement. The concept of cult and sect as revitalization movements within black religion is applied to the Black Muslims and to the sectarian storefront churches by James H. Laue in Chapter 20 and Ira E. Harrison in Chapter 21. Perhaps most intriguing of all are those black Christians who have opted for the formalism of Roman Catholicism. In Chapter 22 Joe R. Feagin analyzes the trends and reasons for this phenomenon.

Part IV rather ambitiously encompasses the ministry and the black power movement. Inasmuch as the leadership (or nonleadership) of the ministry has always been crucial to the role assumed in the community, we felt that the two subjects should be treated together. Chapter 23, an assessment of the Negro church and a highly critical evaluation of the black preacher, is from the important Gunnar Myrdal study. In Chapter 24 W. E. B. Du Bois and Monroe N. Work suggest that the black ministry was well into a prestige crisis less than four decades after the Civil War. The declining appeal of the ministerial profession is reflected in the recruitment difficulties of the seminaries. Walter G. Muelder, in Chapter 25, presents a cogent discussion of the weakness that this trend reveals in the entire complex of black religious attitudes and church structure. The black ministry is no more monolithic, however, than the church itself, and Chapter 26, Ronald L. Johnstone's study of leadership styles among black preachers in Detroit, indicates the potentials and limits of dynamic leadership by the ministry. Johnstone's survey also serves as an introduction to the succeeding readings, which focus on the growing involvement of black ministers in political action and the black power movement. Chapter 27, by Benjamin Mays and Joseph Nicholson, argues that the black preacher is one of the freest individuals in the nation and that the development of a prophetic Christianity may well be his responsibility. Chapter 28, "Letter from Birmingham Jail," should give the reader insight into the goals and methods of the late Martin Luther King, Jr., a Negro preacher who in many ways embodied the ideal envisioned by Mays and Nicholson. In Chapter 29 Joseph R. Washington argues that there must be a new black church that can mold the loyalty of the masses into a unity that will hold until the last barrier to total freedom has been broken. This belief in a socially involved church is seconded in the call to arms by the National Committee of Black Churchmen (Chapter 30). Gayraud S. Wilmore, Jr., and James H. Cone (in Chapters 31 and 32, respectively) register their convictions that black consciousness is the only approach that can save the church as an institutionalized power within the community. The concluding chapter—of Part IV and of the book itself—shows black power in action through the new black ministry of Albert Cleage, Jr.

Religiosity and the Church

In the remainder of this introduction we hope to accomplish two things. First, we hope to present an empirical view of the religiosity of black Americans. Second, we shall offer a brief theoretical interpretation of the black church that we believe may suggest some research possibilities.

The distribution of Negroes[3] and whites by religious affiliation may be found in Table 1. There prevails a persistent stereotype of the Negro as an

TABLE 1

Religion Reported for Persons Fourteen Years Old and Over, by Color and Sex, for the United States: Civilian Population, March 1957

Religion	White		Nonwhite	
	% Male	% Female	% Male	% Female
Protestant	62.4	65.1	85.4	89.4
Baptist	(15.1)	(15.2)	(59.1)	(62.0)
Lutheran	(7.9)	(7.7)	(0.3)	(0.2)
Methodist	(13.1)	(14.1)	(17.0)	(17.5)
Presbyterian	(5.8)	(6.4)	(1.0)	(0.8)
Other Protestant	(20.5)	(21.7)	(8.0)	(8.9)
Roman Catholic	27.8	27.9	6.4	6.6
Jewish	3.6	3.6	–	0.1
Other religion	1.3	1.2	1.5	1.5
No religion	4.0	1.3	5.4	1.7
Religion not reported	0.9	0.9	1.3	0.7
	100.0	100.0	100.0	100.0

Note: Percent not shown where less than 0.1.

Source: Bureau of the Census, Current Population Reports, Series P-20, No. 79, February 2, 1958.

exceedingly religious individual with a penchant for emotional forms of religious expression. E. T. Krueger's comments on black religion are an extreme example. Krueger prefers the word "feeling" for emotion, commenting that the Negro "prefers in religious expression to submerge himself in the engulfing waves of ecstatic feeling produced in the religious crowd." The elements of Negro religion, for Krueger, include "spontaneity, expressiveness, excitement, rhythm, interest in the dramatic, and love of magic." If such accounts were true—and they have little truth—one explanation (as Krueger himself notes) would be the heavy concentration of Negro religious affiliation among the Baptists and Methodist, which in the South have been traditionally revivalistic.[4]

Perhaps the outstanding American community study in the sociology of religion (and one that does much to undermine these stereotypes on black religion) is that conducted by Gerhard Lenski in Detroit during the summer of 1958. We are summarizing some of the observations on the black churches that occur throughout his *The Religious Factor*,[5] because we have based many of our own predictions for our analysis of Gallup Poll data on his perceptions. The general point is that only in devotionalism do Negroes appear to be more religious than whites, according to Lenski's data.[6] When it comes to belief or attendance, Negroes rank between white Catholics and white Protestants and are closer to the latter.

Lenski concentrated his attention on the influences of memberships in groups (degrees of group involvement) and of religious commitments (religious orientations). The degree of group involvement had two measures: associational involvement in the socioreligious group (measured by frequency of attendance at religious services and meetings) and communal involvement (the degree to which the individual's primary relations were limited to his own socioreligious group). Religious orientations also had two measures: doctrinal orthodoxy (assent to prescribed doctrines) and devotionalism (frequency of prayer and seeking God's will).[7]

It is not surprising to find that the communal bond was extremely strong for the Negro Protestant group (as it was also for the Jewish group), whereas it was medium for white Catholics and white Protestants. Only white Catholics had stronger associational bonds than the Negro Protestants. Lenski found that nearly 40 percent of his black sample attended worship services every Sunday and only 5 percent never went to church. Attendance was higher for middle-class than working-class black Protestants.[8]

Religious orthodoxy was most embraced by the Catholic respondents, followed at some distance by Negro Protestants and then by white Protestants. On devotionalism, however, slightly more than two thirds of Negro Protestants ranked high, followed by white Catholics (note quite half) and white Protestants (not quite one third). From his analysis Lenski concludes that "there is likely to be a decline in both doctrinal orthodoxy and in devotionalism in the next generation" for Negro Protestants.[9]

Lenski was also interested in the relationship between the churches and the economic convictions of the believers. He had expected to find an inverse relationship between Negro church involvement and the spirit of capitalism. To his surprise, the relationship was positive. He concluded that "such interaction as occurs among members of the working class within the context of the Negro Protestant churches in Detroit facilitates and stimulates identification with economic values long linked with the *middle class.*"[10]

Lenski's study underlines the importance of the black church to the black community; in addition it suggests that Negro Protestants have been arbitrarily placed by others near the emotional end of the religious expression continuum. There is obviously a need to examine Lenski's findings on a national scale.

In our general exploration of the religiosity of black Americans, we shall first turn to church attendance. Here there is somewhat conflicting evidence.

Norval Glenn has used the responses to a 1957 Gallup Poll to examine white-black differences in attendance; and he found no difference between white and nonwhite Protestants (white Catholics were much more likely to have attended a religious service during the past seven days). Glenn concludes that "there is some [other] evidence that . . . Negroes . . . have stronger religious interests than whites."[11] In comparing attendance for black and white Baptists, however, Lazerwitz found higher rates for the former.[12]

As part of a larger study we have begun analysis of data on black religiosity and attitudes toward society.[13] Using Gallup Poll data, our examination has so far included religious attendance, and the questions of whether the respondents believe that religion is losing its influence, or report having had a religious experience. In the case of religious service attendance—using twelve Gallup studies dating from June 1954 through April 1968—it appears that white Catholics have the highest attendance rate, followed by nonwhite Protestants and white Protestants. The median percentage figures for the twelve studies for attendance within the past seven days are 72 percent for white Catholics, 46 percent for nonwhite Protestants, and 38 percent for white Protestants. Catholics always evidenced the highest attendance, whereas in two of the studies, nonwhite Protestants and white Protestants reversed the positions held when all the studies were combined. When we reran the same data using the responses from nonfarm blue-collar workers, we found the same rankings and comparable percentages. It should be noted, however, that the 1969 Gallup data supported Glenn's finding of approximately equal attendance among white and nonwhite Protestants (with white Catholics maintaining their higher attendance figure).

After observing that a greater percentage of nonwhite Protestants believed that religion was losing influence in American life, Glenn concludes that this might "reflect a decline in the importance of religion among Negroes relative to its importance among whites."[14] In 1957 nonwhite respondents were most likely to report this loss of influence, followed, in order, by white Protestants and white Catholics. By 1962, however, the order had switched to white Protestant, nonwhite Protestant, and white Catholic; and this order remained for data collected during 1965. Perhaps the new ordering during 1962 and 1965 reflected the achievements (apparent and real) of Martin Luther King, Jr.'s war on white attitudes and discriminatory practices. By 1967 nonwhite Protestants were evidencing the same pessimism that white Protestants had shown in 1965. Real equality seemed as far away as ever, and the civil rights movement based on the nonviolent action advocated by Martin Luther King seemed stalemated. The data are summarized in Table 2. But it should be noted that the meaning of this question is uncertain, especially in any black-white comparisons. When black Americans answer this question are they thinking of

TABLE 2

Responses of White Catholics, Nonwhite Protestants, and White Protestants to the Question: "At the Present Time Do You Think Religion as a Whole Is Increasing Its Influence on American Life or Losing Its Influence?"[a]

Religious Racial Group	Year of Survey	Percent Responding[b]			
		Increasing	Same	Losing	(n)
White	1957	82.9	10.4	6.7	(356)
Catholic	1962	59.2	16.2	24.6	(617)
	1965	48.5	16.8	34.7	(274)
	1967	30.9	16.5	˙52.6	(887)
Nonwhite	1957	52.6	7.5	39.8	(133)
Protestant	1962	36.8	35.8	27.4	(190)
	1965	43.4	18.6	38.0	(113)
	1967	23.4	10.1	66.5	(239)
White	1957	73.2	12.1	14.7	(917)
Protestant	1962	47.2	15.9	36.9	(1657)
	1965	18.2	7.3	74.5	(889)
	1967	22.2	14.3	63.5	(1944)
Total	1957	73.7	11.2	15.1	(1406)
	1962	49.4	17.5	33.1	(2464)
	1965	27.0	10.3	62.7	(1276)
	1967	24.8	14.6	60.6	(3070)

[a]*These are Gallup Poll data collected in March 1957, February 1962, February 1965, and March 1967. We are indebted to the American Institute of Public Opinion and to the Roper Public Opinion Research Center for permission to use these data.*

[b]*No responses and responses of "No Opinion" are deleted in calculating the percentages in this table. Such responses are under 10 percent of the total n; the n's as shown have these responses subtracted.*

their own lives and actions, or are they reacting to the apparent influence of professed religion on the actions of whites? Further, are they viewing religion as the churches, specifically, or more broadly as moral values? Whatever its true meaning, the question does not appear to measure amount of influence. Instead, it may measure perception of change in the religious situation.

Krueger's statement that "religion is to the Negro what music and poetry are to the white man"[15] embodies the stereotype of the religious black man. If the stereotype were based in fact, we should be able to assume that Negroes would be more likely to report having had a religious experience. A February 1962 Gallup study asked: "Would you say that you have ever had a 'religious experience'—that is, a moment of sudden religious insight or awakening?" Answering positively were 14.7 percent of white Catholics, 22.2 percent of nonwhite respondents, and 24.8 percent of white Protestants. The percentages for blue-collar (nonfarm) workers are, in order, 16.6, 18.2, and 27.9. The ranking is the same for farmers. Thus, though black respondents apparently are slightly more likely to attend church than are white Protestants, they resemble whites in their tendency to report religious experiences.

Most analyses of the church tend to assume that the church is to a major degree a voluntary association,[16] though investigators differ as to whether churches should be in any sense termed "formal" associations as well. If our assumptions are correct, and the data reported by Lenski seem to support them—that is, first, that Negro religiosity is comparable to that of white Protestants generally and, second, that there is yet an extraordinary degree of at least nominal fealty to the church among blacks—we suggest that the black church may be much more than just a place to relieve tensions or to achieve status that is denied elsewhere, for this may be as true among lower-class white churches or religious associations.

What we have here is an involuntary (or at least semiinvoluntary)[17] communal organization that resembles the phenomenon of the state church.[18] The Negro church gained its foothold during the period in which slavery was the predominant condition of the black people—in which Christianity and the structure of their religion was intrinsically a part of the whole governmental apparatus. The secular and the religious worlds of the slave were hardly separate. After the Civil War, an attempt was made to throw off the yoke of religious enslavement and secure genuine autonomy in religious matters by forming independent black churches. This attempt, in retrospect, seems to have been little more than a gesture. Numerous observers have noted that as the slaves left formal captivity, the church—their major means of institutional protest—became a captive of white society, the same determining power that had formerly enslaved its members.

Because of its other functions—those so often referred to as escape and status-conferring,[19] its sole supervision of rites of passage, and so forth—the black church was able to become deeply entrenched in the black community. At the same time it served largely as a communication link through which white demands were transmitted to the black community. Too seldom were black demands channeled through the church to the white power structure. As the church developed an increasing vested interest in the status quo and passed up opportunities to lead in the protest movements of its black members, some astute observers began to see it as a ponderous, spiritually gutted structure standing in the way of the realization of black goals. This idea may well have been in the minds of such men as E. Franklin Frazier and Joseph Washington when they urged the abandonment of the traditional church and often warned that it was a conservative force hindering integration. For as so often happens with an established church, it ceases to belong truly to the people it serves and becomes instead an instrument of social control. Our interpretation is that the Negro church, racially segregated as it has been, has not only been an attractive institution, but has benefited from certain external forces, especially white racism and the broad social restrictions on Negroes, in maintaining its hold on the community.

In making these observations, we would like to make two things clear. First, though this may occasionally sound like a highly conspiratorial interpretation, we do not mean to imply that the black church was in any way plotting to subvert its own members; it was as much the victim as the betrayer, as its precarious condition in recent years suggests. The villain can be no other than the racist society in which it has been forced to function. Second, we believe that this period of the black church's existence is fast coming to an end. Especially if the black power movement within the church, such as that led by Reverend Cleage (see Chapter 35) is successful, the church will have made the transition from a dependence on the white determined status quo to a true dependence on the loyalty of the black community and a commitment to serve them.

NOTES

1. For example, John Dollard, *Caste and Class in a Southern Town* (New Haven, 1937); Hortense Powdermaker, *After Freedom: A Cultural Study in the Deep South* (New York, 1939); Allison Davis, Burleigh B. Gardner, and Mary R. Gardner, *Deep South* (Chicago, 1941); and St. Clair Drake and Horace Cayton, *Black Metropolis* (New York, 1945).

2. We would like to suggest other volumes that may profitably be used in conjunction with this book. We had originally intended to include a bibliography. Those currently available, however, are of such caliber that we concluded that duplication would be unnecessary. The reader should consult Nelson R. Burr, *Critical Bibliography of Religion in America*, vol. 4 of James Ward Smith and A. Leland Jamison, eds., *Religion in American Life* (Princeton, 1961), 348-381; Elizabeth W. Miller, comp., *The Negro in America: A Bibliography* (Cambridge, 1966); and Morris I. Berkowitz and J. Edmund Johnson, *Social Scientific Studies of Religion: A Bibliography* (Pittsburgh, 1967). The reader may also wish to use this volume in conjunction with a textbook in sociology of religion, of which there are several good ones available: most recently, N. J. Demerath III and Phillip E. Hammond, *Religion in Social Context* (New York, 1969), and J. Milton Yinger, *The Scientific Study of Religion* (New York, 1970). It may also be desirable to use this volume as a companion to works that consider religion with reference to the white church or to other cultural settings. See, for example, Louis Schneider, ed., *Religion, Culture and Society* (New York, 1964), and Richard D. Knudten, ed., *The Sociology of Religion: An Anthology* (New York, 1967). For a variety of reasons the following books should be useful in gaining a perspective on the role of religion in the experience of black Americans: Talcott Parsons and Kenneth B. Clark, eds., *The Negro American* (Boston, 1965); August Meier and Elliott Rudwick, eds., *The Making of Black America* (New York, 1969); Alphonso Pinkney, *Black Americans* (Englewood Cliffs, N.J., 1969); Charles Y. Glock and Rodney Stark, *Religion and Society in Tension* (Chicago, 1965); Rodney Stark and Charles Y. Glock, *American Piety: The Nature of Religious Commitment* (Berkeley, 1968); Louis Schneider, *Sociological Approach to Religion* (New York, 1970); Thomas F. O'Dea, *Sociology and the Study of Religion* (New York, 1970); Clifton H. Johnson, ed., *God Struck Me Dead: Religious Conversion Experiences and Autobiographies of Ex-Slaves* (Philadelphia, 1969); Bruce Hilton, *The Delta Ministry* (New York, 1969); and Carter G. Woodson, *The History of the Negro Church* (Washington, D.C., 1921).

3. Approximately 95 percent of nonwhites are Negro.

4. E. T. Krueger, "Negro Religious Expression," *American Journal of Sociology*, 38 (July 1932): 25, 29-30.

5. Ibid.

6. Gerhard Lenski, *The Religious Factor*, rev. ed. (Garden City, N.Y., 1963), p. 58.

7. *Ibid.*, pp. 22-26.

8. *Ibid.*, pp. 39-41, 49.

9. *Ibid.*, pp. 57-59.

10. *Ibid.*, pp. 7, 122-123, 131.

11. Norval Glenn, "Negro Religion and Negro Status in the United States," in *Religion, Culture and Society*. ed. Louis Schneider (New York, 1964), pp. 623-639.

12. Bernard Lazerwitz, "Some Factors Associated with Variations in Church Attendance," *Social Forces*, 39 (May 1961): 304.

13. The study is being conducted by Raytha L. Yokley, Hart M. Nelsen, and Thomas W. Madron and is supported by PHS Research Grant No. 1 R01 MH 16573 01 from the National Institute of Mental Health. We are indebted to the American Institute of Public Opinion and to the Roper Public Opinion Research Center, Williams College, Williamstown, Mass., for permission to use the data reported here.

14. Glenn, p. 625.

15. Krueger, p. 25.

16. Those who wish to read further concerning the voluntary association are encouraged to turn to a summary, with helpful references: Nicholas Babchuk and Alan Booth, "Voluntary Association Membership: A Longitudinal Analysis," *American Sociological Review*, 34 (February 1969): 31-45. Earlier, Nicholas Babchuk and Ralph V. Thompson, "The Voluntary Association of Negroes," *American Sociological Review*, 27 (October 1962): 647-655, interpreted the Negro church as a voluntary association functioning to release the Negro from "his restrictive social environment" as well as giving the individual a chance "to win applause and acclaim." These authors note that in a study completed in Lincoln, Nebraska, only 12.5 percent of the Negroes in the sample were not religiously affiliated (and these same were also not members of any voluntary association). They note that "Myrdal contends that the wide-spread participation of Negroes in voluntary associations is mainly pathological." We would tend to agree with the authors that the Negro associational pattern "reveals the lag in the Negro adaptation to modern society." We shall extend the argument to state that the Negro church is more of a state (or involuntary) church than a voluntary association. Our view of the black church assumes greater organization within the black community than has been generally recognized. John D. McCarthy and William L. Yancey, "Uncle Tom and Mr. Charlie: Metaphysical Pathos in the Study of Racism and Personal Disorganization," *American Journal of Sociology*, 76 (January 1971), after critically examining the literature concerning the psychological state of black Americans, suggest that a measure of cohesion and solidarity might well exist because of racial conflict and isolation, especially for working and lower-class Negroes. We believe that the black church is both a product of, and helps contribute to, the communal and personal organization of black Americans. Other observers hold quite different views; for example, see William H. Grier and Price M. Cobbs, *Black Rage* (New York: Basic Books, 1968), pp. 196-197.

17. Jeffrey Hadden, "The House Divided," in *The Church, The University, and Social Policy*, ed. Kenneth Underwood (Middletown, Conn., 1969), pp. 275-291, comments that the (white) church is a voluntary association, "that individuals choose to participate of their own volition, and not because of some compelling external force." He notes that the church was less a voluntary association in the past and that "in some social environments very strong informal pressures are exerted to force conformity to a set of socially prescribed behaviors which include participation in a particular religious group." Let us note here that the black church is less a voluntary than an involuntary association, particularly in the smaller communities, where there can be quite strong formal pressure to at least occasionally attend religious services. As Negroes have migrated to the metropolitan centers, the power of the black church as an involuntary association has lessened; however, in this respect, the black church lags behind the white church.

Hadden describes today's white churches by noting that "leadership in a voluntary association . . . is more precarious than in a nonvoluntary organization." Today's clergy who "are more likely to hold liberal views on a whole range of social issues" are on a collision course with parishioners for whom "religion is a source of *comfort* and *help.*" Let us note that until the involuntary power of the black church began breaking up, the black ministry did not find itself in a precarious position. As Myrdal and others have noted, not until fairly recently have black ministers had to compete for their leadership positions because the bulk of educated Negroes tended to be ministers.

18. A comparison of the black church in America to religion in England would be instructive, though such an attempt would surely be beyond the scope of this introduction. We would call attention to the argument by David Martin, *A Sociology of English Religion* (New York: Basic Books, 1967), pp. 106-109, that religion functions to unite societal members under an "umbrella identification." Furthermore, the contemporary state church validates "local *mores,* prejudices and assumptions just at the point when these are in visible flux." This orientation, we would conclude, makes for conservatism, and the church functions, then, as a vehicle for social control.

Parenthetically, this returns us to Hadden's argument. Perhaps the white church is seen by white members as less a voluntary association and more as an "umbrella identification" and a mechanism for ensuring the continuance of the present forms and rules of the society, whereas white ministers view it as a voluntary association which individuals join if they agree with its values. Liberal white ministers can be seen as attempting to move the church in the direction of being a voluntary association, and herein lies the rub described by Hadden—that to attract and keep members reform goals must be toned down, or that there must be "boundaries that are acceptable to a large proportion of the laity."

In comparing white and black churches, the former tends to be more toward the voluntaristic end of the continuum, whereas the latter tends to be more involuntaristic, or like the state church. White minister-laity differences in perception of the church on this continuum have already been noted. Concerning the black church, there appears to be at this time an increasing number of black ministers who realize that the black church must become a voluntary association with goals oriented to ensuring equality, justice, love, and perhaps even the Christianizing of the white society.

19. A central perspective in sociology of religion has been the church-sect theory, consisting of a typology categorizing religious organizations into "churches" or "sects." Most researchers probably view the sect as a religious organization that is basically withdrawn from society, or on the periphery of society. It is especially in the sect that members of socially depressed strata in society can find "the promise of immediate relief from a sense of general deprivation and meaninglessness"; for a more complete explication see Benton Johnson, "Do Holiness Sects Socialize in Dominant Values?" *Social Forces,* 39 (May 1961): 309-316. The reader who wishes to understand in greater depth the sect-church typology should turn to Benton Johnson, "A Critical Appraisal of the Church-Sect Typology," *American Sociological Review,* 22 (February 1957): 88-92; Benton Johnson, "On Church and Sect," *American Sociological Review,* 28 (August 1963): 539-549; Liston Pope, *Millhands and Preachers* (New Haven, 1942), esp. chap. 7; Bryan R. Wilson, "An Analysis of Sect Development," *American Sociological Review,* 24 (February 1959): 3-15; and N. J. Demerath III, *Social Class in American Protestantism* (Chicago, 1965), pp. 37-43.

In this "theory," too often the characteristics used to provide an operational definition of "sectarianism" have been centered in beliefs or ideologies, for example, attitude toward literalism of the Bible and degree of emotionalism and informality shown in the service. Consequently, Negro religion has been stereotyped as generally sectarian (see our earlier discussion of the work by Krueger).

If, instead, we would concentrate on the involuntary associational characteristic of the church and the voluntary organizational aspect of the sect, we would, as a consequence, identify the black church as generally churchlike. We believe that a greater understanding of black religion would result from viewing it from this standpoint.

PART I

Historical Perspectives

1

BLACK RELIGION—1968

CLIFTON F. BROWN

As Clifton Brown suggests, the year 1968 may well prove to have been a
"watershed" year in the history of the black church. Rival stirrings within
the black religious community, from the appearance of caucuses of black
ministers in predominantly white denominations to the rise of anti-Semitism
among the larger black population, indicated that it would not be easy to
develop the kind of unified support that any new directions for the black
church would require. Dr. Martin Luther King, Jr., was murdered, and the
Rev. Albert Cleage, Jr., published *The Black Messiah.* It was perhaps the end
of one era and the beginning of a new one. The subsequent readings in
Part I should provide the reader with some sense of what the church was in
its earlier periods, the dilemmas it faced even then. An uncertain future is
no new experience for the black church.

I

The death of Dr. Martin Luther King and the publication of *The Black Messiah* by Rev. Albert B. Cleage, Jr.[1]—the former representing the end of a
dream, the latter heralding a new hope: these two events, more than any
others in 1968, represented points of departure for black religion in the
United States. Dr. King, the apostle of nonviolence and the symbol of the
Negro's struggle for admittance to the mainstream of the American experience, had held firm to his vision that black and white Americans could and
must live in harmony. Once again, Dr. King was planning to demonstrate that
nonviolence could successfully attack structural racism and provide a valid

Reprinted from *In Black America, 1968: The Year of Awakening,* edited by Patricia W.
Romero (Pioneer Paperbook; Washington, D.C.: United Publishing Corporation for the
Association for the Study of Negro Life and History, 1969), pp. 345-353, by permission
of The Association for the Study of Negro Life and History.

alternative to violence. During December 1967, King's energies were directed toward another march on Washington. The Poor People's Campaign, as the projected march was designated, would either represent the reaffirmation of nonviolence as the vehicle of change or it would represent the swan song of nonviolence as a means and of total integration as the goal of the civil rights movement. April was chosen as the month in which the march was to take place, and the preparations included the involvement of not only blacks but also other ethnic minorities, as well as poor whites.

In March 1968 King's attention was diverted from the planned march to the more immediate problem of a garbage strike in Memphis, Tennessee. On March 28, Dr. King, in support of the strike, led his last march. Ironically this march, led by the champion of nonviolence, ended as a full-scale riot. Looting and the smashing of windows, death and injury, all followed. Shaken and depressed, King flew to Atlanta, but he returned to Memphis on April 3 to lead a second march. On the following day, Thursday, April 4, in the late afternoon, Martin Luther King was shot. Dr. King died an hour later. He was thirty-nine years old. The senseless assassination of Dr. King was tragic—as is the death of any man. Yet for blacks and all other Americans the real tragedy was just beginning. The violent death of Dr. King prompted more violence, and in over one hundred American cities the black ghettoes erupted in a convulsion of rioting, arson and looting. It was the end of the dream—and the dream was not to be recaptured when the Poor People's Campaign finally arrived in Washington.

Young black militants were demanding more direct and forceful means to ameliorate the black man's plight in America. New concepts, often diametrically opposed to King's concepts of Christian love, nonviolence and integration, surfaced in the black community. "We shall overcome" was being replaced as a slogan with such phrases as "Black is beautiful" and "We are not the Black minority but the chosen few." A social movement was turning into a holy cause. With the publication of Cleage's *The Black Messiah,* the "religiocification" of the revolution began in earnest. The religious slave mentality of "pie in the sky someday" was being ousted, or at least challenged, by a new religious orientation that, among other things, emphasized a black messiah, the concept of a black nation as a chosen people and the recapture of the revolutionary imperative in Christianity. The demand for integration into white society, including the white church, was giving way to the demand for separation. Two concepts, one symbolized by Dr. King's unfailing belief in universal brotherhood and redemptive suffering and the other symbolized by Cleage's annunciation of a black theology; two peoples, black and white; two worlds, the ghetto and suburbia—against this background the events in black religion unfolded in 1968.

II

The foundation of black religion in America, conceived as it was against a background of slavery and segregation, provided the black man with the opportunity to be free while still in chains. Black religion produced a gospel of future hope and a theology of the suffering servant. Yet black religion was also a protest movement—a protest against a system and a society that was deliberately designed to demean the dignity of a segment of God's creation.

In the Negro spirituals one can see both the qualities of a gospel of a future hope and the expression of protest against the evils of slavery. No other spiritual illustrated both of these tendencies better than the familiar "When Israel Was in Egypt's Land." The expression of protest is sounded in the first few lines:

> *When Israel was in Egypt's land,*
> *Let my people go,*
> *Oppressed so hard they could not stand,*
> *Let my people go.*
>
> *Go down, Moses,*
> *Way down in Egypt's land,*
> *Tell old Pharaoh*
> *To let my people go.*

Several lines later, a future hope of freedom is expressed. Although this is couched in physical or political terms, it is no more than a symbol of the hope of a complete union with God in a blissful Kingdom of Heaven:

> *No more shall they in bondage toil,*
> *Let my people go,*
> *Let them come out with Egypt's spoil,*
> *Let my people go.*

The theme of future hope is even more pronounced in the spiritual "Heaven":

> *I got a robe,*
> *You got a robe,*
> *All God's children got a robe.*
> *When we get to heaven*
> *Goin' to put on our robe*
> *And goin' to walk all over God's heaven.*

The expression of protest and future hope became institutionalized with the formation of the Negro churches. The first independent Negro church, the African Methodist Episcopal Church, was formed as a result of a meeting

called by Richard Allen in 1816. In 1820 the African Methodist Episcopal
Zion Church severed all connections with the white Methodist Church and
became a separate church.

The Negro Baptist Church did not become an active force in black religious life until after the Civil War. Within all of these churches, the slave
heritage of future hope and of protest had been carried on. However, as
memories of slavery faded and as the Negro churches increasingly reflected
their white counterparts, the protest tradition receded into the background.
In the 1950's, however, with the emergence of Dr. Martin Luther King and
with the growing prominence of the Southern Christian Leadership Conference, much of the protest tradition was recovered. And the form it now
took was that of nonviolent protest. The freedom that had been voiced in the
spirituals was identified with integration—with equality. When integration
failed to become a reality, the protest began to take on more revolutionary
dimensions. Essentially, the Negro church was faced with the question of
whether the church would maintain a more traditional approach to the protest movement or whether it would attempt to remold its position in the
light of the black power movement.

Within the traditional Negro churches (the African Methodist Episcopal
Church; the African Methodist Episcopal Zion Church; the Christian
Methodist Church; the National Baptist Convention of America; the National
Baptist Convention, U.S.A., Inc.; the Progressive Baptist Convention of
America), 1968 seemed to be the year that crystallized the question of
how these denominations could best relate to and identify with the plight
of the black man in America. Though the final solution was, and is, elusive,
the alternatives seemed relatively clear. The first was the pursuit of the
traditional modes of theological and liturgical expression and the continued
advocacy of integration and nonviolence. The second was the creation of
a black theology and the support of radical or even revolutionary methods
of achieving social change. Needless to say, various positions representing a
combination of these two were also found. But these first two alternatives
have represented the two extremes around which the great debate has
centered.

Speaking before an audience of some 15,000 delegates at the eighty-eighth
annual session of the National Baptist Convention, Inc., in Atlanta, Dr. J. H.
Jackson, president of the convention, defended the traditional approach of
Negro churches to the civil rights problem. Comparing black militants to the
Ku Klux Klan, Dr. Jackson lamented the rejection of integration by many
blacks as the most tragic loss in the history of the civil rights struggle.
Dr. Jackson, an opponent of the principle of civil disobedience, further
observed that because of the rejection of the concept of complete integration,

the Negro is now viewed as "one of the most dangerous threats to the orderly conduct and growth of American life."

Dr. Gardner C. Taylor, retiring president of the Progressive Baptist Convention, during the closing session of their convention in Washington, D.C., in September, challenged the delegates to search for the kernel of reality or truth in the separatist movement in the black community. Dr. Taylor raised the question of whether there might not be some validity in the separatist tendencies of young blacks, and suggested that the separatist movement might "provide an awareness of the black man's particular and peculiar spiritual genius." In the course of his address Taylor linked the United States' involvement in Vietnam with the problems of poverty and racism in America. Throughout his speech Taylor questioned the comfortable concepts, outdated attitudes and ineffective practices of American Christians and challenged his audience to seek new and creative responses to the many social, economic and spiritual problems facing the black American.

Bishop Herbert B. Shaw of the African Methodist Episcopal Zion Church, speaking at one of the sessions of the National Committee of Black Churchmen, in St. Louis in November 1968, dramatically and eloquently stated that the Negro church must seek new directions in the future if it is to remain relevant to the black community and true to its God. One of the suggestions made by Bishop Shaw was that the black church identify itself more closely with its African heritage. The Bishop stated, "We must emphasize more about Egypt than that the Hebrews stayed there. We must seek out our brothers in all of Asia and Africa. We must rediscover the truth concerning the descendants of Hagar's son Ishmael as well as those of Sarah's son Isaac for both are sons of Abraham."

Somewhere between the position of Dr. Jackson on the one hand and the positions of Dr. Taylor and Bishop Shaw on the other, were the majority of the members of the Negro church. For them 1968 was a year of uncertainty. The untimely death of Dr. King raised many doubts, not only about the efficacy of nonviolence as a strategy and integration as an end, but also about the function and ethos of the Negro church. Regretfully, a fear was present that to articulate doubt of the effectiveness of traditional black religion would lead to the complete radicalization of the church and the rejection of all familiar and time-honored practices. This often resulted in an increased, if sporadic, involvement in social action without a critical and meaningful reevaluation of the role the Negro church was to play in the future of the black revolution.

The year also saw a growing interest in what might be called the underground, or forgotten, black church—the storefront church. Whatever their denomination (Pentecostal, Holiness, Baptist, and so on), these churches have been found in ghettoes in all American cities, usually identified with the socioeconomic background of their membership. These religious bodies have been a stabilizing influence in the ghettoes. This influence probably has stemmed from the fact that these churches were organized entirely by blacks and have been close enough to their communicants to be able to minister to their personal needs. Generally, storefront churches have a membership of perhaps fifty or less, and more often than not their pastor has been self-ordained.

These churches also often serve the social needs of their members. Many storefront churches have established impromptu day-care centers for children and have collected food and clothing for anyone in need in the community. One pastor of a storefront church in Washington, D.C., summed up the role of such churches in this way: "Many of the people in the community feel they have been forsaken. Many tell you, 'What's the use, nobody cares about me.' Lots of times the smaller churches can reach them when the larger churches can't because the smaller churches are more down to earth in a way the people understand."

III

If the traditional Negro churches have had doubts as to how to respond to the growing militancy and separatism in the black community, such hesitancy was apparently lacking for the black communicants of the so-called "white" churches. Perhaps this difference of attitude lies in the fact that in the traditional Negro churches the power structure has always been black, and if their modes of worship, their theology and attitude toward social action reflected traditional Christianity, it has been, at least, through their own choice. In the case of black communicants of white churches, however, their mode of worship and their theology have reflected a system imposed on them by a hierarchy in which their race has often not been represented, and by a laity of which they have constituted a minority. For the black clergy in predominately white denominations, the problem of racism has been most obvious. Often black clergymen have a second-class status. They often earn less than their white colleagues, and generally they are kept with black congregations, and in the hierarchies they are relegated, if included at all, to token positions. Perhaps most significant is the charge raised by black clergymen that the white church has been more concerned with protecting the interests of the middle class than with its ministry to the poor.

Partly because of inability to accomplish much within the regular channels of these churches and partially in response to a growing sense of black identity, "black power" began to emerge in white churches in 1967. By early 1968 an unofficial black caucus had even been formed in the Roman Catholic Church.

The real significance and potential resulting from the formation of these black caucuses did not really become obvious until the meeting of the Second Annual Committee of Black (formerly Negro) Churchmen in St. Louis, October 29 through November 1, 1968. Present were leaders of all the traditional Negro churches as well as the various black caucuses: the Black Catholic Clergy Caucus, representing fifty-seven of the nation's 130 black Catholic priests; Black Churchmen of the American Baptist Convention; the Coordinating Committee of Black Lutheran Clergymen, formed in May by fifty-six of the eighty-two black ministers in America's major Lutheran branches; the Black Caucus of the Unitarian-Universalist Association; Black Methodists for Church Renewal, representing 300 black ministers, laymen, and bishops; members of the United Presbyterian Church; and the inter-denominational Association for Black Seminarians.

The radicalization within the membership of the committee was evident in the topics and tones of the 300 or so delegates as they discussed many issues in denominational caucuses, workshops, and general sessions. St. Louis alderman Joseph W. B. Clark seemed to capture the mood of the delegates when he said, "We must now reverse this machinery and become black missionaries to the white community, because the Negro problem is not the problem; the problem is the white community."

The separatist tendencies manifested at the St. Louis meeting were the result of the growing cynicism of the delegates toward the white Christian response to the needs and aspirations of the black churchmen. Many delegates expressed the opinion that there was no justification for black churchmen participating in predominately white churches if those churches were not willing to involve themselves in the plight of black people. Hayward Henry, president of the Black Unitarian Causus, clearly indicated the possibility of a separatist movement: "Black churchmen are putting white churches on notice that old paternalistic relationships will not continue. Black people can't stay in mainly white denominations if those groups can't begin to deal with racism and distribution of power. Yes, it is still an open question, but if whites don't answer positively, it could look pretty bad."

Pressures brought by the caucuses within their denominations met with varying degrees of success. The general assembly of the Unitarian-Universalist Association, meeting in late May in Cleveland, voted its Black Affairs Council a budget of $1 million for the next four years. The caucus will receive $250,000 each year and will decide how the money is to be spent. The Methodist Church in October set aside $46,000 for Negro church aid. In

May 1968 the Protestant Episcopal Church approved grants totaling $553,497 to twenty-eight community organizations that represented the interests of minority peoples.

Dr. Cleage's church, the Shrine of the Black Madonna, a congregation of the United Church of Christ, has illustrated two growing tendencies of black congregations in predominately white denominations. The Shrine has shown an almost complete freedom in adapting the traditional symbols of worship to its own needs. For example, above the altar a black madonna and child is depicted in a thirty-foot-high mural. Perhaps more significantly, the Shrine has actively engaged itself in the concerns of the community. The congregation has opened a cooperative supermarket, a clothing center catering to Afro-American clothing, and a gasoline station.

The year not only witnessed the mushrooming of the black caucus movement, but also saw black caucus strategy move beyond national and denominational dimensions. The formation of the Association of Black Seminarians and the caucus of the Fourth Assembly of the World Council of Churches had broad implications for blacks within predominantly white religious structures. Black seminarian caucuses, beginning at Princeton Seminary, quickly spread to many northeastern theological schools. One such caucus, the Black Seminarians of Greater Boston, sponsored the Consultation on the Black Church which was held at Boston University School of Theology on November 6-9, 1968. The consultation, which was national in scope, gave black seminarians at predominantly white schools an opportunity to examine in depth some of the presuppositions that undergird theology in the black church and to discuss how curricula at predominantly white seminaries could better relate to black institutions—historically, theologically, and sociologically.

On July 17, 1968, at the fourth assembly of the World Council of Churches, meeting in Uppsala, Sweden, Bishop Joseph H. Johnson, speaking for the black caucus, rose to protest that only two blacks were among the twenty-one Americans nominated to the council's policy-making central committee. Four black clergymen chosen by the caucus were proposed as substitutes for whites on the list.

The climate for such a move by Bishop Johnson had been set the preceding day, when black novelist James Baldwin addressed the 2,200 delegates and visitors attending the council. Indicting the Church for its racist tendencies and perversion of the teachings of Christ, Baldwin warned, "If you are born under the circumstances in which black people are born, the destruction of the Christian churches, as presently constituted, may not only be desirable but necessary." Though Baldwin's remarks offended some delegates, others, at the conclusion of his speech, gave him a standing ovation.

Determined not to be overtaken by the events occurring in black Protestant circles and feeling that their church had failed to deal adequately with the needs, particularly in ghetto areas, of black people, the Black Catholic Clergy Caucus, composed of priests attending the unofficial Catholic clergy conference on the interracial apostolate in Detroit in mid-April of 1968, denounced the Catholic Church in the United States as "primarily a white racist institution." The caucus, in a list of demands, asked that efforts be increased to recruit Negroes for the priesthood and that a department be established to deal with the Church's role in the black people's struggle for freedom. This type of militant stance by black Catholic clergy was not an isolated incident but in fact represented a trend. As early as February, seven black priests in the Roman Catholic Archdiocese of Chicago had charged that the Church had followed rather than led the demands for the fulfillment of legitimate black aspirations. In the paper stating their position, the priests made recommendations which were similar to the demands of the black priests attending the Detroit conference.

Even within the Roman Catholic religious orders, generally the last organs of the Catholic Church to feel the impact of social change, Black consciousness made itself felt. Indicative of this new spirit was the First National Black Sisters' Conference held at Mt. Mercy College in Pittsburgh. The week-long conclave was attended by some 150 black nuns from seventy-six religious communities. The nuns, often wearing "I am proud to be black" buttons, sought to determine their responsibility to their fellow blacks, to their Church and to their individual religious communities.

IV

Among the most ominous developments in race relations in 1968 were the charges and countercharges of anti-Semitism and white racism that were hurled by black militants and Jews at each other. New York City became the focal point of the growing tensions between black militants and Jews, although such tensions existed in practically every major American city. Many reasons have been given for this. Fear resulting from competition between Jews and blacks for dominance in local neighborhoods has been viewed as one cause. Another possible factor has been the growing presence of blacks in such fields as social work and teaching, fields which have attracted large numbers of Jews. Because of the practice of compensatory hiring to benefit blacks, Jews have found themselves threatened economically.

Another important consideration is the fact that many Southern blacks, like many conservative white Protestants, have had a fundamentalist Christian background. Indicative of this type of background was the concept of the Jews as a people guilty of deicide. Supplementing this heritage has been the fact of economic resentment. In ghetto after ghetto, the storekeeper, the welfare worker, and the landlord have been Jewish. In some instances, the Jewish merchant and landlord have been guilty of overpricing merchandise and of rent exploitation. For many blacks, these men have not been viewed as merely individuals but often as "Jew landlord" and "Jew merchant." The obvious consequence is that the hatred of an individual has been transformed into a hatred of a race.

Finally, as more black militants identified with the Muslim religion, there came the traditional Muslim hostility toward the Jew. This tendency was seen when many militants supported the Arabs in their war with Israel.

The tension between blacks and Jews broke into the open over the decentralization of the Ocean Hill-Brownsville school district in New York. After several Jewish teachers were transferred from their local school, the United Federation of Teachers, comprised largely of Jewish teachers, called a strike. The result was a thirty-six day boycott of classes in three separate city-wide walkouts. Negro parents of school children reacted vigorously, denouncing the striking teachers as "Jew pigs" and carrying signs calling Hitler the "Messiah."

These tensions have troubled both Jewish and black leaders. Black clergymen have been particularly active in the attempt to heal the breach between their community and the Jewish community. In December 1968, in New York, thirteen black ministers issued a statement in which they said: "We decry and denounce any statements emanating from the black community that bear the slightest hint of anti-Semitism. Any word of this kind in no way reflects the attitude of our people. Any person who has concluded that a tide of anti-Semitism is sweeping the black community is terribly naïve." They went on to say that such statements were the product of "exploiters of a minute, minority point of view."

Later in the same week about 200 rabbis and over twenty black ministers from New York City met in an effort to establish an open dialogue between the two groups. In a joint statement issued after the meeting, Rev. Calvin O. Pressly, chairman of the Interfaith City-Wide Coordinating Committee against Poverty, and Rabbi Henry Siegman, executive vice-president of the Synagogue Council of America, observed that although the two communities often had diverse interests, such differences are "no cause for pain or alarm as long as we retain the ability to discuss these differences with one another and to work toward compromises which do not deny the fundamental hopes and aspirations of our respective communities."

V

The trends in black religion in 1968 have indicated, by their nature, by their complexity, and by the manner in which they have found expression, the problem areas or weaknesses of the black religious experience in America. The most crucial of these areas has been denominationalism. This problem existed in both of the chief divisions of the black church—the traditional Negro church and the black membership of predominantly white churches.

The bulk of the black laity belongs to the traditional Negro church bodies. The membership of these denominations comes from every economic, social, and educational level of society. The broad spectrum from which the traditional Negro church draws its membership indicates both its ability to accommodate the diverse elements of black society and its potential to act as spokesman for the black community. Yet because of the nature of the Negro Church, it speaks with many voices and, as with the tower of Babel, confusion and chaos everywhere abound. The Negro church will only be able to assume a forceful and meaningful leadership role in the black community when it is able to speak with one voice.

It was among the black membership (particularly the clergy) of mainly white churches that the most vocal element of black religion was found in 1968. The black caucuses were the agents of this. Yet these caucuses represented only 2 million of the 22 million black church members in the United States. Consequently the indictments, the challenges, and the innovative schemes of the black caucuses lacked the broad power base by which they could have assumed a leadership role in black religion. Furthermore, the black caucuses, too, have often spoken in different voices, reflecting the sad fact that, as in the traditional Negro churches, denominationalism has created barriers which prevent concerted action on common problems.

The social and economic status of the black membership of predominantly white denominations also prevents the caucuses from assuming a leadership role in the black church. With the possible exception of the Roman Catholic Church, black membership in these churches comes from the middle class, a minority group in the black community. And although the middle-class black is interested in and concerned about the economic and social plight of his less fortunate black brother, he is not always able to empathize completely with him. Even when he is able to empathize and to act constructively, the programs initiated often fail because the ghetto black resents aid from someone he considers a deserter—the black middle-class person living in suburbia.

The significance of this, and the great challenge for 1969 and succeeding years, is that until the fragmentation in the black church ceases, duplication of projects, competition between in-groups, misunderstanding, and confusion relating to methods and goals will continue. A unified leadership with the general backing of the black community is the greatest need and the only hope for the survival of the black church as a meaningful expression of the black experience in America.

2

OF THE FAITH OF THE FATHERS

W. E. BURGHARDT DU BOIS

W. E. B. Du Bois—scholar, writer, and activist in the defense of the human dignity and civil and political rights of the black man—wrote this essay on the primary institutional expression of the "inner ethical life" of the Negro people at a critical period in their development. In its earliest stages the church had been the first Afro-American institution Later, when it became first superficially and then internally Christian, it remained the most important of Negro spiritual and social institutions, antedating, as it did for so many, the Negro home. By the opening of this century, however, with the wholesale lynchings of black people, the effective political disfranchisement and civic silencing of the black community in the South and elsewhere, Du Bois saw that the church faced a spiritual crisis comparable to that of its members, who were forced to ive ir ~onflicting worlds as Negroes and as Americans. Could the black church provide a new religious ideal, or were an anti-Christian radicalism or a hypocritical subserviency the only ethical alternatives in white America?

Dim face of Beauty haunting all the world,
Fair face of Beauty all too fair to see,
Where the lost stars adown the heavens are hurled,—
There, there alone for thee
May white peace be.

. . .

Beauty, sad face of Beauty, Mystery, Wonder,
What are these dreams to foolish babbling men
Who cry with little noises 'neath the thunder
Of Ages ground to sand,
To a little sand.

Fiona Macleod

It was out in the country, far from home, far from my foster home, on a dark Sunday night. The road wandered from our rambling log house up the

Reprinted from *The Souls of Black Folk, Essays and Sketches* (Chicago: A. C. McClurg & Company, 1903), chap. 10.

stony bed of a creek, past wheat and corn, until we could hear dimly across the fields a rhythmic cadence of song—soft, thrilling, powerful, that swelled and died sorrowfully in our ears. I was a country schoolteacher then, fresh from the East, and had never seen a Southern Negro revival. To be sure, we in Berkshire were not perhaps as stiff and formal as they in Suffolk of olden time; yet we were very quiet and subdued, and I know not what would have happened those clear Sabbath mornings had some one punctuated the sermon with a wild scream, or interrupted the long prayer with a loud amen! And so most striking to me, as I approached the village and the little plain church perched aloft, was the air of intense excitement that possessed that mass of black folk. A sort of suppressed terror hung in the air and seemed to seize us—a pythian madness, a demoniac possession, that lent terrible reality to song and word. The black and massive form of the preacher swayed and quivered as the words crowded to his lips and flew at us in singular eloquence. The people moaned and fluttered, and then the gaunt-cheeked brown woman beside me suddenly leaped straight into the air and shrieked like a lost soul, while round about came wail and groan and outcry, and a scene of human passion such as I had never conceived before.

Those who have not thus witnessed the frenzy of a Negro revival in the untouched backwoods of the South can but dimly realize the religious feeling of the slave; as described, such scenes appear grotesque and funny, but as seen they are awful. Three things characterized this religion of the slave—the preacher, the music, and the frenzy. The preacher is the most unique personality developed by the Negro on American soil. A leader, a politician, an orator, a "boss," an intriguer, an idealist—all these he is, and ever, too, the center of a group of men, now twenty, now 1,000 in number. The combination of a certain adroitness with deep-seated earnestness, of tact with consummate ability, gave him his preeminence, and helps him maintain it. The type, of course, varies according to time and place, from the West Indies in the sixteenth century to New England in the nineteenth, and from the Mississippi bottoms to cities like New Orleans or New York.

The music of Negro religion is that plaintive rhythmic melody, with its touching minor cadences, which, despite caricature and defilement, still remains the most original and beautiful expression of human life and longing yet born on American soil. Sprung from the African forests, where its counterpart can still be heard, it was adapted, changed, and intensified by the tragic soul-life of the slave, until, under the stress of law and whip, it became the one true expression of a people's sorrow, despair, and hope.

Finally the frenzy, or "shouting," when the spirit of the Lord passed by, and, seizing the devotee, made him mad with supernatural joy, was the last essential of Negro religion and the one more devoutly believed in than all the rest. It varied in expression from the silent rapt countenance or the low murmur and moan to the mad abandon of physical fervor—the stamping, shrieking, and shouting, the rushing to and fro and wild waving of arms, the weeping and laughing, the vision and the trance. All this is nothing new in the world, but old as religion, as Delphi and Endor. And so firm a hold did it have on the Negro, that many generations firmly believed that without this visible manifestation of the God there could be no true communion with the Invisible.

These were the characteristics of Negro religious life as developed up to the time of emancipation. Since under the peculiar circumstances of the black man's environment they were the one expression of his higher life, they are of deep interest to the student of his development, both socially and psychologically. Numerous are the attractive lines of inquiry that here group themselves. What did slavery mean to the African savage? What was his attitude toward the world and life? What seemed to him good and evil—God and devil? Whither went his longings and strivings, and wherefore were his heart-burnings and disappointments? Answers to such questions can come only from a study of Negro religion as a development, through its gradual changes from the heathenism of the Gold Coast to the institutional Negro church of Chicago.

Moreover, the religious growth of millions of men, even though they be slaves, cannot be without potent influence upon their contemporaries. The Methodists and Baptists of America owe much of their condition to the silent but potent influence of their millions of Negro converts. Especially is this noticeable in the South, where theology and religious philosophy are on this account a long way behind the North, and where the religion of the poor whites is a plain copy of Negro thought and methods. The mass of "gospel" hymns which has swept through American churches and well-nigh ruined our sense of song consists largely of debased imitations of Negro melodies made by ears that caught the jingle but not the music, the body but not the soul, of the jubilee songs. It is thus clear that the study of Negro religion is not only a vital part of the history of the Negro in America, but no uninteresting part of American history.

The Negro church of today is the social center of Negro life in the United States, and the most characteristic expression of African character. Take a typical church in a small Virginia town: It is the First Baptist—a roomy brick edifice seating 500 or more persons, tastefully finished in Georgia pine, with a carpet, a small organ, and stained-glass windows. Underneath is a large assembly room with benches. This building is the central clubhouse of a community of 1,000 or more Negroes. Various organizations meet here—the church proper, the Sunday school, two or three insurance societies, women's societies, secret societies, and mass meetings of various kinds. Entertainments, suppers, and lectures are held beside the five or six regular weekly religious services. Considerable sums of money are collected and expended here, employment is found for the idle, strangers are introduced, news is disseminated, and charity distributed. At the same time this social, intellectual, and economic center is a religious center of great power. Depravity, sin, redemption, heaven, hell, and damnation are preached twice a Sunday with much fervor, and revivals take place every year after the crops are laid by; and few indeed of the community have the hardihood to withstand conversion. Back of this more formal religion, the church often stands as a real conserver of morals, a strengthener of family life, and the final authority on what is good and right.

Thus one can see in the Negro church today, reproduced in microcosm, all that great world from which the Negro is cut off by color prejudice and social condition. In the great city churches the same tendency is noticeable and in many respects emphasized. A great church like the Bethel of Philadelphia has over 1,100 members, an edifice seating 1,500 persons and valued at $100,000, an annual budget of $5,000, and a government consisting of a pastor with several assisting local preachers, an executive and legislative board, financial boards and tax collectors; general church meetings for making laws; subdivided groups led by class leaders, a company of militia, and twenty-four auxiliary societies. The activity of a church like this is immense and far-reaching, and the bishops who preside over these organizations throughout the land are among the most powerful Negro rulers in the world.

Such churches are really governments of men, and consequently a little investigation reveals the curious fact that, in the South, at least, practically every American Negro is a church member. Some, to be sure, are not regularly enrolled, and a few do not habitually attend services; but, practically, a proscribed people must have a social center, and that center for this people is the Negro church. The census of 1890 showed nearly 24,000 Negro churches in the country, with a total enrolled membership of over 2.5 million, or ten actual church members to every twenty-eight persons, and in some Southern states one in every two persons. Besides these there is the large number who, though not enrolled as members, attend and take part in many of the activities of the church. There is an organized Negro church for every sixty black families in the nation, and in some states for every forty families, owning, on an average, $1,000 worth of property each, or nearly $26 million in all.

Such, then, is the large development of the Negro church since emancipation. The question now is What have been the successive steps of this social history and what are the present tendencies? First, we must realize that no

such institution as the Negro church could rear itself without definite historical foundations. These foundations we can find if we remember that the social
history of the Negro did not start in America. He was brought from a definite
social environment—the polygamous clan life under the headship of the chief
and the potent influence of the priest. His religion was nature worship, with
profound belief in invisible surrounding influences, good and bad, and his
worship was through incantation and sacrifice. The first rude change in this
life was the slave ship and the West Indian sugar fields. The plantation organization replaced the clan and tribe, and the white master replaced the chief
with far greater and more despotic powers. Forced and long-continued toil
became the rule of life, the old ties of blood relationship and kinship disappeared, and instead of the family appeared a new polygamy and polyandry,
which, in some cases, almost reached promiscuity. It was a terrific social
revolution, and yet some traces were retained of the former group life, and
the chief remaining institution was the priest or medicineman. He early
appeared on the plantation and found his function as the healer of the sick,
the interpreter of the unknown, the comforter of the sorrowing, the supernatural avenger of wrong, and the one who rudely but picturesquely expressed
the longing, disappointment, and resentment of a stolen and oppressed people.
Thus, as bard, physician, judge, and priest, within the narrow limits allowed
by the slave system, rose the Negro preacher, and under him the first Afro-
American institution, the Negro church. This church was not at first by any
means Christian nor definitely organized; rather it was an adaptation and
mingling of heathen rites among the members of each plantation, and roughly
designated as Voodooism. Association with the masters, missionary effort,
and motives of expediency gave these rites an early veneer of Christianity,
and after the lapse of many generations the Negro church became Christian.

Two characteristic things must be noticed in regard to this church. First,
it became almost entirely Baptist and Methodist in faith; second, as a social
institution it antedated by many decades the monogamic Negro home. From
the very circumstances of its beginning, the church was confined to the
plantation, and consisted primarily of a series of disconnected units; though,
later on, some freedom of movement was allowed, still this geographical
limitation was always important and was one cause of the spread of the decen-
tralized and democratic Baptist faith among the slaves. At the same time, the
visible rite of baptism appealed strongly to their mystic temperament. Today
the Baptist Church is still largest in membership among Negroes, and has a
million and a half communicants. Next in popularity came the churches
organized in connection with the white neighboring churches, chiefly Baptist
and Methodist, with a few Episcopalian and others. The Methodists still
form the second greatest denomination, with nearly 1 million members. The

faith of these two leading denominations was more suited to the slave church
from the prominence they gave to religious feeling and fervor. The Negro
membership in other denominations has always been small and relatively
unimportant, although the Episcopalians and Presbyterians are gaining among
the more intelligent classes today, and the Catholic Church is making headway in certain sections. After emancipation, and still earlier in the North, the
Negro churches largely severed such affiliations as they had had with the
white churches, either by choice or by compulsion. The Baptist churches
became independent, but the Methodists were compelled early to unite for
purposes of episcopal government. This gave rise to the great African
Methodist Church, the greatest Negro organization in the world, to the Zion
Church and the Colored Methodist, and to the black conferences and churches
in this and other denominations.

The second fact noted, namely, that the Negro church antedates the
Negro home, leads to an explanation of much that is paradoxical in this
communistic institution and in the morals of its members. But especially it
leads us to regard this institution as peculiarly the expression of the inner
ethical life of a people in a sense seldom true elsewhere. Let us turn, then,
from the outer physical development of the church to the more important
inner ethical life of the people who compose it. The Negro has already been
pointed out many times as a religious animal—a being of that deep emotional
nature which turns instinctively toward the supernatural. Endowed with a
rich tropical imagination and a keen, delicate appreciation of nature, the
transplanted African lived in a world animate with gods and devils, elves and
witches; full of strange influences,—of good to be implored, of evil to be
propitiated. Slavery, then, was to him the dark triumph of evil over him. All
the hateful powers of the underworld were striving against him, and a spirit
of revolt and revenge filled his heart. He called up all the resources of
heathenism to aid—exorcism and witchcraft, the mysterious Obi worship with
its barbarious rites, spells, and blood sacrifice even, now and then, of human
victims. Weird midnight orgies and mystic conjurations were invoked, the
witch-woman and the voodoo priest became the center of Negro group life,
and that vein of vague superstition which characterizes the unlettered
Negro even today was deepened and strengthened.

In spite, however, of such success as that of the fierce Maroons, the Danish
blacks, and others, the spirit of revolt gradually died away under the untiring
energy and superior strength of the slave masters. By the middle of the
eighteenth century the black slave had sunk, with hushed murmurs, to his
place at the bottom of a new economic system, and was unconsciously ripe
for a new philosophy of life. Nothing suited his condition then better than
the doctrines of passive submission embodied in the newly learned Christianity.

Slave masters early realized this, and cheerfully aided religious propaganda within certain bounds. The long system of repression and degradation of the Negro tended to emphasize the elements in his character which made him a valuable chattel: courtesy became humility, moral strength degenerated into submission, and the exquisite native appreciation of the beautiful became an infinite capacity for dumb suffering. The Negro, losing the joy of this world, eagerly seized upon the offered conceptions of the next; the avenging spirit of the Lord enjoining patience in this world, under sorrow and tribulation until the great day when He should lead His dark children home—this became his comforting dream. His preacher repeated the prophecy, and his bards sang—

> *Children, we all shall be free*
> *When the Lord shall appear!*

This deep religious fatalism, painted so beautifully in "Uncle Tom," came soon to breed, as all fatalistic faiths will, the sensualist side by side with the martyr. Under the lax moral life of the plantation, where marriage was a farce, laziness a virtue, and property a theft, a religion of resignation and submission degenerated easily, in less strenuous minds, into a philosophy of indulgence and crime. Many of the worst characteristics of the Negro masses of today had their seed in this period of the slave's ethical growth. Here it was that the home was ruined under the very shadow of the church, white and black; here habits of shiftlessness took root, and sullen hopelessness replaced hopeful strife.

With the beginning of the abolition movement and the gradual growth of a class of free Negroes came a change. We often neglect the influence of the freedman before the war, because of the paucity of his numbers and the small weight he had in the history of the nation. But we must not forget that his chief influence was internal—was exerted on the black world; and that there he was the ethical and social leader. Huddled as he was in a few centers like Philadelphia, New York, and New Orleans, the masses of the freedmen sank into poverty and listlessness; but not all of them. The free Negro leader early arose and his chief characteristic was intense earnestness and deep feeling on the slavery question. Freedom became to him a real thing and not a dream. His religion became darker and more intense, and into his ethics crept a note of revenge, into his songs a day of reckoning close at hand. The "Coming of the Lord" swept this side of death, and came to be a thing to be hoped for in this day. Through fugitive slaves and irrepressible discussion this desire for freedom seized the black millions still in bondage, and became their one ideal of life. The black bards caught new notes, and sometimes even dared to sing—

O Freedom, O Freedom, O Freedom over me!
Before I'll be a slave
I'll be buried in my grave,
And go home to my Lord
And be free.

For fifty years Negro religion thus transformed itself and identified itself with the dream of abolition, until that which was a radical fad in the white North and an anarchistic plot in the white South had become a religion to the black world. Thus, when emancipation finally came, it seemed to the freedman a literal coming of the Lord. His fervid imagination was stirred as never before, by the tramp of armies, the blood and dust of battle, and the wail and whirl of social upheaval. He stood dumb and motionless before the whirlwind: what had he to do with it? Was it not the Lord's doing, and marvellous in his eyes? Joyed and bewildered with what came, he stood awaiting new wonders till the inevitable age of reaction swept over the nation and brought the crisis of today.

It is difficult to explain clearly the present critical stage of Negro religion. First, we must remember that living as the blacks do in close contact with a great modern nation, and sharing, although imperfectly, the soul-life of that nation, they must necessarily be affected more or less directly by all the religious and ethical forces that are today moving the United States. These questions and movements are, however, overshadowed and dwarfed by the (to them) all-important question of their civil, political, and economic status. They must perpetually discuss the "Negro Problem"—must live, move, and have their being in it, and interpret all else in its light or darkness. With this come, too, peculiar problems of their inner life—of the status of women, the maintenance of home, the training of children, the accumulation of wealth, and the prevention of crime. All this must mean a time of intense ethical ferment, of religious heart-searching and intellectual unrest. From the double life every American Negro must live, as a Negro and as an American, as swept on by the current of the nineteenth while yet struggling in the eddies of the fifteenth century—from this must arise a painful self-consciousness, an almost morbid sense of personality and a moral hesitancy which is fatal to self-confidence. The worlds within and without the veil of color are changing, and changing rapidly, but not at the same rate, not in the same way; and this must produce a peculiar wrenching of the soul, a peculiar sense of doubt and bewilderment. Such a double life, with double thoughts, double duties, and double social classes, must give rise to double words and double ideals, and tempt the mind to pretence or revolt, to hypocrisy or radicalism.

In some such doubtful words and phrases can one perhaps most clearly picture the peculiar ethical paradox that faces the Negro of today and is tingeing and changing his religious life. Feeling that his rights and his dearest ideals are being trampled upon, that the public conscience is ever more deaf to his righteous appeal, and that all the reactionary forces of prejudice, greed, and revenge are daily gaining new strength and fresh allies, the Negro faces no enviable dilemma. Conscious of his impotence, and pessimistic, he often becomes bitter and vindictive; and his religion, instead of a worship, is a complaint and a curse, a wail rather than a hope, a sneer rather than a faith. On the other hand, another type of mind, shrewder and keener and more tortuous too, sees in the very strength of the anti-Negro movement its patent weaknesses, and with Jesuitic casuistry is deterred by no ethical considerations in the endeavor to turn this weakness to the black man's strength. Thus we have two great and hardly reconcilable streams of thought and ethical striv-ings; the danger of the one lies in anarchy, that of the other in hypocrisy. The one type of Negro stands almost ready to curse God and die, and the other is too often found a traitor to right and a coward before force; the one is wedded to ideals remote, whimsical, perhaps impossible of realization; the other forgets that life is more than meat and the body more than raiment. But, after all, is not this simply the writhing of the age translated into black— the triumph of the lie which today, with its false culture, faces the hideous-ness of the anarchist assassin?

Today the two groups of Negroes, the one in the North, the other in the South, represent these divergent ethical tendencies, the first tending toward radicalism, the other toward hypocritical compromise. It is no idle regret with which the white South mourns the loss of the old-time Negro—the frank, honest, simple old servant who stood for the earlier religious age of submis-sion and humility. With all his laziness and lack of many elements of true manhood, he was at least open-hearted, faithful, and sincere. Today he is gone, but who is to blame for his going? Is it not those very persons who mourn for him? Is it not the tendency, born of reconstruction and reaction, to found a society on lawlessness and deception, to tamper with the moral fiber of a naturally honest and straightforward people until the whites threaten to become ungovernable tyrants and the blacks criminals and hypocrites? Deception is the natural defense of the weak against the strong, and the South used it for many years against its conquerors; today it must be prepared to see its black proletariat turn that same two-edged weapon against itself. And how natural this is! The death of Denmark Vesey and Nat Turner proved long since to the Negro the present hopelessness of physical defense. Political defense is becoming less and less available, and economic defense is still only partially effective. But there is a patent defense at hand—the defense of deception and flattery, of cajoling and lying. It is the same defense which peasants of the Middle Ages used and which left its stamp on their character for centuries. Today the young Negro of the South who would succeed cannot be frank and outspoken, honest and self-assertive, but rather he is daily tempted to be silent and wary, politic and sly; he must flatter and be pleasant, endure petty insults with a smile, shut his eyes to wrong; in too many cases he sees positive personal advantage in deception and lying. His real thoughts, his real aspirations, must be guarded in whispers; he must not criticize, he must not complain. Patience, humility, and adroit-ness must, in these growing black youth, replace impulse, manliness, and courage. With this sacrifice there is an economic opening, and perhaps peace and some prosperity. Without this there is riot, migration, or crime. Nor is this situation peculiar to the Southern United States, is it not rather the only method by which undeveloped races have gained the right to share modern culture? The price of culture is a lie.

On the other hand, in the North the tendency is to emphasize the radical-ism of the Negro. Driven from his birthright in the South by a situation at which every fiber of his more outspoken and assertive nature revolts, he finds himself in a land where he can scarcely earn a decent living amid the harsh competition and the color discrimination. At the same time, through schools and periodicals, discussions and lectures, he is intellectually quickened and awakened. The soul, long pent up and dwarfed, suddenly expands in new-found freedom. What wonder that every tendency is to excess—radical complaint, radical remedies, bitter denunciation or angry silence. Some sink, some rise. The criminal and the sensualist leave the church for the gambling hell and the brothel, and fill the slums of Chicago and Baltimore; the better classes segregate themselves from the group life of both white and black and form an aristocracy, cultured but pessimistic, whose bitter criticism stings while it points out no way of escape. They despise the submission and sub-serviency of the Southern Negroes, but offer no other means by which a poor and oppressed minority can exist side by side with its masters. Feeling deeply and keenly the tendencies and opportunities of the age in which they live, their souls are bitter at the fate which drops the veil between; and the very fact that this bitterness is natural and justifiable only serves to intensify it and make it more maddening.

Between the two extreme types of ethical attitude which I have thus sought to make clear wavers the mass of the millions of Negroes, North and South; and their religious life and activity partake of this social conflict within their ranks. Their churches are differentiating—now into groups of cold, fashion-able devotees, in no way distinguishable from similar white groups save in color of skin; now into large social and business institutions catering to the desire for information and amusement of their members, warily avoiding unpleasant questions both within and without the black world, and preaching in effect if not in word: *Dum vivimus, vivamus.*

But back of this still broods silently the deep religious feeling of the real Negro heart, the stirring, unguided might of powerful human souls who have lost the guiding star of the past and seek in the great night a new religious ideal. Some day the awakening will come, when the pent-up vigor of 10 million souls shall sweep irresistibly toward the goal, out of the Valley of the Shadow of Death, where all that makes life worth living—liberty, justice, and right—is marked "For White People Only."

3

THE RELIGIOUS LIFE OF THE NEGRO

BOOKER T. WASHINGTON

The practical philosophy of Booker T. Washington emphasized that the Negro who made himself a useful citizen (and did not concern himself for the moment with classical education or the loss of political rights) could win the respect of the whites and a place in their society. Washington's formula for solving the "race problem" was so powerful a force in black-white relations that John Hope Franklin has termed the era of its dominance the "Age of Booker T. Washington." Unlike Du Bois, who saw the church as a central expression of the inner life of the black people, Washington took a less favorable view of its role and was also sharply critical of its often other-worldly orientation. Still, the church could be a powerful tool for instilling a spirit of (Christian) service in the black man if it could be brought into a "more definite connection with the social and moral life of the Negro people."

In everything that I have been able to read about the religious life of the Negro, it has seemed to me that writers have been too much disposed to treat of it as something fixed and unchanging. They have not sufficiently emphasized the fact that the Negro people, in respect to their religious life, have been, almost since they landed in America, in a process of change and growth.

The Negro came to America with the pagan ideal of his African ancestors; he acquired under slavery a number of Christian ideas, and at the present time he is slowly learning what those ideas mean in practical life. He is learning, not merely what Christians believe, but what they must do to be Christians.

The religious ideas which the Negroes brought with them to America from Africa were the fragments of a system of thought and custom, which, in its general features, is common to most barbarous people. What we call "fetishism" is, I suppose, merely the childish way of looking at and explaining the world, which did not, in the case of the people of West Africa, preclude a

Reprinted from *North American Review* 181 (July 1905): 20-23.

belief in the one true God, although He was regarded by them as far away and not interested in the little affairs of men.

But the peculiarity of their primitive religion, as I have learned from a very interesting book written by one who has been many years a missionary in Africa, consists in this, that it sought for its adherents a purely "physical salvation."

✦ In the religion of the native African there was, generally speaking, no place of future reward or punishment, no heaven and no hell, as we are accustomed to conceive them. For this reason, the Negro had little sense of sin. He was not tortured by doubts and fears, which are so common and, we sometimes feel, so necessary a part of the religious experiences of Christians. The evils he knew were present and physical.

During the period of servitude in the New World, the Negro race did not wholly forget the traditions and habits of thought that it brought from Africa. But it added to its ancestral stock certain new ideas.

↰ Slavery, with all its disadvantages, gave the Negro race, by way of recompense, one great consolation, namely, the Christian religion and the hope and belief in a future life. The slave, to whom on this side of the grave the door of hope seemed closed, learned from Christianity to lift his face from earth to heaven, and that made his burden lighter. In the end, the hope and aspiration of the race in slavery fixed themselves on the vision of the resurrection, with its "long white robes and golden slippers."

This hope and this aspiration, which are the theme of so many of the old Negro hymns, found expression in the one institution that slavery permitted to the Negro people—the Negro church. It was natural and inevitable that the Negro church, coming into existence as it did under slavery, should permit the religious life of the Negro to express itself in ways almost wholly detached from morality. There was little in slavery to encourage the sense of personal responsibility.

The attitude of some Negro communities in this respect is very clearly illustrated in the story of the slave who was a "professor" of religion, in the current phrase of the time, but made his master so much trouble by his persistence in certain immoral practices that it was finally necessary to call in a clergyman to try to reform him. The clergyman made the attempt, and sought to bring the terrors of the law to bear upon the slave's conscience.

"Look yeah, Massa," said the culprit, "don't de Scripture say, Dem who b'lieves an' is baptize' shall be saved?"

"Certainly," was the reply, and the clergyman went on to explain the passage to him, but the slave interrupted him again.

"Jus' you tell me now, Massa, don't de good book say dese words: 'Dem as b'lieve and is baptize' shall be saved?' "

"Yes, but—"

"Dat's all I want to know, sar. Now, wat's de use of talkin' to me. You ain't ago'n to make me believe wat de blessed Lord say ain't so, not if you tries forever."

This illustrates one of the difficulties that we have to contend with today. In our Tuskegee Negro Conference, we have constantly to insist that the people draw moral distinctions within the limits of their own communities, that they get rid of immoral ministers and schoolteachers, and refuse to associate with people whom they know to be guilty of immoral practices.

It has been said that the trouble with the Negro church is that it is too emotional. It seems to me that what the Negro church needs is a more definite connection with the social and moral life of the Negro people. Could this connection be effected in a large degree, it would give to the movement for the upbuilding of the race the force and inspiration of a religious motive. It would give to the Negro religion more of that missionary spirit, the spirit of service, that it needs to purge it of some of the worst elements that still cling to it.

The struggle to attain a higher level of living, to get land, to build a home, to give their children an education, just because it demands more earnestness and steadfastness of purpose, gives a steadiness and a moral significance to the religious life, which is the thing the Negro people need at present.

A large element of the Negro church must be recalled from its apocalyptic vision back to the earth; the members of the Negro race must be taught that mere religious emotion that is guided by no definite idea and is devoted to no purpose is vain.

It is encouraging to notice that the leaders of the different denominations of the Negro church are beginning to recognize the force of the criticism made against it, and that, under their leadership, conditions are changing. In one of these denominations, the A. M. E. Zion Church alone, $2 million was raised, from 1900 to 1904, for the general educational, moral and material improvement of the race. Of this sum, $1 million was contributed for educational purposes alone. The A. M. E. Church and the Baptists did proportionally as well.

The mere fact that this amount of money has been raised for general educational purposes, in addition to the sum expended in each local community for teachers, for building schoolhouses and supplementing the state appropriations for schools, shows that the colored people have spent less money in saloons and dispensaries; that less has been squandered on toys and gimcracks that are of no use. It shows that there has been more saving, more thought for the future, more appreciation of the real value of life.

In this connection, it is well to have in mind that the industrial schools have performed a great and useful service, in so far as they have impressed upon the young men who go out from these schools as preachers the importance of learning a trade, something of agriculture, so that they can give the members of their congregations an example of industrial thrift.

At Tuskegee Institute, we insist upon the importance of service. Every student in this department is expected to do, in connection with his other work either as a teacher or preacher, some part of the social and religious work that is carried on under the direction of the Bible Training School in the surrounding country. We are seeking to imbue these young men who are going forth as leaders of their people with the feeling that the great task of uplifting the race, though it may be for others merely a work of humanity, for them, and every other member of the Negro race, is a work of religion.

In this great modern world, where every individual has so many interests and life is so complicated, there is a tendency to let religion and life drift apart. I meet men every day who, honest and upright though they be, have lost in their daily lives this connection with religion, and are striving vainly to regain it. There is no one great dominating motive in their lives which enters into every task and gives it significance and zest.

It is one of the compensations which hardships bring, that the race problem is a thing so real and so present to the Negro people that it enters, as a motive, into everything they do. It is this that makes it possible for them to realize that the acts of every individual have an importance far beyond the measure in which they make or mar his or her personal fortunes.

So soon as a man, white or black, really learns to comprehend that fact, he will cease to whine and complain, and he will be content to do his best, humble though it be, to improve his own condition, and to help his less fortunate fellows.

Slowly but surely, and in ever larger numbers, the members of my race are learning that lesson; they are realizing that God has assigned to their race a man's part in the task of civilization; they are learning to understand their duty, and to face uncomplainingly and with confidence the destiny that awaits them.

4

AFRICANISMS IN RELIGIOUS LIFE

MELVILLE J. HERSKOVITS

In the decades since *The Myth of the Negro Past* first appeared, Melville
Herskovits has remained the foremost proponent of the idea of the survival
of Africanisms among black Americans. Herskovits maintains that, far from
being obliterated by the cultural shock of enslavement, the African cultural
heritage significantly affected the pattern of the black man's acculturation
into American life. In the following selection Herskovits suggests the complexity that lies within the deceptively simple forms of the more emotional black
religious services—as for instance, in the highly structured sermons that
delineate a socially involved God. He also argues that the great appeal of the
Baptist Church to black Americans may well lie in the attractiveness of its
water ritual of baptism to a people with a religious heritage centered in the
West African river cults. For a critique of the controversial Herskovits thesis,
the reader may wish to consult Chapter 17.

In most cities, the services of "shouting" Negro churches are to be heard
over the radio, and I have for some years been following, recording, and
transcribing a sampling of the services of one such church, so that by analyz-
ing the text of the sermons, the world view in terms of the implicit theological propositions that underlie the observed ritualistic practices may be
inductively derived. Many of these churches, including the one under discussion, are of the Baptist denomination, and are so named. The larger churches
are in structure much like conventional white-Protestant-American churches.
Those in attendance are indistinguishable from other Americans in their dress
and bearing. Music is provided by organ or piano, or both. The Bible is cited
as the authority for belief. The broadcasting is smoothly integrated with the
rest of the service. Nothing could be further removed from the West African
setting for polytheistic worship, in the open air, with the prominent placing
of drums and other ritual paraphernalia.

Reprinted from *The Myth of the Negro Past* (New York: Harper & Row, 1941), pp. 208,
232-235, and from the "Preface to the Beacon Press Edition" (Boston: Beacon Press,
1958), pp. xxiii-xxiv. Copyright 1941, 1958 by Melville J. Herskovits. By permission of
the publishers.

Yet there are aspects of the ritual, and of the theology as expressed in the sermons, that at the very least must be regarded as wide deviations from the practices and beliefs of white Baptists. As the service progresses, spirit possession by the Holy Ghost takes place, with motor behavior that is not European, but African. The gospel hymns are sung by a trained choir. There is little singing by the congregation, its participation being the hand-clapping which maintains the rhythm, and the antiphonal responses of "Yes! Yes! Lord," "Yes, Jesus," "That's so," which punctuate the sermon. It is an interesting exercise in ethnomusicology to compare the printed music of these hymns, used by the choir, with transcriptions of them as actually sung, and to note how the scores are manipulated to create quite distinct patterns of harmony and, particularly, of rhythm. Nor is a sociological analysis of the structure of the church group needed to perceive the existence of differences in status and role, because these are immediately apparent in the differences in dress that characterize the special roles of certain members.

The manner in which the supernatural being that rules the universe is conceived in churches of this kind is a subject that has received little or no attention, for the sermons in which these theological concepts are expressed have all too often been dismissed as the illiterate gibberish of preachers who play on the emotions of their congregations and at best are but caricatures of their white counterparts. Yet careful study reveals the sermons to be structurally patterned and rich in imagery. When followed over a period of time, they present a consistent and logical point of view. God, Jesus, and the Holy Ghost are all concerned with the immediate fate of those who worship them. They are disturbed by the fact of segregation and are responsible for its diminution; the Holy Ghost visits with the minister, taking messages to God from those in need of help.

Now, it is simple to find Africanisms in church services of this kind, and their presence is attested by the comments of Africans, as well as Europeans of long experience in Africa, in whose company I have witnessed these rites. But this is only the starting point in the search to understand how Afroamerican groups, through the exercise of that resilience discussed in the pages that follow, have integrated old beliefs with new, reinterpretating both to fit a pattern of sanction and value that functions effectively in meeting the psychological needs of life.

We may begin by treating the organizations that comprise the institutionalized forms of Negro religion. From the earliest times of slavery, it has been the less inhibited, more humble denominations which have attracted Negroes in the United States. Perhaps because this is so striking, a formula which explains it in terms of simplicity, naïveté, and emotionalism has attained a certain currency among students. Thus:

The worship of the Negro is of the simplest sort. He has no appreciation of elaborate rituals, of services consisting of forms and ceremonies. Hence the great mass of colored races have united with either the Methodist or Baptist Churches. These churches have the simplest, least complicated forms of church services, and the Negro naturally gravitated toward them.[1]

The simplicity assumed in this citation, however, is but one of those questionable generalizations encountered again and again in this analysis.

Thus we see how, in assessing the forces that have given Negro religious hysteria its present-day forms, and the extent to which these forces have shaped corresponding modes of behavior among whites, a problem must be faced that is far more complex than is ordinarily recognized. The same conclusion must be reached when another problem of derivation lying in the field of religion is considered. This has to do with the popularity among Negroes of the Baptist Church, which has been stressed by all students of Negro religion. Explanations of this fact, it will be remembered, are couched in terms of the greater democracy of the Baptist Church organization, the greater emotionalism permitted in the services of this church, and that the services of this denomination are closer to the requirements of humbler folk than those of other churches. That the first two of these reasons is congenial to African religious patterns has already been pointed out. Yet neither this fact nor an explanation in terms of the socioeconomic situation of the Negroes under slavery and in postslavery days is of much aid in helping the student understand why the Baptist Church, rather than autonomous "cults," should have had such a great appeal to Negroes, or why denominations other than the Baptist did not attract comparable numbers of followers.

For an answer to this question we must turn to the baptism by total immersion, indispensable for affiliation with the Baptist Church. It will be remembered how, earlier in our discussion of the religious patterns of West Africa, the importance of the river cults was stressed. It was pointed out that the river spirits are among the most powerful of those inhabiting the supernatural world, and that priests of this cult are among the most powerful members of tribal priestly groups. It will be further recalled how, in the process of conquest which accompanied the spread of the Dahomean kingdom, at least (there being no data on this particular point from any other folk of West Africa), the intransigeance of the priests of the river cult was so marked that, more than any other group of holy men, they were sold into slavery to rid the conquerors of troublesome leaders. In all those parts of the New World where African religious beliefs have persisted, moreover, the river cult or, in broader terms, the cult of water spirits, holds an important place. All this testifies to the vitality of this element in African religion, and supports the conclusion, to be drawn from the hint in the Dahomean data, as to the possible influence such priests wielded even as slaves.

In the New World, where the aggressive proselytizing activities of Protestantism made the retention of the inner forms of African religion as difficult as its outer manifestations, the most logical adaptation for the slaves to make to the new situation, and the simplest, was to give their adherence to that Christian sect which in its ritualism most resembled the types of worship known to them. As we have seen, the Baptist churches had an autonomous organization that was in line with the tradition of local self-direction congenial to African practice. In these churches the slaves were also permitted less restrained behavior than in the more sedate denominations. And such factors only tended to reinforce an initial predisposition of these Africans toward a cult which, in emphasizing baptism by total immersion, made possible the worship of the new supernatural powers in ways that at least contained elements not entirely unfamiliar.

The importance of the association of water with African ritual may be further documented to indicate its fundamental character. In ceremony after ceremony witnessed among the Yoruba, the Ashanti, and in Dahomey, one invariable element was a visit to the river or some other body of "living" water, such as the ocean, for the purpose of obtaining the liquid indispensable for the rites. Often it was necessary to go some distance to reach the particular stream from which water having the necessary sacred quality must be drawn; in one instance, at Abeokuta, a bedecked procession of worshippers left a shrine atop a high hill, followed a long path to the riverside over two miles away, and returned before the ceremonies could be carried out at the shrine of the god. On one occasion, in Dahomey, the bed of a sacred stream run dry was "filled" from nearby wells so that this water could be ritually redrawn for use in an especially important ceremony.

Among the Ashanti, pilgrimages to Lake Bosumtwe and other sacred bodies of water regularly occur. And it is on such occasions that the spirit of the river or lake or sea manifests itself, by "entering the head" of a devotee and causing him to fling himself, possessed, into the water. The same kind of possession occurs in the Guiana bush, where the rites of various African tribes for their water spirits impel the one possessed to leap into the river with the strength necessary to swim even against the swift currents of the rapids. Possession by the river spirits in Haiti, or by spirits of snakes that inhabit the water, bring the devotee threshing into the stream near which the rituals are held, and where the deity is thought to reside.

But in the United States, where neither Bosumtwe nor *watra mama* nor Dambalia is worshipped, Negro Baptists do not run into the water under possession by African gods. Their water rituals are those of baptism. Yet it is significant that, as the novitiate whose revelation has brought him to the running stream or the tidal cove is immersed, the spirit descends on him at that moment if at all, and a possession hysteria develops that in its outward appearance, at least, is almost indistinguishable from the possession brought on by the African water deities. The importance of the Biblical concept of "crossing the river Jordan" in the religious imagery of the Negroes, and as a symbol of what comes after death, is a further part of this complex. For, like baptism, the river Jordan embodies a concept in Christianity that any African would find readily understandable. In the transmutation of belief and behavior under acculturation, it furnished one of the least difficult transitions to a new form of belief.

The slaves, then, came to the United States with a tradition which found worship involving immersion in a body of water understandable, and encountered this belief among those whose churches and manner of worship were least strange to them. When, in addition, they found in this group those whites who tended to be closest to the lowly, and thus tended to be the least formidable persons in their new setting, they understandably affiliated with it and initiated a tradition which holds to the present time. The favorable influence of the traditional past, and the new socioeconomic setting were not, however, the only forces that furthered this particular process of reinterpretation. It is not generally recognized that the Cherokee Indians, a tribe with whom Negroes were perhaps more in contact during the days of slavery than with any other except the Seminoles and Creeks, themselves had a well-developed river cult. It was neither African nor Christian, but its mere presence would act to strengthen any river cult foreign to the newly arrived Africans. This Indian rite included total immersion, something which in spirit is not too far removed from the restraints laid on the novitiate of any cult in Africa, or in the rites of certain "shouting" sects where new members "go into mournin'" before baptism. Certainly its presence in the Negro milieu reemphasizes, if this is now necessary, the complexity of the elements that determined the present-day forms of Negro religion wherein baptism plays so prominent a part, and the fact that membership in the church which gives the rite of immersion so large a place in its ritual is the most popular single denomination among Negroes.

NOTE

1. Bertram W. Doyle, "Racial Traits of the Negro as Negroes Assign Them to Themselves," unpublished Master's Thesis, University of Chicago, 1924, p. 90, citing W. J. Gaines, *The Negro and the White Man,* Philadelphia, 1910, p. 185.

5

THE RESULTING PATTERN OF SEPARATION: NEGRO CHURCHES

WINTHROP D. JORDAN

In the previous selections the writers have been debating the character of the Negro's religion, the cultural elements in its makeup. The existence of the Negro church as a physical and spiritual entity has been tacitly assumed. The following reading from Winthrop Jordan's prize-winning study of white racial attitudes may seem to be merely one more instance of the triumph of racial prejudice over Christian ideals. It is also, however, the story of how the white decision that even Christian equality did not require racial togetherness spurred the creation of a separate black church in the North.

That Negroes were generally not welcomed as equal participants among American churches helps account for the development in the years after the revolution of a dramatic and novel variety of separation of Negroes from the white community. Throughout the nation but most obviously in Philadelphia and other northern cities, the "black sheep" of Christ's flock began to "fold by themselves." At least two independent Negro congregations had been founded in the South before the end of the war, but the rush of Negroes into "African" churches began in the same year and in the same city as the Constitutional Convention.

The critical break was led by two prominent Philadelphia Negroes, Richard Allen and Absalom Jones, but they received ample inducement from influential white men. Jones and Allen were leaders of a group of Negroes who worshipped at St. George's Methodist Church. There in 1787 they were told to take seats around the wall and then, one day, in the gallery. Though they complied, one of the church's "trustees" attempted to haul Absalom Jones to his feet during prayer. The indignant Negroes, who had recently

Reprinted from *White Over Black: American Attitudes Toward the Negro, 1550-1812* (Chapel Hill: University of North Carolina Press for the Institute of Early American History and Culture, 1968), pp. 422-426, by permission of The University of North Carolina Press.

subscribed to refurbishment of the church, walked out "in a body" when
the prayer was over. Apparently on their own initiative, but with assistance
from some Quakers, they formed a Free African Society which for a time
showed promise of becoming a very Quaker-like organization. Philadelphia
Friends seem to have been happy over the possibility that Negroes would
develop true religion in an independent but decidedly Friendly way. Although
the Free African Society lasted for more than a decade, it was rendered a
rump in 1791 by the exodus of Jones and Allen, both of whom had been
pupils at Anthony Benezet's school, and a number of their followers.[1] Out of
their efforts soon grew the first Negro Episcopal church in America, led by
Jones, and the African Methodist Episcopal Church, of which Allen became
the first bishop. For some Quakers this exodus seems to have been interpreted
as a defection, for while they were usually happy to see Negroes embracing
other faiths, the Negroes who hoped to establish an Episcopal church told
Benjamin Rush that "Quakers were much displeased with them." This opposition by Quakers, Rush noted in his commonplace book, merely confirmed his
own high estimate of the worth of the project.[2]

The erection of the "African Episcopal Church of St. Thomas" in 1793
occasioned a moving display of interracial harmony. The comptroller-general
of Pennsylvania, John Nicholson, had loaned the Negroes £100 out of his
own pocket, and at least one other prominent Philadelphian gave financial
support. After the roof-raising, on Fifth Street below Walnut one block from
the city jail, there was a festive dinner under some spreading trees at the
edge of town where about 100 white persons, many of them carpenters,
were waited upon by the Negroes. Afterwards about fifty "black people sat
down at the same table" and were waited upon by "Six of the most respectable of the white company." Nicholson and Benjamin Rush and two others
"were requested to set down with them," which they did, "much to the
satisfaction of the poor blacks."

A repast like this was just the fuel to warm the heart of the generous
doctor, especially because his energies were "much fatigued" from tending
the victims of the mounting yellow fever epidemic. Rush had happily devoted
himself to the cause of this church and to the welfare of Negroes generally,
whom he once described as "the scattered appendages of most of the churches
in the city." He was invariably enraptured by public manifestations of interracial brotherhood and noted with satisfaction the progress of Negroes in
letters to his wife and in his commonplace book; he hoped that similar
churches would be established in other states, "and who knows," he asked,
"but that it may be the means of sending the gospel to Africa, as the American
Revolution sent liberty to Europe?" For Rush the separate African churches
had the inestimable virtue of making the black people "happy," but he was

too much the public-spirited physician not to regard them also as instruments
for social hygiene. "It will be much cheaper to build churches for them than
jails," he wrote toward the close of his life. "Without the former, the latter
will be indispensably necessary for them."[3]

Similarly revealing feelings seem to have animated others among the white
supporters of the new Negro Episcopal church in Philadelphia. The building
was finally readied for public worship in July 1794. On a slab of marble on
the outside wall of the church was inscribed, with the best intention, an
appalling irony: "The People That Walked in Darkness Have Seen a Great
Light." The Reverend Samuel Magaw, delivering the opening discourse in
the church, dwelt tediously—and with no greater perceptiveness than the
piece of marble—upon the "darkness" from which Negroes were so fortunately
emerging. Turning from freemen to slaves, Magaw rang the changes on an
age-old theme. "Your present situation," he counseled them, "gives you some
advantages above what others have: yes, and very possibly, above what your
Masters have,—in that your humbleness of mind, your patience, faithfulness,
and trust only in God, will add to the greatness of your future happiness."
He went on to remind the free Negroes of the debt of gratitude they owed
their earthly benefactors, especially to Lay, Woolman, Benezet, Franklin, the
Pennsylvania Abolition Society and, not least, the citizens of Philadelphia.
He cautioned them to guard against pride, which was said to be increasing
among them, and explained with perfect accuracy that "less allowance will
be made for your failings, than for those of other people." Among the virtues
they should cultivate, he suggested, was "an obliging, friendly, meek conversation." Magaw concluded his address by praising the generous character of
Philadelphians.[4]

Plainly Negroes were not alone in deriving warm satisfaction from the
establishment of separate Negro churches. In the ensuing years, the generally
amicable pattern of separation in Philadelphia was repeated, with variations,
in New York, Boston, and other northern cities. The circumstances of origina-
tion varied, and some of the new churches had white ministers at first, but
the trend toward racially separate churches was well under way in the 1790's.
The same process operated in the slave states as well. Not that the now-
familiar arrangement of mutual exclusion had yet been approximated: in
many churches, in one in Wilkes County, Georgia, in 1805, for example,
Negroes and whites attended together. But unquestionably there were an
increasing number of racially exclusive congregations: in Wilmington, Dela-
ware, Negroes erected a church with aid from white persons; in North Carolina
some free Negroes established a church that whites attended and that eventually became all white; in the same state a mixed congregation split apart when
the whites erected a separate church for the Negro members.[5]

Few developments could have been so symptomatic of the changes which white attitudes underwent after the revolution. The splintering of the churches along racial lines was not simply a matter of Negroes recognizing that they would be more welcome elsewhere. It symbolized an increasingly clear-cut and pervasive separation. It meant that the one institution which was at all prepared to accept the Negro as an equal was shattered—completely, as it turned out. The new Negro churches were equal but separate, proto-types of "separate but equal." When Christian equalitarianism ran head on into American racial mores the result was, institutionally and in the public mind, gradual fission along racial lines. Separation was facilitated by the fissiparous character of Protestantism, but it also exposed the waning social strength of religious principles and the power of deep-set social attitudes. Many Americans seemed unable to tolerate equality without separation. This inability proved critical in the years after the revolution, for it raised the question of what would happen to the commitment to equality if separation seemed impossible. If Negroes were going to remain in America and in increasing numbers become free, white men would have every reason to ask more intensely than before the revolution what manner of men these Negroes were. Thus while social relationships between whites and Negroes were undergoing change and examination, the very nature of the Negro was coming under closer scrutiny. Certain aspects of this intense process of assessment become clearest of all in the highly charged writings of one man, Thomas Jefferson, who as much as any single person framed the terms of American assessment of the Negro's physical being and especially of his inherent quali-fications for participation in the white man's community. His answer was physical separation.

NOTES

1. Richard Allen, *The Life, Experience, and Gospel Labors of the Rt. Rev. Richard Allen* (Philadelphia, 1880), pp. 25-26; William Douglass, *Annals of the First African Church, in the United States of America, Now Styled the African Episcopal Church of St. Thomas, Philadelphia . . .* (Philadelphia, 1862); Charles H. Wesley, *Richard Allen: Apostle of Freedom* (Washington, 1935); Charles H. Wesley s. v. "Jones, Absalom," *Encyclopaedia of the Social Sciences;* Henry J. Cadbury, "Negro Membership in Society of Friends," *Journal of Negro History,* 21 (1936): 153-156.

2. George W. Corner, ed., *The Autobiography of Benjamin Rush* (Princeton, 1948), pp. 202-203.

3. The description of the dinner is also Rush's, *ibid.,* pp. 202-203, 228-229; L. H. Butterfield, ed., *Letters of Benjamin Rush,* 2 vols. (Princeton, 1951), 1: 624, 2: 636-637, 639-640, 1071; Rush, *Extract of a Letter from Dr. Benjamin Rush, of Philadelphia, to Granville Sharp* (London, 1792), esp. pp. 3-4. See Douglass.

4. Samuel Magaw, *A Discourse Delivered July 17, 1794 in the African Church of the City of Philadelphia, on the Occasion of Opening the Said Church, and Holding Public Worship in It the First Time* (Philadelphia, 1794).

5. Carter G. Woodson, *History of the Negro Church* (Washington, 1921), chap. 4; Charles C. Jones, *Religious Instruction of Negroes in the United States* (Savannah, 1842), pp. 50-53, 56-58; Ralph B. Flanders, *Plantation Slavery in Georgia* (Chapel Hill, 1933), p. 174; *Minutes Abolition Convention* (1806), 17; John Spencer Bassett, *Slavery in the State of North Carolina* (Baltimore, 1899) Series 17, No. 7-8 in Johns Hopkins University Studies, Herbert B. Adams, ed., pp. 57-58, 60-61.

6

TO MAKE THEM STAND IN FEAR

KENNETH M. STAMPP

In the following passages from *The Peculiar Institution* the reader will find a compelling presentation of the view that the Negro's church provided very little opportunity for training in independent organization and in a sense betrayed him into support of the status quo with the promise of better things in a life to come. Using the setting of plantation slavery for his discussion, Stampp argues that a carefully edited version of Christianity served as a major method of social control that enabled the master class to hold in bondage the souls as well as the bodies of the slaves. In addition, Stampp sees the form of religious expression of the slaves as an unfathomable composite of Africanisms and an enthusiastic religious behavior resembling that of the poorer whites.

"I greatly desire that the Gospel be preached to the Negroes when the services of a suitable person can be procured," wrote a Mississippian to his overseer. Religious instruction "not only benefits the slave in his moral relations, but enhances his value as an honest, faithful servant and laborer," affirmed an Alabama judge.[1] Pious masters regarded their bondsmen as human beings with immortal souls and therefore felt an obligation to look after their spiritual life. Many of them also considered Christian indoctrination an effective method of keeping slaves docile and contented.

When the first Africans were imported in the seventeenth century, some purchasers opposed converting them to Christianity lest baptism give them a claim to freedom. After the colonial legislatures provided that conversion would not have this effect, the opposition diminished. Thereafter most masters encouraged Christian proselytizing among their bondsmen, and conversion proceeded rapidly.

A minority, however, continued to be indifferent. Even in the nineteenth century a southern clergyman complained that some, "forgetful of God and

Reprinted from *The Peculiar Institution* (New York: Alfred A. Knopf 1956), pp. 156-162, 371-377, by permission of the publisher.

eternity," treated their slaves "too much as creatures of profit." In "extensive districts" thousands of bondsmen never heard the voices of those who brought "the glad tidings of salvation to perishing men." Another clergyman was "astonished to find planters of high moral pretensions" who kept their slaves "shut out almost entirely from the privileges of the Gospel."[2]

A few were openly hostile. "Be assured," wrote a North Carolinian, "that religion among the mass of negroes who profess, is nothing more than a humbug." He did not believe "in the efficacy of preaching to negroes and would never contribute a cent for that purpose." A Louisianian considered attempts to convert slaves the "greatest piece of foolishness"; the only way to improve them, he thought, was through "proper discipline." Olmsted met other slaveholders who shared these views. A Mississippian told him that religious exercises excited the slaves so much that it was difficult to control them. "They would be singing and dancing every night in their cabins, till dawn of day, and utterly unfit themselves for work."[3]

Since Nat Turner had been a slave preacher, the Southampton insurrection temporarily increased sentiment of this kind. Its lasting effect was to convince the master class that the religious life of the slaves needed rigid supervision. In December 1831, James H. Hammond resolved "to break up negro preaching and negro Churches." Many years later another South Carolinian was still warning slaveholders, "Do not, I beseech you, send off your negroes to worship . . . by themselves. I have known great mischief to have grown out of such meetings."[4]

The early attitude of certain Protestant sects toward slavery also accounted for some of the surviving suspicion. In the eighteenth century and early nineteenth century, southern Baptists and Methodists exhibited considerable antislavery sentiment. Many slaveholders were therefore reluctant to have the preachers and missionaries of these denominations work among their slaves. But when the southern wings of these churches changed their positions, when southern clergymen became ardent defenders of slavery, the master class could look upon organized religion as an ally. Church leaders now argued "that the gospel, instead of becoming a means of creating trouble and strife, was really the best instrument to preserve peace and good conduct among the negroes." This was a persuasive argument. "In point of fact," recalled one churchman, "it was this conviction that ultimately opened the way for the gospel on the large plantations."[5]

Through religious instruction the bondsmen learned that slavery had divine sanction, that insolence was as much an offense against God as against the temporal master. They received the Biblical command that servants should obey their masters, and they heard of the punishments awaiting the disobedient slave in the hereafter. They heard, too, that eternal salvation would be their reward for faithful service, and that on the day of judgment "God would deal impartially with the poor and the rich, the black man and the white." Their Christian preceptors, Fanny Kemble noted, "jump[ed] the present life" and went on "to furnish them with all the requisite conveniences for the next."[6]

Numerous slaveholders agreed that this indoctrination had a felicitous effect. A committee of a South Carolina agricultural society reported that religion contributed much to "the government and discipline of the slave population." A traveler in Mississippi met a planter who was himself "a most decided infidel" but who nevertheless saw "the advantage of giving religious instruction to slaves." Many claimed that imparting Christian doctrine to impressionable slave children was especially beneficial. It taught them "respect and obedience to their superiors," made them "more pleasant and profitable servants," and aided "the discipline of a plantation in a wonderful manner."[7]

Others noticed a decline in theft when bondsmen "got religion." A Methodist missionary related a slave's confession that the Gospel "had saved more rice for massa than all the locks and keys on the plantation." Moreover, religious services on Sundays kept idle slaves at home and out of mischief. Indeed, one planter even used a Methodist exhorter as an overseer, with gratifying success; another, hearing of it, tried to get one too.[8]

In 1845, a group of distinguished South Carolina slaveholders published a pamphlet illustrating "the practical working and wholesome effects of religious instruction, when properly and judiciously imparted to our negro peasantry." Each plantation, they believed, ought to become a "religious or parochial family," for religion could play a major role in the perpetuation of slavery.

Precepts that inculcated good-will, forbearance and forgiveness; that enjoin meekness and patience under evils; that demand truth and faithfulness under all circumstances; a teaching that sets before men a righteous judgment, and happiness or misery in the life to come, according to our course of faith and practice in the life that now is, must . . . change the general character of persons thus taught.[9]

The master class understood, of course, that only a carefully censored version of Christianity could have this desired effect. Inappropriate Biblical passages had to be deleted; sermons that might be proper for freemen were not necessarily proper for slaves. Church leaders addressed themselves to this problem and prepared special catechisms and sermons for bondsmen, and special instructions for those concerned with their religious indoctrination. In 1847, for example, Charles Colcock Jones, of Georgia, wrote a book entitled *Suggestions on the Religious Instruction of the Negroes in the Southern States,* which was published by the Presbyterian Board of Publications. From his own experience Jones advised missionaries to ignore the "civil condition" of the slaves and to listen to no complaints against masters or overseers. In preaching to the bondsmen missionaries should condemn "every vice and evil custom," advocate the "discharge of every duty," and support the "peace and order of society." They should teach the slaves to give "respect and obedience [to] all those whom God in his providence has placed in authority over them." Religion, in short, should underwrite the status quo.

Owners had various methods of providing religious training. Most of them believed it "pernicious and evil" for slaves to preach at their own services or prayer meetings.[10] Nevertheless, some permitted it. The master or overseer usually attended such meetings, as required by law—and the preacher, naturally, was a trusted slave. In a number of southern towns the bondsmen attended their own churches. Richmond had four African Baptist churches before 1860, each controlled by a governing board of whites and served by a white pastor. In Savannah, Andrew Marshall, a free Negro, was the minister of the First African Baptist Church. Until his death in 1856, Marshall was "greatly respected" by the whites and the "idol" of his slave congregation.[11]

In the regions of small slaveholdings whites and blacks commonly belonged to the same churches; on the large plantations only the domestics accompanied their masters to worship. When there were mixed congregations the slaves sat in the galleries, or were grouped together at the rear. Sometimes they attended special services on Sunday afternoon. Whatever the arrangements, whites admitted Negro members to their churches everywhere in the antebellum South.

The white-controlled churches made an important contribution to the governing of their slave communicants. They disciplined or "excluded from fellowship" bondsmen guilty of such offenses as "disorder," thievery, "selling spirits on the Lord's day at meeting," "unchristian conduct," and "immorality." For instance, the slave Peter, a member of a Presbyterian church in Iredell County, North Carolina, confessed that he had forged a pass. Because forgery and falsehood were such "flagrant crimes," he was suspended from membership and "exhorted to repentence and [a] better life." A year later, Peter applied for the restoration of his church privileges, "professing a deep penitence for his sins, and a strong determination to lead hereafter a life of greater watchfulness and more prayer." Peter was forgiven.[12]

Large slaveholders occasionally built churches on their estates and hired clergymen to preach to their bondsmen each Sunday. The proprietor of a Mississippi plantation maintained a "beautiful little Gothic church" where a resident pastor administered to the spiritual needs of both master and slaves. Other planters, depending upon missionaries who visited their estates periodically, made no provision for regular religious services. Their slaves apparently had mixed feelings about the occasional visitations of the white preachers. One divine noted sadly that some of them made it "a settled point to sleep during sermons."[13]

The best system, many agreed, was one in which the master himself assumed responsibility for the religious life of his slaves. Gathering his "people" around him on the Sabbath, he preached to them from one of the handbooks or read to them from the Scriptures. The advantage of this system, according to a South Carolina planter, was that it created "a feeling of inter-est between the master and the slave." It produced "that happy state of protection on the one part, and obedience on the other."[14]

Whatever form the bondsmen's religious training took, it appeared that piety increased their value. A former slave remembered hearing a Missouri auctioneer expounding the virtues of a female domestic who was up for sale. She was a good cook and an obedient servant. Moreover, "She has got reli-gion!" Why should this have mattered? Because "the religious teaching con-sists in teaching the slave that he must never strike a white man; that God made him for a slave; and that, when whipped, he must not find fault—for the Bible says, 'He that knoweth his master's will and doeth it not, shall be beaten with many stripes!' And slaveholders find such religion very profitable to them."[15] . . .

Most slaves took their religion seriously, though by the standards of white Christians they sinned mightily. In Africa the Negro's world was inhabited by petulant spirits whose demands had to be gratified; his relationship to these spirits was regulated by the rituals and dogmas of his pagan faith. Some of this was in the corpus of "Africanisms" brought to America. But most of it was lost within a generation, not only because of the general decay of Negro culture but also because new problems and experiences created an urgent need for a new kind of religious expression and a new set of beliefs. What the slave needed now was a spiritual life in which he could participate vigor-ously, which transported him from the dull routine of bondage and which promised him that a better time was within his reach. Hence, he embraced evangelical Protestantism eagerly, because it so admirably satisfied all these needs.

"The doctrine of the Savior comes to the Negro slaves as their most inward need, and as the accomplishment of the wishes of their souls," explained a visitor to the South. "They themselves enunciate it with the purest joy. . . . Their prayers burst forth into flame as they ascend to heaven." On many plantations religious exercises were almost "the only habitual recreation not purely sensual," Olmsted noted; hence slaves poured all their emotions into them "with an intensity and vehemence almost terrible to witness." A former slave recalled the ecstasy he felt when he learned that there was a salvation *"for every man"* and that God loved black men as well as white. "I seemed to see a glorious being, in a cloud of splendor, smiling down from on high," ready to "welcome me to the skies."[16]

Like the whites, many slaves alternated outbursts of intense religious excitement with intervals of religious calm or indifference, for both races participated in the revivals that periodically swept rural America. At the emotional height of a revival, most of the slaves in a neighborhood might renounce worldly pleasures and live austere lives without the fiddle, without dancing, and without whisky. But this could not last forever, and gradually they drifted back to their sinful ways.[17] And their masters often drifted with them; for although many used religion as a means of control, many others neglected it between revivals.

Of the Protestant sects, the Baptists and Methodists proselytized among the slaves most vigorously and counted among their members the great majority of those who joined churches. The decorous Episcopalians were ineffectual in their missionary work; even masters who adhered to this sect seldom managed to convert their own slaves. The Presbyterians had greater success than the Episcopalians but far less than the Baptists or Methodists. Indeed, Presbyterian clergymen who preached to the slaves were advised to write out their sermons in advance and to discourage "exclamations," "out-cries," and "boisterous singing." As a result, explained a Methodist, while the Presbyterian parson was composing his sermon the Methodist itinerant traveled forty miles and gave "hell and damnation to his unrepentant hearers." According to an exslave, the Methodists "preached in a manner so plain that the way-faring man, though a fool, could not err therein."[18] So did the Baptists—and, in addition, their practice of baptism by immersion gave them a special appeal.

In the North, Negroes organized their own independent churches; in the South, except in a few border cities, the laws against slave assemblies pre-vented them from doing this before the Civil War. Many slaves attended the white-controlled churches or were preached to by white ministers at special services. This inhibited them and limited both the spiritual and emotional value of their religious experience, because there was an enormous gap between a congregation of slaves and even the most sympathetic white clergyman. As one missionary confessed, "The pastor will meet with some rough and barren spots, and encounter tardiness, indifference, heaviness of eyes and inattention—yea, many things to depress and discourage."[19]

Yet it was from white preachers that the slaves first received their Christian indoctrination. To many bondsmen affiliation with a white church was a matter of considerable importance, and they did not take lightly the penalty of being "excluded from the fellowship" for immorality or "heathenism."

Some white clergymen preached to them with great success. Nor was it uncommon to see whites and slaves "around the same altar . . . mingling their cries for mercy" and together finding "the pearl of great price."[20]

Even so, most bondsmen received infinitely greater satisfaction from their own unsupervised religious meetings which they held secretly or which their masters tolerated in disregard of the law. In these gatherings slaves could express themselves freely and interpret the Christian faith to their own satisfaction, even though some educated whites believed that their interpretation contained more heathen superstition than Christianity. The slaves, observed Olmsted, were "subject to intense excitements; often really maniacal," which they considered to be religious; but "I cannot see that they indicate anything but a miserable system of superstition, the more painful that it employs some forms and words ordinarily connected with true Christianity."[21]

Not only the practice of voodooism which survived among a few slaves in southern Louisiana, but the widespread belief in charms and spirits stemmed in part from the African past. Frederick Douglass learned from an old African (who had "magic powers") that if a slave wore the root of a certain herb on his right side, no white man could ever whip him. Slave conjurers accomplished wondrous feats with "root work" and put frightful curses upon their enemies. A Louisiana master once had to punish a slave because of "a phial which was found in his possession containing two ground puppies as they are called. The negroes were under some apprehension that he intended to do mischief."[22]

But slave superstitions did not all originate in Africa, and it would even be difficult to prove that most did. For the slaves picked up plenty of them from "the good Puritans, Baptists, Methodists, and other religious sects who first obtained possession of their ancestors." (Indeed, more than likely Negroes and whites made a generous exchange of superstitions.) There is no need to trace back to Africa the slave's fear of beginning to plant a crop on Friday, his dread of witches, ghosts, and hobgoblins, his confidence in good-luck charms, his alarm at evil omens, his belief in dreams, and his reluctance to visit burying grounds after dark. These superstitions were all firmly rooted in Anglo-Saxon folklore. From the whites some slaves learned that it was possible to communicate with the world of spirits: "It is not at all uncommon to hear them refer to conversations which they allege, and apparently believe themselves to have had with Christ, the apostles, or the prophets of old, or to account for some of their actions by attributing them to the direct influence of the Holy Spirit, or of the devil." During the 1840's, many slaves heard about Millerism and waited in terror for the end of the world.[23] The identification of superstition is, of course, a highly subjective process; and southern whites tended to condemn as superstition whatever elements of slave belief they did not happen to share—as they condemned each other's sectarian beliefs.

The influence of Africa could sometimes be detected in the manner in which slaves conducted themselves at their private religious services. In the sea islands, for example, a prayer meeting at the "praise house" was followed by a "shout," which was an invigorating group ceremony. The participants "begin first walking and by-and-by shuffling around, one after the other, in a ring. The foot is hardly taken from the floor, and the progression is mainly due to a jerking, hitching motion, which agitates the entire shouter, and soon brings out streams of perspiration. Sometimes they dance silently, sometimes as they shuffle they sing the chorus of the spiritual, and sometimes the song itself is sung by the dancers." This, a white witness believed, was "certainly the remains of some old idol worship." Olmsted reported that in social worship the slaves "work themselves up to a great pitch of excitement, in which they yell and cry aloud, and, finally, shriek and leap up, clapping their hands and dancing, as it is done at heathen festivals."[24]

But again it is not easy to tell how much of their "heathenism" the slaves learned in the white churches and at white revival meetings. One Sunday morning, in Accomac County, Virginia, a visitor attended a Methodist church where the slaves were permitted to hold their own services before the whites occupied the building. "Such a medley of sounds, I never heard before. They exhorted, prayed, sung, shouted, cryed, grunted and growled. Poor Souls! they knew no better, for I found that when the other services began the sounds were similar, which the white folks made; and the negroes only imitated them and shouted a little louder."[25]

A camp meeting in South Carolina provided an equally striking illustration of this point. When the services began, a great crowd assembled around a wooden platform, the Negroes on one side and the whites on the other. On the platform stood four preachers, and between the singing of hymns two of them exhorted the Negroes and two the whites, "calling on the sinners . . . to come to the Savior, to escape eternal damnation!" Soon some of the white people came forward and threw themselves, "as if overcome," before the platform where the ministers received their confessions and consoled them. Around a white girl, who had fallen into a trance, stood a dozen women singing hymns of the resurrection. "In the camp of the blacks is heard a great tumult and a loud cry. Men roar and bawl out; women screech like pigs about to be killed; many, having fallen into convulsions, leap and strike about them, so that they are obliged to be held down." The Negroes made more noise and were more animated than the whites, but the behavior of the two races did not differ in any fundamental way. Except for condemning a "holy dance" which some Negro women engaged in for a new convert, the whites did not appear to think that the Negroes acted in an outrageous or unchristian fashion.[26]

In short, the religion of the slaves was, in essence, strikingly similar to that of the poor, illiterate white men of the antebellum South.

NOTES

1. Ulrich B. Phillips (ed.), *Plantation and Frontier: 1649-1843* (Cleveland, 1910), 1: 112-115; Helen T. Catterall, *Judicial Cases Concerning American Slavery and the Negro* (Washington, D.C., 1926-1937), 3: 238.
2. Charles Colcock Jones, *Suggestions on the Religious Instruction of the Negroes in the Southern States* (Philadelphia, 1847), pp. 7-9, 31; *Southern Cultivator* 9 (1851): 84-85.
3. Ebenezer Pettigrew to James C. Johnston, July 16, 1838, Pettigrew Family Papers: Edwin A. Davis, ed., *Plantation Life in the Florida Parishes of Louisiana, 1836-1846, As Reflected in the Diary of Bennet H. Barrow* (New York, 1943), pp. 323-324; Frederick Law Olmsted, *A Journey in the Back Country* (New York, 1860), pp. 92-93, 107-108.
4. Hammond Diary, entries for December 15, 16, 1831; *De Bow's Review* 24 (1858): 64; Luther P. Jackson, "Religious Development of the Negro in Virginia from 1760 to 1860," *Journal of Negro History* 16 (1931): 206.
5. W. P. Harrison, *The Gospel Among the Slaves* (Nashville, 1893), pp. 149-151.
6. Sir Charles Lyell, *A Second Visit to North America* (London, 1849), 2: 2-3; Frances Anne Kemble, *Journal of a Residence on a Georgian Plantation in 1838-1839* (New York, 1863), p. 57.
7. *De Bow's Review* 7 (1849): 221; 26 (1859): 107; *Southern Agriculturist* 4 (1831): 351-352; Jones, pp. 34-35.
8. Harrison, pp. 205, 210-211; *Farmers' Register* 4 (1837): 574; Howell M. Henry, *The Police Control of the Slaves in South Carolina* (Emory, Va., 1914), p. 139.
9. Quoted in Charleston *Courier*, August 28, 1845.
10. *De Bow's Review* 26 (1859): 107.
11. Jackson, pp. 221-222; Savannah *Republican*, December 15, 1856.
12. Church of Bethany ms. session book.
13. *De Bow's Review* 7 (1849): 221; *Southern Cultivator* 9 (1851): 85.
14. Solomon Northup, *Twelve Years a Slave* (Buffalo, 1853), pp. 97-98; Charleston *Courier*, April 15, 1851.
15. William W. Brown, *Narrative of William W. Brown, a Fugitive Slave* (Boston, 1847), pp. 83-84.
16. Frederika Bremer, *The Homes of the New World* (New York, 1853), 2: 155; Olmsted, p. 106; Henson, *Story*, pp. 28-29.
17. Susan Dabney Smedes, *Memorials of a Southern Planter* (Baltimore, 1887), pp. 161-162; Henry Watson, Jr., to his mother, July 7, 1846, Watson Papers.
18. Jones, pp. 14-15; Carter G. Woodson, *The History of the Negro Church* (Washington, D.C., 1921), pp. 97-98; John Thompson, *The Life of John Thompson, a Fugitive Slave* (Worcester, Mass., 1856), p. 18.
19. Jones, p. 17.
20. Flat River Church Records (Person County, North Carolina); Harrison, pp. 199-201.
21. Frederick Law Olmsted, *A Journey in the Seaboard Slave States* (New York, 1856), p. 114.
22. J. Carlyle Sitterson, *Sugar Country: The Cane Sugar Industry in the South, 1753-1950* (Lexington, Kentucky, 1953), p. 102; Frederick Douglass, *My Bondage and My Freedom* (New York, 1855), p. 238; Hammond Diary, entry for October 16, 1835; Marston Diary, entry for November 25, 1825.
23. Olmsted, *Back Country*, p. 105; Davis, ed., pp. 283-285.
24. Johnson, *Sea Islands*, pp. 149-151; Olmsted, *Seaboard*, pp. 449-450.
25. Emerson Journal, entry for September 26, 1841.
26. Bremer, 1: 306-315.

7

BEYOND THE MASTER'S EYE

RICHARD C. WADE

Though many Northern churches in the postrevolutionary period were encouraging the formation of separate black congregations, even those religious Southerners who approved the Christianizing of the slave population remained skeptical of the propriety (or even safety) of allowing any independent organizations among the blacks. As whites consistently failed to minister properly to the black population, the Negroes were increasingly successful at organizing themselves into religious units, sometimes independently, at other times with some connection to a white congregation. The black religious bodies that Richard Wade depicts provided everything from entertainment and substitute families to decent funerals and leadership training for their members. This selection on the growth of black Christianity in the Southern cities is one aspect of Wade's analysis of the complex relationships resulting from racial accommodation among free blacks, slaves, and whites in the urban South. The reader is also referred to James Cone's important discussion of the relation between antebellum slave protest and Christianity in Chapter 32.

If the homes of some blacks and the grog shops and groceries furnished scattered but persistent centers for the slave's informal life, the churches increasingly provided still another focus. Generally, this activity met with white approval, for it was widely believed that religion sustained rather than threatened slavery. "The Gospel is our mightiest safeguard," a Charleston minister explained; "for it governs in secret as well as in public; it cultivates the conscience, and thus establishes a more vigilant watch over individual conduct than Foucher himself ever accomplished by his unrivalled police." His conclusion was both pointed and typical: "If any community on earth is bound by considerations of personal interest, to encourage the diffusion of sound religious principles among the lower orders, we are that community."[1]

Nor was this mere theory. "The best servants I know, are those who have the most religious intelligence and piety," another asserted.

Those among them who are most intimately acquainted with the Bible, understand best the relation between themselves and their masters, and are best contented with it. The communities where the most prudent and ener- getic measures for the improvement of the colored population have been adopted, have the least trouble in controlling that population.[2]

Religious leaders also thought the opportunities for work among the blacks in the city seemed much brighter than in rural areas. "We know," wrote one of them, "that to negroes in the country, there are insuperable impediments to the full use of the ordinary provision for worship and instruc- tion in parishes and neighborhoods." The reasons for this were not hard to see:

The distance of many plantations from the churches; the insufficiency of the accommodation, were it practical to attend them; the inability of the negroes generally to be reached by ordinary pastoral care– . . . make the fact indisputable, that arrangements for these purposes . . . must be provided *at home*. The Gospel must be carried to them . . . . In our cities and villages [however] opportunities of religious improvement are freely enjoyed by negroes.[3]

This judgment, though accurate in its description of rural problems, was optimistic in its assessment of the urban scene. In fact, in no city did white leadership succeed in meeting either the hopes of slaves or the official responsibilities of their own churches in ministering to the colored population. In part, the failure can be explained by the sheer numbers involved; in the larger towns the scale of the job overwhelmed already overburdened organi- zations. In Charleston, where the effort was greatest, the Reverend Paul Trapier put the question in cold statistical terms. "There are, as it appeared in the census of 1840, about 20,000 slaves in our city and its suburbs [the Neck] ." He calculated that 1,000 were "connected with our six Episcopal Churches," while in all other denominations "it is estimated that more than 5,000 can be accommodated. This leaves an appalling residue of about 14,000." He asked plaintively, "Where are they? What is becoming of them?"[4]

A greater problem than numbers, however, was the difficulty of finding a system of worship and instruction appropriate to the "peculiar institution." "All concur in the confirmation of the improvement effected by religion in the moral condition, docility, and submission to authority, of those slaves to whom it has been communicated," an Episcopal newspaper pointed out. "On the mode of religious teaching only, does a diversity of opinion exist."[5] Should bondsmen attend the same services as the master as part of the family, in the way Catholics did? Others advocated separate worship under white clergymen and tutelage as practiced by some Methodist and Baptist churches. Still others sought a mixture of the two procedures. In any case, the objective was to bring some religious instruction to the blacks without encouraging independent organization among them.

Few doubted the receptivity of the Negroes; indeed it was their enthusiastic response to any overture that continually forced the issue. "Our own security is best consulted not by violent resistance to any original impulse of the heart—not by attempting to extirpate or destroy it—" wrote the Reverend Thornwell in the midst of Charleston's debate on the question, "but by giving it a wise direction and turning it into safe and salutary channels." He even thought it was impossible to prevent slaves from organizing their own churches: "Separate congregations, therefore, they *will* have. If our laws and public sentiment of the community tolerate them, they will be open, public, responsible. If our laws prohibit them, they will be secret, fanatical, dangerous." A prudent policy would save the bondsmen "from secret convocations which the white man cannot witness—we save him from appeals which madden rather than instruct—from a religion which puffs up but does not edify."[6]

While whites debated the proper methods, the Negroes went ahead organizing their religious life as best they could. And the need was deep, for slavery had stripped them of any meaningful pattern of life beyond that of the master and their bondage. The family could furnish none. No tradition could provide roots into a history without servitude. Neither today nor tomorrow offered any expectation of a life without the present stigma. Deprived of nostalgia for the past and unable to discover any real meaning in the present, the blacks sought relief and consolation in a distant time. In the church, with their own kind, amid songs of redemption and the promises of Paradise, a lifeline could be thrown into the future.

"And here rises a poor slave, unlettered, and in the darkest ignorance, so far as human knowledge is concerned," wrote a visitor to a church in New Orleans, "and yet rich in his Christian faith, and as he unfolds a Saviour's love, he sways the hearts of his auditors as no other conceivable theme could move them." It was an unforgettable experience. "My eyes were dim with tears, as in broken language, he spoke of patience under life's cares, and depicted the glory of that world where there shall be no night, and where all tears shall be wiped from every eye." The congregation responded with "an extempore wail, without articulate words, such as I have never heard before from earthly voices."[7]

But other whites who dropped in occasionally to watch the services found them unusual and even shocking. Some believed the worship "a mockery of religion" or, more soberly with Olmsted, "a delusive clothing of Christian forms and phrases" added to "the original vague superstition of the African savage."[8] But these observations missed the significance of religious life for the Negroes. What seemed a burlesque was in fact a reverent, emotional experience. The clapping, chanting, shouting, and sometimes dancing, the fervent response to the minister's preaching, all expressed a longing that had no other sanctioned outlet.

This coming together was of itself important. It was the only colored meeting which needed no special permission; indeed, it had found some approbation among whites. The occasion called for the best clothes, the most proper behavior, the fullest participation. Once there, one was not only a spectator but part of a congregation. The words, the prayers, the exhortations, even while they admonished the sinner, held out the promise of eternal happiness. Put aside for the moment were the burdens of bondage, the daily, fruitless toil, the sense of inferiority. It was no wonder the church was filled at dawn and candlelight on Sunday, and parishioners were active on weekday evenings.

The character of the services reflected these considerations. Many observers described the worship in great detail, but Olmsted's account of a New Orleans meeting was among the most careful and included the familiar elements and sequences. While walking through a "rather mean neighborhood," he was attracted by "a loud chorus" singing in a "chapel or small church." He found there only three whites, one of whom "looked like a ship's officer" and was "probably a member of the police force in undress—what we call spy when we detect it in Europe." The congregation was wholly colored, and the preacher was "nearly black, with close woolly hair. His figure was slight, he seemed to be about thirty years of age, and the expression on his face indicated a refined and delicately sensitive nature. His eye was very fine, bright, deep and clear; his voice and manner generally quiet and impressive."

No sooner had Olmsted been seated than he noticed an old Negro, whom "I supposed for some time to be suffering under some nervous complaint; he trembled, his teeth chattered, and his face, at intervals, was convulsed." He then began to respond to the preacher: "'Oh, yes!' 'That's it, that's it!' 'Yes, yes—glory—yes!'" Others joined him whenever the speaker's voice was "unusually solemn, or his language eloquent or excited." Sometimes the frenzy included "shouts, and groans, terrific shrieks, and indescribable expressions of ecstasy—of pleasure or agony—and even stamping, jumping, and clapping of hands." Olmsted himself found "my own muscles all stretched, as if ready for a struggle—my face glowing, and my feet stamping."

The second preacher was even more extraordinary. "He was a tall full-blooded negro, very black, and with a disgusting expression of sensuality, cunning and variety in his countenance, and a pompous and patronizing manner—a striking contrast . . . to the prepossessing quiet and modest young preacher who had preceded him." Dressed gaudily, he spoke in "a low, deep, hoarse, indistinct and confidential tone." But soon "he struck a higher key, drawling his sentences like a street salesman, occasionally breaking out into a yell with the strength of extraordinarily powerful lungs, at the same time taking a striking attitude and gesturing in an extraordinary manner . . . . This would create a frightful excitement in the people," and they responded with the "loudest and most terrific shouts." Olmsted confessed that he could "compare them to nothing else human I ever heard."

The meeting then returned to the hymns. "The congregation sang; I think everyone joined, even the children, and the collective sound was wonderful." The women "rose above the rest, and one of these soon began to introduce variations, which consisted mainly of shouts of oh! oh! at a piercing height." Many of the others "kept time with their feet, balancing themselves on each alternately, and swinging their bodies accordingly." The preacher now "raised his own voice above all, turned around, clapped his hands and commenced to dance," laughing aloud and "leaping, with increasing agility, from one side of the pulpit to the other." Before he was finished he had thrust aside the other ministers, hurled the Bible into the children's pew, and fallen prostrate across the floor. Shortly thereafter the meeting was closed, and "the congregation slowly passed out, chatting and saluting one another politely, as they went, and bearing not the slightest mark of the previous excitement."[9]

The tumult of the services was simply the most conspicuous aspect of the colored religious life in the cities. More significant was the fact that increasingly Negroes took over basic responsibility for most of the activity of their churches. Of course, formally the law vested supervision and control in white leaders, but the fundamental tasks—recruiting members, finding and supporting ministers, paying rents, and staffing the Sunday schools—fell to the blacks themselves. If this activity had been left to regular denominations, the churches would have scarcely survived, much less flourished. Behind their success lay the enthusiasm of Negroes—slave and free. And throughout urban Dixie colored religious activity burgeoned.

In Richmond the growth is easily traced. In 1823 a number of slaves and free blacks petitioned the legislature for the right to establish a church. The address observed that there had been a "rapid increase of population in the city, especially among slaves and free persons of color." Yet "it has been the misfortune of your petitioners to be excluded from the churches, Meeting Houses and other places of public devotion which are used by white persons." The Negroes had turned to private places "where they are much crowded and where a portion of the Brethren are unable to hear or partake in the worship going on." The congregation consisted of 700 whose names had been submitted to the "Head of Police," who found "no objection . . . to their moral character." The petitioners wanted to build "a House of Public Worship which may be called the Baptist African Church." Realizing they could not expect this "privilege" without "such restrictions and restraints as are consistent" with "the peace and good order of society," they agreed to submit "most chearfully to all regulations." They wanted, however, to choose their own teachers, subject to the mayor's approval.[10]

Many years later, Lyell found the situation greatly improved. The Episcopal church had recently designated a side gallery for the blacks in the hope that masters and slaves "might unite in the worship of the same God, as they hoped to enter hereafter together into His everlasting kingdom." The Negroes preferred other services and few responded, but Lyell was assured that if "I went to the Baptist or Methodist churches, I should find the galleries quite full."[11] By 1856 the Virginia capital had four "African Churches," one of which a Sabbath School convention declared to be "the largest in the world," with a choir "not equalled in America." To these were added several classes for religious instruction carefully supervised so as "not to change the civil status of the negro, or alter relations of masters and servants, or teach them to read." The governor moreover supported the program on the ground that it took from "Northern fanaticism its sharpest weapon."[12]

Every city witnessed the spread of formal Negro organization where slaves and free mingled in religious exercises. Baltimore headed the list with thirteen churches.[13] By 1843 Louisville had four, three Methodist and one Baptist. The latter had a colored pastor and catered to free blacks, though slaves attended too; the others were "under the care" of either the Fourth Street or Brook Street congregations.[14] The city council officially tolerated if it did not encourage this development by passing a resolution in 1835 which permitted Negroes "to worship their God without molestation from any of the city officers, provided they are orderly, and under the supervision of some respectable white man."[15]

Even New Orleans, where the Catholic population was large and itinerant churches many, advertised three "colored congregations" in 1857 with "public services every Sabbath morning upon the oral system with Reverend H. N. McTyre as superintendant."[16] In addition, the African Methodist Episcopal Church owned three chapels scattered across the town with buildings assessed at $15,000, $4,000, and $2,000. The council was less happy about this growth than Louisville's had been and in 1857 passed an ordinance which closed even the authorized separate churches. Three years later, the edict was extended to "all churches where colored persons free or bond, assemble."[17] Yet the four prewar decades had seen an acceleration of Negro religious life both within and outside white organizations in the city.

The Charleston story was the most interesting of any, for it was widely believed that Negro churches had nursed the abortive Vesey plot of 1822. The city's official account of the affair contended that "among the conspirators a *majority* of them belong to the *African Church.*" This congregation, "comprised wholly of persons of color and almost entirely of blacks," had been established in the preceding December. Among other activities it had set up class meetings conducted by a "colored minister or leader as they were termed" for religious instruction and worship. Though the Methodists selected these men, no whites attended the gatherings.[18] The creation of this organization with a separate building just before the Vesey affair led many to associate the two events. And it accounted for a "morbidness" on this topic which could be found "in no other city of the Southern States."[19]

Despite this sensitivity, Charleston's Negroes managed slowly to widen their religious latitude. By 1845 the lowest estimate of church membership was about 6,000, while the highest ran over 8,200.[20] In slavery's last years there were at least 6,000 colored Methodists alone, a figure nearly five times the number of the whites of that denomination. In Trinity Church, out of a total of 2,123 there were only 299 whites, and these, of course, discharged supervisory duties. In 1859 the Presbyterians, finding their own building overcrowded, erected one for the blacks at a cost of $25,000. Immediately it became a thriving center where every Sunday afternoon over 1,000 slaves and free colored people attended.[21]

The range of the churches' concern was not limited to worship. It extended to Sunday schooling for the young, to Bible classes for adults, and to prayers for the sick. Funerals and burial services further involved the churches. Indeed, in death the religious connection took on special meaning. Without it the slave would have been interred without ceremony and with little care in some out-of-the-way cemetery for colored people. The master or the city might provide the plot, and perhaps a wooden slab would mark the spot. But as a member of the congregation the passing was attended with due solemnity. The minister—sometimes white—presided, prayers were offered, and a procession of friends carried the body to be placed in the church burial grounds among other parishioners. Thus the church, for a moment at least, became a surrogate family for the bondsmen. It was little wonder that a leading guidebook for white ministers could observe simply: "Funeral services are much esteemed by the Negroes."[22]

"There was a decent hearse, of the usual style, drawn by two horses; six hacking coaches followed it, and six well-dressed men, mounted on handsome saddle horses, and riding them well, rode in the rear of them," ran Olmsted's account of a Richmond funeral. "Twenty or thirty men and women were also walking together with the procession, on the sidewalk. Among them all was not a white person."[23] In Charleston he witnessed a humbler, similar affair. "The exercises were simple and decorous, . . . and were conducted by a well-dressed and dignified elderly negro. . . . The grave was filled by the negroes, before the crowd, which was quite large, dispersed. Besides myself, only one white man, probably a policeman, was in attendance."[24]

The ceremonies were often held at night to accommodate those who could not get away from work during the day. In such cases the crowds increased and whites, at least, thought a carnival spirit replaced solemn mourning. A Charleston critic contended that "sometimes every evening in the week" Negro funerals, attended by "three or four hundred negroes and a tumultuous crowd of other slaves," made such a racket that they disturbed the neighborhood of the Pitt Street cemetery. "It appears to be a jubilee for every slave in the city," he observed, while concluding ominously that "let it be remembered too that the officiating priests are black men."[25]

On special occasions the gatherings were immense. When a deacon of the Third Colored Baptist Church in Savannah died, a visitor recorded the scene:

> In the procession were four uniformed fire companies. The Porters' Association, of which he was a member, turned out, and wore black scarfs, with white rosettes. . . . A spectator counted fifty-two carriages, well filled, besides a number on horseback, following the hearse. It is estimated that between two thousand and two thousand five hundred colored persons were in the procession.[26]

For most, however, the ceremony was plain and the witnesses few. Yet the religious sanction, the words of the ministry, and the prayers of friends were crucial.

It did not matter so much that the cemeteries were poorly kept. "A few trees, trailing with long moss rise above hundreds of nameless graves, over-grown with weeds," William Cullen Bryant wrote sadly after visiting one in Savannah, "but here and there are scattered memorials of the dead, some of a very humble kind, with a few of marble, and a half dozen spacious brick tombs like those in the cemetery of the whites."[27] What was important was that, when life was finished, the body would not be disposed of like that of a dead animal but the book be closed with some dignity and solemnity.

Colored churches increasingly performed these rites, even though many whites thought it a dangerous extension of their activity. When a Virginia law in 1832 prohibited slaves and free blacks from officiating at funerals, a long petition by Richmond Negroes asked for repeal: "Many colored human beings are inter'd like brutes, their relatives and friends being unable to pro-

cure white ministers to perform the usual ceremony in the burial of the dead."
Eleven clergymen joined in the memorial, explaining that "pressing engagements of white ministers left no time for this function."[28]

Helping in this activity were various church groups. Most important were
small societies called "bands." They cared for the sick and handled the burial
of the dead. Though religious in impulse, they usually existed outside of
church supervision. White ministers knew they existed and worried about
their influence. "They exist among those who are members of every Church
in the City, though without the cognizance or recognition of the constituted
authorities," one observed. Though he appreciated their usefulness because
"there is nothing so dear to a negro than a decent funeral," he feared "they
have been perverted and abused."[29]

The capacity of the blacks to organize their religious life surprised both
visitors and white ministers alike. "To see a body of African origin, who had
joined one of the denominations of Christians and built a church for themselves," Lyell wrote with some awe about Savannah, and "who had elected a
pastor of their own race and secured him an annual salary, from whom they
were listening to a good sermon, scarcely, if at all, below the average of the
compositions of white ministers—to hear the whole service respectably, and
the singing admirably performed, surely marks an astonishing step in civilization."[30] In Richmond, Mrs. Finch was impressed to find the African Baptist
Church "entirely supported and attended by coloured people" and run by
"several intelligent black elders, and deacons."[31]

Local residents sometimes showed great pride in these churches when
visitors inquired about the condition of slaves. But their real response was
more skeptical. It was not only that neighbors complained of the noise that
often accompanied services and classes. More fundamentally, they feared the
independence which separate churches implied. Never certain of what went
on inside, they became convinced that abolitionist literature was circulated
clandestinely and that insurrection was nightly plotted. The churches were,
as one Charlestonian put it, "nurseries of self government" and hence dangerous. The slaves get "excited by the privileges they enjoy, as a separate and
to some extent independent society," warned another.[32]

The fear of white townspeople was in part justified, for in these churches
the Negroes did in fact get some experience in managing their own affairs.
Those most active achieved moreover a special position in both colored and
white communities. Black religious leadership carried a broad status that was
not confined to spiritual matters. Though not ministers in the conventional
sense, the preachers and class leaders were something more than mere slaves.
And the formal connection with white ministers and lay boards gave them
some prestige, at least among the congregation. In the life of these churches

the first signs of traditional Negro leadership were visible in the cities even before the abolition of slavery. Already the church had become the cardinal point of colored affairs.

NOTES

1. *The Religious Instruction of the Black Population. The Gospel To Be Given to Our Servants. A Sermon Preached in Several Protestant Episcopal Churches in Charleston on Sundays in July 1847, by Rev. Paul Trapier, in Charleston S.C. Etc.* (Charleston, 1847), p. 14.
2. "Public Proceedings, relating to Calvary Church, and the Religious Instruction of Slaves; with an Appendix, &c.," *The Charleston Gospel Messenger, and Protestant Episcopal Register* 27 (July 1850): 118.
3. Proceedings of the Meeting in Charleston, S.C., May 13-15, 1845, on the Religious Instruction of the Negroes Together with the Report of the Committee and the Address to the Public (Charleston, 1845), p. 7.
4. *The Religious Instruction of the Black Population,* p. 2.
5. "Public Proceedings, relating to Calvary Church," p. 118.
6. Rev. Dr. James Henley Thornwell, *A Review of Rev. J. B. Adger's Sermon on the Instruction of the Colored Population* (Charleston, 1847), pp. 12-13.
7. John S. C. Abbott, *South and North; or Impressions Received During a Trip to Cuba and the South* (New York, 1860), pp. 75-76.
8. *Missouri Republican,* June 13, 1835; Frederick Law Olmsted, *A Journey in the Back Country* (New York, 1860), p. 109. Frederick Law Olmsted, *A Journey in the Seaboard Slave States, With Remarks on Their Economy* (New York, 1856), p. 266.
9. Olmsted, *Back Country,* pp. 187-196.
10. Petition of Slaves and Free Negroes for Church, Petitions of the City of Richmond to the State Legislature, December 23, 1823, mss., State Library, Richmond.
11. Charles Lyell, *A Second Visit to the United States of North America* (London, 1855), 1:208.
12. *Richmond Enquirer,* May 28, 1857. The next year the First Baptist Church set up an extensive new program; see *Richmond Enquirer,* July 7, 1858.
13. Daniel R. Hundley, *Social Relations in Our Southern States* (New York, 1860), pp. 350-351; Jeffrey R. Brackett, *The Negro in Maryland, A Study of the Institution of Slavery* (Baltimore, 1889), p. 206.
14. G. Collins, *The Louisville Directory for the Year 1843-44* (Louisville, 1843), p. 192.
15. City of Louisville, Journal of the City Council, mss., December 28, 1835. The official latitude was almost enlarged when a move to strike out "orderly" lost, four votes to three.
16. *New Orleans Sunday Delta,* January 4, 1857.
17. *New Orleans Daily Picayune,* May 21, 1858; *New Orleans Daily Delta,* October 13, 1860. One of the colored churches in the Second District had over 1,100 communicants. Rainey, *Myatt & Co's. Directory,* 1857, n.p.
18. *An Account of the Late Intended Insurrection Among a Portion of the Blacks of this City. Published by the Authority of the Corporation of Charleston,* 3rd ed. (Charleston, 1822), pp. 30, 22-23.
19. *The Religious Instruction of the Black Population,* p. 7.
20. *The Religious Instruction of the Black Population,* pp. 2, 8.
21. L. P. Jackson, "Religious Instruction of Negroes, 1830-1860, With Special Reference to South Carolina," *Journal of Negro History* 15 (1930): 100-102.

22. Charles Colcock Jones, *Suggestions on the Religious Instruction of the Negroes in the Southern States* (Philadelphia, n.d.), p. 59.

23. Olmsted, *Seaboard Slave States,* p. 24.

24. *Ibid.,* pp. 405-406.

25. *Southern Patriot* (Charleston), September 19, 1835.

26. Lillian Foster, *Wayside Glimpses, North and South* (New York, 1860), p. 109.

27. W. C. Bryant, *Letters of a Traveller; or Notes of Things Seen in Europe and America,* p. 94.

28. Petition of the Free People of Color to the Virginia State Legislature, Dec. 17, 1834, mss., Virginia State Library, Richmond.

29. *Public Proceedings Relating to Calvary Church and the Religious Instruction of Slaves* (Charleston, 1850), p. 40.

30. Lyell, 2:15.

31. Marianne Finch, *An Englishwoman's Experience in America* (London, 1853), p. 299.

32. Thornwell, *Review of Adger's Sermons on Religious Instruction,* p. 13.

PART II

Differentiation of the Black Church: Residence and Class

8

THE FUNCTION OF THE NEGRO CHURCH

W. E. BURGHARDT DU BOIS

In Chapter 7, from Richard Wade's *Slavery in the Cities, 1820-1860,* the urban black church already showed signs of becoming all things to its members. At the turn of the century Du Bois observed that the Negro church, at least in the city of Philadelphia, had become more of a social than a religious institution. The congregations resembled groups of stockholders with eagle eyes on the budget and a taste for amenable, efficient chairmen of the board. In the churches' list of priorities, Du Bois found that social action held last place, while spiritual mission filled no place at all. This brief selection suggests that the black church continued to function in numerous surrogate roles long after it had ceased to be the only Negro social institution.

The Function of the Negro Church

The Negro church is the peculiar and characteristic product of the transplanted African, and deserves especial study. As a social group the Negro church may be said to have antedated the Negro family on American soil; as such it has preserved, on the one hand, many functions of tribal organization, and on the other hand, many of the family functions. Its tribal functions are shown in its religious activity, its social authority, and general guiding and coordinating work; its family functions are shown by the fact that the church is a center of social life and intercourse, acts as newspaper and intelligence bureau, is the center of amusements—indeed, is the world in which the Negro moves and acts. So far-reaching are these functions of the church that its organization is almost political. . . .

The functions of such churches in order of present emphasis are:

Reprinted from *The Philadelphia Negro* (Philadelphia: Published for the University of Pennsylvania, 1899), pp. 201-207.

1. The raising of the annual budget.
2. The maintenance of membership.
3. Social intercourse and amusements.
4. The setting of moral standards.
5. Promotion of general intelligence.
6. Efforts for social betterment.

1. The annual budget is of first importance, because the life of the organization depends upon it. The amount of expenditure is not very accurately determined beforehand, although its main items do not vary much. There is the pastor's salary, the maintenance of the building, light and heat, the wages of a janitor, contributions to various church objects, and the like, to which must be usually added the interest on some debt. The sum thus required varies in Philadelphia from $200 to $5,000. A small part of this is raised by a direct tax on each member. Besides this, voluntary contributions by members roughly gauged according to ability, are expected, and a strong public opinion usually compels payment. Another large source of revenue is the collection after the sermons on Sunday, when, amid the reading of notices and a subdued hum of social intercourse, a stream of givers walk to the pulpit and place in the hands of the trustee or steward in charge a contribution, varying from a cent to a dollar or more. To this must be added the steady revenue from entertainments, suppers, socials, fairs, and the like. In this way the Negro churches of Philadelphia raise nearly $100,000 a year. They hold in real estate $900,000 worth of property, and are thus no insignificant element in the economics of the city.

2. Extraordinary methods are used and efforts made to maintain and increase the membership of the various churches. To be a popular church with large membership means ample revenues, large social influence and a leadership among the colored people unequaled in power and effectiveness. Consequently people are attracted to the church by sermons, by music and by entertainments; finally, every year a revival is held, at which considerable numbers of young people are converted. All this is done in perfect sincerity and without much thought of merely increasing membership, and yet every small church strives to be large by these means and every large church to maintain itself or grow larger. The churches thus vary from a dozen to 1,000 members.

3. Without wholly conscious effort the Negro church has become a center of social intercourse to a degree unknown in white churches even in the country. The various churches, too, represent social classes. At St. Thomas' one looks for the well-to-do Philadelphians, largely descendants of favorite mulatto house servants, and consequently well bred and educated, but rather

cold and reserved to strangers or newcomers; at Central Presbyterian one sees
the older, simpler set of respectable Philadelphians with distinctly Quaker
characteristics—pleasant but conservative; at Bethel may be seen the best of
the great laboring class—steady, honest people, well dressed and well fed, with
church and family traditions; at Wesley will be found the new arrivals, the
sightseers and the strangers to the city—hearty and easygoing people, who
welcome all comers and ask few questions; at Union Baptist one may look for
the Virginia servant girls and their young men; and so on throughout the city.
Each church forms its own social circle, and not many stray beyond its
bounds. Introductions into that circle come through the church, and thus the
stranger becomes known. All sorts of entertainments and amusements are
furnished by the churches: concerts, suppers, socials, fairs, literary exercises
and debates, cantatas, plays, excursions, picnics, surprise parties, celebrations.
Every holiday is the occasion of some special entertainment by some club,
society, or committee of the church; Thursday afternoons and evenings, when
the servant girls are free, are always sure to have some sort of entertainment.
Sometimes these exercises are free, sometimes an admission fee is charged,
sometimes refreshments or articles are on sale. The favorite entertainment is a
concert with solo singing, instrumental music, reciting, and the like. Many
performers make a living by appearing at these entertainments in various
cities, and often they are persons of training and ability, although not always.
So frequent are these and other church exercises that there are few Negro
churches which are not open four to seven nights in a week and sometimes
one or two afternoons in addition.

Perhaps the pleasantest and most interesting social intercourse takes place
on Sunday; the weary week's work is done, the people have slept late and
had a good breakfast, and sally forth to church well dressed and complacent.
The usual hour of the morning service is eleven, but people stream in until
after twelve. The sermon is usually short and stirring, but in the larger
churches elicits little response other than an "amen" or two. After the sermon the social features begin; notices on the various meetings of the week are
read, people talk with each other in subdued tones, take their contributions
to the altar, and linger in the aisles and corridors long after dismission to
laugh and chat until one or two o'clock. Then they go home to good dinners.
Sometimes there is some special three o'clock service, but usually nothing
save Sunday school, until night. Then comes the chief meeting of the day;
probably 10,000 Negroes gather every Sunday night in their churches. There
is much music, much preaching, some short addresses; many strangers are
there to be looked at; many beaus bring out their belles, and those who do
not gather in crowds at the church door and escort the young women home.
The crowds are usually well behaved and respectable, though rather more

jolly than comports with a puritan idea of church services.

In this way the social life of the Negro centers in his church—baptism, wedding, and burial; gossip and courtship; friendship and intrigue—all lie in these walls. What wonder that this central club house tends to become more and more luxuriously furnished, costly in appointment and easy of access!

4. It must not be inferred from all this that the Negro is hypocritical or irreligious. His church is, to be sure, a social institution first, and religious afterwards, but nevertheless, its religious activity is wide and sincere. In direct moral teaching and in setting moral standards for the people, however, the church is timid, and naturally so, for its constitution is democracy tempered by custom. Negro preachers are often condemned for poor leadership and empty sermons, and it is said that men with so much power and influence could make striking moral reforms. This is but partially true. The congregation does not follow the moral precepts of the preacher, but rather the preacher follows the standard of his flock, and only exceptional men dare seek to change this. And here it must be remembered that the Negro preacher is primarily an executive officer, rather than a spiritual guide. If one goes into any great Negro church and hears the sermon and views the audience, one would say either the sermon is far below the caliber of the audience, or the people are less sensible than they look; the former explanation is usually true. The preacher is sure to be a man of executive ability, a leader of men, a shrewd and affable president of a large and intricate corporation. In addition to this he may be, and usually is, a striking elocutionist; he may also be a man of integrity, learning, and deep spiritual earnestness; but these last three are sometimes all lacking, and the last two in many cases. Some signs of advance are here manifest: No minister of notoriously immoral life, or even of bad reputation, could hold a large church in Philadelphia without eventual revolt. Most of the present pastors are decent, respectable men; there are perhaps one or two exceptions to this, but the exceptions are doubtful, rather than notorious. On the whole then, the average Negro preacher in this city is a shrewd manager, a respectable man, a good talker, a pleasant companion, but neither learned nor spiritual, nor a reformer.

The moral standards are therefore set by the congregations, and vary from church to church in some degree. There has been a slow working toward a literal obeying of the puritan and ascetic standard of morals which Methodism imposed on the freedmen; but condition and temperament have modified these. The grosser forms of immorality, together with theatergoing and dancing, are specifically denounced; nevertheless, the precepts against specific amusements are often violated by church members. The cleft between denominations is still wide, especially between Methodists and Baptists. The sermons are usually kept within the safe ground of a mild Calvinism, with much insistence on salvation, grace, fallen humanity, and the like.

The chief function of these churches in morals is to conserve old standards and create about them a public opinion which shall deter the offender. And in this the Negro churches are peculiarly successful, although naturally the standards conserved are not as high as they should be.

5. The Negro churches were the birthplaces of Negro schools and of all agencies which seek to promote the intelligence of the masses; and even today no agency serves to disseminate news or information so quickly and effectively among Negroes as the church. The lyceum and lecture here still maintain a feeble but persistent existence, and church newspapers and books are circulated widely. Night schools and kindergartens are still held in connection with churches, and all Negro celebrities, from a bishop to a poet like Dunbar, are introduced to Negro audiences from the pulpits.

6. Consequently all movements for social betterment are apt to center in the churches. Beneficial societies in endless number are formed here; secret societies keep in touch; cooperative and building associations have lately sprung up; the minister often acts as an employment agent; considerable charitable and relief work is done and special meetings held to aid special projects. The race problem in all its phases is continually being discussed, and, indeed, from this forum many a youth goes forth inspired to work.

Such are some of the functions of the Negro church, and a study of them indicates how largely this organization has come to be an expression of the organized life of Negroes in a great city.

9

THE NEGRO CHURCH IN THE
NEGRO COMMUNITY

GUNNAR MYRDAL

An American Dilemma is the end product of a comprehensive project to
study the nature of the problem of the Negro in America, which was sponsored by the Carnegie Institution and carried out under the direction of
Gunnar Myrdal. The selection on religion presented here is based primarily on
the published work of Benjamin E. Mays and Joseph W. Nicholson and the
manuscript report of J. G. St. Clair Drake. This survey of the Negro church
analyzes such crucial topics as its role in the black community, its reputed
emotionalism, and the political aspects of the Negro ministry. Though it is
often highly critical of the Negro church and oversimplifies a complex institution, this chapter should serve as an introduction to the problems that will
receive more substantial treatment in chapters 10, 11, and 12.

At least 44 percent of American Negroes were claimed as members of Negro
churches in 1936. Actually, the proportion is considerably higher, for several
reasons [1] Although church membership means different things to different
people, it is quite obvious—not only from total membership figures, but also
from the character of the church service, the religious nature of many of the
Negro's songs, the great use to which the church building is put, the diversity
of voluntary activities organized around the church—that religion and church
play an important role in the Negro community, probably more important
than in the average white community. In this section we shall seek to sketch
this role.

Probably the chief "function" of the Negro church has been to buoy up
the hopes of its members in the face of adversity and to give them a sense
of this community. This is, of course, true of any church, but it is especially
true of Negroes, who have had a hard lot and to whom so many channels of

Reprinted from *An American Dilemma* (New York: Harper & Row, 1944), pp. 935-942,
by permission of the publisher. Copyright 1944, 1962 by Harper & Row, Publishers, Inc.

activity outside the church have been closed. Negroes have had to place their hopes for a better life in religion. As a Negro poet puts it, "Our churches are where we dip our tired bodies in cool springs of hope, where we retain our wholeness and humanity despite the blows of death from the Bosses. . . ."[2] It is this need, perhaps more than anything else, which has attached the Negro so strongly to his church and accounts for his reputation as a religious person. In the colder and more critical words of Mays and Nicholson,[3] "It is not too much to say that if the Negro had experienced a wider range of freedom in social and economic spheres, there would have been fewer Negroes 'called' to preach and fewer Negro churches."

The denominations to which Negroes belong do not tend to have a heavy, formal ritual. It is true that a significant proportion of churchgoing Negroes belong to the formalized Episcopalian and Catholic churches, but the great majority belong to the Baptist and Methodist churches or to the many little sects that have grown up in recent years. Lower-class Negroes more than middle- and upper-class Negroes adhere to these latter churches. The small upper class of Negroes tends to belong to the Episcopalian, Congregational, and Presbyterian churches, since for them a main function of church member- ship is to give prestige.[4]

The religious service in Negro churches is often characterized by extreme emotionalism. The old-fashioned preacher employs gestures, intonation of the voice, sobbing, and words calculated to arouse emotion.[5] His audience aids with interjections at certain points and with stamping of the feet. There is a great deal of choir and congregational singing, and use of musical instru- ments of the percussion type.[6] These "rousements" bring most of the congre- gation into some degree of "possession."

Whites, in searching for rationalizations to justify the subordination of the Negro, have seized upon the fact of religious emotionalism and ascribed it to "animal nature" and even to "excessive sexuality." Even Northerners—or we could perhaps say, *especially* Northerners—have done this, since the Negro's religion is so different from their own, and they are at a loss to account for this behavior. Southerners, on the other hand, are accustomed to seeing extreme emotionalism in many lower-class white churches and revival meetings.

Two things are important in attempting to explain this emotionalism. In the first place, it has been exaggerated. A large minority of Negroes do not attend church, and another large minority do not have emotionalism in their church service. There are wide differences among the various Negro denomi- nations in degree of emotionalism manifested.[7] Emotionalism is uncommon in the upper- and middle-class Negro churches—which are quite like white churches of the same class level in this respect—and it is uncommon in the

Catholic Church and other large, well-established urban churches where there are more lower-class Negroes than middle- and upper-class Negroes. There is a definite trend for Negro youth to avoid the emotional type of church, and the same is true of the social "climbers" of all ages and occupation.[8] Emotionalism is most common in the rural Southern Negro churches and in the "storefront"[9] churches of the cities. These form the great bulk of the Negro churches, but since their congregations are small, they do not include such a large proportion of the Negro churchgoers. But even in the churches of the rural South, emotionalism is declining. According to Mays and Nicholson, revival meetings in the rural South are less successful than they used to be; the professional evangelist is disappearing; and the regular sermons attempt to be more thought-provoking.[10]

The second point is that the great periods of Negro conversion to Christianity were periods when the emotional forms of religion were taking hold of the whites too. In the Great Revival of 1800, it was common to see large groups of whites, gathered in a field upon the advertisement of a traveling revival leader, shouting, crying, laughing, "speaking with tongues," barking, dancing, rolling around, and manifesting all the traits associated with extreme "possession." Negroes occasionally participated, but more often just watched from a distance or had their own imitations with the help of white missionaries.[11] Negroes—and lower-class whites in isolated communities in the South—have retained these religious practices in a relatively subdued form. Negroes have been losing them, but not as rapidly as have whites. Certain practices of the Negro Baptist and Methodist churches—such as permitting persons to become clergymen without having an education—and the geographical and cultural isolation of Negroes in the rural South, have helped to keep the Negroes behind the whites in the trend toward less emotionalism.

It may be that emotionalism in religion is well suited to take the Negro's mind off his degradation and frustration. It is commonly said that it is religion that "keeps him going." The feeling of "possession" is used the world over to produce euphoria when circumstances are unduly unpleasant— although in most groups, drugs and drink rather than religious excitement produce the effect. Whether or not there is any relation between the decline of emotionalism in religion and the growing resentment and caustic bitterness among Negroes could not be proved, although it is plausible.

Just as emotionalism was borrowed from and sanctioned by religious behavior among whites, so were the smaller religious sects taken over by Negroes after they were started by whites. The generation following 1880 saw the origin of a large number of lower-class religious movements, especially among whites in the Middle West.[12] These movements gained most headway, perhaps, among the poor whites and the Negroes of the South. To this group of sects belong the Holiness Church, the Disciples of Christ, the Church of God, and twenty-odd others.[13]

The Negro church is a community center par excellence. In the South, there are few public buildings for the recreation of Negroes, except some of the schools, upon the use of which many limitations are laid. Negroes are usually too poor to build special community centers. Only in large cities does private enterprise provide halls for Negro meetings and recreation. Negro homes are almost always too small to have more than two or three guests at one time. Only the church is left, and in many ways it is well fitted to serve as a community center. It is usually located in the heart of the community it is meant to serve, often closer to most of the homes than is the school. It is owned by the Negroes themselves, and they can feel free to do what they please in it. The white man's respect for religion gives it a freedom from intrusion that is not enjoyed even in the Negro home. In the rural churches, often the preacher himself does not participate in the social activities that go on in his church, since he often has three or four other churches to attend to.[14] In fact, the Negro church is such a good community center that it might almost be said that anyone who does not belong to a church in the rural South does not belong to the community.[15]

The school is often located in a church in the rural South. Lodges and clubs frequently hold their meetings in the church, more often in rural areas than in the cities. Lectures and meetings for discussion of civic problems—including political meetings in the North—are probably most often held in churches. The large Negro churches in Northern, and sometimes Southern, cities often have the full gamut of social and recreational activities that is found in large white churches. (See Table 1.) And, finally, the church, like the barbershop and the pool parlor, is a place to which one wanders when he has nothing else to do.

The denominations to which Negroes predominantly belong—Baptist and Methodist—attempt to exercise a strict control over morals, and have a rather broad definition of morals. For want of a better term, we may say that they have "puritanical" standards of behavior. Negroes have taken over these standards but have modified them somewhat to suit Negro customs and white demands. For example, Negro preachers condemn extramarital sex relations, but they seldom take any specific steps to stop them because usually so many of their congregation engage in the condemned behavior. Too, they dare not say anything against relations between Negro women and white men in the South for fear of physical punishment. In addition to extramarital sex relations, the practices of gambling, drinking, drug-taking, smoking, snuff-dipping, card-playing, dancing, and other minor "vices" are condemned. Sometimes even ordinary sports and picnics come under a religious ban.

TABLE 1

Organizations and Activities of 609 Urban Churches

Organizations and Activities	Number of Churches	Percent Frequency
Preaching	609	100.0
Union services and interchurch cooperation	609	100.0
Missionary societies	609	100.0
Clubs (Social, Educational, Financial)	609	100.0
Sunday church school	608	99.8
Poor relief	590	96.9
Revivals	561	92.1
Choirs	503	82.6
Young People's work	398	65.4
Prayer Meetings	388	63.7
Recreational work	191	31.4
Pastors' aid boards	77	12.6
Gymnasium classes	30	4.9
Church papers	22	3.6
Extension work in missions	21	3.4
Feeding the unemployed	18	3.0
Junior churches	13	2.1
Daily vacation Bible school	10	1.6
Benevolent societies	6	1.0
Clinic (free)	5	0.8
Motion pictures	5	0.8
Cooperate Y.W. and Y.M.C.A.	5	0.8
Girl Scouts	5	0.8
Boy Scouts	5	0.8
Kindergarten	4	0.7
Nurseries (day)	3	0.5

Source: Benjamin E. Mays and Joseph W. Nicholson, The Negro's Church *(New York, 1933), pp. 122-123.*

These injunctions seem to have effect on middle-class Negroes, especially those who are ready to settle down. The upper class among Negroes also tends to avoid some of these practices, but more because they individually want to or because they want to maintain status, rather than because of any specific injunction against them by the church. The bulk of the lower class, and the youth of all classes, seems to pay little attention to them. Females, as greater churchgoers, and as the traditional guardians of morals, obey them more than males.

The Negro church, in respects other than its emotionalism, is like any lower-class white Protestant church. In its relation to the Negro commu-nity, however, the Negro church tends to be different from the white church in relation to its community.

The Negro preacher's stand on problems of caste and on all "political" problems is equivocal. On the one hand, he must preach "race solidarity" because his congregation demands it and because he himself stands to gain if the economic and political situation of his community improves. On the other hand, he is not only a focus of caste pressure, but his position of leadership depends upon the monopoly given him by segregation. Although the Negro preacher is "otherworldly" in his sermons, he has a closer relation to politics than has the white clergyman. In accordance with Baptist and Methodist tenets, he preaches puritanical morals, and yet is often far from exemplary in his own life and sometimes has connections with the underworld. These paradoxes exist because the Negro preacher is not only a clergyman, but also, as Du Bois puts it, "a leader, a politician, an orator, a 'boss,' an intriguer, an idealist."[16] These divergent interests make the Negro preacher shift his actions fairly frequently with respect to controversial questions, so that he appears inconsistent.

Negro preachers usually support Negro business. But at least one case is known where they have received threats from white business competitors for doing so.[17] And there is the fact that the Negro church often receives more money from white businessmen (since there are more of them even in Negro neighborhoods) than from Negro businessmen. In advertising Negro business, preachers use the pulpit as well as written endorsements and the church paper.[18] Some of the Negro businessmen are known racketeers: their legitimate businesses are sometimes a "front" for gambling rackets and even vice. The churches are, of course, officially against such things, but gambling (especially "policy") among the members of the congregation is too widespread to be stamped out, and often the contributions from Negro policy racketeers—especially in the North—are a major source of support for the church. Some Negro ministers in Chicago meet the situation by ignoring the policy playing that goes on; others openly endorse it on the grounds that it provides jobs for Negroes and that "gambling isn't the worst sin." Some spiritualist churches actually give out lucky numbers to be played.[19]

Where Negroes vote, preachers frequently take a stand and use their influences and their pulpit to swing Negro votes.[20] Although the feeling is prevalent among Negroes, as among whites, that clergymen should have nothing to do with politics, the Negro preacher's position as a community leader, as well as his desire to get money for his church and even for himself, often leads him to have some sort of tie with a political machine or candidate. A minister who has a political tie gains in power, since he can "fix" minor difficulties with the law for members of his congregation and sometimes even has control over a few jobs, political or otherwise. Politicians, both white and Negro, realizing that Negroes are in great need and are easily influenced by any display of friendliness or of power, often make use of the large churches even without the minister's express assent. They make an appearance at a church service and conspicuously donate large sums of money at collection time. Many of the church members interviewed by Gosnell did not resent a white politician even in the pulpit, since they felt that the Negro needs all the white influence he can get, and since they do not have time to attend regular political meetings in which they are interested.[21] The church, as the community's most central public institution, seems to many Negroes to take on political functions, as other nonreligious functions, quite naturally.

The Negro community is so poor, and the number of Negro churches so large in relation to the number of churchgoers, that the upkeep of the church is a financial drain. A good portion of the time during an average church service is taken up with the collection, and there is a tendency to emotionalize the collection so as to elicit more money.[22] Both in the South and in the North, there is importuning of white churches, white businessmen, and other white individuals for money to support the churches. Still the average Negro does not get much back from his church in the way of community services.[23] Relatively few of the churches—even the urban churches—offer facilities for recreation, and the amounts spent on charity, education, and social service are pitifully small. This is partly due to the fact that there are too many churches, which makes the overhead expense too high. Too, the urban Negro church often gets itself into great debt when it buys or builds a church edifice. In Mays and Nicholson's sample of urban Negro churches in 1930, 71.3 percent had debts on their buildings.[24] Finally, Negro churches have poor business practices. For all these reasons, and relative to the poverty of the congregation, the Negro church is more expensive to the average Negro than the white man's church is to him. Most Negroes are aware of this fact and are not happy over it.

The Negro church is at once modeled after the white church and yet fitted into the needs and culture of the Negro community. Theology and church service are the same as in white Protestant churches. Emotionalism was borrowed from the whites but has been retained after most whites have abandoned it, and is now considered a Negro "characteristic." Although Negroes do not, on the whole, pay much attention to the moral injunctions of the church, the church has been the major center of community life, and the preacher has been the major leader of the community. But this is changing rapidly as the Negro community becomes diversified, as other professionals are becoming more numerous, as upper and middle classes develop among Negroes, as the minister does not advance as rapidly in education and sophistication as do the youth of his community. The Negro church has declined in relative importance since 1880, and the prospects are for a continued decline. Nevertheless, the Negro church means more to the Negro community than the white church means to the white community—in its function as a giver of hope, as an emotional cathartic, as a center of community activity, as a source of leadership, and as a provider of respectability.

NOTES

The most useful general sources of information on the Negro church that we have found and the ones we have relied upon for most of our factual data are: Benjamin E. Mays and Joseph W. Nicholson, *The Negro's Church* (New York, 1933); and J. G. St. Clair Drake, "The Negro Church and Associations in Chicago," unpublished manuscript prepared for this study, 1940.

1. We have calculated this figure simply by taking the total number of members reported by Negro churches (as reported in the census of *Religious Bodies: 1936*) and dividing it by the total Negro population in 1940. The resulting figure is much too low as a measure of the proportion of Negro church members because: (1) the Negro population grew between 1936 and 1940; (2) some of the smaller Negro churches are overlooked in the census; (3) children are usually not included in the church figures but are included in the population figures. It is also to be noted that the figure cited in the text does not include Negroes who were members of "mixed" churches.

2. Richard Wright, *12 Million Black Voices* (New York, 1941), p. 131.

3. Benjamin E. Mays and Joseph W. Nicholson, *The Negro's Church* (New York, 1933), p. 11.

4. J. G. St. Clair Drake, "The Negro Church and Associations in Chicago," unpublished manuscript prepared for this study, 1940, pp. 388-395.

5. For a discussion of the lower-class Negro preacher, see Drake, "The Negro Church and Associations in Chicago," pp. 366-371.

6. Allison Davis lists the rituals of Negro churches which arouse emotions as follows:

"1. Narration of 'visions' or 'travels' as public evidence of individual's religious conversion.

"2. Highly dramatized baptism in public setting, in a river, creek, or (usually in Old City and its environment) in a hog-wallow.

"3. Communion service in which members shake hands with one another, and march around minister and church officers in a closely packed circle, while they sing and stamp feet.

"4. Communal participation by members in both sermon and *prayers* with antiphonal structure in which members reply to preacher or deacon, or interrupt him. Communal singing, of same antiphonal form.

"5. Funeral service in which all congregation views corpse, and participates in both sermon and prayers; a highly communal service with violent demonstrations such as shouting and 'getting happy.'

"6. Marching of usher board of church, or of visiting usher boards, around seated congregation up to chancel, where donation is made by each member of usher board. Repeated several times, while both usher board and congregation sing.

"7. Intoning, or at times the singing, of sermon or prayer by minister. Use by minister of sobbing technique, or of triumphant laugh in preaching; walking into congregation or elaborate physical dramatization of sermon by preacher.

"8. Devotion of a large part of the service to the collection of money.

"To these may be added rituals of the Sanctified, Spiritualist, Holiness, and other esoteric sects found among both Negroes and whites of the lower-class positions, such as the practices of 'sacred dancing,' rolling in a sawdust pit in state of ecstasy, tambourine playing, reading of the future, healing of the sick, use of images of saints, foot-washing, use of drum and of jazz music, etc." ("The Negro Church and Associations in the Lower South," unpublished manuscript prepared for this study, 1940, pp. 83-84.)

7. "The Methodists and Baptists look down upon the Sanctified, considering their noise and dancing somewhat heathenish." (Powdermaker, *op. cit.,* p. 234.)

8. Drake, p. 434.

9. The term "storefront" churches is commonly used to include churches in residences as well as in stores.

10. Mays and Nicholson, pp. 102, 139, 253.

11. Guion G. Johnson and Guy B. Johnson, "The Church and the Race Problem in the United States," unpublished manuscript prepared for this study, 1940, 2: 217 ff.

12. *Ibid.*, pp. 296-298.

13. *Ibid.*

14. The churches may often be scattered over the countryside, and the ministers have difficulty in getting to them. Mays and Nicholson (p. 251) report that, of 159 rural churches studied, only 5.7 percent of the preachers lived within 10 miles of the church.

15. "Negroes regularly attend church whether Christians or sinners. They have not yet accumulated wealth adequate to the construction of clubhouses, amusement parks, and theaters, although dance halls have attracted many. Whether they derive any particular joy therefrom or not, the Negroes must go to church, to see their friends, as they are barred from social centers open to whites. They must attend church, moreover, to find out what is going on; for the race has not sufficient interests to maintain in every locality a newspaper of its own, and the white dailies generally mention Negroes only when they happen to commit crimes against white persons. The young Negro must go to church to meet his sweetheart, to impress her with his worth and woo her in marriage, the Negro farmer to find out the developments in the business world, the Negro mechanic to learn the needs of his community and how he may supply them." (Carter G. Woodson, *The History of the Negro Church* [Washington, D.C., 1921], pp. 267-268.)

16. W. E. B. Du Bois, *The Souls of Black Folk* (Chicago, 1903), p. 190.

17. Davis, pp. 63-64.

18. Drake, pp. 273-274.

19. *Ibid.*, pp. 274-277.

20. The information for this paragraph on the relation of church to politics is taken from Drake, pp. 231-235, and from Harold F. Gosnell, *Negro Politicians* (Chicago, 1935), pp. 94-100.

21. Gosnell, pp. 94-100. The Northern Negro manifests unusual interest in politics.

22. Davis, p. 85, and Powdermaker, p. 238.

23. The facts in the remainder of this paragraph are taken from Mays and Nicholson, pp. 168-197.

24. *Ibid.*, p. 195.

10

YOUTH AND THE CHURCH

CHARLES S. JOHNSON

When social scientist Charles Johnson scrutinized his people's church in the rural South, he found it to be functioning to meet the needs of a fading generation. Particularly in the plantation areas which were farthest from cities and towns were the youth dissatisfied with their church. Although some remained traditionally loyal, increasing numbers of the young blacks had less need for its brand of escapism, and less patience with an inconsistent moral code which denied them the pleasures which would have relieved much of the tedium of their rural existence. Clearly, the traditional leadership role of the Negro church was in jeopardy before the broadened demands of its disenchanted young.

The church has been, and continues to be, the outstanding social institution in the Negro community. It has a far wider function than to bring spiritual inspiration to its communicants. Among rural Negroes the church is still the only institution which provides an effective organization of the group, an approved and tolerated place for social activities, a forum for expression on many issues, an outlet for emotional repressions, and a plan for social living. It is a complex institution meeting a wide variety of needs.

In order to understand the behavior of rural Negro youth in relation to the church one must appreciate the cultural aspect of their religion. In the case of the Negro living in the rural South the religious conceptions and interpretations of doctrine which he expresses have been conditioned by his level of culture. Religious attitudes, like other social attitudes, are a part of youth's cultural heritage, and bear the stamp and limitation of the carriers of the culture. The first patterns have come from the parents, and these have been reinforced or redefined by the more formal agencies of religious instruction, the most important of which is the church.

Adapted from "Youth in the Church," Chapter 5 of *Growing Up in the Black Belt* (Washington, D.C.: American Council on Education, 1941), pp. 135-140, 145-146, 148, 152, 153, 156, 157, 158, 169, by permission of the publisher. Copyright 1941, 1969 by American Council on Education.

Historically, the formal respect accorded Christianity in America has modified at significant points the expected patterns of treatment for a subject people. Under the slave system, religious gatherings were the first forms of association permitted Negroes, religious teachers were the first leaders allowed to develop, and reading of the Bible was the only tolerated excuse for literacy.

The Negro church came to serve a vital role linked intimately with the status of the race. The doctrine of otherworldliness provided an essential escape from the tedium and tribulations, first of slavery and later of economic serfdom. Educational limitations and the cultural isolation fostered by the rural life of the Negro and by the system of separate social institutions retarded the development of the Negro and stamped him with characteristics associated with the essential patterns of Negro life. Many patterns of religious expression were based upon the practices of white groups not far removed in culture. Frequently, the religious doctrines appropriated were in conflict with pragmatic social values.

The Negro rural church was useful to the older generation of Negroes. The economic homogeneity of the group gave it considerable cohesion. The indifference of the Negro church to current social issues and its emphasis on the values of a future life lent indirect but vital support to the race patterns of the early postslavery period. The formal ban of the church upon dancing, card-playing, and baseball did not seriously trouble the older members because these were not normal expressions of their impulses to recreation and diversion. Other codes of behavior, when in conflict with the folkways of the people, were less conspicuously enforced. The sex mores with which the rural Negro emerged from slavery were a direct result of a situation which prevented an organized family life and the development of personal habits in terms of the standards approved by white society. Through the early period of Negro family organization and the emergence of new values, inconsistencies have appeared between formal codes regarding "illegitimacy," marriage, divorce, and separation, on the one hand, and the requirements for the survival of an "economic family" reinforced by the strength of uncritical custom, on the other. The rural church has been more tolerant of sex mores which violated its codes of conduct than it has of certain forms of recreation such as dancing and card-playing.

The introduction by the school of new values stressing literacy, economic improvement, and urbanization has brought significant changes in the role of the rural Negro church in the community. The institution itself has changed but little, but in its function it has a different impact upon new generations of Negroes. In the setting and atmosphere of a typical church and from observation of the character and content of the regular religious instruction, it should be possible to understand more adequately the nature of this impact and the basis for the religious attitudes of rural Negro youth.

A Regular Church Service

Mount Pizgah Church in Johnston County, North Carolina, is a large, gray, single
auditorium structure, with high ceiling and long horizontal iron bars overhead
to brace the walls. The altar rests at the rear of a small, semicircular platform.
There are four chairs directly in front of the platform which are usually occupied
by the members of the deacon's board. Back of the altar is a large, frayed, and
soiled red plush chair with a high back, in which the minister sits.

The church is filled with perspiring worshippers, both young and old, who
are cooling themselves with fans provided by the undertaker. The women are
dressed in organdy and voile, and the men in wash pants and shirts. A few wear
coats.

After the opening hymn, the congregation is seated; a hard-faced, wiry,
dark man remains standing. He is Deacon Eppse, and he prays thus:

Blessed Jesus, we thank you for life, the greatest blessing in the world, life.
We thank you for the blood that circulates through our bodies. We thank you
for the blood and the air so we can stand on our feet. We thank you for the
loving hand of mercy bestowed upon us; that Thou are in our midst. Prepare
us for our souls' journey through this unfriendly world, and when our life on
this earth is ended receive us into Thy home which art in heaven.

The congregation sings, "We'll Understand It Better By and By." An elderly
brown man of about sixty-five reads the scripture. There are groans and solemn
exclamations from the four men in front of the altar, "Lord have mercy,"
"Amen." The reader interpolates:

We have to slip and straighten up the wick in the candle and lamp. We have
to straighten up a car. Just like we have to straighten up a wick so the light
will burn, and the car so it will run, we have to straighten up our lives so we can
go the way our Lord wants us to go.

They sing:

> Almighty God, Almighty God,
> Hold me in the hollow of your hand,
> I'll be your child, I'll be your child,
> Hold me in the hollow of your hand.

The minister comes solemnly forward to the altar. He is a stout and pompous
man who continuously rubs a large gold watchchain extended across a prominent waistline.

It's a privilege of mine and a blessing to be here, my friends. Since thirty
days ago when we last met many things have been done. Some have gone to
their judgment since that time. Gone to meet their Maker and stand in judgment

before that stern judge. I'm glad God has spared me to be here. There're some who are sick today who desire this privilege we are enjoying. [Amens] Since we met last, death has reigned right here in our neighborhood. As sure as you see a man living, you see a man who is going to die. You look around you and look at some men and they look like the picture of health. The next thing you know they're dead. That makes us know we got to get on our traveling shoes so we can march right up to our heavenly glory.

You know, I'm a lot old times. I'm one of them that don't go in for new fangled things. And one thing, I got that old time religion, that old time religion that works by faith, that purifies your heart. I ain't got no new religion, and I don't want no new religion. Why, don't you know, with this new religion you can't tell how you got it, and you can't tell where you got it? How you going to tell you got religion at all? I got that same old religion, I can go back to where I got it and tell you all about it. I can tell you how I got it and where I got it any time you ask me. And I can go back to that same old spark and refresh myself and come out stronger in my old time religion. That's what I do all the time—go back to that same old spark. It lighted the way for my father and my mother, and it can light the way for me.[Shouts]

He turns attention to his double text: "If a man die shall he live again," and "I am the resurrection and the life," and discourses at length on the life and trials of Job. The sermon then gets down to everyday experience.

Now I've seen men in critical conditions, sometime their fingernails decay and come off and disease is destroying their bodies. Sometimes we say sin causes disease. But it's not always so. Sin in the hearts of men causes disease too. I'll make an example. Job was wrapped in sackcloth and ashes a'praying to God, and his wife said, "Look at old Job. He's no good to himself and nobody else. I'm tired of him being sick, and my children's all forsaken me." But Job heard her, and to Almighty God he said, "Lord, though you slay me yet shall I trust you." Job looked at his wife and his wife said, "Curse God and die!" But Job said to her, "Foolish woman, foolish woman. I brought nothing into the world with me and I'll take nothing out." [The minister wipes his dripping face, and groans and gasps; the congregation groans and shouts.]

Job took his question to Daniel, and Daniel said, "I saw Him as a stone, hewn out of the mountain." But when Job asked him, "If a man die shall he live again?" Daniel said, "I don't know." Job kept on a'going till he come to Ezekiel, and Ezekiel said, "I saw Him as a wheel within a wheel. I saw Him in the haunts of women." But when Job asked him if a man die shall he rise again, Ezekiel said, "I don't know."

But here comes a man from a new country, a man called Jesus Christ. A man that said, "I am the Son of God, the friend of salvation. I am the lowly fisherman from Galilee. I've seen the face of God. I feed the leprosy cast out by yourself. I can cure the incurable disease. I can perform miracles such as the world has never known." And they brought out the leper, the man dying with that terrible disease, the man everybody shunned and let alone to die. And the Nazarene cured him. [Shouts] Blessed be His name! [Shouts and shrieks]

The congregation is now fully stirred, and its fervent chorus of assent punctuates dramatically the minister's spaced phrases. He refers to the loved ones who have departed, and stresses the certainty of death for everyone.

It don't matter how much you know or how high you climb, you got to die. Mr. Roosevelt, the president of this country's got to die, just like you and I. He can run all these things and do all them big things that everybody talks about, but he's got to lay down and die just the same.

The audience becomes sobered, the preacher lowers his voice:

If we fail to live the life in this world, it'll be too late when we come to cross the River of Jordan. It'll be too late then to get ready. Just like you start dressing at home in your room. You got to get dressed at home before you come out in the street, 'cause if you don't when you get out in the street without no clothes, they'll arrest you and take you to jail. It's too late to get dressed up then. Children, let's dress up and get ready for heaven and glory now. Now's the time to get dressed. Don't wait 'til it's too late. Let's be like Paul was when he said, "I've fought a good fight, I've kept the faith, and now I'm ready for glory."

Another deacon prays. The congregation sings a song about "True Religion" that has many verses, one of which runs:

> *Where you going, Elias?*
> *Where you going, I say?*
> *Going to the River of Jordan?*
> *You can't cross there.*

They sing of backsliders and cowards. The minister rises in excitement at the close and shouts, "That song is as true as my hand. It's true, true, true. There's not enough words to say it." He then extends an invitation to join the church; no one responds on this occasion. A deacon takes his place behind the collection table.

Whilst everybody is happy and enjoying this service, we come to you. We know you must have that true religion. But today we want $5.00. We want to get it right at once, quick. Now let everybody push hard while we sing. Let everybody give all he can to the service of the Lord.

The congregation sings a song with verses that could be extended indefinitely:

> *It's the walk that you take*
> *That takes you home.*
>
> *It's the prayer that you pray*
> *That takes you home.*

They raise $4.06. After three hours of this worship they go home. . . .

Only a rough distinction may be drawn between the plantation and the nonplantation areas. On the plantations the social life of the Negro has been historically regimented, and to a large extent some of the influences from that period still survive. In the nonplantation areas, where Negroes engage in mixed farming or tobacco-growing, the influence of towns and cities has been stronger. Thus these Negroes are somewhat less affected by old traditions and habits. The distinction is important in the discussion of Negro youth and the church because of the significant test results which show that respect for the church and the ministry is lowest in the plantation areas and highest in the other areas, varying in direct proportion to proximity to the towns and cities. This conclusion runs counter to the assumption frequently held that the more rural the Negro youth the more attached he is to the church. The rural churches outside the plantation and nearer the cities have their youth problems, but in general they provide a more intelligent ministry and a more progressive Sunday school in the sense that it is more open to new influences and provides more opportunity for participation by youth themselves in the religious exercises. The sermon is still directed to the older people, the church is still dominated by the deacons and other elders, emphasis is still on "old-time religion," and many forms of innocent recreation are still banned; occasionally, however, there is a disposition to provide within the church a substitute for worldly pleasures denied, and at the same time there is, as a result of an improved cultural level, a more serious emphasis upon a code of conduct consistent with the standards of the larger culture.

From the foregoing characterizations of the types of organized religion presented to Negro youth in the rural South we now turn to the reaction of youth themselves to this part of their cultural environment. Pointedly, we ask this question: What are the attitudes of Negro youth toward the rural church?

Attitudes Toward the Church

Several significant factors appear in the attitude of Negro youth toward the church. These observations are based upon a group of tests given to 2,241 Negro boys and girls in the eight counties covered in this study and also upon personal interview data obtained in all of the counties.

Distrust of the Ministry

One test applied to rural Negro youth on their attitude toward the minister was their reaction to the statement, "The preacher tells you to do a lot of things that he doesn't do himself." This was endorsed as true by proportions ranging from 50 percent of the boys in Davidson County, Tennessee, to 93.5 percent of the girls in Coahoma County, Mississippi.

Stereotyped Sermons: The type of sermon presented is criticized by some of the young people. They not only object to the stereotyped sermons, but to the emotional antics of the leaders. A seventeen-year-old Shelby County, Tennessee, girl, daughter of a sharecropper, expressed a preference for useful advice about everyday living. She said:

> I think a preacher out here ought to preach today about things of today. He ought to give the people advice and help them out of their troubles by talking about things that happen today. I don't think a preacher ought to try to preach you into heaven. They had a funeral up at the church the other day, and the preacher tried to preach the body into heaven.

Double Moral Code: The double moral code which belonged to an earlier period of the Negro family is challenged by all types of rural youth, whether seriously as an evil, or in justification of their own indulgences. It seems clear from the comments of these youth that in spite of the persistence of unregulated sex habits in society, the church can no longer give to them the sanction of tolerance. This appears in their expectations of higher moral standards in the ministry. A fourteen-year-old eighth-grade Bolivar County, Mississippi, girl said she "guessed her pastor was all right," but she did not think he was "any better Christian than anybody else." . . .

Conflicts Based on Outmoded Behavior Codes

Rural areas are notoriously lacking in recreational outlets for youth. At the same time, the rural church imposes a strict ban upon dancing, card-playing, baseball, and, in many instances, motion pictures, along with its other moral restrictions. . . . No adequate substitute social activity has been developed by the rural church to compensate for the denial to youth of dancing, card-playing and baseball. . . .

Social Aspects: The social role of the church is still dominant for rural Negro young people. Although they may not "get saved," or believe in the sermons, or take the pastor seriously, and although they frequently look down upon the shouting, the church still provides them with most of their social contacts and approved entertainment. It is still the pivot of social life for Negroes as a group and for youth in particular. . . .

Complete Acceptance of the Traditional Church

Not all rural youth are skeptical of the church and ministers. Some have adopted fully the pattern of their elders in their concept of religion, their deep emotional response to the church, and their adherence to its rigid doctrines, at least in theory. They are firm believers in the church as it exists in the rural areas today, its doctrines, precepts, and premises, and attempt to carry out its prescribed codes of behavior. They regularly participate in the revivals and in other phases of the church program. . . .

Religious Emotionalism and Adolescence: One of the most striking facts about those youth who showed closest approximation to the traditional pattern of the rural church was the consistency in their ages. Most of them were in the early adolescent years around fourteen or fifteen and, incidentally, it was at this age that the most serious emotional shocks were observed in race attitudes and color consciousness.

Some of the most dramatic religious conversions occurred around the ages of twelve and fourteen. These children were deeply stirred by fear of hell, and being "black-marked" by God, and their religious experiences of visions and dreams were similar to those professed by their elders. An eighth-grade Macon County girl, the daughter of an electrician whose community status is very high both economically and socially, provides an excellent example of the sincere, full belief of the converted adolescent who has started "on her way to God" along the traditional path:

> I am a Christian. That was the best thing that happened to me, because now I will go to heaven when I die. I go every second Sunday. The pastor is a good pastor, because he tries to help the sinful folks. I just feel better since I joined church. Feel like I can't sin again. I do better since I joined too. Sometimes I want to talk back to folks, and I think that it is a sin and God will black-mark me, and then I don't say nothing. By black-marking, I mean a record is kept by God, and he puts down a mark every time you do wrong. I ain't afraid to die, and I'm not afraid of dead folks. They can't do nothing to you. I don't care about dying, but I don't want mama to die.

Some of the older youth professed full belief in the church and its teachings but were less intense about it. . . .

Summary

Not very distantly related to the sort of frustration phenomena reported is the current tendency observed in rural areas for traditional congregations to disintegrate and reassemble as "cult" churches. These churches of recent development have the advantages of smallness and homogeneity of membership, of doctrines newly interpreted and vigorously proclaimed, and of new procedures for the resolution of personal tensions in work, family life, and community relationships. In many of these rural communities, and in the towns and cities, the number of "cult" churches continues to grow, and in vigor and practical social value they are an interesting contrast with the traditional institutions.

It is an inescapable observation that the rural Negro church is a conservative institution, preserving in large part many values which, in the general cultural ferment of the Negro group, might well be altered. Its greatest present value appears to be that of providing emotional relief for the fixed problems of a hard life. As one woman put it, "It just seem like I can stand my worries better when I go to church." The secular institutions of the Negro community are changing slowly, but at a more rapid rate than the rural church.

The young people are dividing their loyalties between the church and the school and the overtly questionable agencies of commercial recreation. They require the church less than their parents for emotional release because they are both more mobile and less docile. Increasing literacy and education, and the increased value attached to education, emphasize the distance between themselves and the present church leaders, particularly in the plantation areas. All evidence points to the conclusion that the church will increasingly influence youth as its programs take their needs into account on a new and improved cultural level. Where this has been done, the church has tended to retain its role as a vital social and spiritual force in molding the wholesome and socially acceptable patterns of behavior.

11

BLACKWAYS OF KENT:
RELIGION AND SALVATION

HYLAN LEWIS

Hylan Lewis's portrait of black religion in a small milltown in the South suggests some of the critical functions and weaknesses of an institution that is
forced to serve so many human needs. The impression is unavoidable that
Negro Protestantism in Kent displays some of the characteristics of a state
church, for though it is an integrated part of the round of life and commands
a high degree of nominal affiliation, it elicits the profound involvement of few.
Because the black churches of Kent make minimal moral and spiritual demands
on their adherents, it is relatively easy to conduct oneself as befits a good
churchmember. Nevertheless the churches are constantly faced with the necessity of raising funds and of ministering to the conflicting needs of different
generations. Further, many church-sponsored groups and projects aggravate
an already strong spirit of rivalry among the members and the denominations,
thus precluding much real cooperation in the interests of the black community
as a whole.

The values and virtues of having religion or of acknowledging God are generally taken for granted and are not matters of dispute or discussion. But religion means different things to different individuals and categories of the
population, and the action patterns related to religious experience or belief
vary markedly. For example, the worship form, going to church, is a complex
that involves a variety of activities and meanings. In Negro Kent it is centered
around three active local churches—the Field's Street Methodist Episcopal,
the Mount Prospect African Methodist Episcopal Zion, the Union Baptist—and
around nearby churches in the rural community and adjoining towns.

   If the Negro community of Kent were defined in terms of church atten-

Reprinted from *Blackways of Kent* (Chapel Hill: University of North Carolina Press,
1955), pp. 129-154, by permission of the publisher.

dance, it woulu form a rough circle with a radius of about twelve miles: in addition to the three major local churches, there are six churches in the surrounding rural area which attract regular members and visitors from Kent. Nearly 200 Negroes remain loyal to the rural churches in the communities in which they were born. They attend these churches rather regularly, give financial support, and are buried in the churchyard cemetery when they die. The churches of Kent proper list about 400 active members on their rolls. This means that about three in every five Negroes in Kent have some active church connection, and that about one in three of the active church members is identified with a church outside Kent.

Attendance at regular Sunday morning services averages less than one third[1] of total membership enrolled; attendance at prayer meetings and night services is less. Actually, the Negro churches of Kent are filled only on special occasions: funerals, rallies, communions, and homecomings.

During the course of the year, practically everybody in the community will attend some church one or more times; there are some who attend only once: the annual homecoming, which is as much a social event as a religious one. It is a small minority of regulars who constitute the core of the churchgoing population. Using as a base the estimated Negro population of 1,000, along with available figures on church membership and attendance, the following general picture is obtained:

1. More than 90 percent of the population have been affiliated with some church at some time or another;

2. Less than 60 percent of the population are considered active church members or carried on church rolls;

3. Approximately one fifth of the total population and one third of the active church members retain affiliations with churches outside the community; and

4. On any Sunday morning that is not a special occasion, only one sixth of the total population and approximately one third of the active church members will be found in church.

The relatively small regular attendance at church does not measure its impact on the community, however. In the first place, going to church is highly approved behavior and even the chronic nonchurchgoer will indicate that he should go more often—and goes occasionally; in the second place, there are special church events such as the "annual meeting," communion and homecoming which are more fully attended and which loom large in the anticipation—and memory—of most people. Traditional values involved in the church and the minister are recognized if not fully supported, and the proliferation of church activities and influences throughout the community makes it an important institutional complex.

Going to church involves many values and functions other than those related directly to worship and religion. There is the display and conspicuous consumption factor: in general the best and special clothes are worn; special occasions such as the annual meetings involve new clothes and elaborate preparations. Public recognition and personal satisfactions come to those with special duties and powers—the deacons or trustees, the white-clad and beribboned ushers, choir members and choir leaders, the prayer and collection experts. On those occasions when church attendance is high, the spectator interest is high; many go to see and be seen, to socialize and make and renew contacts. The size of the church area and the pattern of church attendance are dependent upon access to transportation: this involves use of personally owned cars and trucks, ride-sharing, and the hiring of vehicles.

The Meaning of Religion

Merely to say "the Negro is deeply religious" is to be guilty of a bland oversimplification that obscures a wide variety of meanings and activities. Also, it tells little about the content of that religion in the Kent setting.

Salvation and forgiveness—the rewards of the Christian or of the "saved"—are the central themes in local religion. Even among the most "religious," it is rare that the Christian implications of the many acts and decisions involved in everyday behavior are reflected upon or cited. True, moral injunctions and condemnations of certain aspects of secular life are a part of the content of sermons, but these tend to be secondary or incidental to "living like a Christian" or "putting my Jesus first." These latter tend to be in the nature of self-assuring slogans. In ongoing behavior it is the folkways and the mores and individual preferences and predilections that guide and control; of course, the Christian ethic permeates or colors many of the ideal patterns of the society.

Sermons, songs, and prayers, with but few exceptions, stress the reward and salvation features of religion; the punishment feature is often secondary or implied. The positive promise and expectation of salvation from a forgiving God outweigh fear of hell as a punishment for un-Christian conduct. The idea that "the greatest value in life is working to meet your Maker" is reiterated, but religion is otherwordly only in the sense of projection and promise. It is not otherwordly in the sense that it forces or preaches withdrawal from worldly concerns—although it says that these are unimportant. Religion does, however, stress that forgiveness and salvation are possible at but a small price:

prayer and belief loom larger than actual modification of conduct. The following incident illustrates the point:

Several persons were discussing the great religious singers and performers in the community. One person referred to some of the better known ones: "As much whisky as they drinks and the hell they raises, I don't have confidence in none of them." The person's mother answered: "That's where you is wrong. God forgive everything except self-murder; He forgive 'from the stirrup to the ground.' All you got to do is pray. Good thing God ain't like man."

When a definition of a Christian is sought, these themes are stressed: living among the people but living above them (in a moral sense); kindness to one's fellowman—"treating people right"; living like Christ said; following the Bible; and having the spirit of the Holy Ghost. In this connection, it is important to note the emphasis that the most overly devout and confident Christians place upon the individual, and his responsibility for himself alone in terms of salvation. There is a tendency among these confident Christians to stress the fact that they have nothing to do with others, that they must answer for themselves, and that this is the only thing that concerns them.

Religion is something of a reservoir; it is individually tapped and allowed to flow when needed or when ritual or the customary rhythm of life so demand. References to the Bible—which are frequent—are verbal props used to prove, document, underscore, or just to display a kind of erudition. "The Bible says . . ." is an expression used by even the most profane and secular when occasion demands.

Within this general framework there are many belief and action patterns; characteristic variations are related to age, sex, denominations, and individual differences. In religious worship and ritual some persons and groups are active and highly emotional; others are restrained and passive. Likewise, varying amounts of energy and time are devoted to religious activity.

Religion appears to be a much more important aspect of the thought and behavior of older people; religious references sprinkle much of their conversation and they tend to be more numerous and constant in following worship forms and ritual. To a large extent, church activities are oriented around the interests, support, and participation of these older people; effective control of the church is in their hands. Identification with the church is a personal and emotional thing with them. Characteristically, they are aware of the imminence of death.

A widow in her seventies pointed out that she was through working; she was saving herself to meet Jesus. She knew that Jesus doesn't want any tired and broken bodies; she wanted to be fresh so that she can enjoy herself when she gets to heaven. She had been reading Revelations and its description of Judgment Day recently; the way she understood it, all the people who had died were not in heaven yet; they are somewhere in between waiting, and when the day comes all will arise and be judged. She wasn't worried because she had the faith. Although she hadn't been perfect, once she had accepted she had never turned back. She was always going forward; she was certain of her wings.

Expressions like "The Lord will provide," "I'm putting my trust in the Lord," and "I'm ready when my time comes" are characteristically the expressions of elder, mature people. Older people are more likely also to provide the vocal support and "encouragement"—"Amen!" "Preach!" "Ain't it so!" "Yes, Lord!"—for the pastor; they, too, tend to be the public prayer experts. The person who displays marked religious emotionalism is an object of admiration or sympathetic identification among the older persons; among younger persons he may be an object of amusement or curiosity. Emotionalism and overt spirituality are the marks of the "old time religion" with which the elders identify themselves. Many deplore the diminution of religious fervor:

All the spiritual done gone from the church; money done driven it out. . . . Once you could get a revival anytime, but no more. . . . The preachers is different; I ain't got no respect for preachers now.

In the local Baptist church and in the rural regions, the clash between old and new expressions of worship is to some extent crystalized in the conflict over singing styles. The conflict is not as acute among the more sophisticated groups or congregations where worship tends to be more passive. In the Baptist church there are two choirs: the "vocal choir" and the junior choir. In the former, the group is led by the "leader"—who establishes the beat and sometimes lines the numbers—and the singers enthusiastically shout, chant, hum, and at times almost moan songs according to the announced meter and without benefit of instrumental accompaniment. The songs may be spirituals, old-time gospel hymns, or published hymns from the hymnal that have been lined out by the pastor or leader. This kind of singing lends itself to audience participation and mass emotionalism. These are the songs and this the type of singing that developed in a period when many people were illiterate and the piano or organ and the trained musician were rare. These are the songs and this is the style which the older people tend to like; they fit in with their concept of an active, emotional religion.

On the other hand, there is an approach to the more formal choir which sings conventionally arranged numbers to the accompaniment of a piano and

under the direction of a musician leader. The formation of the new choir in
the local Baptist church met significant opposition; even the introduction of
printed hymnals was opposed. This new junior choir is not the official choir
and, when it sings, it sings as if by special dispensation. Although the opposition or resentment comes from the older group and others with vested or
sentimental interests in the old form, there develops even among them some
pride in the new choir; but full peace has not been made because this new
style is essentially vicarious worship. One exchoir leader criticized modern
trends in singing:

You got to git ugly to sing. Some folks wants to look all pretty—keep a
smile—and sing; you can't do that.

Another leader in announcing a song, said:

I like the new songs and the new ways they has of singing them. But I likes
the old songs too; I likes them best. I wants to sing this song just like my old
mother used to sing it. The first time I heard this song, my father sang it.

A younger member of the church commented on the conservatism of the
older members:

They're hard to change; some of them been with the church forty years
and feel they own it. Some change but most of them hold fast.

The control of religious instruments and ritual by older people is explained
by two facts: they participate more and they hold the majority of the church
offices. Spot checks over a nine-month period indicate that upwards of 60
percent of those in attendance at any of the three local churches are persons
over forty; the proportion of younger people at the sparsely attended Sunday
night meetings, the prayer meetings, and church meetings is much less. Of the
six deacons in the Union Baptist Church, four are over sixty-five; six of the
eight deaconesses are over fifty. The Field's Street Methodist Episcopal
Church deviates slightly from the pattern, mainly because, as one officer put
it, "all the older men died off"; but every older man who is active is an officer.
The situation in the Mount Prospect African Methodist Episcopal Zion
Church—the best organized of the three—reveals the general pattern: up until
a few years ago the church had a trustee board of eight men; the youngest was
in the early fifties, the average for the group was over sixty-five. The move to
reorganize the board by introducing younger members nearly precipitated a
split in the church. The newly organized board, that has three members under

forty, averages about fifty-two. None of the seven deaconesses is under fifty.

Women outnumber men in attendance and membership at all three churches.[2] The membership figures:

	Men	Women	Total
Union Baptist	34	82	116
Field's Street M.E.	42	64	106
Mount Prospect A.M.E.Z.	56	97	153

Despite the fact that nominal control and direction are in the hands of the men, women apparently contribute a larger share of the financial and moral support. Church politics is primarily a man's game, but the women wield great indirect power. In a recent, prolonged dispute in one of the churches, the women staged a coup and temporarily assumed authority as a means of forcing a truce between factions in the church.

As a general rule, older people show a greater disposition to active and emotional religious expression; in these age groups sex differences in amount and intensity of expression are less great than among younger groups. If a person is given to overt religious expression in the younger group, the chances are greater that the party will be a female.

Differential Religious Behavior and Change

Religious expression in the three churches[3] varies in quality and quantity. These are not necessarily denominational differences because rural churches of the same denominations show less variability.

The most restrained and passive type of religious behavior is seen in the Field's Street Methodist Episcopal Church. This church has the smallest membership of the three major churches and, on the average, a smaller percentage of its membership attends church regularly. This is the oldest Negro church in the town; it tends to be a "family" church with a relatively few families dominating its membership rolls: one-fourth of the membership—and possibly a larger proportion of the support—comes from two families; the Thorpes and the Roberts. Members of this church tend to look upon it as something of a responsibility that they are duty-bound to discharge, as well as to attend occasionally. It is a taken-for-granted aspect of their way of life rather than the fountainhead of salvation and the place of active religious experience. This is a "sophisticated" congregation. It is the only one of the three churches where the active emotional display known as "shouting" does not occur. "Encouragement" for the minister is meager and restrained. The members tend to be proud of their restrained patterns and particular denominational affiliation; with reference to some of the practices of other churches, members have been heard to say, "We just don't do things that way." They will explain: "We're just plain Methodists—no African, no Colored, no Zion—just straight Methodist." In some quarters, they have been termed "stuck up" or "proud folks." A member of another church referred to them facetiously as the "Black Presbyterians" of Kent (the local white Presbyterian church is probably the most prestige-laden church of the community).

The Mount Prospect African Methodist Episcopal Zion Church is the largest local Negro church. With a membership of slightly over 150, its attendance averages less than fifty. The Mount Prospect members exhibit a liveliness and self-confidence that is not matched by the other congregations: they tend to be something of a we'll-show-them group whose drive to excell is reflected in successful church programs. Their aggressiveness is in part the answer to what they consider the smug pride of the Field's Street group: "Whatever we set out to do, we're more than likely to do it," or "We're all colored; they have had white bishops over them; we ain't never had nothing but colored from the very first beginning." Their public religious behavior is less restrained than that of the Field's Street church and not quite as active and emotional as the Baptists' tends to be. In the middle-class sense, this congregation tends to be progressive and aggressive and the church is one of their vehicles of expression. Their energies incline toward diversion into works incidental to the operation of the church rather than into pure religious expression, as such.

The Union Baptist Church is the only one of the three that has services on alternate Sundays. It is the only local church with a pastor who does not live in the community. The Baptists have a membership list of 116 persons; average attendance for Sunday morning services is between forty and fifty. On the whole, the level of sophistication of this congregation is lower than that of the other two churches. This church is closer to the rural church in ritual and membership than the other two. Its organization is looser, there is greater informality, and religious behavior on the average is more active and emotional. The greater tendency to cling to the old-fashioned ways—which makes some of the members refer to the church as "backward"—and the strength of the conviction that total immersion is the only Biblically approved means of salvation, give the Baptists a more sect-like character than is possessed by any other local group, with the possible exception of the six unorganized members of the "sanctified" group. Incidentally, there are but two Negro Catholics in the community; they worship with the sisters in the chapel of the local Catholic hospital.

Church differences tend to extend to such other forms of religious expression as prayers, communion, revivals, and burials; this is true despite the fact that a basic pattern is present in each. For example, the basic pattern and content of public prayers tend to be the same: humble address to the deity, expression of thanks for past protection and favors, request for blessings on selves and sundry, and conclusion in the name of the Trinity. In keeping with differences in the churches and subject to the skill of the person praying, prayers and the congregational responses to them are likely to be longer and more emotional in the Baptist and African Methodist Episcopal Zion churches.

The responses of the Baptists to communion are greater and more enthusiastic. In all churches, Communion Sunday is a special occasion for which the turnout is large, but the turnout for the Baptists is relatively larger. It tends, in fact, to be a cooperative affair in which members of other churches in the area come to share the fellowship and the ritual. It is a "big turnout day" and one can anticipate that the emotional peak will be high. It is a day on which the more expert and constant religious performers can be expected to perform; these performers are people who are well known and who, at the same time, are conscious of their roles and of what is expected in singing and shouting. Despite the over-all emotional atmosphere and tendency to overt religious expression, it must be remembered that, even in the Baptist church, the bulk of the audience is passive and spectator-like, with the exception of general participation in songs.

It is generally agreed that the effect of revival services on the Kent community has waned. They are held regularly in the local churches, but attendance is small and during the year of the study the number of converts was negligible. The stronghold of the revival is in surrounding rural areas where more of its former force remains. It is significant that the Baptist meetings were the most successful during a year that was poor generally for revivals; at the same time, older participants pointed out that even these meetings did not compare with former times. Revivals for the other two churches were perfunctory and poorly attended. Local churches also have the annual custom of homecoming—a day on which all persons who are able are supposed to return to their home church for all-day reunion services. The ceremonies are topped off with a basket dinner. Enthusiasm and attendance have waned here also.

An essential feature of religion and church membership is the expectation of a church funeral; indeed, it is one of the motives for maintaining church membership. Among the first questions asked after death are "To which church did the deceased belong?" and "Whom do you want to preach the funeral?" In many cases persons indicate long before their deaths the minister they want to preach the funeral. As in the case of other practices, there tends to be a basic pattern within which variations occur. The basic pattern combines these essential steps: return of corpse to the home the evening before the funeral; on the day of the funeral, body and funeral party are driven to the church. (For all exits and entrances, the corpse is borne between parallel rows of women "flower girls" who are usually dressed in white.) The corpse is borne into the church while the church bell tolls and the choir sings or the minister utters an incantation; a song is sung by the choir and audience; a scripture reading and/or prayer is delivered by assisting minister or prominent church member; obituary, acknowledgment of flowers, messages, and testimonies by friends and neighbors are delivered; a eulogy is rendered by the pastor; final view of the remains is taken by the audience; interment follows, with male volunteers filling the grave after final rites.

The quality and the length of each of the above steps depends upon such factors as the importance of the deceased, community reputation, family wishes, and his relation to the church. There are other important variations that are related to custom and denominational or church practice. At the local Baptist church and at rural churches, the casket is opened and the audience files by in sections for a last view. At the other two Kent churches, the corpse will be wheeled to the doorway of the church and members will view the remains as they file out. This is an important distinction that involves taste and sophistication. There are a few who would like to eliminate the viewing of the remains entirely and "do like the white folks."

The chances are high at the Baptist and rural churches, particularly if the relatives of the deceased are persons of limited means, that a collection will be taken as the mourners file by the corpse. It is significant that the "Methodists don't do it that way; they'd rather reach down in their pockets and help out in a case where needed." This practice probably had its beginning as a form of mutual aid—and it undoubtedly still serves such functions—but the interests of the family are not always paramount; the ministers and church officers often insist on this collection. One church officer stopped a group on the way to view the remains and said: "Now the family has not requested this, but the church and the pastor have their expenses; will you please drop in an offering as you pass by?"

The practice is for the pastor to receive $10 or one half of the collection, whichever is more. Occasionally, the family and the church get a portion, and sometimes the undertaker. Instances are cited where a pastor has wanted to take a collection despite the expressed wishes of the family to the contrary.

An indication of a changing attitude toward the church as a source of mutual aid comes from the reaction of an elderly woman to the practice described above; she referred to the traditional dependence upon the church and said:

When some of them gits in trouble, the first thing they do is run to the church. That ain't right and it ain't necessary now 'cause they got societies, pensions and Social Security. The government can take care of them better than the church can; the government can afford it.

The prayer band and the all-night meeting constitute one form of religious worship and expression that lingers and engages the active interest of some members of the population. The two phenomena are significant because they incorporate the most active and expressive features of a type of religious behavior that, despite its prevalence, is on the defensive and will eventually disappear as the young gain control and sophistication increases. The all-night prayer meeting is an institution that survives and has its greatest force in the rural periphery and among the rural migrants to nearby urban centers. Specialists in song and prayer operate with respect to it, giving it continuity and direction. As a "prayer band" or "prayer union" these specialists will travel from church to church. This group constitutes one of the strongholds of the "old-time religion," and the chief participants are mature men and women. Whenever there is an all-night prayer meeting, members of prayer bands within a radius of fifty or more miles gather by bus and car. They wear badges indicating their local band and the number of the band in cases where there are two or more bands in the community. Each local group is organized and has a president or leader; the group has a lodge character. Many husbands and wives participate together.

All-night meetings usually start on Saturday nights and last until dawn Sunday morning. There is an economic aspect to these gatherings, for the collection is usually shared with the local church. The economic aspect explains why the only all-night meeting held during the study in Kent proper was held at one of the minor churches—a denomination which normally would frown upon such activity. The pastor of a congregation of five invited the group in order to get some financial help on his building and maintenance fund. A description of the proceedings and participants follows:

Members of the prayer band came by bus, truck, and car from eight different communities, including Kent. There were about sixty persons—an equal number of men and women—who were the core performers; the age range appeared to be between thirty-five and sixty-five with over half beyond forty. There were about thirty-five spectator-participants.

The schedule and round of activity—praying, singing, testifying, and "shouting" started at 9:00 P.M. and continued until 2:30 A.M., when a recess was called to permit participants to eat the food and drink hot coffee. Activities were resumed at 3:00 A.M. and continued until 6:00 A.M.

The president of the local band, a man in his sixties and an accomplished singer, prayer, and shouter, acted as a roving master of ceremonies who set the pitch and kept things moving. The members of the band proper sat in an irregular circle facing each other. The program consisted of successive cycles of prayer, song, and testimony interspersed with shouting. Representatives

from each of the groups and the audience took turns. The general and recurrent theme in words, songs, and actions was joy and satisfaction in the knowledge that one is a child of God. Standard patterns were: reference to past
troubles, sins, and dramatic experiences; indication of the awareness of the
imminence of death, and an expression of a lack of fear in view of certain
salvation as a child of God.

Prayers, songs, and movements were mixed in a rhythmic pattern: as the
prayer was said or chanted, a song was sung in obligato fashion and a moving
pattern of exhortation was woven. Under such influences, there seemed a real
compulsion to participate actively in some one of the approved ways.

Both men and women "shouted." There were three main types of behavior,
each stylized: the "exploder" broke out suddenly in a violent paroxysm accompanied by shrieks, tears, or moans; such persons usually had to be restrained and often "passed out"; the "jumping jack" jumped up and down
excitedly as if on a pogo stick, singing or talking all the while; if there were
other jumpers in another section of the church, the "jumping jack" usually
proceeded by jumps to join the group; and the "strider" moved quickly
across the floor in somewhat agitated strides, singing, shaking hands, waving
arms, and patting bystanders. Any one person may go through all three phases
in a session; all three types can be seen in action at the same time.

Two of the "star" performers struck themes in their testimony suggestive
of the meaning of religion and of this behavior to them. The first, a man, spoke
of his troubles during the wartime rationing period; he continued and said:
"White folks can ration gas, food, and the something t'eat—but they can't
ration Grace!" The other, a woman, said: "I works all day for the white
folks—in their kitchen and taking care of their children, and just skips around
all day because I'm so happy. . . . I've got Jesus."

It must be emphasized that much of this type of active religious expression
which marks some features of the Kent Negro's religious behavior is highly
stylized and predictable. In the meeting described above, the prayer band
members constitute a team of skilled performers; they are expected to perform and they expect to perform; many of them, in fact, have wide reputa-
tions. In this style of religious expression a premium is placed upon emotion
and action. In this setting freedom of expression and movement are maxi-
mized—every one is moved to some extent by the deeply accented rhythm of
the topical songs and hymns that are sung, by the soulful prayers, and by the
contagion of "the spirit." One person who is a member of a nonshouting congregation observed: "I came to watch the shouting—and to have something
done for my spirit too." The comments by the participants and spectators on
the days following such a meeting were to the effect that "We sure had a good
time down there," "I really enjoyed myself," "You don't want to miss the
next one; it's going to be a big one down at—."

This pattern of expressive religion reveals many of the basic values and
functions of religion on the local scene: personal balm and release, self-
expression, recognition, sublimation, recreation—all are demonstrably in-

volved. These meanings become all the more clear when we realize that many of the chief "actors" and most constant performers in religious activities are persons who in their extrachurch behavior are not the most religious persons in the common meaning of the term.

Auxiliaries operate with respect to church and religious functions in all three churches; they seek to organize the activities of all age groups and of both sexes through such organizations as Sunday schools, usher boards, choral clubs, and "aid" clubs for men and women. These groups represent to some extent training and recruitment devices, but, more importantly, they constitute designs for church control and sponsorship of much social and economic activity; they are important financial arms of the church. There is imitation and some rivalry among comparable groups of the three churches. The duplication and rivalry, particularly in the men's and women's clubs which have important social functions, foster divisiveness and cleavage along church or denominational lines.

Despite certain basic similarities, the differences among the respective clubs are suggestive of the differences in the meaning and functions of religion among the different church groups and to some extent between the sexes. The men's groups have been organized more recently and in the respective churches they parallel and imitate the expressed purposes and programs of the female organizations. The nominal core functions in all groups are church and community aid and uplift. These are well stated in a review of accomplishments of one of the groups:

The Helpful Ladies Club could as well be called a goodwill organization. The club is not only willing to work but is constantly spreading happiness and goodwill in the church and community, whenever and wherever opportunity presents itself. . . .

These are the accomplishments of the club for the past year: we donated $50 to the church's furnace drive, bought plastic tablecloths and curtains to beautify the basement for the annual conference. We purchased a collection table for the offering in the church auditorium. We purchased twenty-five more chairs for the basement making a total of seventy-five chairs by the club. At each rally sponsored by the church, our club made liberal donations. This club also paid on the first Sunday in each month its assessments of $2.

We have sent get well cards to the sick, cards of confidence to the bereaved and flowers in some cases. We sent Xmas greeting to all of our out of town members and to the boys of our church in the service.

Xmas day, the Helpful Ladies sent out thirty or more baskets of fruit, candy and nuts to the sick, shut-ins and aged people of this town of all denominations.

We have worked hard to live up to our success, and credit what we have accomplished to the sisterly love that exists among us, and our ability to work together agreeably.

These might be stated as typical aims and functions, but the groups vary as to the extent of activity and quality of organization and leadership. The state- ment above is a report from what is recognized as the most active group in the community. The incidental functions involving considerations of prestige, display, status, and fraternizing loom importantly among all groups.

The paired groups of the three major churches are:

Women	Men
Helpful Ladies	Young Men's Betterment League
Excelsior Guild	Fraternal League
Missionary Ladies	Fraternal League

In the case of each group, meetings are held every two weeks in members' homes in round-robin fashion. "Having the club" or the "society" is a signifi- cant event for the host or hostess, involving as it does some preparation and expenditure for the usual repast; this feature of the club serves a social func- tion and is the source of some little rivalry.

Certain elements are common to all meetings: the formal religious tone and the ritual of prayers, songs, and Bible verses prior to the business session and formal program; the collection of dues and a decided emphasis upon money matters..Characteristically, the religious tone is stronger and more persistent in the Baptist clubs. Their programs are almost wholly devoted to religious and church problems. Each group has its "lesson" at each session; the lesson is a discussion, led by some member, of a religious or church prob- lem, and is obtained from books that the members purchase. The almost ex- clusive religious and church interest goes far to explain the relative stability of the Baptist men's group, in contrast to the other two men's groups. The other groups—although they operate under the aegis of the church and in their meetings and activities give symbolic and material support to the church—have ambitions for community-wide influence and a larger degree of independence from the church. The indecision that results from these con- flicting purposes makes for ineffectiveness and lack of member interest. The women's clubs do not have the same problem because they are to a large extent controlled by social and status considerations. The only group that has restrictions on membership other than that of church membership is the Helpful Ladies. These ladies vote to admit members and strive to be a prestige group.

The church sponsorship of what, in fact, are social clubs has this effect: the chief forms of noncommercial entertaining are church-related or church- oriented. Teas, suppers, and similar affairs are either sponsored by some auxiliary of the church or are given for the benefit of the church.

Religion and Money

A large portion of the time, energy, and inventiveness invested in religious or church matters is devoted to money raising. The prominence of this aspect of religious behavior makes for a considerable body of criticism and sardonic humor. Pastors recognize this criticism and resistance and defensively apologize for or rationalize the money-raising activity. Whether understood or not, there are good grounds for the church's need of money from the participating individual: a smaller number of participating individuals than formerly, higher maintenance costs, expanded church services, and changing patterns of support for the pastor. The significant clash in values is reflected in the statement of the old lady who said, "All the spiritual done gone out of the church; money drove it out." The usual multiple collections and appeals that are a part of the normal service probably prompted the reaction of a convert to the Jehovah's Witnesses' sect. He said about the sect meetings: "You goes in there and you stays an hour exactly—none of this all-day stuff. And when they's over, you comes out and nobody tries to pick your pocket."

The extremist—but rare—position questions or tries to discredit the entire church institution. This rarely heard position was stated to an appreciative group of idlers in Burton's shed. The opponent of the speaker was defending regular contributions to the church and pastor. The speaker answered:

What's the point of telling a poor man he might go to hell? He done had hell here; if he gets hell, it'll just be hell all the way through for him. Ain't no point in paying a preacher; ain't nothing he can do for you. What you gets, you got to work for yourself.

You can travel from here to California or to New York, and wherever you go, you'll find the biggest thing the nigger is got is a church. They lives in shacks and the finest thing they's got is a church. . . . The trouble is, they pays the preacher, he educates his children to be something; while the nappy head's children eating corn meal and picking cotton.

Resistance and criticism are diffused and have not crystallized. In general, among churchgoers "having my money" is accepted as a necessary part of the pattern. For some it is a matter of competitive pride and prestige; status in the church is often equated with faithfulness of contribution—and to some extent with the amount. A woman leader remarked at one of the innumerable rallies:

We's here to sing and pray and give money. Some folks say that when you talks about money so much you kills the spirit. That ain't so when

you love Jesus; you got to love to give.
I's got my money . . . what I got, I got. What you got, you got.

In general, the devices used for raising money are standardized; frequently, however, some ingenious person or group will develop or import a novel method that is soon imitated. Each of the auxiliaries of the church has a money-raising function. The usual devices used, aside from regular collections and special appeals, are special assessments, envelopes for soliciting, special programs, food-selling, and rallies. The favorite and most effective device is the rally using the theme of the Twelve Tribes or the Twelve Apostles. This device was introduced into the Kent area by a professional fund-raiser from a nearby town who organized the rallies for a fee; the professional is no longer used. The basic pattern is this: twelve groups are organized under captains and given the names of Biblical tribes or apostles. Quotas are set and the groups report at a meeting that is marked by the marching of the tribes, other church members and visitors as a final appeal is made and the monies collected are turned in. Local people refer to these as "the rally," or they say such and such a church is having the "Twelve Tribes" tonight. Other churches and other choirs are invited; the usual practice is for the groups to help each other. The following describes a rally at a nearby church that was participated in by many persons from Kent:

The crowd of more than 300 persons gathered early. While waiting they were led in prayer and song by one of the experts who is one of the more active and fervent leaders in the community. Eventually, fourteen women dressed in white robes appeared; each carried a small stick to which was attached a piece of white cardboard with an Old Testament Biblical name printed on it in large letters: Benjamin, Levi, Zebulun, Asher, Dan, Napthali, Manaseh, Joseph, Issachar, Judah, Simeon, Reuben.

The leader of the group made a fluent and folksy appeal and explanation: "Some folks wants to know why we always has the 'Twelve Tribes' every year, over and over. We has it to raise money so we can fix up things. Look all around you, you can see what we's been doing. And then some folks ain't never seen the 'Twelve Tribes'; we wants them to see it. We wants them to help us: and when they needs us, we'll help them."

Four persons were called upon to help count and check the money. Then the groups were called in order. As each leader got up to lead the march, she would indicate if she had asked a particular choir or church group to march with her; if she had asked a group, she led them around the church singing. If she had not asked a particular choir or church group, she would request one of the song leaders to sing a song for her and invite the entire congregation to join the march and help on her quota. The procession was always led by a man who carried the placard with the name of the tribe; as he approached the table, he would kneel before the minister and would recite a Bible verse. The group leader would place a handkerchief full of money on the table and other members of the congregation who wished to help this particular person followed with their contributions.

This rally raised $505; this plus $335 raised in a special day session made a total of $840.

Earlier, the Baptist church had used a variation on the "Twelve Tribes." "Twelve Gates," all leading to Heaven, were substituted for the tribes. Those who had their quotas could pass by "St. Peter," who was guarding the gate with a sword. All this was not without a point of humor: one lady was too fat to go through the gate; she had to go around. Quotas for the groups were first set at $144 per group; protest resulted in lowering the quota finally to $25. Participants showed anxiety about raising assigned quotas and getting through the gate. They succeeded in raising a total of $918. The Baptists were proud that they had raised more money in their rally than the Methodists had.

The most significant example of interchurch cooperation centered around a competitive rally involving all three major churches. This came on the heels of earlier rallies and heightened criticism of the "money-mad" churches. Each church was to use its own devices to raise $1000 to be used for its own purposes; the church that raised the largest amount was to have its representative crowned "Miss Kent." Each church used the basic rally pattern, only this time leaders representing the forty-eight states were chosen. Over a two-month period, the leaders set up a variety of fund raising projects. The most notable of these was a banquet given "for our white friends" by one of the groups. This was a coup not without some unfavorable reactions in the Negro community, including a fight between two men over the propriety of the event.

There was some resistance to the almost continuous money-raising activities of the churches. The least enthusiastic were the people of the Field's Street Church: they are the smallest church and "we just don't do things in that way." The rivalry between Mount Prospect and Union and the respective pastors provided the chief spark of interest. Mount Prospect won the rally with a total of $1001; Union raised $697; and Field's Street, $490. There were whispered recriminations after the rally about the "unfair tactics" of Mount Prospect.

Aside from underscoring the constant interest in money-raising and the fact that a major portion of church energy is diverted into this channel, this event represents a distortion of the community fund idea—an idea which is a rational answer to the problems of fund raising but that is unlikely of adoption because of rivalries. And it is one of the few intimations of real church cooperation on the local scene. The Presiding Elder called for more such examples and said pointedly: "You folks always talking about getting ready to live in Heaven; you've got to learn to live together in the mud and dirt streets of Kent."

Religion and Needs

Religious conduct appears to be primarily a means of affirming faith and belief in individual salvation. The quality of the expression ranges from the most
passive and perfunctory to the highly active and emotional. Going to church
and having religion are highly approved patterns, and thus social pressure and
prestige are important factors in religious behavior in a community where the
status of everyone is known. The restrained behavior of the more sophisticated
is in keeping with their conceptions of themselves and their emotional demands.
Similarly, the active, emotional behavior of older, less sophisticated, and
marginal persons has meaning in terms of their traditions, statuses, and needs.
Emotional behavior is a link with a more congenial way of life; it supplies
balm, security and a sense of personal worth. The following expressions are
illustrative:

Somebody ought to say something! You done heard this fine Christian
message—and ain't nobody said nothing. I'm going to say something! That's
what I came here for—to say something! I wants to let folks know I got Jesus!
Sometimes you gets gypped here—but Jesus will make it up to you.
You can't ration Grace!

Assuming that the Negro of Kent lives in a relatively "tough culture"—one
marked by significant blocking of wish goals—the free-expression aspects of
his religious behavior parallel the patterned indulgence in whisky, sex, and
tavern behavior, and they serve something of the same function. Religious
expression is a function of social and personal needs as well as tradition: its
manifestations vary roughly with the indices of sophistication, status, and
security. In a Kent that is neither wholly rural nor urban, the old "old-time
religion" persists; but it tends to be on the defensive as educational and urban
influences increase. Some leaders seek to "bring out" the more "backward,"
but there is understandable resistance and inertia. There is still significant
"need" for this kind of religion.

NOTES

1. This figure is based upon an analysis of the attendance records of two of the major
local churches for comparable thirty-five week periods, and upon personal observation
of all churches over an extended period.
2. The figures used throughout this section are as of June 1949.

3. The "sanctified" churches and the Presbyterian Church are left out of this analysis: the former were not active during the period of the study, and the latter had but five members.

12

RITUAL AND STRATIFICATION IN CHICAGO NEGRO CHURCHES

VATTEL ELBERT DANIEL

There has often been a tendency to think of Negro religion as nearly classless, while at the same time exhibiting a basic "lower-class" orientation in the form (ecstatic) and content (escapist) of the service. Vattel Daniel's study of religious life among Chicago Negroes during the late years of the Depression documents a spectrum of types of church services, ranging from the rigidly liturgical to the highly emotional. His research has also revealed the relationship between the type of ritual preferred and the social class and degree of social adjustment of the church member.

Problem and Method

Former studies of the church have not been concerned specifically with a natural and functional classification that shows just how the several types of churches differ in their relationship to social structure, social status, and social situation. They have been concerned mainly with general activities and with external aspects which yield statistical and ecological data,[1] but the functions which churches perform can be interpreted properly only when one realizes fully the nature of the social situations in which various types of worshippers find themselves. The following study shows that Negro churches perform a triple function. Not only do they enable the communicants to express their religious life, but they also enhance the morale of members of a subordinate racial class, and through differentiation in ritual, minister to various classes within the Negro population.

Reprinted from *American Sociological Review*, 7 (June 1942): 352-361, by permission of the publisher.

It is our hypothesis that religious ritual performs different functions for different classes within an urban American Negro population, while at the same time performing a function common to the entire class and one that is also common to all members of the particular denomination or sect with which the individual church is identified. In attempting to determine the relation of ritual and general church behavior in urban Negro churches to the part of the society in which these churches function, we have been concerned primarily with the church's function in the social adjustment of groups of persons. Hence, we have used the sermons, prayers, songs, and behavior in studying ceremonials and beliefs of types of communicants representing class and economic differences in urban Negro life. The types of ritual have been studied as indexes of the degree of adaptation to the social pressures that cause persons and groups to try to conform to the types of religious behavior characteristic of middle-class and upper-class white urban society.

We chose forty churches in that part of Chicago which has the densest Negro population, the selection being made so as to give the necessary distribution as to location, size, denomination, type of ritual, and social class of communicant. Personally instructed research assistants with observation guides obtained written reports of the services of these churches. As far as possible, four reports were received for each church, although not all of them were made by the same fieldworker. After studying these documents, the investigator made several trips to each church and prepared verbatim reports of the services. Particular attention was paid to anything in the sermons, prayers, hymns, and behavior that indicated the social pressures that were affecting the pastor or his people. When possible, special projects were assigned the assistants, and one of them made a case study of her own church.

After the observation documents were prepared, they were used to classify the churches as to ritual and ceremonial. This classification was based upon an analysis of the observation documents into ceremonial, emotional, and ideational elements. Then these types were compared with each other to determine the significance of the differences.

The investigator then interviewed the pastors to find out what they were attempting to do for the worshippers in the church services which they conducted, what were the problems of adjustment to urban life as they saw them, how they thought their type of ritual compared with other types, and what members should be interviewed to find out how successful the pastors were in obtaining their objectives. Particular note was made of statements referring to the class of people attending the churches and the reasons why certain classes of persons attended certain churches. Five thousand interviews[2] obtained from 1937 to 1939 were used to determine a class system of Negroes on Chicago's South Side. The general life of each class was then related to its life in the type of church which it frequented. An attempt has been made to show that type of ritual is a function of type of life in the part of the society in which one finds oneself.

Classification and Comparison of Ritual Types

The use of ritual as a key concept in the study of Negro church life has several advantages. Among them are the following: ritual can be objectively recorded; these records, instead of merely listing barren details, give portraits of an ideal-forming institution in action, featuring four types of worshippers, (1) the crowd that dances, (2) the group which indulges in demonstrative assent, (3) the congregation which prefers sermon-centered services, and (4) the church with formal liturgy. We have named these types of worshippers (1) ecstatic sects or cults, (2) semidemonstrative groups, (3) deliberative churches, and (4) liturgical denominations.

In our classification of churches according to ritual and ceremonial, we have used the following criteria: emotional demonstrativeness, thought content of sermons, prayers, hymns, and the use of liturgy. We have kept in mind, however, that emotional demonstrativeness is not always crowd behavior in the extreme sense. When it is prescribed, expected action, it is a part of a type of ritual. In applying it as a criterion, we rated the actions of the worshippers in terms of the characteristics of the act. These characteristics of emotional demonstrativeness are frequency, intensity, and speed, length or duration, and the number of persons participating. Thought content of ritual elements was studied or analyzed as to otherworldliness as opposed to emphasis upon current problems; conflict with established denominations as contrasted with a positive statement and application of doctrine; and reference to rural background and homely illustrations, rather than to facts of history and of general literature. The liturgy test was used to determine the opportunity for spontaneous action or the lack of such opportunity, because of the obligation of following a prescribed order of service adopted by the denomination. It soon became evident that there would be marginal cases that would have to be decided on the predominance of some particular type of behavior that would cause them to be placed in certain categories. In these cases, the opportunity for the exercise of emotional demonstrativeness, the use of this opportunity, and the frequency, intensity, duration, and universality of the demonstrations were the deciding factors.

The Interpretation of Observation Documents

After classifying the churches as liturgical, deliberative, semidemonstrative, and ecstatic on the basis mentioned above, the observation documents were analyzed into ceremonial, emotional, and ideational elements, and a synthesis was made of those that were characteristic of each church type. The items listed in the analysis include equipment in relation to atmosphere for worship; the order of service, including the use of liturgy; sacerdotalism; types and themes of music and prayer; the message of the minister; formal invitations to join the church; the offering; and the presence and degree of emotional demonstrativeness.

We prepared tables showing liturgical orders of services; hymns of five liturgical services; sermons of five liturgical churches; sermons of fourteen deliberative churches; orders of the semidemonstrative services; hymns of twelve semidemonstrative services; sermons of twelve semidemonstrative services; ecstatic behavior in semidemonstrative services; order of the ecstatic services; hymns and songs of nine ecstatic services.

The synthesis of common elements in the ceremonials of liturgical churches is given in Table 1. In differentiating liturgical churches from the other types, we stressed liturgy and sacerdotalism because these aspects have the greatest influence over the others.

TABLE 1

Ritual Elements of Five Liturgical Services

Classification	Elements
Equipment	Altars, candelabra with lighted candles, vestments, organs, hymn boards, prayerbooks, special hymnals; in some cases, shrines and stations of the cross; stained glass windows and statues add to the effect of the setting upon the worship; comfortable pulpit seats and pews.
Liturgy and sacerdotalism	A rigidly prescribed ritual; activity of the priest predominates.
Hymn themes	Adoration; better life; comfort; resurrection; absolution; communion.
Prayer themes	Confession, absolution, consecration, oblation, implication, humble access, Thanksgiving; a prayer for the whole state of Christ's Church (*Kyrie Eleison*); prayer of Simeon (*Nunc Dimittis*).
Sermon topics	"The Church and Fiery Trials"; "The Great Supper"; "The Holy Catholic Church"; "The Prayer of Consecration"; "Easter Day"; etc.

Table 2 summarizes the elements analyzed from verbatim accounts of the deliberative service. The distinguishing phase of the deliberative church service is the sermon, and the others are usually planned with reference to it.

TABLE 2

Elements of Ritual in Fourteen Deliberative Churches

Classification	Elements
Equipment	Stained glass windows; vestments; vases of flowers; organs; hymn boards; special hymnals; collection plates or baskets.
Liturgy and sacerdotalism	Formality without a great amount of liturgy; activity of the pastor shared by ministerial and lay assistants.
Hymn themes	Desire for better life; adoration; working; fighting for the Lord.
Prayer themes	Invocation; meditation; divine aid; daily life; church attendance; work; confession; absolution; consecration.
Sermon topics	"The Triumphal Entry"; "Evidences of Life"; "Knowing God"; "Prayer"; "What Kind of Gospel Does Today Need?"; "Building a New World for God"; "The Miracle of Christ"; "Replenishment"; "Transfiguration"; "Dead Folks Walking Around"; "The Failure of the Church"; "Man"; "God's House"; "The Work of a Son."

Table 3 gives semidemonstrative patterns of public worship, which patterns are in sharp contrast to the formal ritual of the liturgical churches and the non-liturgical formality of the deliberative congregations. In the semidemonstrative church much emphasis is placed upon the prayer pattern and themes, emotional lay participation, picturesque preaching, conspicuous offerings, and regimented usher service.

The greatest departure from the liturgical and deliberative church services is noted in Table 4 which classifies elements of worship of the ecstatic sects.

Ritual, Belief, and Social Situation

The Traditional Negro Church

It is not sufficient simply to describe the liturgical, deliberative, semidemonstrative, and ecstatic services in urban Negro churches, for "if we are to have a sociology of religion, it must come through observation of religion in action among other social forces."[3] Since one of the important functions of these churches is to minister to various classes within the racial group through differentiation in ritual, it was necessary for the investigator to study these

TABLE 3

Analysis of Twelve Semidemonstrative Services

Classification	Elements
Equipment	Varies from stained glass windows to those covered with colored paper; vestments for two choirs, and uniforms for ushers; vases of flowers; organs or pianos or both; comfortable pulpit seats, with pews varying from the standardized type to both straight-back and folding chairs; collection plates or baskets.
Liturgy and sacerdotalism	Even when an attempt is made to follow a definite order of service, there is a high degree of informality; not only is the activity of the pastors shared by official ministerial and lay assistants, but in many cases, any active member of the congregation may "raise" (or begin) a hymn or be called upon to lead in prayer.
Hymn themes	Adoration; salvation; comfort; better life; joy; heaven; faithfulness; prayer; and, less frequently, resignation, unity, work, and death.
Prayer pattern and themes	Usually poetical prose with themes of invocation; confession; forgiveness; meditation; consecration; patience; mercy; and especially, supplication for aid to the preacher; church members and officers; the sick and distressed; those present as well as those absent.
Sermon topics	"Wisdom"; "The Ten Virgins"; "The Peril of Knowing Too Much"; "Spiritual Mountain Climbing"; "A Great Experience"; "The Value of Knowing, Believing, and Trusting the Living God"; "An Invitation and Its Refusal"; "Love"; "None Given"; "The Folly of Our Excuses."
Emotional lay participation	Assents and shouts of approval in response to statements made by the minister in the sermon; running, dancing, and swooning during the sermon or immediately after it has been concluded; any of these patterns of behavior during the singing of a gospel song, spiritual, hymn, or a special number; crying or showing any evidences of emotion mentioned above at the time that a member of one's family or a close friend "becomes converted" in the church; "amens" and other forms of assent during a fervent prayer.
Invitation and reception of new members	Techniques include the singing of an invitational hymn led by the choir and followed by the pastor's earnest entreaty, which is often related to the sermon theme and varies from a simple statement to a prolonged, persistent persuasion, or techniques calculated to cause embarrassment, emulation and fear to those who fail to respond positively.
Offerings and usher services	Preliminary offerings for missionary or benevolent purposes, and the main offering to provide income to pay church expenses; the latter offering is received in plates or baskets passed by highly regimented, neatly uniformed ushers who also function in seating the congregation.

TABLE 4

Elements of Worship in Nine Ecstatic Cults

Classification	Elements
Equipment	Varies from stained glass windows of edifices to painted or curtained show windows of stores; most of these have mottos on the walls; some have vestments for choirs and ushers' blue armbands with gilt lettering; usually there is a vase of flowers and a piano together with other instruments of percussion, such as drums, tamborines, triangles, and sometimes a wind instrument, usually a trumpet; comfortable pulpit seats with pews varying from the standardized type to both straight-back and folding chairs; collection plates or baskets.
Liturgy and sacerdotalism (or their opposites)	A high degree of informality; even when a special ritual is followed, it is highly theatrical and it is recognized by rapid and rhythmic movement; at times, in some of the cults, the ecstasy becomes so great that pandemonium reigns.
Hymn themes	Comfort; ecstasy and holiness; heaven; salvation; adoration; loyalty; steadfastness.
Prayer ritual and themes	Two sects use the Lord's Prayer only. In one of these, all stand with raised hands and little fingers interlocked, repeating the prayer in unison. In a third cult, the entire congregation, standing with hands raised, pray rapidly, loudly, and differently. Some of the prayers are conventional in type, and include the following: invocation; divine aid; adoration; confession; absolution; consecration.
Sermon patterns and topics	Some conventional sermons and themes, but usually the sermons are simply pastoral expositions of scripture passages read by members of the congregation, a verse at a time. The principal emphases are sexual sins and their consequences; healing by fasting and prayer; God helps the poor.
Emotional lay participation	Varies from verbal assents to a state of ecstasy in which each member "receives the Holy Ghost." The saint-making ritual is sometimes used for making believers "saints." In most cases, the frenzy includes yelling, tapping, stamping, shouting, and, in some instances, running and jumping, including the type which resembles the movements of a jumping jack. Loud praying while standing with hands uplifted, and speaking in tongues while in a similar position constitute the climax of the ecstatic behavior, although this was not so prevalent as were the rhythmic hand-clapping and foot-patting.
Special aspects of cult rituals	The hand-raising ceremony, in which the right hand is raised, sometimes both hands, as devotees pray loudly; speaking in tongues, in which the believers repeat rapidly and loudly unintelligible symbols; footwashing, which is the final ceremony in admitting members received into the cult; healing ritual, in which the sick are anointed with oil and surrounded by a praying, singing, and dancing group; saint-making ritual, in which believers are supposed

TABLE 4 (continued)

Classification	Elements
Special aspects of cult rituals (continued)	to receive the Holy Ghost, after white-robed saints kneel with them and pray loudly, accompanied by rapidly repeated rhythmical assent, while the pianist plays a revival hymn; baptizing of sacred objects—at the end of a regular baptismal service, members bring sacred objects which are also baptized and blessed.
Testimony stereotypes	Many believers of the church find stereotyped expression in lay testimony. Conceptions include those of praising the Lord because He is risen; of thanking Him for providing for every need; of the old-time religion as the religion of exhilaration; of faith-healing; and of the second advent, or of "soon" coming of Jesus.

classes of persons representing different types of social participation based upon economic life, family background, education, and other factors. In doing this, he found that the function of religious ritual in the life of the urban Negro varies according to the class with which the worshipper is identified.

The traditional Negro church followed a ritual quite similar to that designated as semidemonstrative, but the emotional and cultural advancement of the urban Negro led to the establishment and development of liturgical and deliberative churches. Not only did some of the liturgical churches become more ritualistic and some of the deliberative churches more sedate, but even some of the old-line denominations adopted a formal ceremonial which left many migrants from the rural South after 1916 with a feeling that they were not at home in them. Therefore, they developed pentecostal, spiritual, and spiritualist churches in which they celebrated the Christian tradition with an abandon which led to an ecstasy that had a more satisfactory effect upon them.

Negro Classes and Life in the Church

Passing over the superficial, commonsense criteria of class based on appearance and manner of speech, we have used occupation, income, consumption, education, philosophy of life, pattern of behavior, associational activity, and family life as bases for grouping. The upper class includes the leading business men and women, statesmen and politicians, as well as the professional class. The professional class comprises not only physicians, ministers, and attorneys, but also dentists, pharmacists, editors, teachers, librarians, social service workers, engineers, architects, and concert artists. The business class consists of insurance company executives and other important enterprisers. Statesmen and politicians may be differentiated as congressmen, state legislators, aldermen, ward committeemen, although some of the latter are in lower groups.

The most important elements in upper class status are found in activities which are not centered in the church. Thus, churchgoing is not an important activity for many persons of the upper stratum. Except in the cases of those who belong to middle-class or lower-class churches for business reasons upper-class persons who attend church regularly are inclined to devote themselves to those of the ritualistic or of the deliberative type, and largely to Episcopal, Presbyterian, and Congregational churches, which churches have become known as the churches of the social elite. Generally speaking, upper-class behavior means manifesting self-control.

The upper middle class is characterized by conservatism, conformity, thrift, industry, and ambition. The upper-middle-class person is deeply interested in civic affairs, particularly those which affect his racial class. His participation is noted for its sincerity and dependability and he does much of the work for which upper-class leaders receive credit. In this class are placed the less successful professional and business men and women, minor executives, government employees, the more advanced clerical workers, and important politicians who do not qualify for higher status. While the personal service types have been lowered in the social scale, government employees (and more specifically postal employees), because of income, education, and other factors, have moved steadily upward. The upper middle class shows the greatest variety in church as well as in associational interests. It frequents the Congregational, Episcopal, Presbyterian, and some of the Methodist and Baptist churches. It is quite similar to the upper class in its choice of ritual and ceremony, but is more faithful in attendance. This attendance is often for social reasons as well as for spiritual uplift, since some of the recreation of the older group is organized under the auspices of the church.

Differences between the upper and lower middle classes are those of point of view, family connection, education, and occupational status. Occupations indicative of lower middle-class status are tailor, waiter, orderly, houseman, bellman, hairdresser, dressmaker, salesclerk, barber, cashier, worker in one of the industries, and in some cases, domestic service. In the lower middle class, we have the strongest supporters of the semidemonstrative churches, large and small. Those who can do so, often join the larger churches because of their prestige, while persons with little money are more comfortable in the smaller Baptist and Methodist churches. On the other hand, there are both respectables and nonrespectables who consider deep religious devotion a symbol of lower-class status, and religion an "opiate" foisted on them by the upper classes of the larger society, and thus seek to show their urbanity and freedom, sometimes by indifference and nonparticipation, and at other times by open resentment. Opposed to this attitude of the heretic, that of the devotee evidences almost a blind belief in God's power to rectify immoral conditions without the conscious mediation of man.

The most distinguishing marks of the lower class are low income and low educational status, with all these imply. Two implications are poor environment and poor ways of conducting oneself. Because the economic depression has reduced persons of various classes to a relief status, crudity and ignorance, indicative of lack of gentility or of poor ways of conducting oneself may well be chosen as criteria. Since this class comprises marginal workers, consisting mainly of common laborers and domestic servants, it furnishes the majority of unemployed persons and relief clients, since too large a percentage of the meager income has been spent for certain items of furniture (an aspect of conspicuous consumption), for food and liquor, or for other media of dissipation. There is practically no associational life among lower-class men, while lower-class women of the respectable type find their most satisfying associational contacts in church clubs. Yet some associational relationships are afforded by labor unions, by clubs of migrants from the same southern states, and by protest groups among the unemployed. There are two contrasting attitudes toward religion and the church on the part of those in the lowest class. Some persons are antagonistic and condemnatory, even blasphemous. Others are religious devotees who put to shame the average churchgoer of the upper and middle classes. Many of these manifest a high standard of morality, and have their associational and leisure time activity within the church. Members of this category are found in large numbers in the Baptist, Pentecostal, and Spiritual congregations. Since the beginning of the depression, those of the lower class who have been recipients of the charity of the Catholics have often become interested also in their ritual, but the most frequent lower-class religious group is a sect, characterized by emotional demonstrativeness, and usually housed in a storefront building.

Summary

Former studies of the church have not been concerned specifically with a natural and functional classification that shows just how the several types of churches differ in their relationship to social structure, social status, and social situation. In this study, we have made such a classification and have found through an analysis of the type of life lived outside the church that the type of ritual engaged in, reflects the life of the society of which the worshipper is a member. The social nature of the bizarre behavior of the ecstatic sects prevents that type of isolation that accentuates inferiority and takes the devotee into a world where temporarily he can live above the handicaps of everyday life. The congenial informality of the semidemonstrative church groups affords fellowship, personal recognition, and tension release, so consoling to the former ruralite in the urban situation. The members of the deliberative and of the liturgical churches seem already to have adjusted themselves to city life and their church services stress meeting squarely the issues of life rather than seeking escape through emotional release.

In determining the relation of ritual and general church behavior in urban Negro churches to various classes within the Negro group, we have been concerned primarily with the part which types of churches play in the social adjustment of types of persons. Hence we have used the sermon, prayers, songs, and behavior in studying the ceremonials and beliefs of types of communicants representing class and economic differences in urban Negro life. The functions which churches perform for Negroes can be interpreted properly only when one realizes fully the nature of the social situations in which Negroes of different social status find themselves in the social structure of our nation. These churches serve a triple function. Not only do they enable the communicants to celebrate the Christian triumph, but they also render a distinct service to them as members of a minority group, and through differentiation in ritual, they minister to various classes within this group. As Holt has said:

There is an intimate relationship between personal feeling of success or failure and the social situation in which the individual is living. There is a close relationship between personal feeling of depression or exhaltation and the prevailing type of religion in which the individual is participating. . . . If we are to have a sociology of religion, it must come through observation of religion in action among other social forces.[4]

NOTES

1. Extensive church studies have been made by H. Paul Douglass, Arthur E. Holt, Samuel C. Kincheloe, and those who have been trained by them. For studies of Negro urban churches, see Robert L. Sutherland, *An Analysis of Negro Churches in Chicago,* doctoral dissertation, University of Chicago, 1930; George H. Hobart, *The Negro Churches of Manhattan, New York City* (New York, 1931); Paul W. Bare, *The Negro Churches in Philadelphia,* master's thesis, Drew University, 1931; Rothe Hilger, *The Religious Expression of the Negro,* master's thesis, Vanderbilt University, 1931; Benjamin E. Mays and Joseph W. Nicholson, *The Negro's Church* (New York, 1933); Edith Lockley, *The Negro Spiritualist Churches of Nashville,* master's thesis, Fisk University, 1935; Dan Dodson, *The Ethnic Church,* master's thesis, Southern University, 1936; Ida Rowland, *Study of Rituals and Ceremonies of Negroes in Omaha,* master's thesis, Omaha University, 1938; Raymond J. Jones, *A Comparative Study of Cult Behavior among Negroes,* master's thesis, Howard University, 1939. The theses of Hilger, Jones, and Lockley deal with religious expression of cults, although the church upon which Mr. Hilger's study is based belongs to an old-line denomination and Mr. Bare stresses particularly the churches of the store-front type. While Mr. Sutherland begins with a helpful classification, he does not base it primarily on ritual.

2. From W.P.A. Project 3684, *Chicago Negro Community Study.*

3. Arthur E. Holt, "Case Records as Data for Studying the Conditioning of Religious Experience by Social Factors," *American Journal of Sociology,* September 1926, pp. 227-236.

4. Holt, p. 227.

13

THE NEGRO CHURCH AND ASSIMILATION

E. FRANKLIN FRAZIER

With the prospect of an integrated American society in mind, the late black sociologist E. Franklin Frazier has attempted to predict how the Negro church would function in competition with its white counterpart. Frazier seemed to think that the church could not survive as a spiritual and social refuge for Negroes of any class. Among the lower classes the religious heritage would be diffused into such semisecular groups as the gospel singers. The upper strata of black society would tend to adopt the religious focus of whites and use the Negro church for business reasons or else abandon it altogether. Inasmuch as Frazier has rather cynically pronounced the Negro church "responsible for the so-called backwardness of American Negroes," he may well have read the signs of its demise with a satisfaction unshared by many members of the black community.

The Walls Came Tumbling Down

We have studied the transformations which have occurred in the Negro church and in the religion of Negroes as the result of urbanization. We have seen how the migrations of Negroes to cities have tended to uproot the traditional organization of the Negro community and changed the outlook of Negroes. As the result of the social disorganization of Negro life there has been a reorganization of life on a different basis in order to meet the demands of the city. Life in the cities of the North has brought a larger measure of freedom from racial prejudice and discriminations which had characterized race relations in the South. This new freedom has enabled Negroes to enter more into the mainstream of American life. Since this new freedom has been due partly to broad changes in the economic and social organization of American life, the Negro in the South benefited from these changes. The success which Negroes have achieved in breaking down racial barriers has been due partly to their own efforts. They

Reprinted from *The Negro Church in America* (New York: Schocken Books, 1964), pp. 68-81, by permission of the publisher. Copyright 1964 by the University of Liverpool.

have carried on a constant struggle in the courts and they have influenced to some extent public opinion. As the mid-century drew to a close a distinguished white woman, who had been associated with their struggle, could look back at the success which Negroes had made in breaking through racial barriers and say in the words of the well-known Negro spiritual, "the walls came tumbling down."[1]

However, as the racial barriers are broken down and Negroes increasingly enter into the mainstream of American life, the traditional organization of Negro life is constantly being undermined. The so-called process of integration, which is only an initial stage in the assimilation of Negroes into American society, does not have the same effect on all parts of the social structure of the Negro community. The extent and the nature of the participation of Negroes in the wider American community is determined first by their class position. Negroes in the Black Belt or rural counties in the South where they constitute 50 percent or more of the population are still almost completely isolated from the main currents of American culture. Although lower-class Negroes in cities, who include those engaged in domestic and personal services and those employed as unskilled laborers, have more contacts with American life, they are still more or less confined to the Negro community. As Negro workers acquire skills and become members of labor unions, they begin to enter into the mainstream of American life. This is, of course, more characteristic of Negro workers in the North than of those in the South. Many Negroes in the North who are employed as white-collar workers and in technical and professional occupations enter even more fully into the main currents of American society. Not only does their work enable them to share more fully in American culture but they associate more freely with their white fellow workers than any other section of the Negro population.

The second factor and a factor of equal importance, which determines the nature and extent of the participation of Negroes in the wider American community, is their own institutional life. The system of racial segregation in the United States has resulted in an almost complete duplication of the institutions of the American community within the Negro community.[2] We shall begin by considering those institutions which embody the secular interests of Negroes. As Negroes have moved from the world of the folk, they have established insurance companies and banks which have a purely secular end. These institutions are becoming a part of the different associations of insurance companies and banks and they are subject to state supervision. Then there are many other kinds of business enterprises, many of which cater especially to the personal and other needs of Negroes, and thus supply services often refused by white establishments. Negroes are expected to patronize these various so-called "Negro" businesses because of "racial loyalty." There is a National Negro Business League and numerous Negro chambers of commerce. Among the more successful Negro businesses should be included the Negro weekly newspapers which have circulations running into the hundreds of thousands.

Then there are certain cultural institutions among which are included the various secret fraternal organizations such as the Masons, Odd Fellows, and the Elks. In this group we would also include the various college Greek letter societies for men and women. Although they would not qualify as institutions, there are numerous social clubs which may be considered along with the cultural institutions. The most important cultural institution is, of course, the Negro church. It embodies, as we have seen, the cultural traditions of Negroes to a far greater extent than any other institution.

As "the walls of segregation tumble down," it is the institutions which embody the secular interests of Negroes which are being undermined more rapidly than those representing their cultural interests. As white establishments cater to the personal needs of Negroes there is less need for what is known as "Negro" businesses to supply such services. Moreover, as the large corporations and other so-called white business enterprises employ Negroes in all capacities, there is less need for an association of people engaged in "Negro" businesses. Likewise, as white newspapers carry more news concerning Negroes and employ Negro journalists, the Negro newspapers decline in circulation as the foreign language newspapers have done. Although schools are cultural institutions, the segregated Negro public schools and state colleges will become less important.

The situation is different in regard to the cultural institutions within the Negro community. There are some privately supported Negro educational institutions with deeply rooted traditions in Negro life that resist the trend toward the integration of the Negro. On the other hand, as Negro professors are increasingly taken on the faculties of so-called white colleges and universities and Negro students are admitted to such institutions, Negroes are joining the mainstream of American life. When one comes to the Negro church, which is the most important cultural institution created by Negroes, one encounters the most important institutional barrier to integration and the assimilation of Negroes. White churches may open their doors to Negroes and a few Negro ministers may be invited to become pastors of white churches; the masses of Negroes continue, nevertheless, to attend the Negro churches and the Negro church as an institution continues to function as an important element in the organized social life of Negroes.

The Church Is No Longer a Refuge

The strength of the Negro church as a barrier to the integration of Negroes into the main currents of American life should not be overestimated, especially since the process of integration has not progressed very far. Moreover, it is necessary to differentiate the situation in the North from that in the South. In the South the Negro has scarcely begun his struggle to participate in the secular and public institutions of the American community. On the other hand, in the border states and in the North there is much larger participation of Negroes in the secular and public institutions of the American community. In the South the lives of Negroes still revolve about the activities of the Negro community. Even where they gain entrance into labor unions, they are excluded from the "social" activities of these organizations. In the North Negroes are included increasingly in the "social" activities of the various labor unions. Nevertheless, in the North the proliferation of organizations which provide for the "social" needs of Negroes indicate the extent to which Negroes are still outsiders, so to speak. Moreover, the ecological or spatial segregation of Negroes, which is often the result of impersonal economic and social forces rather than prejudice and discrimination, tends to maintain the separate institutions of the Negro community. The church is the most important of these institutions in which the masses of Negroes find a refuge within white society which treats them with condescension if not contempt.

But the Negro church can no longer serve as a refuge as it did in the past when the majority of Negroes lived in the South under a system of racial segregation and the majority of the Negroes in the South lived in rural areas. Willy-nilly Negroes are drawn into the complex social organization of the American community. This is necessary for mere survival. Recognizing the need for a more complex social organization to serve the needs of urbanized Negroes and at the same time taking cognizance of the fact that Negroes were still excluded from labor unions, a Negro sociologist proposed that the Negro church, being the largest organized unit of Negro life, incorporate some of the functions of the new forms of organized social life which are required in the city.[3] It is apparent, however, that this proposal was impractical since the Negro church could not perform the functions of the new types of associations necessary to life in the city.

It was inevitable that the Negro should be drawn into the organized forms of social life in the urban environment. As a consequence, the Negro church has lost much of its influence as an agency of social control. Its supervision over the marital and family life of Negroes has declined. The church has ceased to be the chief means of economic cooperation. New avenues have been opened to all kinds of business ventures in which secular ends and values are dominant. The church is no longer the main arena for political activities which was the case when Negroes were disfranchised in the South. Negro political leaders have to compete with the white political leaders in the "machine" politics of the cities. In a word, the Negroes have been forced into competition with whites in most areas of social life and their church can no longer serve as a refuge within the American community.

We have seen how Negroes in the established denominational churches developed secular interests in order to deal with race prejudice and discriminations to which they are exposed when the "walls of segregation come tumbling down." We have seen how lower-class Negroes have reacted to the cold impersonal environment of the city and of the large denominational churches by joining the "storefront" churches and the various cults. These all represented their reaction to the crumbling traditional organization of Negro life as Negroes are increasingly cast afloat in the mainstream of American life where they are still outsiders.

The Gospel Singers

Although the lower strata in the Negro community do not participate to the same extent as the upper strata in the main currents of American life, they are nevertheless increasingly assimilating the manners and customs of American society. There is thus achieved a certain external conformity to the patterns of American culture.[4] They continue to be influenced in their thinking and especially in their feelings and sentiments by the social heritage of the Negro which is represented by the spirituals and religious orientation toward the world contained in the spirituals. The masses of Negroes may increasingly criticize the church and their ministers, but they cannot escape from their heritage. They may develop a more secular outlook on life and complain that the church and the ministers are not sufficiently concerned with the problems of the Negro race,[5] yet they find in their religious heritage an opportunity to satisfy their deepest emotional yearnings.

Out of the revolt of the lower strata against the church and the growing secularization of Negro religion there has come an accommodation between traditional Negro religion and the new outlook of Negroes in the new American environment. This accommodation is symbolized by the gospel singers. The songs which the gospel singers sing have been described as a compound of "elements found in the old tabernacle songs, the Negro Spirituals and the blues."[6] Since the Negro has become urbanized, there has been an amazing rise and spread of "gospel singing." This has been attributed, and correctly so, to the fact that, "As Negro churches have become more European in decorum and programme, the great mass of less Europeanized Negroes began to look elsewhere for full vented religious expressions in music and preaching."[7] The important fact is that although the gospel singers have gone outside the church for a congenial form of religious expression, they nevertheless remain in the church and are a part of the church. Recently when a gospel singer died and her funeral was held in a large Baptist church in the nation's capital, it was reported that 13,000 persons viewed her remains, 1,000 persons jammed the church, and another 1,000 lined the sidewalks outside the church. Dozens of gospel-singing groups came from neighboring areas and as far away as Pennsylvania and Illinois. The white owner of a broadcasting company flew from Ohio to attend the funeral. Between 150 and 200 cars accompanied the body to the cemetery.[8]

More important still for us here is the fact that the gospel singers symbolize something that is characteristic of Negro religion from the standpoint of assimilation. Some of the so-called advanced Negro churches resented these gospel singers and refused to permit them to sing within their churches. They have gradually become more tolerant and let down the bars as the gospel singers have acquired status and acceptance within the white world. Such well-known gospel singers as Mahalia Jackson, Rosetta Thorpe, and the Ward Sisters have been accepted as "artists." The gospel singer not only sings to the Negro world but sings to the white world. One of the famous Ward Sisters stated that the gospel singing is popular because "it fills a vacuum in people's lives. For people who work hard and make little money it offers a promise that things will be better in the life to come."[9] She was thinking, of course, of Negroes but the gospel singers sing to white America as well. This is indicated by their hold on the record industry and their popularity on radio and television programs.

Gospel singing has, of course, become commercialized and that is another indication of the relation of Negro religious life to assimilation. It indicates in a sense the terms on which the Negro is being assimilated. Moreover, white men in the South are beginning to imitate the Negro gospel singers. And Negro gospel singing is often featured as a part of the programs on television. Thus, the religious folk songs of the Negro are becoming secularized despite the fact that the singing of them in secular entertainment is a concession to the so-called religious revival in the United States. The gospel singers, then, unlike the cults, do not represent a complete break with the religious traditions of the Negro. They represent or symbolize the attempt of the Negro to utilize his religious heritage in order to come to terms with changes in his own institutions as well as the problems of the world of which he is a part.

In a sense, therefore, the attempts of the Negro to resist segregation in the sit-down strikes in the South represent the same falling back upon his religious heritage in time of crisis. This movement on the part of Negro students in the South is supposed to be based upon the nonviolent resistance movement of Gandhi.[10] Some of its intellectual leaders like the Reverend Martin Luther King may use Gandhi's nonviolent resistance as an ideological justification of the movement, but Gandhism as a philosophy and a way of life is completely alien to the Negro and has nothing in common with the social heritage of the Negro. As Negro students go forth singing the spirituals or the gospel hymns when they engage in sit-down strikes or sing their gospel songs in response to violence, they are behaving in accordance with the religious heritage of the Negro.

Then there is another aspect of this movement which needs to be considered in relation to the changes in the religion of the Negro. Because of the improvement in their economic conditions, an increasing number of Negro students are able to attend the colleges for Negroes in the South. They are being drawn from those strata in the Negro population closest to the rural background and who, therefore, are closest to the folk heritage of the Negro. Education, or more specially the opportunity to attend college, is the most important factor enabling Negroes to achieve middle-class status. Moreover, the leaders of this movement have seen something of the world because of their army or other experiences, or their parents have had similar experiences. In their revolt against the racial discrimination they must fall back upon the only vital social heritage that has meaning for them and that social heritage is the religious heritage represented by the spirituals which are becoming secularized.

The Religion of the New Middle Class

... Here we are interested in the religious outlook of the new Negro middle class which has become important among Negroes during the past twenty years or so. It is this class whose outward appearance and standards of behavior approximate most nearly the norms of the white American society. Moreover, Negroes who have achieved middle-class status participate more largely than any other element in American life. It is for this reason that we shall focus attention upon the new middle class in studying the changes in the religious life of Negroes as they are related to the assimilation of Negroes into American society.

The growing importance of the new middle class in the Negro community is due to the continual differentiation of the population along occupational lines. Therefore, the new middle class is composed almost entirely of those persons who derive their incomes from services rendered as white-collar workers and as professional men and women. Despite the dreams of Negro leaders, fostered by the National Negro Business League at the turn of the century, that Negroes would organize big industries and large financial undertakings, Negroes have not become captains of industry nor even managers of large corporations. So-called "Negro" business continues to consist mainly of small retail stores catering to the personal needs of Negroes. There are a small number of insurance companies, small banks, and newspapers which constitute their larger business enterprises. The owners and managers of these enterprises constitute the upper layer of the middle class while the increasing number of Negroes in skilled occupations constitute its lowest stratum. For reasons which have been indicated, in the North and West about 25 percent of the Negro population is able to maintain middle-class standards while in the South only about 12 percent are in this position.

The new Negro middle class is a new phenomenon in the Negro community because it has a different economic base and a different social heritage from the relatively small middle class which had become differentiated from the masses of Negroes by the first decade of this century.[11] This older middle class was an "aristocratic" élite in a sense because its social status and pre-eminence were based upon white ancestry and family and its behavior was modeled after the genteel tradition of the Old South. The upper layer derived their incomes from land but the majority of the members of the élite were employed in a large variety of occupations including positions as trusted retainers in white families. The new middle class has a different occupational basis and occupation is one of the important factors in determining status.

Since the opening of the century there had been a faith among middle-class Negroes in "Negro" business as a means of solving their social as well as economic problems. This faith was somewhat as follows: as Negroes became businessmen they would accumulate capital and give employment to Negroes and once Negroes possessed wealth, white men would respect them and accord them equality. The new middle class has accepted without the critical attitude which experience should have given them, the faith in "Negro" business as a way to social and economic salvation.

Since the emergence of the new middle class involves the rise of the more ambitious and energetic elements among the masses of Negroes to middle-class status, this new class does not possess the genteel tradition of the older middle class. This new class is largely without social roots except the traditions of the Negro folk represented in the spirituals. But as these Negroes rise to middle-class status they reject the folk heritage and seek to slough off any reminders of their folk inheritance. However, since their rise to the middle-class status has enabled them to marry into families with the genteel tradition of the old middle class, there is often a confusion of "aristocratic" folk values. It is for this reason that many middle-class Negroes exhibit in their manners and behavior the characteristics of both a peasant and a gentleman. Among this new class there is much confusion as to standards of behavior and beliefs. There is a constant striving to acquire money in order to engage in conspicuous consumption which provides the outward signs of status and conformity to white American standards. They all possess the same goal, which is acceptance into the white community and they all profess, at least, a desire to be integrated into the white community.

Integration for the majority of middle-class Negroes means the loss of racial identity or an escape from the lowly status of Negroes and the contempt of whites. With integration they began to remove as much as possible from the names of their various organizations anything that would identify them as Negroes. This even extended to their church organizations. The Colored Methodist Episcopal Church became the "Christian" Methodist Episcopal Church. It is significant, however, that when the middle-class leaders in the African Methodist Episcopal Church attempted to take "African" out of the name and substitute the word "American," there was a revolt on the part of the masses who demanded that "African" be retained. This incident is indicative of the general attitude of the middle class toward the African background of the Negro. While there is some outward profession of pride in African independence and identification with Africa, the middle class rejects identification with Africa and wants above all to be accepted as "just Americans." It was the new middle class which was rising to importance in the 1920's that was most bitterly opposed to the Garvey movement which had as its goal the identification of Negroes with Africa and African interests.[12] Middle-class Negroes seize upon identification with Africa only as a means of compensating for their feeling of inferiority and improving their status in the eyes of American whites.

Despite the fact that middle-class Negroes conform to the standards of whites and accept without question the values of American society, they are still rejected by the white world. They feel this rejection more keenly than lower-class Negroes who participate less in the white man's world and conform to the standards of their own separate world. Moreover, because of their position, middle-class Negroes have an ambivalent attitude toward their identification as Negroes. On the one hand, they resent the slightest aspersion upon Negroes. When placed in competition with whites they have feelings of inadequacy and when they find themselves in close association with whites they have feelings of insecurity though they may clamor for integration into the white world.[13] They are status seekers in a double sense; they strive to keep up with the expectations of their class in the Negro community and they seek or hope to gain status in the white world. In order to maintain high standards of consumption often both husband and wife work but they constantly complain of the "rat race" to maintain life as they would live it. They live frustrated lives despite their efforts to compensate for their feelings of inferiority and insecurity. They have little time for leisure and the enjoyment of what they call the "cultural" things of life. As a matter of fact, they have little appreciation of music or art and they read very little since reading has not become a tradition in the new middle class.

Their ambiguous position in American society together with their recent rise to middle-class status are reflected in the religious behavior and attitudes of middle-class Negroes. There is first a tendency for middle-class Negroes to sever their affiliation with the Baptist and Methodist churches and join the Presbyterian, Congregational, and Episcopal churches. The middle-class Negroes who continue their affiliation with the Baptist and Methodist churches choose those churches with intelligent ministers and a relatively large middle-class membership. As a consequence there is a solid core of the Negro middle class that continues to be affiliated with the Negro church. However, middle-class Negroes continue their affiliation with the Negro church for a number of reasons. Their families may have been associated with the churches and the churches which they have known since childhood provide a satisfying form of religious worship. Although many middle-class Negroes continue to be affiliated with the church, the church is no longer the center of social life for them as for the lower class. They are members of professional and business associations and Greek letter fraternal organizations, though "social" clubs constitute the vast majority of these other forms of organized social activities. Some are thus able to satisfy their striving for status outside the church. But for others it is necessary to leave the Baptist and Methodist churches and join the Presbyterian, Congregational, and Episcopal churches in order to satisfy the desire for status.

The striving for status and the searching for a means to escape from a frustrated existence is especially marked among the middle-class Negroes who cannot find a satisfactory life within the regular Negro church organization. This probably accounts for the fact that during the past two decades middle-class Negroes have been joining the Catholic Church.[14] Sometimes they send their children to Catholic schools where they will receive a discipline not provided in the public schools for Negroes. Very often after joining the Catholic Church with the expectation that they will escape from their status as Negroes, they find that they are still defined as Negroes by whites. Some middle-class Negroes in their seeking to find escape from the Negro identification have gone from the Catholic Church to the Christian Science Church and then to the Bahaist Church. Moreover, there is a tendency among middle-class Negroes to be attracted to Moral Rearmament, hoping that they would find a group in which they could lose completely their identification as Negroes and escape from their feelings of inferiority and insecurity. A small intellectual fringe among middle-class Negroes have affiliated with the Unitarian Church. But some of them may still attend more or less surreptitiously the Methodist and Baptist churches on Friday nights.

This type of dual church affiliation is more characteristic of Negro professional men who affiliate with churches mainly for social and professional reasons. Some professional Negroes affiliate with a church which their friends or middle-class Negroes attend, and at the same time affiliate with churches attended by the lower class who are their clients. They are representative of the growing number of middle-class Negroes who have a purely secular outlook on the world. Some of them express contempt for religion and do not attend church though they may pretend to have some church affiliation. Since they have neither an intellectual heritage nor a social philosophy except a crude opportunism which enables them to get by in the white man's world, they may turn to all forms of superstition. This is because they are still haunted by the fears and beliefs which are a part of their folk heritage. They are often interested in "spiritual" and "psychic" phenomena. Very often the real religious feelings and faith of middle-class Negroes are expressed in their obsession with poker and other forms of gambling.[15]

The religious behavior and outlook of the middle-class Negroes is a reflection of their ambiguous position as Negroes rise to middle-class status and become increasingly integrated into the American community. To the extent that they are becoming really assimilated into American society, they are being beset by the religious dilemmas and doubts of the white middle-class Americans. On the other hand, for the masses of Negroes, the Negro church continues to be a refuge, though increasingly less of a refuge, in a hostile white world.

NOTES

1. Mary White Ovington, *The Walls Came Tumbling Down* (New York, 1947).

2. See E. Franklin Frazier, *The Negro in the United States* (New York: The Macmillan Co., rev. ed., 1957).

3. See the proposal of Dr. George E. Haynes of the Federal Council of Churches, quoted in St. Clair Drake and Horace Cayton, *Black Metropolis* (New York: Harcourt, Brace & Co., 1945).

4. See "Racial Assimilation in Secondary Groups," in Robert E. Park, *Race and Culture* (Glencoe, Ill., 1950), chap. 16.

5. See Drake and Cayton, pp. 650-654, concerning the rebellion of the lower classes against the church.

6. Arna Bontemps, "Rock, Church, Rock," in Sylvester G. Watkins, ed., *Anthology of American Negro Literature* (New York, 1944), p. 431.

7. Willis Laurence James, "The Romance of the Negro Folk Cry in America," *Phylon*, 16 (1955): 23.

8. See *Washington Afro-American*, April 5, 1960, for featured article on front page concerning death and funeral of Thelma Greene, at which a member of the Robert Martin Singers of Chicago sang a solo, "God Specializes," causing a number of persons to faint and to be carried out by nurses.

9. Interview with Clara Mae Ward in Winston-Salem, who claims she is the only gospel singer ever to have visited the Holy Land. "Singing for Sinners," *Newsweek*, 50 (September 2, 1957): 86.

10. See "The Revolt of Negro Youth," *Ebony*, May 1960.

11. E. Franklin Frazier, "The Negro Middle Class and Desegregation," *Social Problems*, 4 (April 1957): 291-301.

12. See Frazier, *Negro in the United States*, pp. 528-531.

13. E. Franklin Frazier, *Black Bourgeoisie* (Glencoe, Ill., 1957), pp. 216 ff.

14. The recent increase during the past twenty years in the number, which remains relatively small, of lower-class Negroes in the Catholic Church has been due to aid provided them during the *Depression years* and the better educational facilities, as compared with the public schools, provided them by the Catholic Church.

15. E. Franklin Frazier, *Black Bourgeoisie* (Glencoe, Ill.: Free Press, 1957), pp. 209 ff.

14

THE POWER OF THE CHURCH

KENNETH B. CLARK

Although Kenneth B. Clark is scarcely more optimistic than E. Franklin
Frazier in his assessment of the probable future of the Negro church, he does
take a considerably more positive view of its potential prophetic role. The
church has always been a center of protest as well as a refuge from oppression,
just as its ministers have been community crusaders as well as fashionable congregational status symbols. Nevertheless, Negroes must inevitably ally themselves with agencies holding recognized power in the larger society. Clark
concludes that the black church, itself a victim of the ghetto and up to now
essentially powerless, may become a casualty of its members' move in a competitive, nonsegregated world.

Have the churches of Harlem themselves any power—real or latent—to stimulate and direct constructive social change? Or are they, too, victims of the
ghetto?

The need of the average Negro to compensate for the daily subservience
and emotional restraints imposed upon him by his inferior status can be satisfied either in the bars, on the streetcorners, or in the churches.

Established Negro churches, the many storefront churches, and the sporadic Negro quasireligious cult groups, like Father Divine's and the late Daddy
Grace's followers, play chiefly a cathartic role for the Negro. These churches
and cults and their leaders provide an opportunity for their followers to "let
off steam," to seek release for emotions which cannot be expressed in overcrowded homes or on the job. The Negro church is a social and recreational
club and a haven of comfort for the masses of Negroes. Within the church, a
Negro porter or maid can assume responsibilities and authority not available
to him elsewhere. Only there can he engage in political intrigue and participate
in financial decisions open to whites in many other aspects of their lives. Here
the Negro domestic exchanges her uniform for a "high-fashion" dress and en-

Reprinted from *Dark Ghetto* (New York: Harper & Row, 1965), pp. 174-182, by permission of the publisher. Copyright 1965 by Kenneth B. Clark.

joys the admiration and envy of other friends. The value of the church in providing personal affirmation and self-esteem for Negroes is great enough to
permit them to tolerate almost any degree of personal, theological, or educational inadequacy upon the part of their minister, so long as he holds the
church together as a successful social and financial institution. Prominent
Negro ministers of Negro churches are indulged by their congregations. They
are permitted considerable personal freedom, and they are often given presents of clothing and cars. They are symbols of the social and civic success of
the church and give the members of their congregation the vicarious satisfaction of relationship to an important church and identification with an influential minister.

This is the source of both the power and the weakness of the Negro church
in the ghetto. The potential power of the Negro church lies in the fact that it
does attract large numbers of the masses of Negroes. The weaknesses of the
Negro church, however, cannot be ignored: They are inherent in the general
pathology of the ghetto of which the Negro church is a part. Among its more
flagrant weaknesses is the fact that its potential strengths can all too easily be
dissipated by preoccupation with trivia, with competitiveness, suspiciousness,
and a desperate struggle for the empty status, bombast, and show of the
ghetto world.

Many Negro ministers have, nevertheless, managed to mobilize the positive
power potential of their churches and have harnessed it to the democratic and
idealistic ideologies of religion for effective racial protest and action. It was
inevitable that, in addition to their escape function, Negro churches would
have a direct protest role. The dream of heaven that sustained Negroes for so
long has been transformed into hope for life on earth. The roles of such Negro
ministers as Adam Clayton Powell, Martin Luther King, Jr., Ralph Abernathy,
and Fred Shuttlesworth in the Negro protest movement reflect the historical
and unavoidable relationship between Negro religion and Negro protest. The
role of the Negro church in the early stages of the Negro movement may have
owed its strength to the fact that the Negro church was the only institution
in which the Negro was allowed that degree of autonomy and freedom from
white domination which permitted even a minimal degree of organization for
a sustained protest movement. The Negro was required to finance and build
his own churches. He hired and paid his ministers without any major help
from the white community. In all other aspects of life—in all economic, educational, and other institutional contacts—even under a pervasive and rigid
biracial and segregated system, the Negro was still dependent upon white
financial control. His schools were controlled by white authorities or white
philanthropy. His job, his business, and his home were controlled by white
industries and banks. His rights as a citizen were determined by white politi-

cians and government officials. Only in the most segregated of social institutions, the church, was he able to exercise that degree of personal and racial freedom necessary for the initial stages of an effective campaign against racial injustices. The Negro church, therefore, cannot be understood primarily in traditional theological terms, but rather in terms of the religion of race. For the Negro, his church is his instrument of escape, his weapon of protest, his protective fortress behind which he seeks to withstand the assaults of a hostile world and within which he plans his strategies of defiance, harassment, and, at times, his frontal attacks against racial barriers. The ministers and laymen of the white Christian churches are responsible for making the Negro churches effective as vehicles of racial protest by their historic unwillingness to incorporate Negroes into their houses of Christ and by their inability to share with the Negro his passion and action for justice and equality. One of the earliest civil rights controversies, dating back to the beginning of human slavery in the New World, was the argument whether the African slaves should be taught to read and converted to Christianity. A paradox of Protestantism, the dominant religion of the early North American colonists, was the need to reconcile the practical fact of human slavery with the ideals of Christian brotherhood. The advantages of slavery demanded that the religious and moral conflicts of the early American Christians be handled by the comparatively simple device of denying to the African slave the status of a fully developed human being. The contemporary Negro churches, whether in an all-Negro denomination or as part of a white denomination, are concrete symbols and citadels of this exclusion and rejection.

Given the special origin of the Negro church and Negro personal need, one must be prepared for the possibility that in spite of very compelling religious and idealistic reasons for desegregation of American churches, the church is likely to be the last of the social institutions to be effectively integrated. Paradoxically, bedrock resistance to desegregation may be found more among Negroes than among whites, for only in the church have many Negroes found a basis for personal worth. If one demands that the Negro give up the Negro church before total integration is achieved, on the grounds of consistency with the goals of the civil rights movement, the demand will be rejected, for the Negro has managed to salvage some personal self-esteem from his church, and until he achieves such self-esteem elsewhere he will not give up this, his last and only sanctuary.

This point is no less true merely because there exist, in the larger community, churches with interracial congregations. Such churches tend to offer themselves as examples of the type of religious democracy toward which all other churches should strive. An analysis of the social class structure of the membership of such churches would probably reveal that the members are well above the American mean in social, economic, and educational status. The chances are that Negro members of interracial churches are of the uppermiddle classes or upwardly mobile groups, probably superior even to the average white member of the church in educational background. The interracial church outside the ghetto is a social instrument for the upwardly mobile and upper-middle-class Negro who uses the fact of his membership as additional evidence of his success. He therefore tends to demand of the church that it protect this image of himself above any other ideal. Any issue which would tend to remind the Negro of his racial identity would necessarily come in conflict with the basic needs which he sought to satisfy by joining. Even to discuss race may shatter the delusions of denial and the fantasies of acceptance which are part of his identification with the interracial church. Such Negroes are nonetheless able to derive satisfaction through their jobs and personal success and are less dependent upon the church for a more basic psychological support than are the masses of Negroes. Segregated Negro churches in the ghetto not only serve the needs of whites but of Negroes, too; and therefore there are no genuinely interracial churches in the heart of any Negro ghetto, and there cannot be. If the ghetto churches were genuinely interracial the needs of Negroes for self-esteem and for escape would remain unfulfilled.

The Negro intellectual, on the other hand, tends to reject the church altogether as a multiple symbol of fantasy. He tends to regard the church as basically irrelevant to the hard and difficult realities of race. He tends to emphasize the fact that the church has, historically, compromised on moral social issues, obscuring them by abstruse theological debate. In his view, the churches have, in a sense, sought to have the cake of moral leadership and eat it, too, refusing to come in conflict with those power groups that support racial injustice, determined to hold on to their major contributors, who are usually conservative, fearing to offend them by commitment to social change. It has seldom dared to question the validity of the uses of power by the princes of power. This looks like hypocrisy to the Negro intellectual, and as a result he often rejects not only the church as an institution, but religion itself.

The church as an institution has not yet found the formula for effecting change without alienating its strongest supporters. If any reconciliation or resolution of this conflict is possible it would seem to depend on the ability of the church leadership to state clearly and unequivocally the terms for such resolution which are consistent with the basic moral and theological positions of the church and thereby to assume the risk that the practical controllers of power within the church will accept, comply with, and use their power to reinforce this position, rather than rejecting it as in many Southern and Northern churches. But even if, in response to this challenge, the lay leaders of the church oppose its stand for justice, the moral strength of the church would have been affirmed and the issue between the demands and the direction of practical economic and political power on the one hand and moral and spiritual power on the other hand would be clarified. The façade of power which the church now presents would be removed, and the church would be forced to develop a genuine prophetic role. The fact that the churches are the most pervasive social institutions in the Negro ghetto, and the fact that churches do not hold primary power in American society, are cruelly related. If religion were a powerful social force, either the white society would have to restrict church strength in Northern Negro communities—witness the bombings of Negro churches in the South—or the ghettos themselves would be transformed.

Religion in Harlem, as among Negroes generally, is primarily Protestant, though the number of Negro Catholics has been gradually increasing in recent years. For many Negroes, in a reversal of the pattern some immigrant groups have followed, to become a Roman Catholic is part of a move to a higher status because of the association between poverty and inferiority and their Protestant past.

The number of Negro Roman Catholics, from 1953 to 1963 rose from roughly 450,000 to 700,000, an increase of 55 percent. Yet nationally, among 237 Roman Catholic bishops, none is Negro; and in New York City, there is no Negro priest among the 433 priests in charge of parishes serving approximately 80,000 Negro Catholics.

There are some large and prosperous Negro churches in Harlem and some distinguished churchmen. The majority of Negro church members belong to segregated Negro denominations (Negro Baptist and Negro Methodist, including African Methodist Episcopal, A.M.E. Zion, Christian Methodist Episcopal,[1] and Wesleyan Methodist) and most of the rest either to evangelical sects or to churches belonging to white-controlled denominations (Presbyterian, Protestant Episcopal, Lutheran, and Congregational). The former are segregated by decision of the white denominations to live apart, though the Methodists are now moving slowly toward abolishing their Negro Central Jurisdiction; the latter by the same kind of *de facto* segregation, justified by geography, that affects the city's school system.

In the past, Negro church leaders have tended to concentrate their energies on building and maintaining the institution itself, but as the civil rights movement gained in impact and Southern Negro ministers took leadership in the struggle for justice, Northern Negro ministers, affected by a newly stirring social conscience, began to assume a firmer role in attempting to influence social change. The segregated denominations, which raise their own funds and control their own affairs, have, doubtless in part for this reason, been able to provide most of this leadership. One does not find a similar leadership within the evangelical sects like the Pentecostal and Holiness, perhaps because these are oriented more to the next world than to this. Negro ministers whose churches belong to white-dominated denominations have a tougher decision to make. They must pay attention to the opinions of their national hierarchy. They are less free. Seeking to avoid the charge of "Uncle Tom" churches, with its attendant loss of status in both Negro and white communities, they often try to support themselves without help, though this pressure inevitably means that the time and energy and funds spent on providing an educated ministry, a dignified setting, a well-run institution, are not available for social action. "Negro work" does not receive priority in Protestantism; and Protestantism, less unified than either Roman Catholicism or Judaism and less identified than Catholicism and Judaism with the needs of recent immigrant and refugee groups, has been far less effectively organized to help Protestants of low income and persistent need, and particularly Negro Protestants. Yet the vast majority of Negroes in the urban ghettos, as well as elsewhere, hold on to the Protestant faith that has served their spirit while it has neglected their other needs as human beings.

In the wider uses of power, the Negro churches have played a peripheral role. Only rarely has a Negro churchman been accepted in a position of influence by the wider community. One such occasion was the election in 1964 of the Reverend Edler Hawkins to be moderator of the United Presbyterian Church in the United States, the first and only Negro chosen to head a white-dominated denomination. Hawkins is not well known to whites, but in Harlem he has been regarded as forward-looking and sound and not at all as one of the flamboyant Negro religious leaders.

In the Protestant Episcopal Church, despite the fact that large numbers of Negroes belong—especially members of the so-called middle and upper classes—and despite the presence of a number of highly trained and educated Negro Episcopal priests, there are only two Negro bishops nationally: One is Bishop John Burgess of greater Boston; the other has been relegated to missionary work in Liberia. The Episcopal Church has spoken forcefully on race, but acted timidly and inconsistently in the march toward racial justice, reflecting conflict within the church itself on its role in society. A number of hospitals, agencies, and schools identified with that denomination continue to exclude or segregate Negroes. The 1960 denominational budgets for race relations and alcoholism were the same—$7,500—both of obviously low priority. When an advisory committee on intergroup relations was appointed in 1960 to report to the Department of Social Relations of the National Council, its critical findings were never presented and debated openly. The House of Bishops, to whom the committee appealed in 1961, felt at the time that it had a more urgent matter than race to discuss, a matter later revealed to have been concerned with the personal behavior of Episcopal priests.

Within the Methodist body, two separate denominations have existed; one, the segregated Negro Central Jurisdiction is now a matter of considerable embarassment to liberal white Methodists who led a "kneel-in" at the 1964 General Conference to try to stir the denomination's conscience to prompter action. The vote was to abolish the Central Jurisdiction over a three-year transition period. Some Negro Methodists have and will continue to resist its abolition just because the parallel Negro hierarchy makes possible Negroes' achievement of power. But in 1964, two Negroes were chosen as bishops, among the forty-four in the Methodist Church, to serve integrated jurisdictions; one, Bishop Prince A. Taylor, Jr., of New Jersey; the other, Bishop James Thomas of Iowa.

Open competition in religion, as in other areas of life, is always hard for Negroes themselves to face. Yet the very satisfactions of segregation reinforce it. The transition from a closed society to an open, nonsegregated one requires that Negroes and whites both surrender the advantages of the closed society for the dangerous but hopefully more rewarding open competitive society.

NOTE

1. In response to the Supreme Court's 1954 decision, the C.M.E. denomination changed its name from Colored Methodist Episcopal.

15

RELIGION: OPIATE OR INSPIRATION OF CIVIL RIGHTS MILITANCY?

GARY T. MARX

Much of the controversy over the role of the Negro church has centered in the question whether it has inhibited or promoted social protest among Negroes. From a survey conducted in 1964 by the Survey Research Center, University of California, Berkeley, Gary Marx has attempted to determine the actual connection between religious involvement and civil rights militancy. His analysis of the metropolitan sample of Negroes supports the assumption that an otherworldly religious orientation is incompatible with militant protest. Nevertheless, as he notes, there is a "social gospel" strand present in the black church. For the purposes of this study militancy has been measured by a summated index of positive responses to eight items, including "Would you like to see more demonstrations or less demonstrations? (More)," and "Negroes who want to work hard can get ahead just as easily as anyone else. (Disagree)." For a listing and discussion of the items the reader can turn to Marx's *Protest and Prejudice,* pages 40-48.

> Let justice roll down like waters, and righteousness like a mighty stream. *Amos 5:24*

> The white folks like for us to be religious, then they can do what they want to with us. *BIGGER THOMAS*

> Did we not straitly command that ye should not teach in this name? And behold, ye have filled Jerusalem with your doctrine.... Then Peter and the other apostles answered and said, We ought to obey God rather than men. *ACTS 5:28*

Reprinted from *Protest and Prejudice,* rev. ed. (New York: Harper & Row, 1969), pp. 94-105, by permission of the publisher. Copyright 1967 by The Anti-Defamation League of B'nai B'rith.

> But God . . . is white. And if his love was so
> great, and if he loved all his children, why
> were we the blacks, cast down so far?
>   *JAMES BALDWIN*

. . . Being religious may be regarded as one kind of institutional affiliation or it may be seen as a psychological phenomenon. Because it relates to both these areas, and because of the crucial bearing of the Negro church on the civil rights struggle, religion is considered separately.

The relation between religion and political radicalism is a confusing one. On the one hand, established religious institutions have generally had a stake in the *status quo* and hence have fostered conservatism. The otherworldly orientation of the masses, particularly as expressed in the more fundamentalist branches of Christianity, has been seen as an alternative to the development of political radicalism. On the other hand, as the source of both universal humanistic values and the strength that can come from believing one is carrying out God's will in political matters, religion has occasionally played a positive role in movements for radical social change.

This dual role of religion is clearly indicated in the case of the Negro American and race protest. Slaves are said to have been first brought to this country on the ship *Jesus Christ.*[1] Despite occasional controversy over religion's effect, most slave owners eventually came to view supervised religion as an effective means of social control. Stampp, in commenting on the effect of religion, notes:

> Through religious instruction the bondsmen learned that slavery had divine sanction, that insolence was as much an offense against God as against the temporal master. They received the Biblical command that servants should obey their masters, and they heard of the punishments awaiting the disobedient slave in the hereafter. They heard, too, that eternal salvation would be their reward for faithful service. . . .[2]

In discussing the period after the Civil War, Myrdal states: "Under the pressure of political reaction, the Negro church in the South came to have much the same role as it did before the Civil War. Negro frustration was sublimated into emotionalism, and Negro hopes were fixed on the afterworld."[3] A large number of other analysts, in considering the consequences of Negro religion after slavery until the early 1950's reached similar conclusions about its conservative effect.[4]

However, the effect of religion on race protest throughout American history has by no means been exclusively in one direction. While many Negroes were no doubt seriously singing about chariots in the sky, Negro preachers such as Denmark Vesey and Nat Turner and the religiously inspired abolitionists were actively fighting slavery in their own way. All-Negro churches first came into being as protest organizations, and later some served as meeting places where protest strategy was planned or as stations on the underground railroad. The richness of protest symbolism in Negro spirituals and sermons has often been noted. Beyond this symbolic role, the all-Negro church brought together in privacy people with a shared problem. It was in the church that many leaders were exposed to a broad range of ideas legitimizing protest and obtained the *savior faire,* self-confidence, and organizational experience needed to challenge an oppressive system. A recent commentator states that the slave churches were "the nucleus of the Negro protest."[5] And another, that "in religion, Negro leaders had begun to find sanction and support for their movements of protest more than 150 years ago."[6]

Differing perceptions of the varied consequences religion may have on protest have continued to the present time. While there has been very little in the way of empirical research on the effect of the Negro church on protest,[7] the literature on race relations is rich with impressionistic statements which generally contradict each other about how the church either encourages and is the source of race protest or inhibits and retards its development. For example, two observers note: "As primitive evangelism gave way to a more sophisticated social consciousness, the church became the spearhead of Negro protest in the Deep South,"[8] while another indicates that "the Negro church is a sleeping giant. In civil rights participation its feet are hardly wet."[9] A civil rights activist, himself a clergyman, states: "The church today is central to the movement. . . . If there had been no Negro church, there would have been no civil rights movement today."[10] On the other hand, a sociologist, commenting on the more involved higher-status ministers, notes: "Middle class Negro clergymen in the cities of the South generally advocated cautious gradualism in race activities until the mid-1950's when there was an upsurge of protest sentiment among urban Negroes . . . but most of them [ministers] did not embrace the most vigorous techniques of protest until other leaders took the initiative and gained widespread support."[11] Another sociologist states: "Whatever their previous conservative stance has been, the churches have now become 'spearheads of reform.'"[12] Still another suggests that

the Negro church is particularly culpable for its general lack of concern for the moral and social problems of the community . . . it has been accommodatory. Fostering indulgence in religious sentimentality, and riveting the attention of the masses on the bounties of a hereafter, the Negro church remains a refuge, an escape from the cruel realities of the here and now.[13]

Thus one faces opposing views, or at best, ambiguity in contemplating the current effect of religion. The quietistic consequences of religion are all too well known, as is the fact that only a relatively small segment of the Negro church is actively involved. On the other hand, the prominent role of the Negro church in supplying much of the ideology of the movement, many of its foremost leaders, and a place where protest can be organized, can hardly be denied. It would appear from the bombings of churches and the writing of Martin Luther King and other religiously inspired activists that, for many, religion and protest are linked.

Denomination

It has been long known that the more fundamental sects, such as the Holiness groups and the Jehovah's Witnesses, are relatively uninterested in movements for concrete secular, political, or social change.[14] Such transvaluational movements, with their otherworldly orientations and their promise that the last shall be first in the great beyond, are said to solace the individual for his lowly status in this world and to direct attention away from efforts at collective social change. While only a minority of Negroes actually belong to such groups, the relative percentage belonging is higher than among whites. Negro literature is rich in descriptions of these churches and their position on race protest.

Table 1 shows data on civil rights militancy which are consistent with past research on political radicalism among sects. The percentage of respondents scored as militant is about twice as high among members of the more conventional religious groups than among those who belong to sects. The percentage militant increases from only 15 percent for the sects to 43 percent for Episcopalians. It is perhaps ironic that those individuals in largely white denominations (Episcopalian, Presbyterian, and Catholic) appear somewhat higher in militancy than those in Negro denominations, in spite of the greater civil rights activism of the latter. This was true even when social class was held constant.

TABLE 1

Militancy by Religious Denomination[a]

	Episco- palian	United Church of Christ	Presby- terian	Cath- olic	Meth- odist	Baptist	Sects and Cults
Militant	43%	42%	36%	36%	28%	25%	15%
Number	(23)	(12)	(25)	(107)	(141)	(657)	(106)

[a]*Twenty-five respondents are not shown in this table because they did not specify a denomination or belonged to non-Christian religious groups or other smaller Christian groups.*

In their comments, some of which were noted earlier, members of the less conventional religious groups clearly expressed the classical attitudes of sects toward participation in the politics of the secular world. An automobile serviceman in Philadelphia stated, "I, as a Jehovah's Witness, cannot express things involving the race issue." A housewife in the Far West ventured, "In my religion we do not approve of anything except living like it says in the Bible. Demonstrations mean calling attention to you, and it's sinful."

The finding that persons who belong to sects are among the least likely to be militant was to be expected. Clearly, for most people, this type of religious involvement rules out the development of radicalism. But what of religious Negroes in the more conventional churches, which may put relatively less stress on the afterlife and encourage various forms of secular participation? Are the more religiously inclined within these groups also less likely to be militant?

Religiosity

The study measured several dimensions of religious involvement: the importance of religion to the respondent, the orthodoxy of his religious belief, and the frequency of his attendance at worship service.[15] Even with the sects excluded, irrespective of the dimension of religiosity considered, the greater the religiosity, the lower the percentage militant (Table 2).[16] Militancy increases

TABLE 2

Militancy by Subjective Importance of Religion to Respondent[a]

Religion Is	Percent Militant	Number
Extremely important	22	(664)
Quite important	34	(194)
Fairly important	44	(96)
Not too important	56	(18)
Not at all important	62	(13)

[a]*Members of sects are excluded here and in all subsequent tables in this chapter.*

consistently from a low of 22 percent among those who said religion was "extremely important" to a high of 62 percent for those who indicated that religion was "not at all important" to them. For those high in orthodoxy (having no doubt about the existence of God, the devil, or an afterlife), only 20 percent were militant, while for those totally rejecting these ideas 57 percent indicated concern over civil rights (Table 3). Militancy is also inversely

TABLE 3

Militancy by Religious Orthodoxy[a]

	High 6	5	4	3	2	1	Low 0
Militant	20%	26%	25%	24%	42%	41%	57%
Number	(284)	(158)	(210)	(129)	(110)	(51)	(42)

[a]*Having no doubt about the existence of God, the devil, and the afterlife were each scored two, being fairly certain in acceptance of these beliefs was scored one, while having some doubts was scored zero.*

related to frequency of attendance at worship service.[17] As seen in Table 4, while 18 percent of those who attend church more than once a week are high on militancy, 32 percent who attend less than once a year are high in militancy.[18]

TABLE 4

Militancy by Frequency of Attendance at Worship Service

Attend Church	Percent Militant	Number
More than once a week	18	(79)
Once a week	26	(309)
Once to several times a month	28	(354)
Less than once a month to once a year	34	(178)
Less than once a year	32	(61)

These items were strongly interrelated and have been combined into an over-all measure of religiosity. Those scored as very religious in terms of this index attended church at least once a week, felt that religion was extremely important to them, and had no doubts about the existence of God and the devil. As one moves down the index, frequency of church attendance, the importance of religion, and acceptance of the belief items decline consistently until for those scored not at all religious church is rarely if ever attended, religion is not considered personally important and the belief items are rejected.

Observing the effect of this measure on civil rights concern, it can be seen that militancy increases from a low of 19 percent for those labeled very religious to a high of 49 percent for those considered not at all religious (Table 5).

Religiosity and militancy are both related to age, sex, region of the country raised in, and denomination. Older people, women, those raised in the South, and those in Negro denominations were more likely to be scored as religious and to have lower percentages scoring as militant. Thus it is possible that the relation of religiosity to militancy is simply a consequence of the relation of both religiosity and militancy to some third factor. However, it can be seen

TABLE 5

As Religiosity Increases Militancy Decreases[a]

	Very Religious (11, 12)	Quite Religious (7-10)	Not Very Religious (3-6)	Not At All Religious (0-2)
Militant	19%	24%	33%	49%
Number	(209)	(485)	(166)	(124)

[a]*Those for whom religion was extremely, quite, fairly, not too, and not at all important were scored 4, 3, 2, 1, and 0, respectively. Those with scores of 6, 5 and 4, 3, 2 and 1, and 0 on the orthodoxy index were scored 4, 3, 2, 1, and 0, respectively. Those attending worship services more than once a week, once a week, once to several times a month, less than once a month to once a year, and less than once a year were scored 4, 3, 2, 1, and 0, respectively.*

that even controlling for these factors the finding remains the same (Table 6). Even among older people, women, those raised in the South, and those Negro denominations, the greater the religiosity the less the militancy. This finding persists even when observed in light of . . . the indexes of Exposure to Values Legitimating Protest, Social Class, Social Participation, and Subjective Predisposition to Militancy.

TABLE 6

Militancy Related to Religiosity by Age, Sex, Place of Upbringing, and Denomination

	Index of Religiosity							
	Very Religious		Quite Religious		Not Very Religious		Not At All Religious	
Age								
18-29	20%	(25)	28%	(110)	35%	(55)	43%	(37)
30-44	22	(54)	31	(161)	37	(59)	53	(58)
45-59	21	(63)	21	(117)	24	(33)	52	(21)
60+	13	(67)	11	(96)	26	(19)	—	
Sex								
Women	18	(133)	21	(286)	32	(76)	42	(38)
Men	20	(76)	28	(199)	33	(90)	52	(86)
Where Raised								
Deep South	16	(122)	19	(255)	25	(61)	38	(29)
Border states	29	(49)	28	(104)	31	(42)	54	(35)
Non-South	16	(38)	32	(126)	41	(63)	60	(52)
Denomination								
Episcopalian, Presbyterian, or Congregationalist	17	(12)	39	(23)	46	(13)	58	(12)
Catholic	10	(10)	31	(49)	40	(20)	54	(28)
Methodist	35	(23)	20	(76)	36	(28)	50	(12)
Baptist	17	(161)	23	(325)	30	(101)	46	(68)

Note: Percent militant; number of respondents shown in parentheses.
[a]*Three out of six respondents scored as militant.*

The incompatibility of piety and protest that these data show is evident in comments offered by respondents. Many religious people hold beliefs that clearly inhibit race protest. For a few, segregation and a lowly status for Negroes are somehow God's will and not for men to question. Thus a house-wife in South Bend, Indiana, in saying that civil rights demonstrations had hurt Negroes, added, "God is the Creator of everything. We don't know why we all dark-skinned. We should try to put forth the effort to do what God wants and not question."[19] A Negro spiritual contains the lines, "I'm gonna wait upon the Lord till my change comes." Rather than seeing segregation as God's will, our respondents more frequently stressed that God, as absolute controller of the universe, would bring about change in his own way and at his own time. In indicating her unwillingness to take part in a civil rights demonstration, a Detroit housewife said, "I don't go for demonstrations. I believe that God created all men equal and at his appointed time he will give every man his portion; no one can hinder it." And in response to the question about whether or not the government in Washington was pushing integration too slowly, a clerk in Atlanta said, "You can't hurry God. He has a certain time for this to take place. I don't know about Washington."

Others who desired integration and immediate social change felt that, since God was on their side, man need not do anything to help bring it about. Thus a worker in Cleveland gave as his reason for desiring fewer civil rights demon-strations: "With God helping to fight our battle, I believe we can do with less demonstrations." And in saying that Negroes should spend more time praying and less time demonstrating, an Atlanta clergyman added, "Praying is demon-strating."[20]

Although the net effect of religion is clearly to inhibit attitudes of protest, many religious people are nevertheless militant. A religious orientation and a concern with racial protest are certainly not mutually exclusive. Given the active involvement of some churches, the singing of protest spirituals, and the ideology of the movement as it relates to Christian principles of love, equality, passive suffering,[21] and the appeal to a higher moral law, it would be surpris-ing if there were only a few religious people among the militants. A study of Southern Negro CORE activists indicates that less than one person in ten never attends church while almost six out of ten attended church weekly.[22] A religious orientation and a concern with racial protest are certainly not mutu-ally exclusive, and some of those in our study would no doubt agree with Thomas Jefferson that "resistance to tyranny is obedience to God."

However, what determines whether religion leads to an active concern with racial matters or results in quietism?

The classical indictment of religion from the Marxist perspective is that, by focusing concern on an afterlife, the evils of this life are ignored. However,

there are important differences among religious institutions and among individuals in the importance they give to otherworldly concerns. Like most
ideologies, both religious and secular, Christianity contains many themes,
which, if not in contradiction, are certainly in tension with one another. Here,
no doubt, lies part of the explanation of religion's varied consequences for
protest. One important strand of Christianity stresses acceptance of one's lot
and glorifies the afterlife. However, another is more concerned with the realization of Judeo-Christian values in the current life. Martin Luther King clearly represents this "social gospel" tradition.[23] When one's religious involvement includes
temporal concerns and acceptance of the belief that men as well as God have
a role in the structuring of human affairs, then, rather than serving to inhibit
protest, religion can serve to inspire and sustain it. This religious inspiration is
clearly present in the writings of King and others.

However, among sect members and the religious with an otherworldly orientation, religion and race protest, if not mutually exclusive, are certainly
what one observer has referred to as "mutually corrosive kinds of commitments."[24]

Until such time as religion loosens its hold over these people, or comes to
embody to a greater extent the belief that man as well as God can bring about
secular change, and focuses more on the here and now, religion would seem
to be an important factor working against the widespread radicalization of
the Negro public.

NOTES

1. Louis Lomax, *When the Word is Given* (New York, 1964), p. 34. And in another
context it has often been noted that when the missionaries came to the lands to be colo-
nized, they had the Bible and the indigenous people had the land. When they left, they
had the land and the native people still have the Bible.

2. Kenneth Stampp, *The Peculiar Institution* (New York, 1956), p. 158.

3. Gunnar Myrdal *et al., An American Dilemma* (New York, 1944), pp. 861-863.
About the North he notes that the church remained far more independent "but on the
whole even the Northern Negro church has remained a conservative institution with its
interests directly upon other-worldly matters and has largely ignored the practical problems of the Negroes' fate in this world."

4. For example, Dollard notes that "religion can be seen as a mechanism for the
social control of Negroes" and that planters have always welcomed the building of a
Negro church on the plantation while looking with less favor on the building of a school
(John Dollard, *Caste and Class in a Southern Town* [Garden City, N.Y., 1957], p. 248).
A few of the many others reaching similar conclusions are Benjamin E. Mays and Joseph
W. Nicholson, *The Negro's Church* (New York, 1933); Hortense Powdermaker, *After
Freedom* (New York, 1939), p. 285; Charles Johnson, *Growing up in the Black Belt*
(Washington, D.C., 1941), pp. 135-136; St. Clair Drake and Horace Cayton, *Black
Metropolis* (New York, 1962), pp. 424-429; George Simpson and Milton Yinger, *Racial
and Cultural Minorities,* rev. ed. (New York, 1958), pp. 582-587. In a more general con-
text, the social control consequences of religion have been noted throughout history

GARY T. MARX   159

from Plato to Montesquieu to Marx to Nietzsche to Freud to contemporary social theo-
rists.

5. Daniel Thompson, "The Rise of Negro Protest," *Annals of the American Academy
of Political and Social Science,* January 1965, p. 26.

6. Liston Pope, "The Negro and Religion in America," *Review of Religious Research,*
Spring 1964, p. 145.

7. The empirical evidence is quite limited. The few studies that have been done have
focused on the Negro minister. Thompson notes that in New Orleans Negro ministers
constitute the largest segment of the Negro leadership class (a grouping not necessarily
the same as "protest leaders") but that "the vast majority of ministers are primarily interested in their pastoral role. . . . Their sermons are essentially biblical, dealing only tangen-
tially with social issues" (Daniel Thompson, *The Negro Leadership Class* [Englewood
Cliffs, N.J., 1963], pp. 34-35). Studies of the Negro ministry in Detroit and in Richmond,
California, also stress that only a small fraction of Negro clergymen show any active concern with the civil rights struggle. (R. L. Johnstone, "Militant and Conservative Community Leadership Among Negro Clergymen," doctoral dissertation, University of Michigan,
1963, and J. Bloom, "The Negro Church and the Movement for Equality," master's thesis,
Department of Sociology, University of California in Berkeley, 1966).

It is worthy of mention that, although the number of cases was small, the Negro ministers in our sample had the lowest percentage militant of any occupational group. With
respect to the sons of clergymen, the situation seems somewhat different. While the myth
of the preacher's son gone bad is almost a part of American folklore, one would think
that a comparable myth might develop within the Negro community—that of the preacher's son gone radical. Malcolm X, James Baldwin, A. Philip Randolph, Martin Luther King,
James Farmer, Adam Clayton Powell, Elijah Muhammad, and a number of others had
clergymen as fathers. To be taken into consideration is that clergymen make up a relatively larger segment of the Negro middle than of the white middle class.

8. Jane Record and Wilson Record, "Ideological Forces and the Negro Protest,"
Annals of the American Academy of Political and Social Science, January 1965, p. 92.

9. G. Booker, *Black Man's America* (Englewood Cliffs, N.J., 1964), p. 111.

10. Rev. W. T. Walker, as quoted in William Brink and Louis Harris, *The Negro Revolution in America* (New York, 1964), p. 103.

11. N. Glenn, "Negro Religion in the United States," in L. Schneider, ed., *Religion,
Culture and Society* (New York, 1964).

12. J. Fichter, "American Religion and the Negro," *Daedalus* (Fall 1965), p. 1087.

13. E. U. Essien-Udom, *Black Nationalism* (New York, 1962), pp. 357-358. Many
other examples of contradictory statements could be offered, sometimes even in the
same volume. For example, Lee stresses the importance of religion for protest while Logan
sees the Negro pastor as an instrument of the white power structure in a book published
to commemorate 100 years of emancipation (Carleton Lee, "Religious Roots of Negro
Protest," and Rayford Logan, "Educational Changes Affecting American Negroes," in
Arnold Rose, ed., *Assuring Freedom to the Free* (Detroit, 1964).

14. Liston Pope, *Millhands and Preachers* (New Haven, 1942), p. 137; J. Milton
Yinger, *Religion, Society, and the Individual* (New York, 1957), pp. 170-173.

15. These dimensions and several others are suggested by Charles Y. Glock, "On the
Study of Religious Commitment," *Religious Education—Research Supplement,* July–
August 1962, pp. 98-100.

16. One of the items in the militancy index (the question of praying as against demon-
strating) might be seen to lead to a certain amount of circularity in Tables 2 to 6. However, it is noteworthy that even when this item is deleted from the militancy index the
results are the same (Gary T. Marx, "Religion: Opiate or Inspiration of Civil Rights Militancy Among Negroes?" *American Sociological Review,* February 1967).

17. There is a popular stereotype that Negroes are a "religious people," and social
science research has shown that they are "overchurched" relative to whites, that is, the
ratio of Negro churches to the size of the Negro population is greater than this ratio for
whites. Using data from the nationwide survey of anti-Semitism, a brief comparison of
the religiosity of Negroes and whites was possible. When the various dimensions of religiosity are examined, holding the effect of education and region constant, Negroes appear
as significantly more religious *only* with respect to the subjective importance assigned to

religion. In the North whites were more likely to attend church at least once a week than were Negroes, while in the South rates of attendance were the same. About the same percentage of both groups had no doubts about the existence of God, and while Negroes were more likely to be sure about the existence of a devil, whites, were more likely to be sure about a life beyond death. Clearly then, any assertions about the greater religiosity of Negroes relative to whites are unwarranted unless one specifies the dimension of religiosity being measured.

18. The study also made use of an additional measure of religious involvement, membership in church organizations. . . . As membership in organizations increased, so did militancy. Church organizations were purposely excluded because the relation between degree of involvement in a church organization was the opposite of that noted for most other types of organizations. Thus, among those belonging to none, one, two, or three or more church organizations, the percentage militant decreases from 28 percent to 23 percent to 15 percent to 8 percent, respectively. Thus, organizational involvement in churches serves to decrease militancy, unlike the pattern noted for other types of involvement.

19. Albert Cardinal Meyer notes that the Catholic bishops of the United States said in their statement of 1958: "The heart of the race question is . . . religious." ("Interracial Justice and Love," in M. Ahmann, ed., *Race: Challenge to Religion* [Chicago, 1964], p. 126). Viewed from the perspective of the activist seeking to motivate Negroes on behalf of the civil rights struggle, this statement has a meaning which their excellencies no doubt did not intend.

20. The study of ministers in Richmond, California, referred to earlier, offered similar findings. While almost all of the ministers in the study were opposed to discrimination, very few had taken concrete action, in part no doubt because of their belief that God would take care of them. One minister noted, "I believe that if we all was as pure . . . as we ought to be, there would be no struggle. God will answer my prayer. If we just stay with God and have faith. *When Peter was up, did the people march to free him? No. He prayed, and God did something about it* [italics added] " (Bloom).

21. A discussion of nonviolent resistance as it relates to Christianity's emphasis on suffering, sacrifice, and privation may be found in James W. Vander Zanden, "The Nonviolent Resistance Movement Against Segregation," *American Journal of Sociology,* March 1963.

22. In the North the same figure, four out of ten, report never attending as indicate that they go to church weekly. (Ingeborg B. Powell, "Ideology and Strategy of Direct Action: A Study of the Congress of Racial Equality," doctoral dissertation, University of California in Berkeley, 1965, p. 207.)

23. "Any religion that professes to be concerned with the souls of men and is not concerned with the slums that damn them, the economic conditions that strangle them, and the social conditions that cripple them is a dry-as-dust religion." He further adds that "such a religion is the kind the Marxists like to see—an opiate of the people" (Martin Luther King, *Stride Toward Freedom* [New York, 1958], pp. 28-29).

John Lewis, a former SNCC leader and once a Baptist divinity student, is said to have peered through the bars of a Southern jail and quoted the New Testament: "Think not that I am come to send peace on earth. I came not to send peace, but a sword" (Matthew 10:34).

24. Rodney Stark, "Class, Radicalism, and Religious Involvement," *American Sociological Review,* October 1964.

PART III

Cult, Sect, and Church: Religious Alternatives to Traditional Negro Protestantism

16

THE NEGRO AND
HIS RELIGION

ARTHUR FAUSET

In this chapter on the religion of the American Negro, Arthur Fauset disputes some commonly held notions about the Negro, his church, and the current movement into cults. Fauset denies that there is any particular natural affinity between religion and the black American; further, he avers that Negro religion is predominantly an American institution that grew in response to the American situation of the Negro. Far from viewing the movement to cults as flight from reality, Fauset argues that it is the new cults that may well realize the potential latent in Negro religion for protest against social, political, and economic evils. Fauset's analysis should assist the reader in his evaluation of the socioreligious movements described in the following chapters.

The "Religiosity" of the American Negro

The religiosity of the Negro often is taken for granted. Not only is this a popular opinion, but important social scientists intimate and even emphasize the fact.

To take two outstanding examples, there is the sociologist, Robert E. Park, who states,

> I assume . . . the reason the Negro so readily and eagerly took over from the white man his heaven and his apocalyptic visions was because these materials met the demands of his peculiar *racial temperament* [italics mine] . . . .[1]

Reprinted from *Black Gods of the Metropolis* (Philadelphia: University of Pennsylvania Press, 1944), pp. 96-104, 107-109, by permission of the publisher.

Herskovits, the anthropologist, has been quoted above as stating:

Underlying the life of the American Negro is a deep religious *bent* [italics mine] that is but the manifestation here of a similar drive that, everywhere in Negro societies, makes the supernatural a major focus of interest. The tenability of this position is apparent when it is considered how, in an age marked by skepticism, the Negro has held fast to belief. . . .

According to the same author, because religion is such a controlling factor in the life of the average Negro,

everywhere compensation in terms of the supernatural is . . . immediately acceptable to this underprivileged folk, and causes them, in contrast to other underprivileged groups elsewhere in the world, to turn to religion rather than to political action or other outlets for their frustration.[2]

The inference to be drawn from such opinions is that there is something in the Negro amounting almost to an inner compulsion which drives him into religious channels. Some facts and figures on the relation of the American Negro to his church, as compared with the relation of white people to their churches, might be suggestive in this connection.

In their highly revealing study of religion among American Negroes, Mays and Nicholson have disclosed that if we choose to be guided by the proportion of Negroes and whites in the United States who attend church, Negroes can scarcely be considered more religious than whites.[3] Actually the proportion of white men attending church is higher than that for Negroes. The following figures refer to all church members in America over the age of thirteen years: Negro women, 73 percent, Negro men, 46 percent, white women, 62 percent, white men, 49 percent. Thus it becomes apparent that more than 40 percent of Negroes never attend church at all; and this compares with the total nonchurchgoing population of America which according to Mays and Nicholson is 42 percent; but what is more significant, considerably less than half the Negro men attend, and this is below the proportion for white men. Nevertheless the opinion of the universality of religious attitudes among Negroes, as contrasted to whites, persists.

It would seem that Herskovits' observation that "in an age of skepticism, the Negro has held fast to belief" requires some modification.

It may be contended that the Negro holds fast to his belief (presumably is constrained by his heritage to cling to his belief) whether or not he is a church member. This contention is subject to question. Indeed, results of this study, and particularly suggestions in the testimonies of cult members, warrant more than a faint suspicion that many Negroes who find their experience in the more orthodox evangelical churches a disappointment move into the cults. It does not seem too great an assumption to imagine that for the remainder of those disappointed communicants who leave the more orthodox churches but do *not* enter the cults, many drop their belief altogether (for most practical purposes, that is, since relatively few people actually become out-and-out atheists) as well as their membership.

Hence, to the extent that Parks' suggestion of "temperament" and Herskovits' analogous use of the term "bent" imply an almost instinctive participation by American Negroes in religious pursuits, these opinions need to be received with considerable caution.

The Negro Church as an American Institution

There can be no doubt, of course, that the church, and consequently to a degree religion, have played conspicuous roles in the lives of a vast majority of American Negroes, today and in the past. This degree of influence does not find its exact counterpart in the white man's religious experience.

As far as the Negro is concerned, Mays and Nicholson properly have pointed out that

relatively early the church, and particularly the independent Negro church, furnished the one and only organized field in which the slaves' suppressed emotions could be released, and the only opportunity for him to develop his own leadership. In almost every other area he was completely suppressed. . . . Thus, through a slow and difficult process, often involving much suffering and persecution, the Negro, more than three quarters of a century prior to emancipation, through initiative, zeal and ability, began to achieve the right to be free in his church. He demonstrated his ability to preach; and this demonstration convinced both Negroes and whites that he was possessed of the Spirit of God. . . .[4]

The point to be noted is that the development of the Negro's church came as a result of the Negro's need in America for a place to express himself in various ways; it did not result from some inexorable law peculiar to his nature; neither did such a law, or as Herskovits expresses it, a "drive," constrain the Negro then or later "to turn to religion rather than to political action or other outlets for his frustration."

The two "nationalist" cults in this study are the clues in a consideration of Herskovits' assumption. What kind of people struggle politically? Obviously people who have certain political concepts. Such concepts, to result in action, cannot be divorced from life, but like the religion of the Negro according to Herskovits' characterization, it must bear an "intimate relation to life," involving the "full participation of the communicants."

Stated in political terms, in order for a people to act politically there must be political concepts, and these concepts must be made concrete by means of a political organ or organism, such as a political organization (party) or a political identity (nation). Political struggles of a national group inevitably involve that group's national identity. The struggle then becomes one in terms of that national identity, national homeland, or national unity.

It is just this quality of national identity which until very recently has been lacking in the psychology of the Negroes in America. Perhaps every other sizable group in America does have such a national identity, but because of the historical factors involved in the transfer of the Negro people from Africa to America, and possibly because of the infiltration of blood from practically all the other groups in America into the veins of the Negro group, with a corresponding confusion of national emphases, the Negroes in the United States have not been conscious of those national roots which are so marked in the thinking and traditions of such elements in the American nation as the Germans, Poles, or Irish.

The black Jews and the Moorish Americans understand some of this. The black Jews would remind American Negroes of their ancient name and their ancient land. "Without a national name," they say, "there can be no future for a people. Therefore you must not be called Negroes, colored, jigaboos, etc." Having sounded this political note, they are impelled by the logic of their thinking to emphasize the political aspect of their life in America, even though essentially they are a religious group.

The Moorish Americans go even further than the black Jews. After positing the fact that the "name" is the first prerequisite, they go so far as to claim the American continent for themselves, contending that this land is merely an extension of Africa. "For a people to amount to anything," they maintain, "it is necessary to have a name [nation] and a land." Although this assumption of the American continent as an extension of their own Africa may be nothing more nor less than a political expedient, we may assume that the words fall short of action only because the Moors do not have the means to make their beliefs real.

Most American Negroes, however, have not been influenced by such convictions. Consequently they have lacked strong political motivation. For such as these, Africa has not been their land, since they were uprooted spiritually as well as physically. They were not bothered by the names attached to them; if they were called Negro, colored, Afro-American, black, it was all pretty much the same thing. But neither has America been their land, since it was all too obvious to them that they were merely second-rate citizens. Inevitably in the past these great masses of Negroes have been relatively inert politically.

In recent years, however, there has been developing, more and more, the conviction among the masses of Negroes that America *is* their land. Today many Negroes point with pride to the fact that not even the Pilgrims may claim priority to them as settlers in the land.[5] Impressed by the increasing strength of their numbers, and beginning to appreciate the potential position of power which inheres in being the largest so-called minority group in the country, the conviction is growing among the masses of Negroes that they, as well as the Italians, Poles, Jews, Germans, and any other national groups in America, are Americans.[6]

Pari passu with this developing national pride, political consciousness and enormously increasing political action are manifesting themselves. It is no mere fortuitous circumstance that with the decline in the proportion of orthodox churchgoers indicated by Mays and Nicholson, there is an increase in the proportion of Negroes who are entering the trade unions, organizing by means of consumer cooperatives, economic boycotts, protest groups of various kinds, and those who are otherwise girding for political action.

This latter trend is no more the result of "temperament" or "bent" than is the association with religious attitudes which scholars so often ascribe to the Negro. Clearly it signifies that because of the exigencies of the times, affecting not only the Negro but the entire nation, the need for wholesale political action at last is being felt and understood among the masses of Negroes.

A mechanism for action would logically follow. It is only natural for such a mechanism to utilize the religious organization as one means of bringing about the desired end. What we witness here would seem to be a continuation of the very kind of adaptation of an institution to a given need against which the slaveholders hoped to safeguard themselves by forbidding Negroes to congregate even for purposes of religious worship. Consequently, it should come as no surprise to find in the cults, as Reid pointed out,[7] particularly in those like the Moors, the black Jews, and the Father Divine Peace Mission Movement, leaders who are aware of these pressing needs and allow the sails of their religious barks to be trimmed accordingly. Thus the Negro church maintains its American tradition.

The African Heritage

Common sense requires us to believe that everything cultural which the Negro brought over with him from Africa could not have been eradicated from his heritage, despite the centuries since he left Africa, the thousands of

miles which have separated him from the ancestral homeland, and the eroding
influences of an overwhelming and inescapable superculture.[8] Nevertheless,
if we do not go all the way with Frazier and Park in their almost wholesale
assertions that there are no African religious survivals to speak of, neither can
we accept every chance correspondence which might appear to indicate survival.[9] Certainly for the United States, where the European influence in both
form and content of the worship is so marked as to be undeniable, we are not
inclined to accept mere correspondence between American Negro and African
practice as conclusive indication of African origin. The historical evidence
must be present to support these clues, or so it appears to me, and much of
what we observe in the cults studied here seems to confirm this position.

Thus it is a question whether Herskovits is correct in emphasizing the
importance of the influence of the African river cults in the religious development of the American Negro. According to him, Negroes flocked to the
Baptist Church because this form of worship was so readily associated in the
minds of the Negroes with their own river cults in West Africa, and "particularly in view of the fact . . . that river-cult priests were sold into slavery in
great numbers."[10] Were this the deciding factor, it seems to me there should
be fewer Negroes in the Methodist groups, and probably none in the other
denominations which have reduced the baptismal flow to a mere trickle
through the fingers. What is to be said of the Father Divine cult, with its
thousands of followers who do not practice baptism? We should recall the
fact that Father Divine himself probably spent his youth in that part of the
South and among the very Negroes of that section who normally would be
expected to cling to the most primitive attitudes regarding a ritual which was
once so important and of such great significance. Besides, there are the
Moorish Americans, another group of Negroes whose southern origins might
be expected to result in a conservation of this ritual, but to whom the idea
has become almost foreign in their Moslem form of worship.

It probably is true, as Herskovits indicates, that the elaborateness of the
death ceremonies among some Negroes is an African survival. Yet in at least
three of the cults studied we find that the entire association with the idea of
death offers radical departures from well-known West African attitudes and
practices.

The Moorish Americans maintain the same calm reserve in the presence of
death which we have observed with regard to the most ordinary and simple
questions of their faith. They regard death merely as a transition in which
the body quietly dissolves in order to make way for the departure of the soul
to Allah. Usually the body is held for three days, then there is a simple service
at which a prescribed chapter of the *Holy Koran* is read, after which burial
takes place. Sometimes after the burial there is a feast to celebrate the transi-

tion of the spirit from this world to the abode of Allah.

The black Jews take death in their stride. As soon as a member of the flock dies, the body is required to be taken immediately to an undertaker's establishment. The family of the deceased goes into seclusion until after the burial. Meantime all members except very close relatives and perhaps some person designated by the prophet are forbidden to view the remains. The body is to be disposed of as soon as possible.

In the Father Divine cult, it is actually a disgrace to die. Death carries with it the penalty of being charged with having failed to fulfill the requirements of the evangelical life. The dead person becomes an outcast. It has been reported that the potter's field has become the resting place of some members of the Father Divine cult, for the simple reason that no relative or near one would claim the body of the deceased whose unfaithful living habits had required the intervention of the death angel.

None of these attitudes toward death discloses that fear of consequences so characteristic of certain West African tribes, who believe that to permit the soul of the departed to roam at large as a result of improper burial rites is certain to invite misfortunes on living members of the family of the departed one.

Even the tendency of the cults to manifest a disproportionate leader emphasis, which Herskovits has noted as an African phenomenon, does not appear to be prima facie evidence of African influence. Mary Baker Eddy, Joseph Smith, and Ann Lee are only a few leaders of predominantly white religious groups in America whose preeminent place in the regard of their adherents is the same as that of the Negro cults.

"Are Negro 'shouts' due to the exposure of Negroes to the white revivalist movement?" asks Herskovits. "Or is white revivalism a reflex of those African-isms in Negro behaviour which, in a particular kind of social setting, take the form of hysteria?"[11] He probably is the first scholar to suggest that it was the African influence on American Negro worship which conditioned the Southern white camp-meeting, instead of the other way round, as numerous former students of the problem have expressed it.

In a study of Northern cults there is no means of determining in what way. if any, the relation between Southern white and Negro practice developed; therefore confirmation or refutation of Herskovits' position cannot be indicated here. Still, the absence of various indications of African influence which have been noted in Northern cult worship, including even music in the case of the Moors, does warrant our holding in reserve the opinion which Herskovits advances. His answer to the problem is a novel and extremely interesting one, but undoubtedly a great deal more evidence than he is able to present must be adduced before his theory can be accepted.

By way of conclusion to a very interesting series of questions which arise whenever we are dealing with this matter of African survivals, I am con-strained to cite two performances of religious worship which I observed recently in New York City. If there is any moral, the reader must gather it from the performances themselves:

One evening on Lenox Avenue I heard the noise of singing and shouting emanating from a second-floor hall. I mounted the steps and entered the place, which was called Mother Horn's Pentecostal Church.

An altar service was in progress. A number of women, most of them clad in flowing white robes, were swaying before an improvised altar. Presumably these were angels, for they were praying for and administering admonitions to certain unsaved men and women who were in varying stages of prostration, some of them having fallen on one or both knees to the floor, or, in the case of a few persons, lying prostrate as if in a cataleptic trance.

There was much moaning and groaning and weeping by the unsaved, accompanied by quotations from the scriptures, shouts, admonitions, speak-ing in tongues, and what in some instances appeared to be exorcising, by the white-clad angels.

But the significant fact in all this performance was that of all the members who were participating the most vociferous was the minister, conspicuous by his incessant yelling from the platform; and no one was more involved in the peculiar rites of administration to the prostrate sinners than a certain woman who, I learned later, was a leader in this particular sect. But both of these leaders were members of the white race, while most of the other per-ticipants were Negroes.

There was one male devotee who approached me and spent a good part of the evening endeavoring to save my soul, alternately clapping his hands rhythmically, genuflecting, and dancing to the music which was being sung and played constantly, calling out in strange tongues, and assuring me over and over that never in all his life had he entered into such profound happiness as now since he had found his Lord and Savior. That man undoubtedly was a full-blooded American Indian. . . .

Summary of Findings

The data in this study, while admittedly limited, offer the following indica-tions:

1. It is a fair inference that the apparent overemphasis by the American Negro in the religious sphere is related to the comparatively meager participa-

tion of Negroes in other institutional forms of American culture, such as business, politics, and industry, a condition which is bound up intimately with the prevailing custom of racial dichotomy which restricts the normal participation of Negroes in many avenues of American life. On the other hand, the study does not present adequate grounds for believing that there is an instinctive religious "bent" or "temperament" which sets apart the American Negro from other Americans in his quest for the satisfaction of basic urges or needs through religious processes.

2. Because the American Negro's experience in other institutional or "secular" forms is limited, the one institution with which he is closely identified tends to act as a channel for various kinds of expression. Thus the Negro leader finds in the church a mechanism preeminently suited to the needs of leadership along numerous lines. It seems reasonable to suppose that many of these leadership expressions would not develop within the framework of the religious experience of the Negro if the outlets for expression in other institutionalized life in our culture were more normal.

3. Negroes are attracted to the cults for the obvious reason that with few normal outlets of expression for Negroes in America due to the prevailing custom of racial dichotomy the cults offer on the one hand the boon of religion with all its attendant promise of heaven either here or above or both; and on the other hand they provide for certain Negroes with imagination and other dynamic qualities, in an atmosphere free from embarrassment or apology, a place where they may experiment in activities such as business, politics, social reform, and social expression; thereby these American Negroes satisfy the normal urge of any member of our culture who wishes to contribute positively to the advancement of the group.

4. The personality of the leader of the cult frequently is a very substantial determining factor in the attractiveness of the particular cult to its member.

5. The American Negro religious cult exercises rigid taboos over certain features of the private lives of its members, frequently reaching into the most intimate details of their lives. Sex inhibitions are of paramount importance in most of the cult groups.

6. American Negro religious cults practice forms of endogamy, in some instances proscribing even with regard to race. But in the Father Divine cult, where marriage is strictly forbidden, there is much greater social catholicity within the cult.

7. Singing, dancing, shouting, clapping the hands, etc., while generally characteristic of American Negro cult worship, are not essential features. The Moors definitely contradict such an assumption.

8. There is much greater use of the place of worship for religious purposes by the American Negro cult than by the more orthodox evangelical churches.

9. There is an indication that as American Negro cults become more intent upon social, economic, and political problems, the literal adherence to the Bible as a book of reference diminishes. The most rigid adherence to the Bible is by the cults which have the least notable political or economic programs, and conversely, those cults with original economic, social, and political programs tend to develop their own sets of rules, even going so far as to discard the Bible almost entirely.

10. The theory that Negroes in the United States demonstrate survival characteristics of African influence in the form, ritual, and spirit of their religious worship must be received with considerable caution. That there is a modicum of such influence undoubtedly is true, but this is overwhelmingly outweighed by American cultural influences.

As a concluding observation, we surmise from these evidences, with other general observations of the American Negro's religious life, that the Negro church is still to be reckoned with as a positive factor in the further social, political, and economic development of the American Negro. But it would be wrong, we believe, to interpret this conclusion as a substantiation of Herskovits' impression that the Negro religious "bent" impels him to "turn to religion rather than to political action or other outlets for his frustration."[12]

Because of historic reasons, obviously the American Negro church will continue to act as an important social mechanism for Negro leadership and for the masses. But for the very reason that Negro leaders still find it neccessary to have recourse to the church mechanism (bearing in mind, however, that other mechanisms such as the trade union, cooperatives, etc., now appear on the threshold) it is also clear, as the evidence of some of the cults indicates, that the American Negro church is likely to witness a transformation from its purely religious function to functions which will accommodate the urgent social needs of the Negro masses under modern stresses of politics and economics. Is it fantastic to imagine that, as time passes, the American Negro church may bear a relationship to the original religious institution of our memory somewhat analogous to the relationship which the modern drugstore bears to the nineteenth-century apothecary shop?

The earlier quoted observation of Ira De A. Reid[13] with regard to the cults in particular is very pertinent in this connection. The discernible response of these cults to certain dynamic urges which motivate the American Negro's present-day psychology undoubtedly has more than passing significance. The original revolutionary potential of the American Negro church may again be in evidence in these phenomena. Thus a Negro Baptist clergyman has utilized the religious mechanism in order to have himself elected to the council chambers of New York City, another one to the legislative halls of Pennsylvania.

The activities of Father Divine in the political and economic fields, to use a notable example among the cults, are suggestive evidences of the continuing dynamic character of the American Negro's religious experience in a milieu which has made the unique unfolding of that experience compulsory and inevitable.

NOTES

1. Robert E. Parks, "The Conflict and Fusion of Culture," *Journal of Negro History* 4 (1919), p. 128.
2. Melville J. Herskovits, *The Myth of the Negro Past* (New York: Harper and Row, 1941).
3. Benjamin E. Mays and J. W. Nicholson, *The Negro's Church* (New York, 1933), p. 201, based on U.S. government religious census of 1926.
4. Mays and Nicholson, p. 3.
5. The first Negro slaves arrived at Jamestown, Virginia, in 1619.
6. Such organizations as the National Association for the Advancement of Colored People, the National Negro Congress, the International Brotherhood of Sleeping Car Porters, and movements like the Black Star movement of Marcus Garvey, are replete with historical evidences of this development of a national consciousness which has been increasing rapidly in recent years.
7. Ira De A. Reid, *In a Minor Key* (Washington D.C., 1940), p. 85.
8. Herskovits has recorded the following evidences (as he believes) of African influence on Negro ritual in North and South America: (1) spirit possession; (2) dancing with African steps and identical motor behavior; (3) singing that derives in manner, if not in actual form, directly from Africa; (4) references to crossing the River Jordan (which he relates to African river-crossing); (5) wakes; (6) shallow burials; (7) passing of small children over coffin; (8) inclusion of food and money in coffin; (9) fear of cursing; (10) improvisation of songs of ridicule. See Melville J. Herskovits, "Provenience of New World Negroes," *Social Forces,* 12 (1933): 247-262.
9. Probably the most thorough, and certainly the most painstaking, treatment of most of the instances of correspondence is recorded in Herskovits' most recent work, *The Myth of the Negro Past.* For the author's bold spirit of scientific inquiry and his careful statement and elucidation of the facts, there can be nothing but the highest praise and deepest appreciation, although there are certain inferences and conclusions by the author which we are compelled to treat with reserve.
10. Melville J. Herskovits, "Social History of the Negro," *Handbook of Social Psychology,* 1935, pp. 256-257.
11. Herskovits, *The Myth of the Negro Past,* p. 225.
12. See Herskovits, *The Myth of the Negro Past.*
13. There are indications that a new church is arising among Negroes, a militant church, one that is concerning itself with the problems of the masses. Sometimes it is the old-line Protestant church, sometimes a younger denomination, sometimes a Catholic congregation—and sometimes a community church. Its leaders organize and take part in aggressive social movements for the public and the race's weal. Led, in a few urban and rural centers, by outstanding men who are trained and practiced in religious thought as well as in economics, this church is vital. Yet it cannot be said that today even this church is an influential factor in the lives of the whole Negro working population. Extremely significant in Negro life, however, has been the inordinate rise of religious cults and sects. Even before the depression one noted this tendency. . . . Today, Father Divine, Daddy Grace, Moslem sects, congregations of Black Jews and the Coptic Church, have been added to the church organizations existing among Negroes. Their influence and reach are enormous and significant—perhaps more socially adapted

to the sensationalism and other unique characteristics of city life, and the arduousness and bitter realities of race, than the prayerful procrastinations of the church institutions they now supplant. Ira De A. Reid, *In a Minor Key* (Washington, D.C., 1940), pp. 84-85.

17

THE KINGDOM OF
FATHER DIVINE

HADLEY CANTRIL and MUZAFER SHERIF

The Kingdom of Father Divine, a society in microcosm, provided one alternative to those finding little satisfaction in an otherworldly church. The "children" of Father Divine wanted heaven on earth, not in the hereafter. In return
for great sacrifices of material goods, relationships in the outside world, and
even health, the Kingdom promised higher status for blacks, meaning in life,
and a resolution of all the plaguing uncertainties of the larger world. The
authors see this group as one of a variety of fascistic expressions of dissatisfaction. Unfortunately, Father Divine and other such saviors offered a milieu
too startlingly in conflict with the real world to enable the believer to function in both.

The Kingdom as a Microcosm

"Father Divine is God!"

Whether whispered, spoken, sung or shouted hysterically, these words are
believed by hundreds, even thousands, of people. They may be heard almost
any afternoon or evening at the main kingdom of heaven, housed in an ordinary brick structure forming part of a crowded street in the center of New
York's Harlem. During the past few years the street has been more crowded
than ever, for now Father Divine's cars and busses with their placards of
"Peace," "We thank you, Father," and "Father Divine's peace mission" are
lined along the curbing. Nearby laundries, cafeterias, and small shops, otherwise like most of their kind, display signs of "Peace," "Special attention given
to FATHER DIVINE children. I thank you." On Saturday and Sunday after-

Reprinted from *Journal of Abnormal and Social Psychology,* 33 (1938): 147-167.

noons and evenings moving crowds fill the sidewalk in front of kingdom head-
quarters. Sooner or later most people are inside.[1]

The doors of the kingdom are always open. In the small corridor leading
to the upstairs assembly hall we face a brightly colored sign: "The relaxation
of your conscious mentalities is but the reconception of God's omniscience."
The hall itself is filled with believers, sitting on simple wooden benches. Most
of them are Negroes, with a sprinkling of whites. White visitors are easily
recognized. They are given seats or ushered to the platform at the front of
the hall.

The room is filled with crude banners. High overhead are stretched in
silver letters "Father Divine is Dean of the Universe." The followers (or
"children," as they call themselves) are singing the verse:

> *Father Divine is the captain*
> *Coming around the bend*
> *And the steering wheel's in his hand.*

The song has five verses. Singing is accompanied by a small brass band. No
one officially leads the "children." It is unnecessary. A few already know the
song, and the rest soon catch the simple rhythm. The crescendo increases
with each verse. At the end of this song, a large, middle-aged colored woman
testifies how Father cured her bad knee, which specialists had been unable to
help. Some listen, others close their eyes and moan. Shouts of "Isn't it wonderful!" "He's so sweet!" and "We thank you, Father!" are frequent. One or two
hysterical Negroes walk around dazed and shouting, occasionally falling. The
testimony ends with the first line of another song, sung with great feeling by
the testifier. It is immediately picked up by others. The band catches the
tune. Soon all are singing:

> *One million blessings,*
> *Blessings flowing free,*
> *Blessings flowing free,*
> *There are so many blessings,*
> *Blessings flowing free for you.*

As the song continues (substituting "billion" and "trillion" for "million"),
some begin to sway; shouting becomes more frequent, a white man jumps up
and down praising Father, the rhythm is emphasized by the clapping of the
children. Still no one is leading them. This song ended, there is another
testimonial. A man castigates himself for his former sins. He was an
adulterer. He had stolen food and money. He had been a drunkard.
Someone told him about Father. He came to hear him and was immediately cured of his evil ways. He intersperses his testimony with "I do
thank you, Father. You are so wonderful." Other children confirm his

belief. They listen intently to his confession. He talks for about ten minutes, exhausting himself with the vitality of his speech. He sits down, wipes his face, puts his head on his knees. Someone begins to sing:

Now don't let me say it, unless I mean it.
Oh! Don't let me say it, unless I mean it.
For I know it will manifest just as I've seen it,
Since you are here, Sweet Father.

It has eleven verses and a chorus. The last verse is sung loudly, with clapping and many outbursts, some of the children tap dancing, some crying, some laughing.

This spontaneous flow of songs and testimonials continues for hours on end. There is perfect freedom to do what one wants—to sing, shout, cry, sway, jump, meditate, testify, or dance. Frequently the eyes turn to the many banners on the wall where homemade signs tell us:

Father Divine is God Almighty. The same one that John said, "there would come one greater yet and I will baptize you with the holy ghost and fire."

Out of one people Father Divine made all men, therefore races, colors, creeds, distinction, divisions, nationalities, groups, segregation, nicknames, classes, and all such abominations must come to an end. All these things are of the flesh and no flesh shall glorify itself in the presence of the almighty Father Divine. Man's day is done. God alone shall reign. This is his day of reign. Thank you Father.

Our justice and truth is called in the expression of the Father. Peace.

Peace, peace, peace! Father Divine is the wonderful counselor, Prince of Peace. At his name all war shall cease.

We turn to our colored neighbor and ask him when Father Divine is coming. He looks at us blissfully and says, "He's here." "Where?" He points at random: "He's there, there, everywhere. He's in your heart." Another follower notices our dilemma and advises us to go downstairs to the banquet table. Father speaks there, if he speaks at all. Many have already gone down. It is about 11 P.M.

The banquet hall is filled. A large horseshoe table takes up most of the space, and around it are seated about a hundred children. Another hundred or more are standing in the crowded spaces nearby. There is one conspicuously vacant place at the head of the table, near which sit several well-dressed Negroes and one white. We are told they are Angels. They seem more self-possessed, more patient, more intelligently alert than the rest. On the table in front of the Angels are great platters of turkey, chicken, cold cuts, fruit, and bread. The air is close and sticky.

This room, too, is lined with banners, proclaiming such sentiments as:

Father Divine is the only redemption of man.
Father Divine is God and a little child shall lead them.

In general the group downstairs is more orderly, more unified than it was upstairs. Still there is no leader present. Yet here is a self-contained microcosm bound together by a common set of norms.

Factors Creating and Sustaining the Microcosm

The testimonials which continue show that within the microcosm basic needs are satisfied. Children who live outside the kingdom also tell how Father has provided for them. One woman says, "I thank you, Father Divine, God almighty, for what you have done for us since coming in contact with the Peace Mission. Thank you, Father. My brother was ill and suffering pain and covered with sores. In two weeks' time he was able to work without pain or sores. Truly there is nothing to do but to thank you, Father." Another ends her testimonial in song:

> Father I thank thee, Father I thank thee,
> Father I thank thee, for what You've done for me.

The testimony of Life Dove—a pretty young Negress—is received enthusiastically:

People have been talking about God for many years, but today, a God whom you can't see or never have any personal contact with just doesn't fill the bill. A promise of some home far beyond the clouds, with milk and honey flowing freely, really isn't what it takes to keep going down here, on terra firma. If God can't take care of me here and now, then how can I know or even believe He'll do so very much after I'm dead and gone. . . . Now, all in all, I ask you, what more of a God do you want, than one who'll give you shelter, food to eat, clothes to wear and freedom from sickness, worry and fear? Now isn't that wonderful![2]

In return for the benefits they receive, supposedly everything the children have is Father's—their money, their services, their thought, their love. Those who come to live in one of the numerous kingdoms give Father their property, their insurance, their extra clothes, their savings—everything. Most of those who live outside the kingdoms give him something after providing minimum needs for themselves.

Even more important for the unity of the microcosm is the common "positive attitude" Father has inculcated in them. They are told constantly "to visualize Him, so they can realize Him, so they can materialize Him." "If you concentrate your thoughts and your energy and your mentality in the Positive direction you must produce and receive the results of the POSITIVE-NESS, which will be SUCCESS and PROSPERITY and HARMONY, where the negative direction will cause the result to be the expression of negation with all of its expressions and from all of its angles. You see, that is the Mystery."[3]

The effect of the positive attitude—constantly thinking of Father and thanking him—is to cause the thought to enter

the sub-conscious mentality so that your very sub-consciousness got it, then and there, you had it. Now isn't that wonderful? As you had it, so you have it. By this, you can speak the Words into "tangibilization" or outer expression "visibilated" and cause mankind to observe that which you have been thinking. This is a beautiful thought, is it not—the great Universal Brotherhood of man and the conscious recognition of the FATHERHOOD of GOD, and the realization of the PRESENCE of both it and them—of both HIM or HE and them.[4]

To protect the "positive attitude" and to make it easier to cultivate, Father has strictly forbidden his children to have any direct outer contact with possible sources of "negative attitudes"—those which would shift concentration from him to something else. The children are forbidden to read any newspapers or magazines except those published by Father. They must read only the books Father or his Angels recommend. They must listen to no radio programs except when Father broadcasts. They are not allowed to attend moving picture shows. Their senses, as well as their services and thoughts, are Father's.

The unity of the microcosm is further preserved and emphasized by the almost complete break most of the children in the kingdom have made with the outer world. For one thing, all dates appearing in any publications are followed by the letters ADFD—Anno Domini Father Divine, although some of the followers interpret the letters more simply as "Always Divine Father Divine." The new frame of reference is further established by the rebirth of the follower. Since he is "reborn" when he enters the kingdom, his age is reckoned from that date. He gives up, furthermore, his former name and identity, receiving another name by revelation and thereby severing a whole host of past associations, personal and social values. The new name is a "kingdom" name which fits the pattern of the new world: Quiet Devotion, Glorious Illumination, Crystal Star, Job Patience, Celestial Virgin, Fineness Fidelity, Flying Angel, Rolling Stone, Quiet Love, Wonderful Devotion.

With the disappearance of the old identity goes all thought of race, color, or vocation. "All God's children are equal." "In God's sight there is no difference in color." No one is allowed to use the words "black," "white," or "Negro" in the kingdom. One speaks of "A person of the darker (or lighter) complexion."

A new vocabulary has been created to express the wonderfulness of Father. Father sets the pace in coining words and phrases; the children imitate him. Another extract from one of Father's messages shows some typical "kingdom" words.

It is a privilege to realize GOD as INFINITE, EVER-PRESENT and OMNIPOTENT, and yet INCARNATABLE and REPRODUCIBLE and REPERSONIFIABLE, as HE has been PERSONIFIED. GOD would not be OMNIPOTENT, the same today, yesterday and forever, if HE were not REINCARNATABLE. GOD would not be the same today, yesterday and forever, if HE were not REPERSONIFIABLE. Now isn't that wonderful?

("Truly wonderful!" assert the children.)

Parents who join the kingdom are separated as man and wife. They generally leave their children behind in the outer world to fend for themselves. More frequently a single parent (usually the mother) enters the kingdom, forgetting and giving up completely children and spouse. Worldly habits such as smoking and drinking are taboo. There is no cohabitation in the kingdoms. The general positive attitude is sufficiently dynamic to overcome these specific, worldly behavior patterns. All signs of bodily afflictions such as glasses, trusses, or crutches are thrown away. Ailments are forgotten. No medical or dental attention is allowed.

The isolation achieved by the follower when he breaks thus from the outer world in his change of name, his reckoning of time, his contacts, his habits, his thoughts, and his close personal associations, makes it possible for him to form a new frame of reference very similar to that of the other children around him. The deliberate cultivation of the "positive attitude" keeps the children psychologically united. During the meetings they are kept overtly together by the simple words of the songs, the simple melodies of their particular variety of spirituals, and, above all, by the simple rhythms which instill the behavioral accompaniments of clapping and swaying and often lead to a more exaggerated physical activity.

Individual Differences and Conflicts within Microcosm

But within the boundaries of this small world are still found differences and conflicts characteristic of any group of people. An observer will notice the differential enthusiasms of the followers: A few are hysterical, many are excited, some are calm and deliberate. Inquiry reveals that there are differential sacrifices: Though most of the children give all they possess and earn, some withhold a small portion, while others keep their material things to themselves. The testimonials, too, reflect varying degrees of enthusiasm and sacrifice. Father's rewards are meted out unequally because of his realization that different children have different values for his purposes. One finds within the kingdoms individuals seemingly possessing no more personality traits in common than one would expect from any group of similar size chosen at random. A high degree of intelligence is displayed by some of the followers; a few are obviously below the average. In short, we may hazard the guess that within the microcosm the psychologist would probably find an almost normal distribution curve for any measurable trait or capacity.

Rivalries and schisms develop in heaven as they do elsewhere. Jealousy is often shown by those who are not so close to Father as some others. An Angel sitting at the right hand of God is envied by all. Father's alleged sexual intrigues with certain Angels create friction among those intimately acquainted with the machinations of the kingdoms. More obvious rivalries and potential schisms develop in some of the meetings when a controversy ensues over the interpretation of Father's words. One follower may preach Father's gospel in a way which is inconsistent with the meaning another follower has derived. If a quarrel seems imminent, an Angel will intervene and point out, "Father wants only praise. Preaching is His exclusive right," or, "It is Spirit that makes you praise Father this way or that way." Hereupon the controversy stops; all seem satisfied with the explanation and the Angel sings, "Father writes on the wall," temporarily dissolving dissension.

To avoid sectarianism within the kingdoms, Father teaches his children to tell all their secrets to him alone. His chief Angels spread the doctrine of peace and serve as spies. For example, a possible rupture in the Los Angeles kingdom was prevented by Faithful Mary ("Angel No. 1"), who went from New York as Father's personal missionary. To these Western brethren she explained:

Father says when you write something about his works and criticize, you are trying to knock him and he will expose you. Because whenever you have anything you want God to know personally, you will tell God alone. You may know when you are writing up something and putting it in the paper you want every one to know about it. Now if you loved Father, in the mortal consciousness, and you had a sister who got pregnant, or broke a leg, as we called it in the South, don't you know you would not have it established in the paper, because you wouldn't want any one to know it?[5]

Father is well aware of the dangers of controversy, against which he warns his children. They must align themselves with "cosmic forces" or the cosmic forces will destroy them. "God will express dissatisfaction, or dissatisfaction in what you are doing, if you will reflect or manifest dissatisfaction. Now, isn't that Wonderful—for the reaction of your thoughts and actions may be manifested in the atmospheric conditions of the weather. It is indeed Wonderful! This has been the experience of all Religions. The Cosmic Forces of Nature through the Ages, worked according to the conscious mentality of the people. When their minds were antagonistic and conflicting one with the other, the atmospheric conditions would be exhibited from that angle of expression. Now isn't that Wonderful!"[6]

The cosmic forces are all on Father's side. He can turn them against dissenters, who thus are caused to sicken and to die. "If man works inharmonious to Me we believe the Cosmic Forces of Nature will destroy him."[7] These mysterious forces are the causes of wars, floods, tornadoes, race riots, storms, pain, and disease. They can be brought under the control of the individual to work for his personal satisfaction and happiness only when there is "harmony in his conscious mentality."

Polarization Around Concrete Symbol

Father's children, then, are likely to quarrel individually or in groups during his absence. The "cosmic forces" may tend to catapult some of them away from the kingdom's center of gravity. But as the time for Father's appearance approaches, all differences dissolve. The developing crescendo of the songs in the banquet hall downstairs and the general increase in excitement indicate that personal identity is being submerged in a common value. All thoughts are centered on Father. All eyes are searching for a concrete focal point—found in the empty chair at the head of the table. The songs themselves reflect the intense need for the symbol of this common feeling:

> *Father, I love you, Father I do.*
> *Father, I love you, Father I do.*
> *Father, I trust you, Father I do.*
> *Father, I trust you, Father I do.*
> *Father, I need you, Father I do.*
> *Father, I need you, Father I do.*

Father arrives. His entrance is greeted with an uproar. He is an unusually short, well-dressed Negro about sixty years old, though he looks younger. He sits down. Dishes of hot food are brought him which he blesses by starting on their way around the large table. Sometimes Father pours coffee. All the while there is more singing, interspersed with more testimonials. Father seems unmoved by all of this turmoil. He pays absolutely no attention to the praises heaped upon him. The most glowing testimonial fails to excite him. He knows that it is unnecessary to respond to each song or testimonial. He knows that he is already the idol of the people, a symbol already created by their intense feeling. And since the idol is strong in the minds of the children, it needs no support from the outside. He eats and chats with his neighbor though he may somewhat nervously drink many glasses of water while undergoing this bombardment of adoration. Those at the table eat heartily as Father has told them to do. When one person finishes his meal, another takes his place. After an hour or so of eating, most of the children are happily replete.

Now that Father has satisfied their hunger, the followers appear blissfully content. Satiety has further dulled all critical processes. The unity of their attitudes, their full stomachs, and their fatigue make them more suggestible than ever. Their testimonials and songs show that all ego identities have broken down. They are one with God.

Father rises to speak. His opening words sustain the identity in the minds of the children. "Peace, everyone." "Peace, Father," shout the children. "Here you are and there I am, there I sit and here you stand, and yet I sit and stand as well as sit in the midst of the children of men. As you are so am I and as you may be, so am I that you might be partakers of the Nature and the Characteristics of Christ."[8] Or

Here we all are again, just the way we should be, just as I am. When I say "Here we all are again," it means nothing less than the consciousness of the Allness of God in the likeness of man, and the nothingness of man, where such a recognition stands. Now isn't that wonderful? A place wherein you can stand, where all the Allness of God and the nothingness of matter will be a reality to you.[9]

For several minutes he directly sustains their belief that he is God and that they are part of him:

Oh, it is a privilege to live in the Land of the Living, where God Himself according to the Scripture, shall be with us, and shall be your God and you shall be His People, for the Mouth of Spirit is Speaking. Oh, it is a privilege to realize, every positive spoken word can and will be materialized if you will allow such to be, by the sacrifice of your life for that which you have spoken."[10]

There is no doubt in the minds of the children that they are face to face with God. "We believe every word you say, Father," they shout from time to time. Father reassures them in their belief, explaining that "by your intuition you know it is true."

The message may last an hour. The delivery of the message, like the testimonials and the singing, is dramatic. But Father's exit, like his entrance, is business-like, in spite of the praises which follow him to his car outside or to his office on the top floor of heaven.

Father's mysterious movements add to his divinity. He has a private airplane to speed him through the heavens. One never knows when or where he will appear. The statement that he was never born, but was "combusted" in Harlem about 1900 is generally known to the children.[11] His letters, which they read in their papers and magazines, are the letters of no ordinary individual. All of them have the same ending: "This leaves ME as I hope you are and all who are concerned may also be, Well, Healthy, Joyful, Peaceful, Lively, Loving, Successful, Prosperous and Happy in Spirit, Body and Mind, and in every organ, muscle, sinew, vein and bone and even in every atom, fibre and cell of MY Bodily Form." At the 1936 International Righteous Government Convention it was moved and passed that "Father Divine is God." There were no dissenting votes.[12]

Since he is God, all are under his power—city, state and federal officials, kings, premiers, and popes. His publications reproduce his letters to Mayor LaGuardia, President Roosevelt, the Pope, Gandhi, and other celebrities. Occasionally city or state officials come to speak at his meetings, but Father, as would be expected, always steals the show. If Divine has not yet demonstrated his control of individuals outside his microcosm, at least those within it are acting under his direction. Before the 1936 presidential election Father repeated in sermon after sermon that his fellowers should not vote until he had told them how to vote.

Hold your HANDS. I say, STAY your HANDS, until you find the man that will stand for RIGHTEOUSNESS, TRUTH and JUSTICE for 'He that waits upon the Lord shall renew his strength.' Now isn't that wonderful! Now I know you are enthusiastic, and filled with the spirit of Politics for RIGHTEOUSNESS, yet I believe every one of you will HOLD YOUR HAND; will STAY your HAND, until you get the Command.

"Yes Father," cry the children. "Since," as Father said, "not one of the major parties, officially and nationally, or conventionally, has come to me and accepted of my righteous government platform, we must stay our hands."[14] His command—repeated hundreds of times—was apparently effective, for the Harlem polls were virtually deserted on election day.[15]

Impact of External World on Microcosm

The world that Reverend Divine has created, the world in which he is God, the world in which his commands are obeyed is essentially a microcosm within a larger world organization. It has its own standards, its own norms. Yet even in the moments of greatest frenzy, in the geographical center of the Kingdom of God, *the realities of the outside world may be seen to intrude.* One notices that the testimonials of white children are listened to more attentively than those of the Negroes. When a white visitor enters, or wants to pass in the crowd, children of the darker complexion politely make way for him. The class consciousness and servility of the Negro have become so ingrained that they pervade a heaven where one of the strongest tenets is that there shall be no thought of race or color.

Because of the glaring discrepancies between the beliefs and standards of the kingdom and those of the harsher world outside, it would be expected that a follower's exit from the former world and his entrance into the latter would be fraught with difficulties. Most of the children spend their weekdays working in a society where Father Divine is not God, where there are rigid differentiations regarding color, race, and class. What happens when the devout follower leaves the kingdom on Sunday night?

Father is aware of the possible difficulties arising from the fact that he demands all of a follower's love and thought and also commands him to do his work well. "Do your job conscientiously but think constantly of me." Both of these tasks can be accomplished simultaneously, says Father, "if you don't let your right hand know what your left hand is doing." Those who have menial or routine jobs are apparently quite able to think about one thing while doing another. The discrepancies between the two world orders are not seen by the more ignorant believers. But anyone in a responsible position requiring concentration and intelligence finds it almost impossible to visualize Father and at the same time to perform efficiently. Happy Star, a trusted housekeeper in a family to which she is devoted, was completely unable to reconcile the two duties successfully. She reported,

It drove me almost crazy to try to plan a dinner for the family and guests and at the same time relax my conscious mentality. And sometimes when Mr. X. (head of the house) would ask me something, I would say 'Peace. Thank you, Father.' This embarrassed me to death. I did not know what to do. I tried to resist Father's hypnotic powers and kicked myself for going to the kingdom and giving up my salary. But I kept going.

A responsible butler reported that he found it difficult to be alert in his duties and at the same time to think always of Father. Furthermore, his teeth were aching, his eyes were bad, and he was constantly constipated. Since Father had forbidden any medical or dental attention as well as the use of drugs, and since the butler was giving Father all of his monthly wages, he could do nothing to remedy his condition. And yet, though he became skeptical of the movement, he did not leave for several years.

Why is it difficult for intelligent children to escape Father's influence? They all give the same answer—fear. Father is all-powerful. He has told them that the cosmic forces are on his side, that he has power of life and death. Several incidents have served to strengthen this belief. In June 1932, Judge Smith sentenced Father to jail. Three days later the judge died. When asked about this Father said, "I hated to do it." Will Rogers made some unfavorable remarks about Father in a radio broadcast. His airplane crash soon followed. Huey Long refused to see one of Father's Peace Mission delegations. A few days later he was assassinated.[16]

This fear of Father pervades the kingdom. Blessed Life, who finally left heaven, had been one of Father's chief Angels until Father got all his money. Then he was gradually moved from the head to the foot of the table. Soon he had a very menial position in the kingdom, and Father no longer paid attention to him. He grew skeptical. Sores developed on his legs. He was not able to speak to his wife when they met at the meetings. Why could he not talk to her as to any other sister? He was lonesome and desperately unhappy. The bed-mate, with whom Blessed Life had been sleeping for weeks, died of tuberculosis. His wife finally communicated with him secretly, helped him overcome his fear, and the two escaped. But many in the kingdoms have no outside connections, no money, no job, and remain in agony.

This condition may partially account for some of the psychopaths taken from the kingdoms to Bellevue Hospital. It certainly accounts for the fact that one is likely to remain a follower even with rapidly growing doubts. The only people who remain happy are the poor and the ignorant who have lost nothing by the transfer of allegiance.

Incompatibility of the Two Worlds

Some of the more courageous and intelligent children do leave the kingdoms. For them adjustment is difficult. Happy Star finally left but admitted later that it was eighteen months before she realized that no harm would come to her. Although a conservative, refined Negress she said it was hard to "hold myself in" when she was no longer under Father's spell. She wanted to do in excess all that Father had forbidden—smoke, drink, have sexual relations with her husband. Mrs. Y. is also a backslider. For Father she had given up her small savings, her family, her friends, her reputation as a reliable cook. When she left the kingdom she had nothing to depend on. Her husband would not take her back. Penniless and worried, she realized that she had "been a fool" and didn't know where to turn next. She must make a new life for herself. She does not like to talk about her days in the kingdom. She is filled with her hatred of Father, "not for what he did to me," she says, "but for what he is doing to all the poor souls in there now."

These cases could be multiplied. They all illustrate the complete incompatibility of Father's microcosm and the world of reality. One collapses when the other is entered. Compromise is impossible. Behind this fact lies the explanation of Father Divine's following. His children are people who want to escape the world of reality, where their needs are not satisfied, and enter into a new world, where they will have material and psychological comfort.

Here are some typical biographical snatches gathered at random from conversations with children in the kingdom:[17]

Mrs. A. (Negress about thirty-five). "I'm happy now, but while I was down yonder in Alabama, I was bowded with trouble. My children give me so much trouble, I just liked to worry myself to death, but since I been living in this consciousness, I know that Father is God, and he takes care of his own. They wan't my children nohow; they was God's all the time, so I've give them up mentally, cause I know God will take care of them. Two boys and a girl. The boys by my first husband and the girl by my last. Them boys was all the time getting in trouble, and the white folks is so mean down there, 'til it kept me worried. But they ain't like that in the kingdom. It's just wonderful. Everybody is the same. . . . I didn't know about Father down there, that is not 'til I come to New York, but he caused me to come here to him. One day I just pitched down everything, and left, and I got work and a woman on the job told me about Father and I came and been coming ever since. I don't worry about nothing now. Thank you, Father."

Mrs. I. (Negress about forty). "I made up my mind that I was going to New York, where I could see God in the flesh. I told Jim that I was going to leave California. He didn't want to come, so I left him. He wan't no good nohow, but I had been living with him a long time. We was supposed to be married by the laws of the world, but according to God's law we was living in adultery. . . . No, I don't miss him none. He wan't nothing but a worry all the time. When we left Florida with our white folks, I had to do most everything, then when I got sick, he acted like he was mad cause I had to stop working. Men don't mean you no good in this world, and the sooner you find that out the better off you are. Put your trust in God, and he will give you everything, or else he removes it from your consciousness."

Many of the songs suggest past or present troubles:

> *Father's going to save this soul of mine:*
> *Yes, He is, I know He is.*
> *Father's going to heal this body of mine:*
> *Yes, He is, I know He is.*
> *Father's going to feed me all the time:*
> *Yes, He is, I know He is.*

Others express conscious gratitude for the escape:

> *I have found Heaven, Heaven at last.*
> *I leave behind me all of my past.*
> *I come to rest on his sacred breast.*
> *I thank you Father.*

Reasons for Existence of Microcosm

1. Escape from Material Hardships

It is not difficult to see why Father Divine should flourish in Harlem, famous for its congestion, poverty, high rents, and general squalor.

In many tenements basic sanitary facilities are unknown. Open fireplaces are used to heat congested railroad flats. In 1931 the death rate from tuberculosis was three times as high in Harlem as in New York City as a whole. The infant mortality rate in central Harlem was the highest for any district in Manhattan. Other diseases were disproportionately high. The National Urban League reported in 1932 that in a single block in Harlem 70% of the tenants were jobless, 18% were ill, 33% were receiving either public or private aid and 60% were behind in their rent. There were practically no recreation facilities for the children, except on the streets. In 50 cases picked up at random only one was found to have contact with organized recreation. In three years the ownership of Harlem real estate by negroes had decreased from 35% of the total to 5% of the total.[18]

Bewildered and hopeless souls living under these conditions readily surrender to a god who literally provides them what they have always craved—food, shelter, peace, security.

They are anxious to believe and to follow a God who says, "I am lifting you, and all humanity out of the ruts, the mirks, and mires, out of human superstition, out of lacks, wants and all human limitations, out of all the depressions and off of the welfares and other public charities into the reality of God's PRESENCE, where there is a FULL and a PLENTY for all of His Children."[19]

When they compare their days in the kingdom with their days outside, the contrast appears heavenly indeed. Father encourages the children to believe that heaven is on this earth, not on another one.

> Men have used Religion to keep you in poverty! They used Religion to bind you in Slavery! But I have come to break their bands and set the prisoner free. . . . All that they have surmised and all that they have striven to get you to visualize, I have brought down from the sky. We are not studying about a God in a sky. We are talking about a God here and now, a God that has been Personified and Materialized, a God that will free you from the oppressions of the oppressors and free you from the segregations of the segregators. . . .[20]

To the poor, the oppressed, and the segregated these words are an answer to life-long prayers and needs, momentarily bringing the individual's level of accomplishment and performance up to his level of aspiration.

2. Meaning Provided

The provision of a certain material comfort, the promise of security, prosperity, and health, are explanation enough for the faith of many followers. One finds in the kingdoms, however, some children who even before coming to him have had material comforts, security, health, and comparative freedom. The desires Father satisfies in them are somewhat less elemental but none the less real. For one thing, Father gives meaning to the environment in which they live. Complexity, confusion, hopelessness, and purposelessness are changed into simple understanding, peace, happiness, and a faith in the abstract principles embodied in the person of Father. A middle-aged white fisherman from the coast of Oregon, Humble by name, has crossed the continent several times to spend a few days in the main kingdom. He already had food, shelter, security, the material comforts of the middle class. But the state of the world had troubled him. He could make nothing out of changing economic and social conditions. Somehow he heard of Father. Now he says,

> As you study this movement more and get to know Father better, you will become convinced, as I am, that Father has the only solution for all political, economic, and social problems of the present day. I believe Father is God in the same sense that I would call a man who knew the laws of mathematics and was able to control mathematical formulas and equations, a mathematician. Father knows the laws of the universe and is able to control cosmic forces—something that only God can do. Therefore, Father must be God.

For Humble and many others of his class, Father provides an escape from a tortuous mental confusion caused by complex, conflicting circumstances. He gives meaning to the individual life and to the world. It is perhaps largely for this reason that one finds in the movement so many "joiners"—people, many of them whites, who have been Baptists, Holy Rollers, Christian Scientists, and Theosophists before coming to Father. Their search for a solution to the meaning of life leads them from one formula to another.

3. Status Raised

Even more important in explaining the adherence of many middle-class followers, especially Negroes, is the fact that in Father's movement they are given a status which they have always craved and which has always been denied them in spite of their comparatively large bank accounts. A well-paid, healthy cook of the darker complexion related how Mother Divine[21] called for her with her big car and chauffeur and how Father called for her husband with his Rolls Royce and chauffeur. "We felt like we were big shots," the wife confessed. Their status was raised from that of servant to that of their employer or anyone else who might ride behind a chauffeur. They were, furthermore, riding with God and the wife of God.

The Reverend M. J. Divine is sincere and aggressive in his fight for Negro equality. His "righteous government" platform demands legislation in every state "making it a crime to discriminate in any public place against any individual on account of race, creed, or color, abolishing all segregated neighborhoods in Cities and Towns, making it a crime for landlords or hotels to refuse tenants on such grounds; abolishing all segregated schools and colleges, and all segregated areas in Churches, Theatres, public conveyances, and other public places." It further demands "legislation making it a crime for any newspaper, magazine, or other publication to use segregated or slang words referring to race, creed, or color."[22]

This elevation of social status, even if temporary, is a sufficient reason for many people to follow Father's movement. For where else can the servile Negro or the outcast white so easily find a real democracy? Who else is so openly fighting for Negro equality? Only the Communists, for whom Father directed his followers to vote in 1932 but from whom he has now severed all relations.

Father encourages self-respect by familiar devices. He makes good use of *prestige suggestion.* For example, in the *World Herald* we read:

FRENCH COUNTESS VISITS FATHER DIVINE. Joining the *ever-increasing list of celebrities* and *important figures* from *every* walk of life that have visited FATHER DIVINE since HE has made HIS Head-quarters in New York, is the "Comtesse Roberte de Quelen." The tall stately, *blond* Countess, on an extended vacation from her Chateu Historique de Surville in Montereau, France, was one of FATHER DIVINE'S guests, Monday night. Finally overcome

by the Wonderful SPIRIT of FATHER, and the beautiful singing and enthusiastic testimonies of the Angels, plus the sumptuous banquet, the Countess
arose and literally beaming, said "I love this place, and I love you all!"[23]

Such words from foreign, white nobility obviously enhance the egos of followers with circumscribed environments and limited opportunities.

The *impression of universality* is maintained in sermons, publications,
and slogans. On the back cover of every *Spoken Word* (a semiweekly publication) the Kingdom peace missions are listed. We find that there are thirteen
in Harlem, twenty-five throughout the rest of New York state, ninety others
scattered over the United States, and twenty-two in other parts of the world,
including Australia, British West Indies, Canada and Switzerland. Significantly
enough, at the end of the list we read, "Because of the unknown number of
FATHER DIVINE connections throughout the world, the above is but a partial
list for reference." A banner in the banquet hall assures the children—
"20,000,000 people can't be wrong. We thank you Father." In a parade held
in January, 1936, a large banner informed spectators that there were
22,000,000 people in the movement. By September of that year the number
had increased to 31,000,000. The actual number of the following is almost
impossible to ascertain. Estimates range from 3,000 to 25,000.

Whatever the exact membership of the group may be, there is no doubt
that the norms of the kingdom are accepted by thousands of individuals. An
official investigation of the movement, ordered by a New Jersey judge, summarized as follows the reasons for its growth:[24]

1. Search for economic security.
2. Desire to escape from the realities of life and impoverished conditions.
3. Search for social status.
4. Instinctive search for God and assurance of a life hereafter.

The first three of these conclusions are similar to those outlined above as
basic causes for the movement's appeal. The committee's fourth conclusion,
however, will not withstand psychological scrutiny. It would be more accurate
to substitute for the phrase "instinctive search for God" the idea that individuals are constantly seeking to give meaning to their environment, and that
when a meaning rooted in the realities of the world cannot be found, the
individual either creates and reifies for himself a symbol that will satisfactorily resolve his conflicts or accepts from his culture some preëstablished
symbol around which to relate his environment meaningfully.[25] The last
phrase of the committee's conclusions—"assurance of a life hereafter"—does
not seem to square with actual facts. Father Divine, as we have seen, preaches

that the Kingdom of Heaven is on this earth, not beyond it, and that those who completely align themselves with cosmic forces will have everlasting life.

The Microcosm as a Prototype

This interpretation of the cult allows it to serve merely as one example of a great variety of escape mechanisms now observable among individuals of various nations, colors, and classes who seek an easy resolution of their own mental conflicts—some closure from free-floating, incomplete meanings. Father Divine's movement is similar, serves the same psychological function as Theosophy, Buchmanism, the Townsend Plan, Nazism, and other such mass movements.[26] It differs only in content, and in the particular conditions that have created the confusion and suffering from which the followers seek an escape. An observer of the Oxford Group, for example, confirms this impression with his statement:

They (the Buchmanites) seem to have been struggling with the complexities of life rather than with any distortion of their own souls. They are relieved to transfer to God this struggle with a complex civilization. The more complete the surrender to God, the more complete the escape from worry and fear. In this escape, lies the great attraction of the Oxford Groups.[27]

Dr. Buchman, in turn, advocates Fascism, another variation of the same theme. "The world needs the dictatorship of the living God. . . . Human problems aren't economic. They're moral. . . . They could be solved within a God-controlled democracy, or perhaps I should say a theocracy, and they could be solved through a God-controlled Fascist dictatorship. . . . I thank heaven for a man like Adolf Hitler."[28] And the Nazis sustain a similar fiction that "there is something mystical, inexpressible, almost incomprehensible, which this unique man (Hitler) possesses, and he who cannot feel it instinctively will not be able to grasp it at all. We love Adolf Hitler, because we believe deeply and unswervingly that God has sent him to us to save Germany."[29]

The disparities between any microcosm and the larger world macrocosm become more acute as the discrepancies increase between basic and derived needs satisfied in the two worlds. We have already noted the collapse of Father Divine's microcosm when a follower reenters the world of reality. The same phenomenon is apparent when one observes the disillusionment of a former Buchmanite, Townsendite, Theosophist, Christian Scientist, or Nazi. Frictions between microcosm and macrocosm will continue until one of two things occurs. Either the microcosms themselves must be patterned to fit the needs of an individual living in our modern world, or the conditions in the larger macrocosm must be changed to provide the satisfactions and meanings now artificially derived in the microcosms.

NOTES

1. More complete biographical accounts of the Reverend M. J. Divine and both historical and descriptive accounts of his movement may be found in R. A. Parker, *The Incredible Messiah* (Boston, 1937); John Hosher, *God in a Rolls Royce* (New York, 1936); and S. McKelway and A. J. Liebling, "Who Is this King of Glory?" *The New Yorker*, June 13, 20, and 27, 1936.

2. *The Spoken Word*, August 18, 1936, p. 21. This is a semiweekly publication of the Peace Mission. Weekly magazines are *The World-Herald* and *The New Day*. The kingdom's newspaper, *The New York News*, is published each Saturday.

3. Hosher, pp. 167f.

4. *The New Day*, July 9, 1936, pp. 4f.

5. Hosher, pp. 153f.

6. *The Spoken Word*, August 11, 1936, p. 5.

7. Hosher, p. 121.

8. *The Spoken Word*, August 18, 1936, p. 17.

9. *Ibid.*, May 30, 1936, p. 17.

10. *Ibid.*, July 7, 1936, p. 17.

11. Hosher, p. 259.

12. *Ibid.*, p. 238.

13. *The Spoken Word*, June 20, 1936, p. 5.

14. *The New York Times*, November 4, 1936.

15. *Ibid.*

16. Hosher, p. 177.

17. The writers are indebted to Miss Esther V. Brown, a colored student who mixed freely with the "children" in the kingdom and gathered many case histories.

18. Hosher, pp. 88f. See also, Parker, pp. 34-59.

19. *The Spoken Word*, August 18, 1936, p. 29.

20. Hosher, p. 233.

21. Mother Divine occasionally appeared with Father as his wife, although she was generally kept in the background. She recently died in a charity hospital, apparently forsaken by Divine, who will not admit that sickness and death can come to a real follower.

22. *The Spoken Word*, June 20, 1936, pp. 11ff.

23. *The World-Herald*, January 7, 1937. Italics ours.

24. Committee report to the Honorable Richard Hartshorne, Judge, Court of Common Pleas, Essex County Court House, Newark, N. J., December 11, 1933, p. 35.

25. See C. K. Ogden, *Bentham's Theory of Fictions* (New York, 1932); H. Vaihinger, *The Philosophy of "As If"* (New York, 1925); T. W. Arnold, *Symbols of Government* (New Haven, 1935).

26. For an account of several recent movements, see L. Whiteman and S. L. Lewis, *Glory Roads* (New York, 1936); also C. W. Ferguson, *Fifty Million Brothers* (New York, 1937).

27. Hugh O'Connor, The Oxford Groups, *The New York Times Magazine*, July 18, 1936.

28. *New York World Telegram*, August 26, 1936.

29. Quotation from a speech by Hermann Göring, reported in F. L. Schuman, *The Nazi Dictatorship* (New York, 1935), p. 122.

18

NEGRO "JEWS" IN THE UNITED STATES

HOWARD M. BROTZ

The quest of the black Jews for a usable past represents a departure from such utopian cults as the Father Divine movement. These lower-class blacks, many of them migrants, have emphasized pride of race and ancestry and their pre-Christian religion and have rejected such symbols of their depressed status in American life as the old light-skinned elite, the religion of the slave-holders, and typical lower-class behavior. The reader is also urged to consult Howard Brotz's later reflections on the black Jews as well as his comments on the role of black nationalism in altering the situation of blacks in America in *The Black Jews of Harlem: Negro Nationalism and the Dilemmas of Negro Leadership* (New York: Free Press, 1964) and in his introduction to *Negro Social and Political Thought 1850-1920* (New York: Basic Books, 1966).

Introduction

The "black Jews" in the United States are a variant of a number of Negro groups whose members believe that the "so-called Negro is misnamed, that they have recovered their true identity and religion that had been robbed from them by the slavemasters, and that Christianity is the religion of the whites." These groups were all founded in the northern metropolises during the past thirty years by charismatic prophets who constructed the outlines of these "true" religions. They include—besides the "Black Jews"—"Moors," "Moslems," "Coptic Egyptians," etc.[1] Apart from the appeal of mysterious and strange rites and apocalyptic prophecy to unsettled individuals suddenly conscious of a sense of weakness, their ideologies are, as we shall show, a

Reprinted from *Phylon*, 13 (December 1952): 324-337, by permission of the publisher. Paper read at the Spring Meeting of the Committee for the Scientific Study of Religion, Harvard University, April 26, 1952.

"rational-type" repudiation of the premises of the status of the Negro in American society that is of profound impress to their adherents. They have endowed themselves, a group of low social status, with honored descent from what is evaluated by them as an honored (nonwhite) group and in such terms that they not only have nullified the shame of slavery but feel superior, or at least equal, to whites. In addition to the religious sects elaborating this theme, this apolitical, self-indulgent nationalism has also been the mainspring of several secular groups such as the Ethiopian World Federation and the Back-to-Africa Movement of Marcus Garvey. Though the latter did have an ostensibly political program, viz., the "Redemption of Africa," the number of Negroes who emigrated was infinitesimally small. Of far greater importance to the masses in the movement were the uniforms, the parades, and the paramilitary honorifics which they bestowed upon themselves.

Although the Garveyites in no way eschewed the name "Negro" as did the religious sects, they endowed it with the honor derived from the conception of themselves as the descendants of a great African race of whom the "pure" members were black. What was common to all these groups is what may be termed an "explosive" sense of the past, experienced as a conversion, transmitted by dynamic, prophet-like leaders outside of kinship groups or other traditional social relationships. It is thus not subject to the restraints of institutionalized expectations and aspirations in the extent of its demands upon the present.

The Emergence of the Commandment Keepers

The largest and most well known of the black Jewish cults in Harlem today is the Commandment Keepers Congregation of the Living God, called more familiarly among the membership by the name of their "lodge": the Royal Order of Aethiopian Hebrews, the Sons and Daughters of Culture, Inc. The group was organized by its present leader, "Rabbi" Wentworth Arthur Matthew, an alert, forceful, and intelligent man, fifty-eight years of age, dark brown, who though claiming a "D.D." as well as a Ph.D. degree, is self-educated beyond elementary levels.

Matthew came to New York from the West Indies in 1913, when the large-scale emigration of propertyless Negroes from the South and the West Indies to the metropolitan areas of the North had begun. The change for these immigrants in the pattern of biracial relations produced the effect upon them that has been elsewhere observed to be a consequence of a rapid improvement in the conditions of life. It served to make the migrants critical of their status, to generate on the one hand demands for deference and other values beyond those which they had newly acquired and on the other hand resentment against the existing order for failure to fulfill these new aspirations. The disruption and instability of the family and other primary groups in this stratum of Negro society, depriving the individual of a stable supply of affection, was an additional source of the aggressiveness that was projected upon the hostile world in the rising race consciousness of the times.[2] One of the principal ideological expressions of the emerging racial solidarity was a concern about ancestry. The atmosphere was filled with ideas about the origins of the Negro—the revaluation of the Negro as a race with a dignified past that antedated the period of slavery. As early as 1910 a book called *The Black Man, the Father of Civilization: Proven by Biblical History*[3] was in circulation, and the Garveyites were shortly to incorporate this same theme.

The rise of such dark-skinned charismatic leaders as Garvey and Matthew, who indulged the dark-skinned Negro lower class with symbols augmenting their self-esteem, is also related to several facts about the status structure of Negro society. First, color distinctions within Negro society intensified their identification with symbols of blackness. The light-skinned Negro élite, for example, outspokenly repudiated Garvey's "Black Zionism;" this he vilified as "mulatto treachery." Second, the élite of that time prided themselves upon "culture," family background, and modest expenditure and would not engage in the conspicuous consumption of goods that would command the respect of the Negro masses. Third, the élite were not wealthy enough to endow internal social service organizations with funds or, in general, to supply the material indulgences in money and jobs which the Negro masses came to demand. The things which the masses respected lay outside of Negro society, thus increasing their feeling of inferiority; and with the unwillingness of the old Negro élite to supply the type of symbolic indulgences demanded by the masses, there was no one, apart from the nationalist leaders who eventually emerged, with whom they could identify. From their point of view Negro society had no "head."[4]

During his first six years in New York, Matthew did odd jobs throughout the city. It is probable that he had occasional employment with nearby Jewish synagogues, for lower Harlem at that time was a densely Jewish neighborhood. Attracted by the Garveyites, he finally came in contact with another dark-skinned West Indian named Arnold Ford who propagated the doctrine that the "so-called Negroes were really the Children of the House of Israel"; Ford had attempted to persuade the Garveyites to adopt Judaism as their creed. Matthew, "realizing" that he was a Hebrew, organized his own congregation with a nucleus of eight men. He, as had Ford before him, took some Hebrew lessons from an immigrant Jewish teacher to whom he presented himself as a Jew. Matthew also acquired details of orthodox Jewish ritual, the names of Jewish institutions, as well as a few words of Yiddish from this unidentified man who was apparently of Hasidic background. Calling himself "rabbi," he purchased Jewish ritual materials—an ark, a scroll, prayer shawls and books, skullcaps—and rented rooms on 135th Street where he established his "synagogue" and "rabbinical college." He put out a sign that Hebrew was taught, and also spoke on streetcorners where he conducted healing and preached the following doctrine:

> During slavery they took away our name, language, religion, and science, as these were the only possessions the slaves had, and they were pumped full of Christianity to make them more docile. The word Negro is a badge of slavery which comes from the Spanish word *niger* meaning black thing. Those who identify themselves with Negroes identify themselves with black things, not human beings. Though some say that the word Negro comes from the Niger River, people are named after land, not water. All so-called Negroes are the lost sheep of the House of Israel which can be proved from scripture and they all have birthmarks that identify their tribe. Jacob was a black man because he had smooth skin.[5]

He attracted a small number of men and more particularly middle-aged women, like himself dark-skinned, recent migrants, and dissatisfied with their conditions of life, who in turn brought friends of theirs to see the services. As his reputation grew, others sought him out:

> If someone calls me a Negro, I let them know what I am, so they will know what they are too. During slavery and darkness they took our name away from us. But all nations have names—Negro is not the name of a nation. If we'd find out about the people that Jesus spoke about, the lost sheep, he meant the House of Israel. When a man is lost and doesn't know his name, it's like amnesia toward his nationality. I knew who I was before I came to Rabbi Matthew. I spoke on streetcorners, wrote a book called *Marks of a Lost Race*, explaining the war through scriptures, you know. There were two of us. This buddy went back to his wife, but I couldn't go back to mine. The spirit got me. Well one night Matthew's name was revealed to me and I came up here. Later on I brought my wife. Since I've joined, it has enlightened me a whole lot. When I stand before the Torah and hear what God told our fathers and mothers, and what we've lost, what we would have if we followed the law, it's made me a new person. Rabbi Matthew is the only man that's got something that benefited our people. I broke up my home to come up here. That's something. Not till we turn back like Rabbi Matthew will our trouble cease. They say we've advanced since slavery, but we're still in back of the whites. But return to one leader and let him point out the way and let him take up the burdens he knows how. The Gentiles elect men to exercise authority over you. But the one who grows up great among you, like Rabbi Matthew, let him be your servant. I feel better since being with Rabbi because I've come back to my customs.[6]

When I came to this country, my grandfather had always told me about
the Hebrew language, that it was his language. We had books at home about
the Hebrew children, Hebrew people. I didn't find anyone until someone
invited me to come up to the synagogue. When I came there I saw placards
on the wall with Hebrew on them and I said to the rabbi, "Do you teach
this?" and I began and here I am. I took private lessons from him and believe
I was the first black woman to teach Hebrew in the western Hemisphere.
Besides before I joined, whenever I lived in an apartment house, I hardly ever
knew anybody in the house. I was sick for nearly a year because I kept the
ice bag on my face for such a long time that I froze my face. The doctor told
me to keep it on for two hours at a time and I even slept with it. I was practically blind in one eye, but the rabbi went down to the drug store and got
something and washed my eye out with it, and I can see much better now. I
was very sick for nearly a year, didn't get out of that bed for eight months.
But the students came up here and took their lessons from me right in my
room.[7]

Among those whom he did convert it appears that he stirred them to
think about their ancestry and stimulated them in so doing to find some clue
in their life which gave them proof that he was right. One of the individuals
whom either he or Ford may have inspired joined a neighboring Jewish
synagogue on 116th Street in the belief that he was of Jewish ancestry. This,
however, is the only case known to the writer in which a Negro joined a true
Jewish organization. This was resisted and disapproved of by the cult leaders.

During the depression the group could no longer pay the rent of the
synagogue and it fell amost totally apart. Matthew had to take a job as a
janitor. Since then it has slowly grown, beginning with the inner core who
never left the fold, to its present size of approximately 200. It now occupies
the second floor of a tenement house on 128th Street and Lenox Avenue and
above this are two floors where the elderly women rent rooms.

There are records of at least eight other black Jewish cults which originated
in the New York metropolitan area during the period 1919-1931, the leaders
of which were all acquainted and in several cases associated with each other
as congregations would emerge, fail, split, reorganize with substantially the
same membership. Several of the self-appointed "rabbis" took "Jewish"
names: Mordecai Herman, Ishi Kaufman, Israel Ben Yomen, Israel Ben
Newman, Simon Schurz. There were bitter rivalries among the "rabbis" who
differentiated themselves from each other by variations in doctrine and practice. Some permitted the eating of pork; others did not. Most of them accepted
Jesus as a "black Jew who was lynched by the Gentiles." The group which had
incorporated the least of Jewish ritual was that of Elder Robinson's who ran
a "baby farm" in New Jersey. He was later convicted of violation of the Mann
Act and of misuse of his parishioners' funds. All the "rabbis" conducted mis-

sionary activities along the whole length of the eastern seaboard and there are isolated "black Jews" in smaller towns today who responded to this evangelism and occasionally solicit money from Jews. There is also a group in Philadelphia under "Prophet" Cherry who denies that the black Jews are Ethiopians.

Most of the congregations disintegrated as groups with the death of the leaders. In the 1930's Ford emigrated to Africa where it is alleged he became a "Mohammedan"; he died there. From then on it has been Matthew who has received most attention from whites and who is referred to in the press from time to time as the "leader of Harlem's orthodox Jews."

The Ritual and Beliefs of the Cult Today

Jews in the New York area, from the first days of these cults, have expressed a recurrent interest in them, under the impression that they are, might be, or must be Jews. This interest has opened up contacts for Matthew which would hardly be accessible to the ordinary storefront preacher (or to the "Moors"). He has been invited to lecture before Jewish organizations on "The Anthropology of the Black Jews and Their Relations to the Fairer Jews," and there are usually to be found a dozen Jewish visitors at the services each week for whom the third row of seats is set aside. The possibility of financial support as well as recognition from Jews has motivated Matthew to convince them of the legitimacy of his qualifications. When Jews are present, he states from the pulpit, "We are strictly 'koshered' and all males amongst us are circumcised." He also attempts to give Jewish observers the impression that all of his flock were born Jews (while at the same time asserting that he was the first black Jew in America).

Though on the whole most reporters and observers have taken his statements as the truth, these contacts with Jews have occasionally resulted in repudiation for him and at least in one instance in public embarrassment. He is thus suspicious of protracted questioning about his background, extremely sensitive about the question "How did you become a Jew," and hostile toward those who call his group a Negro cult. These contacts have, however, furnished Matthew with a minute entree to Jewish society and culture; and many of the speculations of Jews themselves about the origin of these groups have spurred the cult leaders in their quest for "rational" proof of what they felt to be their true identity. In the early 1920's, for example, both Matthew and Ford were visited by a representative of a Jewish organization who thought they might be Falashas, a tribe of Ethiopians who believe that they are descended from King Solomon and the Queen of Sheba. It was through this visit that they first

learned of Falashas and this legend. Although the observer thought they were
"misled," they from thenceforth "realized" that they were Falashas or as they
more characteristically define themselves, Ethiopian Hebrews, and added a
belief in descent from Solomon and Sheba to their ideology. (Ethiopia, it
may be noted, is a country with which Negroes outside these sects are widely
identified. Not only is it the only country in Africa with a nonwhite ruler
but it is also as Claude McKay has observed "the wonderful Ethiopia of the
Bible" to the American Negro masses. The fact, too, that Haile Selassie calls
himself the "Lion of Judah" has convinced Matthew that he is really a
Falasha who does not eat pork.)

Matthew "codified" the main beliefs of the cult and published them—"The
Twelve Principles of the Doctrines of Israel with Scriptural Proof"—around
1940 in the Minute Book of the Commandment Keepers, which also contains
the curriculum of the Ethiopian Hebrew Rabbinical College and the "Anthropology of the Ethiopian Hebrews." The ritual, the worship service, and even
their basic theological conceptions have never departed very far from that
which was familiar to these people in their childhood religious experience.
The spontaneous sermon, the hymns (Protestant hymns with Old Testament
references), the frequent collections of money; testimonials, the enthusiasm,
the fervent trust in an omnipotent God who will take care of everything "in
his own good time," the explicit concern with love and friendship, the prayers
for authorities (from president to sheriff), the scaling down of demands in
gratitude to God for mere existence or the continued use of one's limbs
(quite in contrast to their racial mission)—all these are characteristic of the
pariah religiosity of the lower-class Negro church, organized around self-
appointed, untrained, and uneducated preachers with a "call," in groups
which have considerable flexibility in practice. Within the tradition of this
church Matthew, like the other cult leaders, has fashioned his own form of
worship that is a curious syncretistic blend of the most diverse religious
patterns and other cultural forms which exist in a metropolis.[8]

Services are held on Saturdays, both mornings and afternoons, and on all
Jewish holidays. As each member enters the door on the second floor marked
"Synagogue," he or she fervently kisses the *mezzuzzah* (miniature scroll) on
the door and then takes his seat where he meditates quietly over Phillip's
Hebrew Prayerbook or speaks in a hushed voice to his neighbor until the
service begins. Members greet each other with "Shalom." The men, who sit
in the front, wear skullcaps and prayer shawls; the women behind them wear
the white garb generally worn by "saints" in the Holiness churches with the
Hebrew word for Zion embroidered on their garments. Those who can, read
from the Hebrew prayerbook; and the high point of the service occurs when
all the males file up to the altar to recite in Hebrew their name, the tribe which

Matthew has assigned them upon "examination of their bodies for critical birthmarks," and a blessing.[9] This is followed by a march of all the males around the "synagogue' behind the "rabbi" who carries the scroll, all singing "Round the Walls of Jericho." This, as are Matthews' extemporaneous sermons and prayers, is the occasion for a considerable degree of euphoria: handclapping, "halleluiah's," "Thank God's" "Glo' to God's," etc.

These distinctive rites are not only the sacred practices of a group of people predisposed to seek something sacred but also the basis of a feeling of superiority to whites who are regarded as a doomed group in their salvationary doctrine:

> Christianity violates the Ten Commandments, keeps the Sabbath on the wrong day, and is full of idolatry. It was with Israel that God made the covenant and it is Israel who will be resurrected when the Messiah comes. Only Israel has the Cabbalistic Science. And Hebrew is the Lord's language, the language spoken by Adam and Eve in the Garden of Eden. We are the elect of Israel. This is the Gentile Age and it is coming to an end as did all other ages.[10]

This theme is of especial importance within those meetings of the cult when white visitors are absent and Matthew and the other cult leaders articulate the free-floating antiwhite hostility of the urbanized Negro masses such as is evident in the following:

> Q. Have you been in this country very long?
> A. Yes, I saw what the crackers did to our boys in the First World War.[11]

Their religion is also ambivalently the basis of explicit self-differentiation from other Negroes as they move in the world outside the cult. The men grow beards to the extent possible. They do not work on Saturday and they wear their skullcaps at work. When asked about this by whites, they deny that they are Negroes. Those who went into the armed forces declared themselves as Jews (although assigned at that time to segregated companies) and occasionally attended religious services. Within Negro society they maintain their identity in contacts with nonmembers, though regarded on the whole as cranks. The elderly women who reside over the synagogue have few or no primary group connections outside the cult. Note this in the following:

> Q. Do you have any contacts with colored people outside the group?
> A. Yes. They kinda scorn at me. They scorn at my sons too. They make fun of me, say, "He try to call himself a Jew." But it doesn't bother me because I know myself. Most of the people I know are outside the group, but I don't eat in their homes.[12]

Q. Same as above.

A. None. They don't speak my language. But I feel friendly to certain groups. The only way I go anywhere is if they have a program. They patronize us and we go to theirs.[13]

Magic

Their religious practices also contain an important magical component vis-à-vis two concerns that are fairly widespread among uneducated urban Negroes of rural origin. These are health—physical and mental—and affection. For example, apart from an increased susceptibility to respiratory diseases under slum conditions during the cold winters, evidence suggests that dissatisfaction increased the migrant's sensitivity to body pain and concern with ailments. The ability to heal was, as noted, part of Matthew's charisma from the beginning of his career. The foods tabooed in this cult, according to "the rules for eating koshered foods" are primarily pork but also duck, frankfurters, crabs, catfish, lobsters, and bear, which are regarded as "unhealthy":

We are the healthiest congregation on Manhattan Island, because we don't eat pork. I didn't need to get vaccinated for smallpox because there isn't any pork in my blood. Of course, some of you have been here only a few years and still have a lot of pork in your system. Also, the reason we don't have evil thoughts is because we eat clean food.[14]

(The "Moors" also regard pork, catfish, and crabs, which Professor Hughes has suggested were the staples of their former diet, as "poisonous.") The food taboos are adhered to with tenacity. Sister Judith said that she used to love bacon but today cannot even stand the smell of it, although one of the members did not realize for three years after joining that bacon is pork.

On Monday nights Matthew lectures at the rabbinical college on "The Cabbalistic (sic) Science of the House of Israel," among other subjects. This is a set of secret Hebrew formulas, unknown to the Gentiles (whites) by which one can "cure rheumatic (sic), restore sight, bring back life to dead babies, keep oneself from going crazy in the middle of the night, change the bad minds of people to good, make enemies your friends, etc." The essentials of this are that there are four angels who work in three hour shifts around the clock: nine to twelve, twelve to three, and so on. In order to get a response from the right angel one has to call his name in Hebrew while he is "on." The Cabbalistic science, too, like the rest of their practices, is the basis of explicit self-differentiation from the stereotype of the Southern, rural Negro:

Cabbalistic science is one of the branches of mental telepathy. Those who thought it conjuring had a dark cell in their minds. This is an angelic science— has nothing to do with rabbit's foot, spiritualism, or conjuring spirits out of a graveyard. The spiritualists set you against your best friends, lead you into the numbers racket. Use dirt and filth—dead man's fingers, grave dirt. Cabbalistic things are parchment. The science of Israel is a big thing. It's why we use *talesim*, candles, and incense. The Catholics faintly imitate us. Do you think the three Hebrew boys who went into the fiery furnace went in saying, "Lawdy Jesus?" They knew how to pray. They went into the furnace annointed with the oil of life, which we can't take up tonight, and they tell me that when they came out they didn't even smell of smoke.[15]

Though members of the cult will use the Cabbalistic science independently to relieve, for example, a severe headache in the middle of the night, Matthew will step in, among cases of illness among the women within the inner circle, to apply his magical techniques personally. He is reluctant to allow any of these to consult physicians; they seem to accept his authority so long as they remain in the group.

Social Structure

The group presents in general the outlines of a typical charismatically led sect— the extraordinary individual surrounded by followers without any other con-flicting primary group authorities. The essentials of the leader's charisma in this case rest on his role as a protective conferrer of indulgences, both material and symbolic. Seventy percent of the members of the cult, who are predomi-nantly of West Indian origin, are women, about half of whom do not have husbands in the group and are either alone or with child or grandchild. To the lone immigrant women who, as Matthew states, "didn't know anything about American ways," he supplied such skills as filling out application forms and advice about getting onto relief rolls during the Depression. Some of the women entrusted their entire savings to him. He also has a telephone and transmits requests for day workers. He has taken the lead in buying land and building houses in suburban Babylon, L.I., and in connection with this formed the lodge which is legally incorporated. About ten of the members have so far bought homes.

To the group Matthew presents himself as a protector and states that he has "rescued them from ignorance, brought them where they are today, given them back their name, language, and religion." He also states that "he had a dream in which it was revealed to him that he was born to lead," and he has fashioned a legend about his own ancestry to the effect that he "was born in

Africa, the son of a Falasha cantor who migrated from Ethiopia to Lagos."
Some of the other cult leaders similarly claim birth in Addis Ababa or elsewhere in Africa. The members on their part regard him as a "chosen man of
God, the man who rescued them from the fallacy of ignorance, has given
them all they know, and has taken care of them when they were sick."

Matthew has undivided control of the finances of the group and of its
affairs in general, apart from two small subgroups of "Willing Workers" which
maintain their own treasuries and turn over surpluses at the end of the year.
These are social circles, primarily preoccupied with visiting and caring for
sick members. The principal subgroup, the Hebrew School or Rabbinical
College, has no autonomy at all. The rabbi is the "principal" and "dean" and
teaches the children himself three afternoons a week. Adults, who pay a
dollar a week, attend during the evenings. On Mondays the rabbi lectures. On
Wednesdays and Thursdays they study Hebrew and are divided into graduated
classes under three women teachers who constitute the "faculty." All of the
lessons begin and end with a prayer service at which others besides the rabbi
officiate. It is in the rabbinical college that new members are gradually initiated into the lore of the cult and those who wish are trained for "ordination"
and for the degrees of "D.D." and "M.H.D.," Master of Hebrew Doctrine.
Diplomas for these are awarded annually in a graduation ceremony at which
the members wear caps and gowns which they own, and during this evening
Matthew is addressed as "Dean" in speeches from the "faculty" and graduating class. At another ceremony during the year he ordains new rabbis.
What is of interest here is that there are no formal, objective standards of
competence in this training process. Some of the students know as much or
more than the teachers. Students "advance" and are awarded their "degrees"
when Matthew "decides" they are charismatically qualified, and those who
do not press demands to obtain these degrees remain as students for long
periods of time. It is also of interest that two of the teachers confided to the
writer that they know as much as Matthew. It must be recalled that these
churches are in a tradition in which qualifications for religious leadership are
self-judged (the "call"). It is also true that many of the members know large
sections of the Bible by memory and have had experience in preaching or
have developed oral skills in giving testimonials and other spontaneous communications of religious experience before entering the cult.

Notwithstanding the proliferation of subordinate "rabbis" and officers,
who derive in all but a few minor posts, their titles, and degrees from Matthew,
none of them has any real ritual functions, makes any decision of major
importance within the group nor even gives very much advice. The group is
a "love" group in which those closest to the "rabbi"—the "Mothers," "willing
workers," "true gold members"—have the greatest honor. The "faculty" and

others in the inner circle render "service" without any rational remuneration, and their identification with Matthew is so great that equalitarian demands are suppressed.

As their actions show, Matthew and the other cult leaders were men bent upon a profound quest for power and prestige in the small worlds within which they moved. Matthew has fantasies of vast bureaucratic hierarchies of which he is the head; and when from time to time he sees himself in this image, he produces constructs not only of an elaborate internal organizational structure with myriads of subcommittees but also of an extensive interlocal network of congregations of 500,000 black Jews in the western hemisphere of whom he is the "Chief Rabbi with credentials from Haile Selassie." He also has fantasies of being consulted by diplomats, distinguished rabbis, judges before announcing their verdicts; of sending telegrams of indignant protest to the State of Israel "for excluding Falashas on the grounds that syphilis was endemic among them"; and of getting individuals on trial acquitted. He has transformed fleeting contacts with individuals and institutions into recognition and friendship.

Although he is granted undivided authority in the corporate affairs of the group, he is denied commensurate deference from Negro society outside the cult. His lack of education and family background, his dark skin color, and his erratic religious affiliation would be judged negatively by the old Negro élite; and with his lack of wealth and appropriate style of life he would not rank very high in the esteem of the nouveaux riches doctors, businessmen, entertainers, exprizefighters, and exnumbers kings who are the new Negro élite (and the first monied élite in American Negro society). In his relations with the white world his denial that he is a Negro has not resulted in markedly different treatment by whites. His windows were broken, for example, when he first moved out to Long Island. Even his relations with Jews, from whom he gets perhaps the only deference outside the cult, are marked by his fear of ridicule; and within the cult he counteraccuses the Jews of "being 80 percent reformed, eating bacon, changing their names, etc." (Some of the other cult leaders consider the white Jews outright frauds, "the products of intermarriage.") It is also true that the constant application of charismatic logic is strenuous. When the writer asked Matthew what he thought of the "Moors," he answered, "They're just a Negro cult who don't want to admit that they're Negroes."

One evidence of Matthew's anomalous role and position is his attempt to intensify his demands for deference within his group; he constantly warns against the temptation of repudiating his authority and wisdom. There has been, in fact, a secession organized by three of the "rabbis" whom Matthew ordained, all of whom were married men. They wanted more of a share in determining the affairs of the sect and the disposition of the revenues. With twenty-five other members they set up their own "synagogue" nearby. One of these three "rabbis" formed his own group a year later. These deviant bodies are smaller groups—sixty members in one, twenty-five in the other—and the rituals of both vary slightly from Matthew's group.

Personal and group experiences have intensified Matthew's aspirations to differentiate himself and his followers from the white stereotype of the Southern, rural Negro. Inculcation of the "proper" standards of behavior in these respects constituted 40 percent of the thematic content of his sermons and addresses to his group. The main criterion of this differentiation is personal "regularity": restraint, neatness, conformity with the mores and avoidance of trouble with the police, steady work habits, etc. For example:

People learn Negro habits. We have to emphasize a certain aloofness. This gives us dignity and self-respect, which makes us an example. The kids, for example, play with Negroes. But I tell them, keep your things tidy in school. Apologize quickly if something goes wrong and don't talk back to your teacher. Don't act up like Negroes. Among the Negroes there were conscientious objectors and other crazy things.[16]

You women who go out to work, make your bed in the morning. Don't say you'll make it when you come back because you don't know how you'll come back! They'll judge you according to the state of your domicile.[17]

Matthew is also preoccupied with the necessity of strict parental control over children in order to prevent delinquency and crime. For example:

Children must be punished but it's not always necessary to use a strap. Some mothers just don't know how to take care of their children, always take the side of the child against the teacher. No wonder they learn to disobey If you can't handle your children, give them to me. And there won't be any marks on them either. I'm a juvenile officer of this precinct, and if I can't handle them, I'll take them to the police station. One policeman told me that there's more law on the end of his nightstick than in all the books. The worst thing that can happen is that when you are out, someone comes into your house and destroys your furniture or mugs you, puts a bullet through your head. Or when you're in the house, you hear a knocking on the door: "Matthew, come on to the station. Your son is wanted for murder!" Better the child should be dead right now.[18]

In his explicit statements and in his behavior Matthew serves as a model to his group; however, his behavior hardly conforms to the fashions of more privileged groups. Patterning themselves after Matthew, the men dress entirely in black except during the summer when they wear the white uniforms of hospital attendants.

It was previously noted how their religious practices are the basis of explicit self-differentiation from the Negro lower class, particularly white

stereotypes of it. Sister Judith Reid stated with evident pride in her address to
the graduating class, "Hebrew is not a language which is spoken in the street."
Although enthusiasm exists in their worship service, it is far less than the
practices prevailing in the Holiness churches. The black Jews abstain from
possessions, swooning, speaking in tongues, and excessive screaming, all of
which Matthew regards as "niggeritions."

In the starkest contrast to the antiwhite sentiments he verbalizes, Matthew
has stated that he never has any troubles with whites, even in the South. There
is no juvenile delinquency among the children of the members, nor is there
rule-breaking of the type which occurs among the "Moslems" whose rejection
of American culture has been much more radical than that of the black Jews—
draft evasion, withdrawal of children from the city schools, and, in the past,
human sacrifice. Of importance is the fact that the members are known as "good
workers." Although data on this subject are scanty, they strongly suggest that
the self-esteem which individuals derive from membership in all these nationalistic religious sects has resulted in modification of behavior in the direction
of personal stability. It has not, however, significantly affected the range of
their occupations. The elderly women are domestic day-workers, the younger
women semiskilled workers in light industry or clerks. The men include
besides domestics and semiskilled clerks, a few artisans and proprietors of
small stores.

Limitations of space permit only the following remarks on the nature of
their status-oriented behavior. One conclusion is that it is not modeled after
the behavior of known individuals in higher strata of Negro society. At the
risk of some oversimplification it may be said that reflection about the existence of superior Negro social strata is so vague, and the primary group tie
within the cult is so strong, that effective aspirations to rise are not generated.
(This is wholly apart from whatever effects adherence to the apocalyptic
aspects of their religious beliefs have on their behavior.) Sexual propriety—so
crucial a basis of differentiation to the respectable upper strata of Negro
society—is not of any real importance to the members of the cult and is the
basis neither of exclusion nor of positive prestige. Matthews makes a rare
reference to "you women without husbands" but with regard only to the
extra care they need to exercise in the rearing of their children. It is without
moral opprobrium. In the sphere of consumption practices, there is no vying
for status according to middle-class criteria. Even the few who are able to
afford a middle-class standard of living and have purchased homes have gone
out to build a residential colony.

A second conclusion with respect to status behavior is that in the spheres
in which it appears that they have incorporated standards which prevail in
Negro and white society, such as the prestige-worthiness of education, they do

not compete with others outside the cult. The standards of achievement have been fitted into the charismatic structure of the group. They award their own degrees and honors.

Their status-oriented behavior is thus essentially a reaction against a countermodel; it is compatible with their sectarian withdrawal and the rejection of the dominant culture. They obtain stable grants of the deference they demand only from other members of this cult who have likewise radically repudiated their identity in American society.

NOTES

1. See E. D. Beynon, "The Voodoo Cult Among Negro Migrants in Detroit," *American Journal of Sociology*, 43 (May 1938): 894-907; Howard M. Brotz, "The Black Jews of Harlem," unpublished master's thesis, Department of Sociology, University of Chicago, 1947; Arthur H. Fauset, *Black Gods of the Metropolis: Negro Religious Cults of the Urban North* (Philadelphia, 1944).

2. It may also be true that Negroes during their first days in the North experienced some degree of guilt in the release of antiauthoritarian behavior, as for example, in "daring" to approach whites as equals in even such anonymous situations as riding in the front of a streetcar.

3. James M. Webb, *The Black Man, the Father of Civilization: Proven by Biblical History* (Seattle, 1910).

4. See E. A. Shils, "The Bases of Social Stratification in Negro Society," unpublished manuscript prepared for the Carnegie-Myrdal study of the Negro in America.

5. Personal interview with Matthew.

6. Personal interview with Robert Smith.

7. Personal interview with Judith Reid.

8. The black Jews may be accurately regarded as sects of Christians who pressed their identification with the figures of the Old Testament to the extreme belief that they themselves are Jews. This is not unique in Anglo-Saxon religious history. What is probably the prototype for this development within English Puritanism occurred in seventeenth-century England when various Puritan extremists held and were prosecuted for "Judaistic" opinions, based on the literal interpretation of the Old Testament, arising in similar fashion out of an intense identification with and enthusiasm for the figures of the Old Testament drama. Some practiced circumcision, observed the seventh-day Sabbath, and taught the "distinction of meats." Others claimed that they were destined to lead the Chosen People back to the Promised Land. About 1650 Thomas Tany, a London silversmith, discovered that he was a Jew of the tribe of Reuben, and announced the imminent rebuilding of the Temple at Jerusalem with himself as High Priest. (See Cecil Roth, *A History of the Jews in England*, 2d ed. [London, 1949], pp. 149-150, 281.) The practice of Judaism, however, is based not directly upon the literal Bible but upon a body of traditional rules—the oral law—that is the outgrowth of cumulative interpretation of the written law. An essential component of Judaism, furthermore, particularly since the exile, is self-enclosure—"build a fence around the Torah"—which has entered into the day-to-day behavior of the modern Jews to make them a minority group, conscious of its separateness in strange lands not its own. It is doubtful if the radical Puritan philo-Semites understood the nature of the difference in both these respects between the early Hebrews and Jews of the contemporary world, and were confused when they came in contact with actual Jews. One notes this even today among fundamentalist Puritans whose ambivalence toward Jews rests at least in part upon the fact that they are thinking of two different sets of people. Even Matthew occasionally forgets that he

is a "Jew" and engages in explicit anti-Semitism, i.e., in which Jews, regarded as a group "apart," are charged with negative group characteristics.

9. No one reads Hebrew correctly and only a quarter do so at all. Matthew's extemporaneous "Hebrew" prayers, to the accompaniment of a piano, are sheer gibberish. The use of the prayerbook is also defective by Jewish criteria with large sections omitted. The members exchange pleasantries with each other in a pseudo-Hebrew that functions essentially as a cult code. All this, however, is of no great analytical importance; the structure of the group would not be affected by modification toward greater conformity with Jewish criteria in the respects noted. At a nearby group, for example, they do read Hebrew correctly.

10. Sermon, Matthew.

11. Personal interview with James Hayes, very meek-mannered West Indian, who had been with the group only two months.

12. Personal interview with Arthur Collins, who had recently joined.

13. Personal interview with Judith Reid, who resides in the building.

14. Matthew, Lecture to the rabbinical college.

15. *Ibid.*

16. Personal interview with Matthew.

17. Sermon, Matthew.

18. *Ibid.*

19

THE BLACK MUSLIMS AS A PROTEST MOVEMENT

C. ERIC LINCOLN

In the following chapter C. Eric Lincoln examines the paradox of the Black Muslims, a well-organized, religion-based black nationalist cult which has usually found itself beyond the pale of "respectable" Negro protest—not only in the eyes of whites, but of many blacks as well. The message of the prophet, Farad Muhammad, who appeared in Detroit in 1930, attracted many Negroes who had become increasingly despairing under the postwar oppressions of white society, North and South. Since the assassination of the militant young Minister Malcolm X and the appearance of other black nationalist movements, such as the Black Panthers, which have appropriated much of the Muslim platform of black supremacy, the group has attracted considerably less attention. Writing during the early 1960's, Lincoln believed that in spite of the failures of white society, which had elicited such an extreme protest response, the continued acceptance of the ideal of American democracy by most black Americans would doom such a movement to the fringes of the fight for equal rights. Further material on the movement may be found in Lincoln's *The Black Muslims in America* (Boston: Beacon Press, 1961, E. U. Essien-Udom's *Black Nationalism: A Search for an Identity in America* (Chicago: University of Chicago Press, 1962), and *The Autobiography of Malcolm X* (New York: Grove Press, 1964).

The social movement called the "Black Muslims" is symptomatic of the anxiety and unrest which characterizes the contemporary world situation. It is not an isolated phenomenon; for it has its counterparts in Asia, in Africa, in South America, in Europe, and wherever the peoples of the world are striving for a realignment of power and position. Such conditions of social anxiety generally follow in the wake of major disturbances in the power equilibrium, or in the anticipation of such disturbances. Wars ("hot" or "cold"), major

Reprinted from *Assuring Freedom to the Free,* ed. Arnold Rose (Detroit: Wayne State University Press, 1964), pp. 220-240, by permission of the publisher.

political changes, in short, whatever is perceived as a threat to the continued existence of the group, or the values without which existence would be interpreted (by the group) as meaningless, contributes to a condition of anxiety which may well be reflected in various forms of conflict—of which the protest movement is one.

We may restate our thesis in another way: Whenever there is an actual or a felt discrepancy in the power relations of discrete systems or subsystems, a condition of social anxiety will emerge.

A protest movement is an expression of the pervasive anxiety and discontent of a group in negative reaction to what is perceived as a discrepancy of power. Power is the control over decisions. The protest movement is a reaction protesting that control, or the character of its expression.

Conflict may also derive from a persistent inequity in the distribution of scarce values within a society. By scarce values I mean such tangibles as jobs, food, houses, and recreational facilities (*resource scarcity*); and such intangibles as status, recognition, respect, and acceptance (*position scarcity*).[1]

Such conflict may exist at one of several possible levels: It may be (1) *latent,* with the subordinated group unorganized in the recognized presence of a vastly superior power. The conflict may be (2) *nascent,* a situation in which an organization for conflict is in existence or under development, but the conflict has not yet become overt. Again, conflict may be (3) *ritualized* by the contending parties, thereby assuming a nonviolent expression. Very often conflict is (4) *suppressed,* by proscription of the organizations of the subordinated group, or by force or the threat of force. In extreme circumstances conflict becomes (5) *violent,* resulting in the destruction of life and property.[2]

The Black Muslims are a symbol and a product of social conflict. They represent a point at the extreme edge of a spectrum of protest organizations and movements which involves, directly or indirectly, probably every Negro in America. The spectrum of protest begins on the near side with the conservative churches, then shades progressively into the relatively more militant congregations, the Urban League, the NAACP, the SCLC, the SNCC, CORE, and finally the unknown number of black nationalist organizations of which the Black Muslim movement is the largest and the best known. The organizations mentioned do not exhaust the roster of protest by any means. Some of the protest movements have sizable membership in spite of their amorphous character. Some have no more than ten or twelve members. Some do not even have names.

But almost every church, every social club, sorority, or fraternity, every business or civic association doubles as a protest organization. The effort is total, or very nearly total. In some cities the protest membership is quite fluid, with individuals moving freely from group to group within a defined range as they become more activist-oriented, or perhaps less certain of the final efficacy of the action groups. The wide range of affiliative possibilities is both functional and dysfunctional to the protest interests. Because there are many organizations, there is greater opportunity for a wider variety of personal expression than was possible when the Urban League and the NAACP had the field to themselves. However, the supply of leadership material has not kept pace with the proliferation of movements and organizations. The most effective leadership remains concentrated in a few organizations, while the energies and enthusiasms of a good number of the lesser-known protest groups are dissipated for want of planning and direction. Theirs is an inarticulate protest—unknown and ineffective.

The Black Muslims are among the best organized and most articulate of the power movements. In terms of their immediate internal objectives, they have a highly effective leadership, some of which has been recruited from the Christian churches and retrained by Elijah Muhammad to serve the cause of black Islam. Their newspapers and magazines are superior in layout and technical quality to much of the Negro press; and their financial support of the movement is probably higher in proportion to income than that of any similar group. Yet, the Black Muslims are not generally acceptable to the spirit of protest which has won universal respect and frequent admiration for some other members of the Negro's spectrum of protest. To understand why this is so, it will be fruitful to offer some analysis of the circumstances out of which the movement was born, the character of its membership, and the nature of its goals.

The psychological heritage of the Black Muslim movement, in common with that of all other Negro protest organizations, is at least as old as the institution of slavery in America. Protest has been a distinctive although frequently a subdued thread widely distributed across the whole fabric of white-black relations throughout the history of white and Negro contact in America. The successive roles of masters and bondsmen, masters and slaves, white men and freedmen, majority and minority groups, have been successive arrangements of hegemony and subordination in which the Negro's role vis à vis that of the white man has not changed. From time to time, especially since World War II, there have been varying degrees of adjustment *within the system of arrangements,* but the power relationship has remained constant. Hence, the capacity of Negroes to affect decisions relating to themselves and the system of values they hold to be important is not appreciable.

Even the Negro's limited capacity to affect decisions and produce change depends primarily upon the conscience and the convenience of the white man, rather than upon any existing corpus of power possessed by Negroes. Indeed, it is unlikely that the Negro will ever have a dependable share in the control

of the decision-making apparatus of his country until he either controls a significant segment of the economy, or a much larger percentage of the vote
than he does at present. His inordinate dependence upon "protest" derives
precisely from his failure to achieve the more dependable protection for his
interests that comes from sharing the white man's power rather than appealing
to the white man's conscience.

A protest movement is an aggressive expression of a subordinated group. It
is the organization of the resources of the subordinated group to resist the
coercive power of the dominant group, or to challenge the morality or the
justice of the expression of that power. The Negro did not wait until he was
delivered in America to begin his protestation of the white man's concept of
the black man's "place" in the caste system to be established here. Available
records show that no fewer than fifty-five slave revolts occurred at sea between 1700 and 1845. During the height of the slave period—the 200 years
from 1664 to 1864, there are recorded accounts of at least 109 slave insurrections which occurred within the continental United States. Since it was
customary to suppress all news and information concerning revolts lest they
become infectious, it is reasonable to assume that the reported cases were of
some magnitude, that very many cases were not reported, and that some
cases which were reported have not yet been made available to research.

Protest was not limited to armed insurrection. The rate of infanticide was
high. Suicide became a problem of such magnitude as to require the slave
owners to devise "the strongest arguments possible" (supported by religious
and social taboos) to reduce the rate of self-destruction. Sabotage of live-
stock, machinery, and agricultural produce was not unknown. "Taking" (from
the white man, as distinct from "stealing" from each other) was routine. Running away was a form of protest so common as to have been considered a
disease. Southern physicians described its symptoms in the journals of the
period and gave it the name monomania—"disease [it was said] to which the
Negro is peculiarly subject."[3]

As slavery became increasingly profitable, the slavocracy became concerned
to offer a moral justification for its peculiar institution. At the same time, it
sought to inculcate the illiterate slaves (as it sought later to indoctrinate the
freedmen and their abolitionist friends), with an image of the Negro shrewdly
designed to discourage protest and to encourage resignation and accommodation.
This was the "Myth of the Magnolias," so called because it was usually accompanied by a fantasy of banjo-strumming darkies lounging peacefully under
the sweet-scented magnolias behind the big house—happy and contented in
their station, and forever loyal to the kindhearted master and his arrangements for their mutual felicities. The Magnolia myth explained the Negro's
condition in terms of "his *natural docility,* his *instinctive servility,* and his

inherent imbecility." It alleged that the Negro's "docile nature" led to his
willing acceptance of his condition of bondage, and that his "instinctive servility" made him an ideal slave—a being equipped psychologically to submit
his will completely to that of another; who senses his own inferiority, and
who willed that his body be at the complete disposal of the more sophisticated
will of his master. His alleged "imbecility" derived, it was argued, from an inherent incapacity to be creative, or to learn at a level beyond the simple activities of a child. This was a principal intent of the Magnolia myth—to perpetuate
an image of the Negro as being inherently intellectually inferior, and therefore incapable of mastering the complex requirements of adult citizenship and
self-determination. The Negro was a child who could never grow up. He would
never be "ready." This was the image he was required to accept of himself.
This was the image the world was asked to accept.

The historians, the novelists, the politicians, and a varied assortment of
other myth-makers have done America a great disservice. Each repetition of
the myth makes it more difficult for those segments of the white majority
who believe it to understand the behavior of Negroes; and each repetition of
the myth increases the determination of the Negro minority to belie it. Both
science and history have discredited the Magnolia myth, but the protest movements provide the most dramatic refutation. There are, for example, no docile
Muslims. There are no servile students participating in the sit-ins. And considering its success before our highest tribunal, it is hard to believe that the legal
staff of the NAACP is a council of imbeciles.

The Magnolia myth with local modifications remains a pervasive influence
in our society. Our information media have done little to refute it. The editors
of the texts we use to educate our children have done even less. It has remained then to the Negro to destroy the myth himself. The Black Muslims
have gone a step further and have created for themselves a countermyth, *the
myth of black supremacy.*

The Black Muslim movement had its beginning in the black ghetto of
Detroit. The time was 1930. It was the first year of the Great Depression—a
time of hunger, confusion, disillusionment, despair, and discontent. It was a
period of widespread fear and anxiety. Between 1900 and 1930 2.25 million
Negroes left the farms and plantations of the South. Most of them emigrated
to selected urban areas of the North—New York, Philadelphia, Chicago, and
Detroit being among the most popular destinations. The Negro population of
Detroit, for example, increased 611 percent during the ten years of 1910 to
1920. During the same period, the total Negro population in the North increased from a mere 75,000 to 300,000, an increase of 400 percent.

Floods, crop failures, boll weevils, and the revival of the Ku Klux Klan all
served to hasten the Negro's departure from the South. One hundred Negroes

were lynched during the first year of the twentieth century. By the outbreak of World War I in 1914, the number stood at 1,100. When the war was over, the practice was resumed—twenty-eight Negroes being burned alive between 1918 and 1921. Scores of others were hanged, dragged behind automobiles, shot, drowned, or hacked to death.

The Negroes who left the South were temporarily welcomed in the North, although the congenialities of the North have always been of a most impersonal sort. Many industries sent agents into the South to lure the Negroes North with promises of good jobs. But the Negro was soon to find that it was his labor, not his presence, that was wanted. It was a common practice for the agents to purchase tickets for whole families and to move them en masse for resettlement in the great industrial cities. The war had drained away the white manpower needed to build the ships, work the steel, pack the meat, and man the machines; and it had also cut off the normal supply of immigrant labor from Europe.

After the war was over, the Negro's welcome wore thin. It became increasingly hard for Negroes to get jobs except as strikebreakers. Soon there were not enough jobs to go around, and thousands of Negroes were fired and replaced with white men. There was not enough housing, and most Negroes were crowded into the black ghettos in the most deteriorated part of the inner city. Landlords and law-enforcement agencies alike were unsympathetic. But still the Negroes came out of the South. Few had skills; many were illiterate. All were filled with hope for something better than what they had left. Soon there was hunger and crime and delinquency—and trouble with the police. The bright promise of the North had failed. Hope turned to desperation. In desperation is the onset of anxiety.

It is an interesting historical phenomenon that when a people reach the precipice of despair, there is so often waiting in the wings a savior—a messiah to snatch them back from the edge of the abyss. So it was that in Detroit there appeared in the black ghetto a mysterious Mullah who called himself W. D. Farad Muhammad. He had come, he told the handful of Negroes who gathered to hear him, from the holy city of Mecca. His mission, as he described it, was "to wake the 'Dead Nation in the West';[4] to teach [them] the truth about the white man, and to prepare [them] for the Armageddon." The Armageddon? What did this apocalyptic concept have to do with the problems of the Negro in America? Farad was explicit on the point: In the Book of Revelation it is promised that there will be a final battle between good and evil, and that this decisive battle will take place at Har-Magedon, "the Mountain of Megiddo," in the great plain of Esdraelon in Asia Minor.[5] But the Bible has a cryptic message for the initiated of black Islam (even as it has for more familiar sects). The forces of "good and evil" are the forces of "black and white." "The valley of Esdraelon" symbolizes "the wilderness of North America." The Battle of Armageddon is to be the black man's final confronta-tion of the race which has so long oppressed him.

At first Farad (who was at the time thought to be a prophet, but who was after his departure recognized as Allah himself) met from house to house with small groups of Negroes. He went about his mission as unobtrusively as possi-ble, listening to the problems of the destitute Negroes, sharing whatever they had to offer him. A contemporary convert recalls his *modus operandi*:

He came first to our house selling raincoats, and afterwards silks. In this way he could get into the people's houses. . . . If we asked him to eat with us, he would eat whatever we had on the table, but after the meal he began to talk. . . .[6]

What he had to say must have been electrifying. Another Muslim describes his first encounter with the Prophet as follows:

Up to that time I always went to the Baptist church. After I heard that sermon from the Prophet, I was turned around completely. When I went home and heard that dinner was ready, I said: "I don't want any dinner, I just want to go back to the meetings." I wouldn't eat my meals but I [went] back that night and I [went] to every meeting after that. . . . That changed everything for me.[7]

The fame of the Prophet spread and he soon established in Detroit the first of the temples of Islam. As his following increased he grew more bold in his attacks upon the habits and the culture symbols the Negroes had always taken for granted. In the first place, he taught his followers that they were not "Negroes," but "black Men." The word "Negro" was alleged to be an in-vention of the white man designed to identify his victims better and to sepa-rate them from their Asian and African brothers. Further, the so-called Negro was not an American, but an "Asiatic," for his forefathers had been stolen from the Afro-Asian continent by the white slavemasters who came in the name of Jesus. Christianity, the Prophet taught, was a white man's religion, a contrivance designed for the enslavement of nonwhite peoples. Wherever Christianity has gone, he declared, men have lost their liberty and their free-dom. Islam was declared to be "the natural religion of the black Man." Only in Islam could the so-called Negroes find freedom, justice, and equality.

Little by little the Prophet began to enlighten these disillusioned migrants from the South about their true history and their place in the future. Black Man was the "original man," he taught. On the continent of Afro-Asia black civilizations flourished "long before the white man stood up on his hind legs and crept out of the caves of Europe." Further, the white man was pictured as "a devil by nature." He is, the Prophet taught, the physical embodiment of the principle of evil, and he is incapable of doing good. Further, said Farad, "the white man is the eternal adversary of the one true God whose right and proper name is Allah."

By "tricknology" the blue-eyed devils had enslaved the black man, the chosen people of Allah. The devils had taken away the slaves' native language (which was Arabic), and forced them to speak a foreign tongue. The white devils had taken away their names (i.e., their identity), and given them European names (which are to be hated as badges of slavery). Above all, the cruel slavemasters took away their natural religion (which is Islam) and made them worship a blue-eyed Jesus with blond hair, telling them that this was their God.

The so-called Negroes, although unknown to themselves, comprised "The Nation of Islam in the West." They had been brainwashed and given a false image of themselves by their white teachers, especially the Christian preachers who lulled them into submission by promising them a home "over Jordan" when they would no longer hew the wood and draw the water for the white man's comfort.

"The wheel must turn," the Prophet insisted. The Nation of Islam had a manifest destiny. The Armageddon must come. It would come as soon as the black man in America learned who he himself was, and accepted the truth about the white man, which the Prophet had been sent to declare.

Not all of Farad's energies were spent in attacking the white man. He taught his followers cleanliness and thrift. He persuaded them to give up liquor and such "unclean" foods as pork, cornbread, peas, possums, and catfish, bidding them to separate themselves from the habits they acquired in slavery. He established a school where home-making, Negro history, Arabic, and other subjects of interest to the Muslims were taught. He demanded that his followers be clean at all times, bathing at least once each day. He taught them to give an honest day's work for an honest day's pay. He taught them to be respectful of others, and above all, to respect themselves. They must obey "all constituted authority," but they must require an eye for an eye and a tooth for a tooth. The *lex talionis* was the law of survival.

The Prophet's first appearance in Detroit is dated as July 4, 1930, and no one remembers seeing him after June 30, 1934. There are many legends, but no authentic information on where he came from, or where he went. But four years of preaching left a legacy of good and evil for 8,000 Negroes who had come to call themselves Muslims.

In the troubled times of the early 1930's men and women everywhere were looking for some panacea to save them from the desperate circumstances of the Depression. Large numbers of people found that they could not cope

rationally with the excruciating anxiety—the uncertainties with which they
were confronted from day to day. Some escapists leaped from the rooftops
of the very buildings which were symbols of more stable times. Some clairvoyants, who thought they could discern the wave of the future in Marxist philosophy, found their panacea in the Communist party. The Negro's escapism
tended to be of a more practical nature. Instead of taking the long route to
heaven, he built himself "heavens" here on earth in the cults of Father Divine
and Daddy Grace.

The followers of Farad were both escapists and clairvoyants. Farad himself
was the messiah who had come to lead the so-called Negroes into the millen-
nium which was to follow the Battle of Armageddon. He was the Prophet who
had foreseen and foretold the Golden Age that would be theirs when the black
nation in the West had thrown off the yoke of the white slavemasters. But
Farad had disappeared.

The Prophet had not left himself without a witness. Very early in his brief
ministry in Detroit he had attracted the admiration and the loyalty of a young
Negro from the town of Sandersville, Georgia. Elijah Poole, son of a Baptist
minister, was already embittered by the harshness of race relations in the
South when he left Georgia and migrated to Detroit with his family in the
early 1920's. In Detroit, his disillusionment with the "promised land" was
almost immediate, for he soon discovered that the limitations which prescribed
his place in the North differed only in degree from the familiar pattern of
circumscription in the South. For a time, better jobs were available in the
North, but Poole was soon to discover that job security operated on a racial
basis. Housing was more strictly segregated than in the South, and living conditions in the black ghetto were often worse than they had been in the sharecropper's cabin. The lynchings in the South had their counterparts in the race
riots of the North. There seemed to exist a universal conspiracy to make life
in America as untenable as possible for Negroes.

The belittling paternalism of the South had been replaced by the cold indifference of the North, and Elijah Poole found himself and his family with no
better chance of assimilation in the great "melting pot" of the North than he
had left in the South. As a matter of fact, his daily contact with foreign-born
elements speaking in strange "un-American" accents and wearing "foreign"
clothes increased his feelings of isolation and resentment. He saw the jobs of
Negroes taken from them and given to white men who had not fought for this
country, and who in some cases had fought against it. Inevitably, the Georgia-
born Poole arrived at the conclusion that even in the North the color of a
man's skin, not the fact of his citizenship nor the quality of his intrinsic worth,
was the determining factor in all his social relationships.

Elijah was now ready for the racist doctrines of Wali Farad. From their first meeting he became the Prophet's most dedicated apostle and his chief amanuensis. Farad had identified the black man's oppressor in terms never before heard in the Negro community. He had exposed the white man as a devil—a *literal* devil, created on the Isle of Patmos by a mad scientist whose name was Yakub. This was the secret of the white man's power, his cruelty, *and* his vulnerability. Allah had given the devil a certain time to rule, and the time of the devil was up. *The black man must prepare himself for the Armageddon!* Poole was impressed. Farad had the explanation of the white man's cruelty as well as the key to his power. Eventually, Farad entrusted his mantle and his mission to Elijah. He made Poole First Minister of Islam and put the Muslim school, the training of ministers, and the highly secret FOI (the Fruit of Islam, the leadership training corps "for the coming Armageddon") under his direction. Later, Poole was sent to Chicago to found Temple No. 2, the present headquarters of the movement.

In recognition of Poole's dedicated leadership, Farad relieved him of his "slave name" (i.e. "Poole") and honored him with the Muslim name "Muhammad." Thereafter, Farad's public appearances were progressively less frequent until the day of his final disappearance.

Under Elijah Muhammad, the new "Messenger of Islam," the movement spread from the initial temple in Detroit to almost every major city in the country where there is a sizable Negro population. In most of these cities there is a temple; in others, where the movement is less strong, there are missions. Where there are no missions there are likely to be representatives of the movement who are in contact with the Muslim leadership in nearby cities.

The black ghetto is the principal source of Muslim recruitment. There, in the dirty streets and crowded tenements where life is cheap and hope is minimal, where isolation from the common values of society and from the common privileges of citizenship is most acute, the voice of the messenger does not fall upon deaf ears. So often, his is the only message directed to the pimps, the prostitutes, the conmen, the prisoners, the excons, the alcoholics, the addicts, the unemployed, whom the responsible society has forgotten. It is a voice challenging them to recover their self-respect, urging them to repudiate the white man's religion and the white man's culture, daring them to believe in black supremacy, offering them a black God and a black nation, promising them that the day will come when "we will be masters . . . and we are going to treat the white man the way he should be treated,"[8] demanding of them that "if anyone comes to take advantage of you, *lay down your life!* and the Black Man will be respected all over the Planet Earth."[9]

"Never be the aggressor," the voice proclaims, "never look for trouble. But if any man molests you, may Allah bless you."[10]

"We must take things into our own hands," the messenger insists. "We must return to the Mosaic law of an eye for an eye and a tooth for a tooth. What does it matter if 10 million of us die? There will be 7 million of us left and they will enjoy justice and freedom."[11]

Such is the challenge of Elijah Muhammad who is hailed by his ministers as "the most fearless black man in America." His followers are, with few exceptions, from America's most underprivileged class. They are denizens of the black ghetto. To them, the voice of Elijah Muhammad is a voice raised against injustice—real or imagined. Muhammad is a paladin who has taken up the cudgel against the "devil" responsible for all of their miseries and their failures. The resentments and the hostilities that breed in the ghetto are finally brought to focus upon a single object—*the white man.* Outside the black ghetto there are Muslim units in many of the state and federal prisons across the country. Here the movement finds its prison audiences to be ready made and highly receptive, for the racial character of the law-enforcement agencies, the courts and the custodial personnel, is a key factor in sharpening the Negro prisoner's resentments and his sense of persecution.

I have tried to present a developmental background for the Black Muslim movement against which we may now more profitably examine their demands as a protest group. Generally speaking, the movement has been a protest directed at the whole value construct of the white Christian society of which the Black Muslims feel themselves (as Negroes) to be an isolated and unappreciated appendage. Hence, the burden of their protest is against their "retention" in a society where they are not wanted. This is the soft side of the "Armageddon complex" which looks to the removal of the source of their discomfiture rather than to going anywhere themselves. Mr. Muhammad teaches that "the white man's home is in Europe," and that "there will be no peace until every man is in his own country."

In a recent issue of the official Muslim newspaper, *Mr. Muhammad Speaks,* the Muslims stated their protest in the form of the following ten propositions:

1. We want freedom. We want a full and complete freedom.
2. We want justice. Equal justice under the law. We want justice applied equally to all, regardless of creed or class or color.
3. We want equality of opportunity. We want equal membership in society with the best in civilized society.
4. We want our people in America whose parents or grandparents were descendants from slaves, to be allowed to establish a separate state or territory of their own. . . .
5. We want freedom for all Believers of Islam now held in federal prisons. We want freedom for all black men and women now under death sentence in innumerable prisons in the North as well as the South.

We want every black man and woman to have the freedom to accept or reject being separated from the slave master's children and establish a land of their own. . . .

6. We want an immediate end to the police brutality and mob attacks against the so-called Negro throughout the United States.

7. As long as we are not allowed to establish a state or territory of our own, we demand not only equal justice under the laws of the United States, but equal employment opportunities—NOW!. . . .

8. We want the government of the United States to exempt our people from ALL taxation as long as we are deprived of equal justice under the laws of the land.

9. We want equal education—but separate schools up to 16 for boys and 18 for girls on the condition that the girls be sent to women's colleges and universities. We want all black children educated, taught without hindrance or suppression.

10. We believe that intermarriage or race mixing should be prohibited. We want the religion of Islam taught without hindrance or suppression.

These are some of the things that we, the Muslims, want for our people in North America.[12]

Some of the proposals of the Muslims are obviously unrealistic, and we need not discuss them here. Other tests and demands of the Black Muslims as stated in the foregoing propositions do not seem unreasonable. I do not know any Americans who do not "want freedom," for example. Justice under the law, equality of opportunity, and freedom of worship are all "approved values" in our society, and they find their sanctions in the American creed. Further, they are objectives which are implicit in the programs of all other movements within the Negro spectrum of protest. What, then, are the factors which qualify the Muslim protest movement and make it unacceptable to the general American public?

The fundamental differences between the attitudes, the behavior, and the goals of the Black Muslims as compared to other Negro protest organizations may be explained in terms of their differing degrees of dissociation deriving from the unusual anxiety and frustration incident to their status in the American social arrangement. Negroes, as a caste, are *all* outside the assimilative process, and they exhibit from time to time the frustrations which are the corollaries of their marginality. However, the dissociation of the Muslim membership from the larger society, and even from the general Negro subgroup (which ordinarily seeks to identify itself with the American mainstream), may be considered extreme. In reacting to the unique pressures of their day-to-day experiences as low-caste Negroes in a white-oriented society, the Muslims have abandoned the fundamental principles of the American creed and have substituted in its place a new system of values perceived as more consistent with the realities of their circumstances.

It is meaningless to label the Muslims as "un-American," for the American creed is not a legal or constitutional document against which the political loyalty of a group may be measured.[13] The American creed is a common set of beliefs and values in which all Americans have normally found consensus. It is a body of ideals, a social philosophy which affirms the basic dignity of every individual and the existence of certain inalienable rights without reference to race, creed, or color. The roots of the American creed are deep in the equalitarian doctrines of the eighteenth-century Enlightenment, Protestant Christianity and English law. For most of us, it has been the cultural matrix within which all discordant sociopolitical attitudes converge, and from which derives the great diversity of social and political interpretations which makes democracy possible in a society of widely variant populations.

The Black Muslims, by the nature of certain of their goals and institutions, have excepted themselves from the aegis of the American creed. The Black Muslims repudiate American citizenship in favor of a somewhat dubious membership in a mystical "Asiatic" confraternity, and they are violently opposed to Christianity, the principles of which are fundamental to our understanding of the democratic ideal. Not only do they resist assimilation and avoid interracial participation in the life of the community, but the Muslim creed assigns all nonblacks to the subhuman status of "devils" (and promises to treat them as such); the sustaining philosophy is one of black supremacy nurtured by a careful inculcation of hatred for the white man and his characteristic institutions. By their own choice the Black Muslims exclude themselves from the body of principles and the system of values within the framework of which Americans have customarily sought to negotiate their grievances.

Other groups advocate white supremacy, resist the assimilation of Negroes and others, and practice hatred rather than love, yet they retain an idealistic loyalty to the principles of the American creed. The point is that although the creed is violated constantly in practice, it remains an *ideal* to which all give their asseveration—in which all believe, and from which we continue to derive our laws and our moral values in spite of our failures to honor them completely.

The Black Muslim movement does not conceive itself to be in violation of the principles and values of the American creed. Rather, the movement views itself as having substituted new principles, new values, and a new creed based on a radically different interpretation of history from that expressed in the American creed. Muhammad promises a new order based on the primacy of a nation of black men with a manifest destiny under a black God. His is a nation radically different from those now shaping the existing American society. In spite of the fact that the Black Muslim movement shares at some points the immediate goals of the lesser Negro protest movements, its oppugnance to traditional values limits its general acceptability as a protest organization. The action impact of the movement on the general Negro community has been negligible considering the fact that most of America's 20 million black citizens live under conditions considerably more iniquitous than those which at other times and places have been productive of the gravest social consequences. This is not to suggest that Negroes are not aware of the movement. They are. And there are important pockets of sympathy among Negroes for the Muslims as a class more oppressed than other Negro classes, and a certain covert admiration for their militant, nonaccommodative stance against the traditional aggressions of the white man.

Nevertheless, the depth of the Negro's commitment *as a class* to the democratic procedures implicit in the American creed has operated successfully to contain the Muslim movement—eliminating it as a serious threat to racial peace or national security. But the Black Muslims remain a somber symbol of the social callousness that is possible even in an equalitarian democracy. Such movements do not "just happen." The Muslims are the most insistent symptoms of the failure of this society to meet effectively the minimum needs of one tenth of its population to find a meaningful level of participation in the significant social values most Americans take for granted.

The Muslims represent that segment of the Negro subgroup who, being most deprived of traditional incentives, have finally turned to search for alternatives outside the commonly accepted value structure. They are the products of social anxiety—people who are repeatedly frustrated in their attempts to make satisfactory adjustments in a society unaware of their existence except as the faceless subjects of statistical data. As Negroes, their future was unpromising. As Muslims, theirs is a creed of futility. As Americans, the responsibility for what they are, or what they will become, is our own.

NOTES

1. " 'Resource scarcity' is a condition in which the supply of desired objects (or states of affairs) is limited so that parties may not have *all* they want of anything." " 'Position scarcity' is a condition in which . . . a role cannot be simultaneously occupied or performed by two or more actors, and different prescribed behavior cannot be carried out simultaneously." (Raymond W. Mack and Richard C. Synder, "The Analysis of Social Conflict—Toward an Overview and Synthesis," *Journal of Conflict Resolution,* 1, no. 2 [1957]: 218.)

2. See St. Clair Drake, "Some Observations on Interethnic Conflict as One Type of Intergroup Conflict, *Journal of Conflict Resolution,* 1, no. 2 (1957): 155-178.

3. See Melville J. Herskovits, *The Myth of the Negro Past* (Boston, 1941), pp. 86-109.

4. I.e., American Negroes.

5. "Armageddon" is Greek transliteration from the Hebrew "Har-Magedon."

6. Eradmann Beynon, "The Voodoo Cult Among Negro Migrants in Detroit," *The American Journal of Sociology*, 43 (July 1937-May 1938): 895.

7. *Ibid;* p. 896.

8. *Chicago's American,* February 22, 1960.

9. See "Tensions Outside the Movement," in C. Eric Lincoln, *The Black Muslims in America* (Boston, 1961), pp. 135-178.

10. C. Eric Lincoln, *The Black Muslims in America* (Boston, 1961), p. 5.

11. *Chicago's American,* February 23, 1960.

12. July 31, 1962.

13. For an excellent interpretation of the American creed see Arnold Rose, *The Negro in America* (Boston, 1957), pp. 1ff.

20

A CONTEMPORARY REVITALIZATION MOVEMENT IN AMERICAN RACE RELATIONS: THE "BLACK MUSLIMS"

JAMES H. LAUE

James Laue, noting that the social scientists have finally "discovered" the Black Muslims, has used the theory that the Muslims are a "revitalization movement," aimed at constructing a more satisfying culture for black Americans, to suggest that the nation of Islam has done some "discovering" of its own. Though this too was written before the death of Malcolm X, Laue argues that the Muslims are quickly learning the methods of adaptation for survival, of toning down their rhetoric in order to attract more sympathy from black intellectuals and less hostility from the "host" white population. Even though black Americans subscribe to the American value system, their psychological deprivations may eventually allow such black nationalist movements, with a more sophisticated appeal, to come in out of the "fringe" of the protest movements.

Rarely do empirical cases seem so made to order for a particular sociological theory as does the Black Muslim movement for Anthony Wallace's formulation of the "revitalization movement."[1]

The "Lost-Found Nation of Islam in North America" is a mushrooming sect of Negro Americans led by some of the country's angriest young men. A politicoreligious organization preaching black nationalism and claiming "hundreds of thousands" of members throughout the United States, the Muslim movement is productively viewed in Wallace's revitalization terminology as "a deliberate, organized, conscious effort by members of a society to construct a more satisfying culture." There is no question that Negro Americans have been trying to do this since slave times: the Black Muslims stand out as a contemporary and highly organized example of this effort.

Although black nationalist groups have been a force in United States racial

Reprinted from *Social Forces*, 42 (March 1964): 315-323, by permission of the publisher.

patterns for most of the twentieth century—particularly in the northern ghettos—interest in the Muslims is only now beginning to grow among American social critics, popular pulp writers, and social scientists. The first scholarly work on the movement was C. Eric Lincoln's *The Black Muslims in America.*[2] Then in 1962 E. U. Essien-Udom's *Black Nationalism: A Search for an Identity in America* appeared.[3]

While Lincoln and Essien-Udom give considerable attention to the historical and psychological dimensions of the movement, the specifically sociological implications are yet to be explored. In this [essay], then, Wallace's theory is juxtaposed with what we know about the Muslims in hopes of clarifying the theory and operationalizing it as a guide for sociological research on the Movement.

A Note on Method: I Am a "Gray"

Since I am a "gray" (or "grayboy"—the hep Negro's terminology for the white man, signifying status as a mutation from the pure black), I cannot get in to Muslim temple meetings. It is hardly necessary to say that this is a decided research disadvantage! Research on the movement in the past three years has taken me into a number of temple-type situations, however; one of the chief sources of information presented in this [essay] has been participation in a number of informal discussion groups with several young Muslim members.

Combined with this participant observation have been documentary research on Muslim publications,[4] analysis of various semipopular articles and television programs, and attendance at public meetings regarding the movement. On two occasions I have seen the Muslims' musical tragicomedy, *Orgena* ("A Negro" spelled backwards), finding in the two performances differences which are presented later in this analysis. The most productive forms of research, finally, have been interviews and dialogue with leaders and students of the movement,[5] among them Minister Malcolm X, heir apparent to the top position in the movement.

The Theory of Revitalization Movements: "A More Satisfying Culture"

Wallace's definition of a revitalization movement as a "deliberate, organized, conscious effort by members of a society to construct a more satisfying culture" implies an organismic analogy and the corollary principles of stress and homeostasis. Society is seen as an organic system which is constantly exposed to stress induced in its component subsystems. The total system maintains itself by providing mechanisms sufficient to handle this stress.

Wallace finds each member equipped with what he calls a "mazeway"—a mental image of self, society, nature, and culture through which values operate in maintaining social order.

Whenever an individual who is under . . . chronic stress receives repeated information which indicates that his mazeway does not lead to action which reduces the level of stress, he must choose between maintaining his present mazeway and tolerating the stress, or changing the mazeway in an attempt to reduce the stress. . . . It may also be necessary to make changes in the "real" system in order to bring mazeway and "reality" into congruence. The effort to work a change in mazeway and "real" system together so as to permit more effective stress reduction is the effort at revitalization; and the collaboration of a number of persons in such an effort is called a revitalization movement.

Wallace sees six types of movements reported in the literature which can be classified under the revitalization rubric:

1. *Nativistic:* emphasis on elimination of alien persons, customs, and values.
2. *Revivalistic:* emphasis on reinstitutionalization of customs and values thought to have been in the mazeway of previous generations.
3. *Cargo cults:* importation of alien values, customs, and material into the mazeway via a ship's cargo.
4. *Vitalistic:* importation of foreign elements, but ships and cargo are not the necessary mechanisms.
5. *Millenarian:* an apocalyptic world transformation engineered by the supernatural.
6. *Messianic:* participation of a divine savior in human flesh in the mazeway transformation.

The most prominent historical cases to which Wallace points are the origins of Christianity and Islam, and the Ghost Dance and the Peyote cult of American Indian tribes.

Revitalization movements move through five ideal-typical stages in what Wallace calls the "processual structure":

1. *Steady state:* Chronic stress within the system varies within tolerable limits as culturally recognized techniques for satisfying needs operate efficiently.
2. *Period of increased individual stress:* "Individual members of a population . . . experience increasingly severe stress as a result of the decreasing efficiency

of certain stress-reduction techniques." The population may, according to Wallace, be " 'primitive' or 'civilized,' either a whole society or a class, caste, religious, occupational, acculturational, or other definable social group." Some of the elements responsible for lowering efficiency of stress-reduction mechanisms may be changes in the physical environment, military defeat, socioeconomic distress, political subordination, acculturational pressures, and epidemics.

3. *Period of cultural distortion:* Individual maladjustments combine to produce internal cultural distortion. "The elements are not harmoniously related but are mutually inconsistent and interfering." Stress reproduces itself and anxiety rises as the incongruities of the mazeway are perceived. Life is no longer meaningful.

4. *Period of revitalization:* Total cultures or subsystems on the way to disaster are frequently rescued—or, at least delayed—by the revitalization movement. The theory specifies six functional problems at this point: mazeway reformulation, communication, organization, adaptation, cultural transformation, and routinization.

5. *New steady state:* A new *Gestalt* is in operation, both for the members of the revitalized group and the host and/or neighboring cultures. Wallace's formulation here clearly implies that the movement has been institutionalized.

The Muslim Movement Today: "Those Who Know Aren't Saying"

The Muslim movement, according to the most accurate guesses, encompasses less than 100,000 members (some estimates run as low as 5,000) organized in some eighty "temples of Islam" throughout the country. Muslim leaders do not release exact membership figures—and their refusal to do so adds to the aura of uncertainty about Muslim strength which gives the movement so much leverage in the American racial situation today. "Only Allah knows," smiles Malcolm X, who, like most Muslims, has rejected his "Christian name" and substituted the symbol of an unknown quantity. "Those who know aren't saying, and those who say don't know!"

But the sociological significance of the movement has less to do with numbers than with mood—the militant mood and new sense of urgent activism growing in Negro Americans at all class levels in the last decade. For while the number of fully participating members is uncertain, there is no uncertainty about the way hundreds of thousands of Negroes respond to the Muslims' stark and straightforward articulation of "the problem" and its causes—

white evil and intransigence. There is no question that Negroes have been
ready to hear this for a long time.

Leadership

There is no doubt that Malcolm X is the Muslims' driving organizational
force. But the movement is formally centered around the Messenger, the
Prophet of Allah—the Honorable Elijah Muhammad. The Messenger, a
Georgia-born, light-skinned man in his middle sixties, is the ideal-typical sha-
man; he is believed to have had a mystical association with God himself, and
"believes in and follows Allah 100 percent."[6]

Membership

Membership is predominantly male and lower class. Selected men belong to
the Fruit of Islam, a "secret army"[7] which acts as a security force at temple
meetings and speeches by the leaders. The FOI is rigorously trained in military tactics and strategy and, while it will not initiate aggression, it responds
with force to any encroachments on its honor. One FOI member was killed
and many injured in a recent struggle with police who attempted to break up
a temple service in Los Angeles. The FOI is thus symbolic of the Muslim pre-
scription to "act like a MAN!"—and by such an orientation the leaders are
working to restore the Negro male emasculated by American discrimination
to the head of a patriarchal family structure.

Historical Development

The Muslims are one of a long line of black nationalist groups which have
made the scene (in the words of the brothers) in America in the last half-
century. A number of these groups work the streets of Harlem and other
Northern ghettos today: the Muslims are the largest. The most important fore-
runners of today's Muslim movement were the Moorish Science Temple movement of Noble Drew Ali and the Universal Negro Improvement Association of
Marcus Garvey—a "Back to Africa" group.[8] Both hit their peak in the World
War I era, and have small followings today.

Today's Muslims stem most directly from the work of Wallace D. Fard, who
appeared in Detroit in 1930 as the incarnation of Allah.[9] Elijah Poole, who
had recently moved to Detroit, ". . . came under the spell of Fard, who, he
recalls gratefully, took him 'out of the gutter . . . and in three-and-a-half years
taught (him) the knowledge of Islam.' "[10] Renamed "Elijah Muhammad" by
Fard, the enthusiastic migrant established a mosque in Chicago in 1932, where
he later sheltered Fard from the police. When Fard disappeared in 1934 (there

were rumors that Muhammad had induced Fard to offer himself as a human sacrifice[11]), Muhammad was the logical successor. Under his guidance, the movement grew slowly and maintained a position among the many sects competing for the marginal, disgruntled Negro. Malcolm X was converted while in prison in 1947 (many Muslim members are former convicts, addicts, and social derelicts), and his organizational ability and quick wit have been central to the movement's phenomenal growth in the last few years.

Values: The Religious-Historical Identity

The Muslims claim to be a branch of orthodox Islam, accepting most of the Koran and ". . . only the parts of the Bible which are divine."[12] The Genesis story of the creation is true—for the white man only—and the Muslims have the date placed somewhere around 6,000 years ago. But the black man was created 66 trillion years ago, and the white man is only here as the result of an albino mutation produced by an evil black scientist who succeeded in breeding out the pure black strain.

Muhammad preaches black nationalism (which is often interpreted as black supremacy) and black union against the white world. "The white man has robbed you of your name, your language, your culture, and your religion," Muslims are told. Through this treacherous stripping of the "so-called American Negro" of his heritage, the white man has succeeded in subjugating the black man—whose *real* language is Arabic, whose *real* religion is Islam and whose *original* homeland is the Nile valley in Northern Africa. "The white man was still living in caves in Europe and eating meat raw while our forefathers lived in luxury in flourishing civilizations on the banks of the Nile," continues the Messenger.

Values: The Secular Program

The Muslims say they want several states of their own to set up a separate black nation. If the United States does not repent for its treatment of this nation-within-a-nation, Allah will strike down the oppressor. The Armageddon date was originally set for 1914, but Allah granted a seventy-year extension.[13]

I am convinced from a number of conversations with Muslim leaders, however, that what they *really* want is access to the vices and virtues enjoyed by white Americans. The Muslims' puritanical ethical prescriptions place them in the mainstream of the dominant American middle-class value system. Members are enjoined to run their businesses like the white man, protect their women, abstain from alcohol and tobacco, and give generously to the "church" (many Muslims donate one third of their livelihood to the temple). And nowhere is the neat, well-mannered, humble model of an American family attending church better exemplified than in the Muslim family going to three or four temple meetings per week. Significantly, the demanding discipline of the Muslims has made them more successful than any other civic, religious, or governmental agencies in social rehabilitation of Negro convicts, prostitutes, addicts, alcoholics, disorganized families, and slum homes. But also significantly, the wave of press attention to the movement has chosen to play down these achievements.

Muslim women are placed on a pedestal (and are the subject of a song popular in the movement, "Black Gold") while the white man is blamed for the long history of miscegenation under slavery and segregation. Many women in the movement enroll in the Muslims Girls Training and General Civilization Class, where they are ". . . taught how to sew, cook, keep house, rear their children, care for their husbands, and how to behave at home and abroad."[14]

Ritual Behavior

Temple meetings are quite subdued compared to many lower-class Negro religious gatherings. Members are searched before entering the mosque, and are not admitted if they have alcohol on their breath. Some altar settings present the star and crest of Islam opposite a silhouetted lynching scene backed by the American flag and the cross, with a sign asking, "Which Will You Choose?" Sermons are customarily long. In addition to temple attendance, most orthodox followers bathe and pray five times a day.

Aesthetic Expression

Minister Louis X of Boston, a former calypso singer, is the artist of the movement; *Orgena* is his product. The show has played in most of the large Eastern cities, including return engagements in New York and Boston. It depicts the glorious ancient culture of the black man, his enslavement by white colonializers and slavetraders, and the trial of the white man—who finally confesses that he is the devil, and is dragged off stage under the death sentence. The play is punctuated by several of Minister Louis' songs, including "A White Man's Heaven is a Black Man's Hell," which presents Muslim theology attractively backed by a calypso beat. A recording of "White Man's Heaven" is now in national circulation by the movement, and acts as a potent recruiting force.

The Muslims as a Revitalization Movement:
The Shaping of a Substitute Identity

The Muslim movement is one of several alternative avenues of expression for the angry, sensitive, disillusioned Negro in America today. He is thoroughly Americanized at the value level, but frustrated at the personality level be-cause of lack of institutionalized channels of cultural achievement. While the closed-system nature of the dominant white culture in the nineteenth century dictated clowning, self-hate, and neuroticism as adjustive techniques, the more aggressive channels of protest safely available today include enhanced striving, in-group aggression, prejudice against out-groups, and militancy.[15] The particu-lar cluster of mechanisms demonstrated in the Muslim movement involves all of these, plus denial of membership—substitution of identity as a "Muslim" for identity as a "Negro."

The psychological stances represented by these reactions are all part of the Black Muslims' unique mazeway. They have been translated into a coherent movement, which exhibits elements of five of the six types of revitalization movements Wallace suggests:

The *nativistic* phase of the movement emphasizes elimination of the white slavemaster and his evil system, to be replaced by an all-black nation-within-a-nation—in which contact with the white's alien customs and values is neither desirable nor possible.

Consequently, in *revivalistic* fashion the Muslims hope to institute the pat-terns of ancient Islamic society as they idealize it—an example of the Golden Age approach of every people who have ever suffered cultural disorganization.

From our perspective on the "outside," we can also call the Muslim move-ment a *vitalistic* effort, stressing importation of foreign elements. But it is clear that the Muslims do not accept this "importation" terminology, for the germ of the core values they espouse is inherent in every black man, they say; he is phylogenetically a Muslim, and automatically superior to his white counterpart.

The *millenarian* emphasis of the movement is very strong. Minister Mal-colm and the Messenger state time and again that Allah will engineer a Babylon-type demise of the white man if he does not repent in time.

And, while Fard was the official incarnation and Muhammad only a sha-manistic prophet, Muslim leaders know that many members do not make the distinction, and indeed view the Messenger as a *messianic* figure actually par-ticipating in the divine.

Viewing sociological theory as an organizing, economizing, and operationalizing endeavor, we may now specify the points of congruence and variation between Wallace's outline of the "processual structure" and the historical development of the movement:

1. Steady State

While the terminology of "steady state" and "new steady state" which Wallace uses may be a necessary theoretical distinction, it implies too much of a revolutionary character for the revitalization movement, and suggests an almost qualitative split between steady state$_1$, the flux phase, and steady state$_2$. For societies and their subgroups are *never* in a state which can be differentiated as "steady" when compared to another given state. Groups and ideologies dance in and out of power and influence, forming a dynamic matrix whose continuity is violated if we arbitrarily slice out chunks surrounding certain "movements." Social changes in the "movement" form should not be conceptualized as mutations of a former order (which the "*new* steady state" terminology implies), but rather as logical maturations with discernible etiological bases. We would do better to label these periods simply "stage 1" and "stage 2"—with the intervening processes seen as mediating developments leading to the new stage of systemic equilibrium.

Viewed in this light, it is appropriate to specify some of the dynamic social patterns which bred and nurtured the Muslims. Most obvious is Negroes' irrepressible dissatisfaction with their disproportionate share of the benefits from the expanding American economy—benefits which are paraded before all citizens every day via the mass media. Equally important is the failure of the old philosophical and religious systems to provide meaningful rationalizations for Negroes' nonattainment of deeply internalized democratic goals. The tight white opportunity structure becomes intolerable when a minority member is able to objectify his position and see what he is being denied. And finally—but by no means exhaustively—the emergence of African nations is *the* most specific model for American Muslim militancy today. Muslim leaders press for an identification with the African spirit of black revolt but carefully avoid any implication of actually returning to African ways, thus avoiding Garvey's mistake by recognizing that Negro Americans are too thoroughly middle class in their values for any "Back to Africa" approach to succeed.

2. Period of Increased Individual Stress

I am saying, then, that the "breakdown of stress-reducing mechanisms" for Negro Americans has been occurring since the first slave arrived, and that the breakdown has led to protests of varying intensity throughout the years.[16] In the last few years American society has not been able to provide stress-reducers at a rate rapid enough to satisfy its increasingly heterogeneous population structure. The system has not been able to institutionalize deviant channels of adjustment as they have appeared.

Negro Americans have experienced in varying degree the status-deprivation of which we talked in the last section. But, as Wallace rightly points out, the initial consideration of a substitute mode of adjustment often *increases* stress because of lack of feedback about the effectiveness of this alternate stance. The Muslims have avoided this pitfall by some highly successful advertising of the restructured identity they offer. They have worked in prisons and on the streets of Harlem and other large cities, first convincing potential converts of their totally deprived state as "so-called American Negroes," then presenting a totally new identity, ready made and ready to put on. It is an active, life-consuming identity, not a "pay-your-membership-fee-without-necessary-commitment-to-action" stance, which for years has been the folk-level format of the now threatened and allegedly nonmilitant NAACP.

3. Period of Cultural Distortion

Regressive individual responses to deprivation long have been at a level which produces distortion in the Negro subculture. Crime, alcoholism, addiction, prostitution, and family disorganization have made their mark on the Negro American community. Mr. Muhammad's missionaries have capitalized on this cultural distortion, winning many of their converts from the lowest planes of society. "Look at these acts you committed as a Christian, as a so-called Negro," preach the ministers. "Then look at *our* people, who have rejected their slavemaster and their slave religion, and have thrown off the vices taught by the blue-eyed devils."

4. Period of Revitalization

The first important functional task in revitalization is *mazeway reformulation*. Wallace proposes that this reformulation generally depends on a restructuring of elements and subsystems already current in the system—elements which are articulated, combined, and operationalized by the prophet as guides to action. While the Muslims claim to preach a doctrine entirely alien to America, their position becomes a thinly veiled acceptance and rephrasing of American ideals, as suggested above.

The revitalization period usually originates in "one or several hallucinatory visions by a single individual. A supernatural being appears to the prophet-to-be, explains his own and his society's troubles as being entirely or partly as a result of the violation of certain rules, and promises individual and social revitalization if the injunctions are followed and the rituals exercised." Muhammad *did* receive instructions from a supernatural being (Fard), but as far as we can determine, it was in the flesh and not hallucinatory communication.

After "the dream," the prophet moves to *communicate* his insights, fulfilling the second functional requirement of the revitalization process. The two doctrinal motifs hypothesized for this stage are manifested by the Muslims: "that the convert will come under the care and protection of certain supernatural beings" (Allah); and that "both he and his society will benefit materially from an identification with some definable new cultural system" (Islam, of the Black Muslim variety). Disciples readily assume the responsibility for communicating the word; in the Muslim case, followers like Malcolm X and Louis X have become recruitment agents with charisma at least equal to that of the Messenger—although neither of them would (or could) admit it, of course.

Wallace's discussion of the *organizational* phase of the revitalization stage hinges on what Weber calls the problem of succession: the prophet must transfer his charismatic qualities to other individuals and the organization to effect legitimation of his cause. Muhammad is certainly regarded as an unquestionable authority, sanctioned by the supernatural. His movement has already moved out of the cult stage, since the leadership structure is sufficiently developed to ensure its maintenance when Muhammad dies, even though a good deal of conflict may result as the hierarchy adjusts. The disciplinary action of the Fruit of Islam, the unifying force of *Orgena* whereever it is produced and the organizational ability of Minister Malcolm combine to give the Muslim movement a solid bureaucratic structure that makes Negro rights organizations and lower-class religious groups envious.

Perhaps the most important phase of the revitalization process is *adaptation,* and it seems to be the major area of the theory upon which elaboration is necessary. Wallace suggests three aspects of this process: doctrinal modification, political and diplomatic maneuvers, and force. Muslim doctrine has undergone drastic modification in the last few years as the membership has broadened, but, contrary to the theory, most of the alterations have been engineered by Malcolm X rather than the prophet.[17]

Some of the major doctrinal modifications which may be seen in the Muslims' sect-to-church drive are:

1. The black supremacy doctrine is being softened in an effort to attract Negro intellectuals. A former *Orgena* focus on problems of the Negro in America, for instance, is now tempered with strong emphasis on colonialism in Asia and Africa. In fact, it now is "colonialism" rather than "the white man" which is sentenced to death in *Orgena.*

2. Relationships with other Negro rights groups are improving. Malcolm X

has called former NAACP legal head and now Federal judge Thurgood Marshall a "twentieth-century Uncle Tom" loudly and often, but the Muslim leader has accepted a number of speaking engagements at local NAACP chapters in the last two years. Too, former vehemence against the sit-ins and Martin Luther King, Jr., was absent in a recent television debate which found Minister Malcolm consciousiy trying to tone down his criticism for a national audience.[18] And following the Los Angeles police slaying of a member in 1962, the Muslims readily cooperated in a protest rally with the NAACP, the Congress of Racial Equality, and local Negro ministers—indicating a new level of synthesis not possible only a few years earlier when the Muslims had reached neither their current level of national prominence nor their desire for a broader-based "church" status.

3. Muslims are reemphasizing the religious character of the movement in response to charges that the Islamic orientation is merely a gimick and cloak for political motives. Minister Malcolm's Harvard Law School Forum speech in 1961 focused around the Muslims as a *religious* movement—a radical change from an address at Boston University a year earlier. At the same time, the Muslims are not condemning Christianity with their former gusto—at least publicly—as exemplified in open debates and the most recent performances of *Orgena*.[19]

In discussing force as an adaptive technique, Wallace suggests that as organized hostility develops, emphasis in the movement frequently shifts from cultivation of the ideal to combat against the unbeliever. I find this ingroup ideal vs. outgroup combat syndrome more cyclical than lineal, however. For a time, the main task of the Fruit of Islam was "guarding the Black Nation against 'trouble with unbelievers, especially with the police.'"[20] In 1960 and 1961, with the environment perceived as less hostile, the emphasis had moved back to ingroup solidarity and uplift, including policing errant members and performing as a drill team at performances of *Orgena*. But more recently, in response to increased extrasystemic challenge from prison wardens and police as the movement seeks to expand, the FOI has redirected its efforts and training toward outside forces.[21]

The Muslim movement today is clearly in the "adaptive" phase of revitalization, and promises to remain there for several years. The proposed phase of *cultural transformation*—acceptance of the movement as a legitimate mode of social adjustment by a controlling portion of the host population—may come rapidly if the Muslims continue to adapt their doctrines in true third party style.

Routinization—the tragedy that befalls all revolutions—occurs on both integrative (internal) and adaptive (external) planes, although the theory stresses only the integrative aspects of this process. For Wallace, routinization takes place only after the desired transformation has occurred. Perhaps the gravest immediate challenge to rapid rationalization will occur when the ailing Muhammad dies, for a power struggle between Malcolm X and others is certain unless the Messenger makes a definite pronouncement regarding his legitimate successor.[22]

5. New Steady State

After my earlier strong objections to the nondynamic implications of the "steady state terminology" and analysis of the Muslims as professional discontents, we may conclude that the nation of Islam cannot logically reach anything resembling a "new steady state"; it would go out of existence first.

There is one more aspect of the theory which deserves clarification—Wallace's qualification that the revitalization terminology is best applicable to a movement which is completely successful. His position here indicates that his data and interpretations derive necessarily from "dead" movements—a characteristic of postdicting which sociology has found hard to overcome. This approach would thus limit analysis considerably, since many powerful and socially disruptive movements do not reach even the adaptive phase. The Muslim movement, on the other hand, is one of a number of researchable in-process movements that offer a dynamic context in which theory can be checked as it is built.

The success or failure of a revitalization movement depends largely on the relative "realism" of the doctrines, according to Wallace. I think that this formulation must be modified to include the *degree to which the leaders make known their doctrinal positions to power elements of the host population.* Many movements fail, says Wallace, because wildly unrealistic predictions which do not come true result in mazeway disintegration of the members. The Muslims have learned this lesson well: They purposely keep predictions and interpretations vague to save themselves embarrassing refencing later. More and more in the last years, Malcolm X has been hedging on questions concerning relations with other groups, black supremacy, the battle of Armageddon, and Muslim action plans for the future. He is ever-ready with "Only Allah knows," to counter a prying or threatening question regarding the nature and destiny of the movement.[23]

Prospects for Future Research: "Pretty Soon, Man"

The Muslim movement is becoming increasingly aware of its public face— and particularly its image with intellectuals. In the next few years, then, the movement should be more and more amenable to social scientific research. The chief requirement for the social scientist who wishes to successfully execute such research, of course, is the proper skin color! Even these barriers may be loosening, however, for recently when I half-jokingly asked Malcolm X, "When are you going to let me in to a temple meeting?" he half-seriously replied, "Pretty soon, man. Maybe pretty soon."

Now that the facts concerning the etiology of the movement are surfacing, a major longitudinal research study charting the sect's drive toward institutionalization is called for. Here, for instance, the Weberian may find a twentieth-century case of an underdeveloped nation-within-a-nation (the Negro subculture in American society) already exhibiting the religiously sanctioned asceticism to which Weber attached such great importance as motivator and justifier of this-worldly economic activity.

Intensive comparative studies are also needed. As one hypothetical framework for this kind of research, we can view the Muslim movement as analogous in origin and development to the Peyote cult. Antecedents of both Peyotists and the Muslims were aggressive and uncompromising in their orientation to the host population.[24] Indian Ghost Dances at the turn of the century were harsh and unrelenting ritual rejections of the encroaching white culture: earlier black nationalist groups like the Garvey and Moorish Science movements were soon doomed to obscurity by their failure to adapt even marginally to the host population. Just as the emergence of the Peyote cult offered a more readily syncretic alternative for frustrated and hostile Indian Americans, so the Lost-Found Nation of Islam presents today a workable and sufficiently flexible identity for an ever-expanding group of militantly disenchanted Negro Americans.

NOTES

1. A. F. C. Wallace, "Revitalization Movements," *American Anthropologist*, 58 (April 1956): 264-281. The few direct quotations concerning Wallace's theory which appear in this paper are taken from these pages.

2. C. Eric Lincoln, *The Black Muslims in America* (Boston, 1961).

3. E. U. Essien-Udom, *Black Nationalism: A Search for an Identity in America* (Chicago, 1962).

4. The most important source of current information is a tabloid called *Muhammad Speaks,* formerly issued in Harlem and now published in Chicago. The magazine has moved from an emphasis on white brutality to its current format offering general information (cooking tips, for instance) as well.

5. I am especially indebted to W. Haywood Burns and William Strickland, formerly of Harvard College, who have contributed many of the insights presented in this paper. Several conversations with Mr. Lincoln and Mr. Essien-Udom have lent additional material and interpretation. And Ministers Malcolm X of New York, Louis X and Rodney X of Boston, Jeremiah X of Atlanta and Brother John Ali of Chicago have given many hours of conversation to expand my understanding of the Nation of Islam.

6. Malcolm X, speech at Harvard Law School, Cambridge, Mass., March 24, 1961.

7. Lincoln, p. 199.

8. For a discussion of the Muslims' antecedents and other current black nationalist groups, see Lincoln, chap. 3, and Essien-Udom, chaps. 2 and 3.

9. See E. D. Beynon, "The Voodoo Cult among Negro Migrants in Detroit," *American Journal of Sociology,* 43 (May 1938): 894-907.

10. Lincoln, p. 181. This account is also symbolic of the conversion experiences of most members in the movement today.

11. *Ibid.,* p. 182.

12. Malcolm X, speech at Boston University School of Theology, Boston, Mass., May 24, 1960.

13. No one knows whether George Orwell, in 1984, had the same vision!

14. Lincoln, p. 128.

15. Gordon W. Allport analyzes these and other "traits due to victimization" in *The Nature of Prejudice* (Garden City, N.Y., 1958), chap. 19.

16. This point is documented in a number of sources, including James H. Laue, "Race Relations Revolution: The Sit-In Movement," mimeographed, 1961, and Louis Lomax, *The Negro Revolt* (New York, 1962).

17. While Muhammad continues to make crude antiwhite statements (many of which find their way into the media), Minister Malcolm spends much of his time with Negro and white intellectuals trying to take Muhammad's foot out of the movement's mouth.

18. "Open Mind," presented on educational television, WGBH-TV, Boston, Mass., April 30, 1961.

19. It should be made clear that while the Muslims have a powerful ethicopolitical program, they must be viewed sociologically as primarily a religious endeavor—a system of beliefs and rituals about ultimate problems (the nature and purpose of existence, death, meaning, right ethical norms, etc.) organized in and for a community of believers. Their this-worldly asceticism is, in fact, quite similar to that of the American Puritans of the eighteenth century.

20. Lincoln, p. 200.

21. For an interesting discussion of this cycle, see Essien-Udom, chap. 11.

22. While this manuscript was in press, Malcolm X was censured by Muhammad for intemperate public remarks about the death of President Kennedy. Some observers saw the action as a suspension, designed to remove Minister Malcolm from competition with Muhammad's sons for leadership after the Prophet dies. But Mr. Lincoln, following a conversation with Malcolm X in January 1964, said the incident was "a more or less routine display of hierarchical power," and that "similar sanctions are applied continuously in the temples at a less public level." Minister Malcolm was, in fact, on his way to an important meeting with Muhammad at the time—one month after the censure.

23. Malcolm X exercises this unbeatable theological one-upsmanship in interpretation of past events, too. He linked, for instance, the crash of a Belgian airliner in 1961 with the same-day announcement of the assassination of Congo leader Patrice Lumumba, and suggested that the 1962 crash killing 120 Georgia cultural leaders was also part of Allah's plan for retribution against the white world. With very little tongue-in-cheek I suggest that Malcolm X's connection of these events has unwittingly offered a Muslim formulation of a new F-item. Note the Similarity of these linkages with item 10 of the original F-scale, which was designed to test for "superstition and stereotypy": "It is more than a remarkable coincidence that Japan had an earthquake on Pearl Harbor Day, December 7, 1944." (Adorno et al., *The Authoritarian Personality* [New York, 1950], p. 235.)

24. See Bernard Barber, "A Socio-Cultural Interpretation of the Peyote Cult," *American Anthropologist,* 47 (October-December 1941): 673-675.

21

THE STOREFRONT CHURCH AS A REVITALIZATION MOVEMENT

IRA E. HARRISON

In his assessment of the religious situation in 1968, Clifton Brown noted that there was a growing interest in the "underground" or storefront black church. Since the work of Arthur Fauset on sects and cults of the cities of the 1940's, very little research has been directed toward this little-understood segment of the black church. An exception is the following study by Ira Harrison. Working independently but using the same theory as that which James Laue applied to the Black Muslims, Harrison here suggests that the storefront church helps to "revitalize" black migrants to Northern cities from the rural South by "refurbishing" their rural religious practices to an urban, often depersonalized society.

Though one occasionally discovers the term "storefront" church in the literature on the urban environment, the data on how they begin, who attends, what kinds of activities prevail within these churches, and the differences among various types of storefront churches are not always clear. This [essay] will report the findings of an exploratory study of sixteen storefront churches in Syracuse, New York,[1] and will suggest that storefront churches may be viewed as a revitalization movement in the manner stated by Anthony F. C. Wallace. That is, storefront churches are "deliberate, conscious, organized efforts by members of a society to create a more satisfying culture.[2]

In 1961, the Youth Development Center of Syracuse University conducted a series of surveys of storefront churches in preparation for a larger study on social mobility. This survey was conducted in two phases: one consisting of a survey of storefront churches; the other consisting of a survey of nonstorefront churches and the establishing of extended participant observation with one

Reprinted from *Review of Religious Research,* 7 (Spring 1966): 160-163, by permission of the author and the publisher. This is a revision of a paper presented at the Northeastern Anthropological Conference, McMaster University, Hamilton, Ontario, on March 21, 1964. I would like to express my appreciation to Dr. Helen Icken Safa for her comments and suggestions.

storefront church from September 1961 to May 1962, on a part-time basis. The method used was participant observation. A tape recorder was used to record church services on several occasions. This survey resulted in an extensive annotated bibliography on storefront churches, a typology of Negro churches in Syracuse, and several working papers.

Storefront churches are not new to Syracuse. A 1937 report on the Negro in Syracuse comments that:

> Hundreds of Negroes, are so depressed by the monotony, sordidness and dreary toil of their daily life so worried by economic problems, and so deprived of normal forms of recreation and emotional outlet, that they are forced to seek relief from these problems in the vicious "storefront" churches which flourish in the Negro communities.[3]

A master's thesis on the Negro community in 1943, a continuation of the 1937 report, also mentions storefront churches:

> These are a kind of fly-by-night affair, small irregualr congregations built largely about the personality of some individual leader, finding a home for the moment in an otherwise vacant "storefront" or similar building and often passing out of the picture as quickly as they come in.[4]

The history of storefront churches in Syracuse parallels that of Negro migration from the South. The 1937 report listed the Negro population as 2,400, 62 percent of whom migrated from Virginia, North Carolina, Georgia, Florida, and other southern states. The 1943 report reveals that 380 male migrants out of 494 migrants who came to Syracuse to work in defense plants between 1940-1942 came from South Carolina, North Carolina, Georgia, Florida, Virginia, Alabama, Tennessee, Louisiana, Mississippi, and Kentucky. Between 1950 and 1960, the Negro population in Syracuse more than doubled, increasing from 5,058 to 12,251 persons, or 142 percent. Much of this influx was directly from the southern states and indirectly, via the migrant farms of upstate New York.

Moreover, in 1950, 93 percent of Syracuse's Negro population lived in a ghetto-like slum area near the center of the city, whereas in 1960, only 72 percent of the Negro population of Syracuse lived in this area. Many storefronts have changed location in an attempt to follow the movement of people out from the center of the city, just as the church followed them from the South. Blackwell, writing about Cleveland storefront churches, says that: "The Negro 'storefront' church tends to follow the same direction that the mass of the Negro population takes. And by the same reasoning, the creation of new churches is due to the increase in population."[5] Thus, the storefront church may also be seen as an urban manifestation of the Negro's rural heritage. I have heard many storefront church members speak of "back home," referring to Virginia, South Carolina, and Alabama. I also heard that most of the membership of one storefront and the minister are from Montgomery, Alabama. During one church service, the pastor asked, "Where was Sister Green?" A male member stood up, looked around, and said, "She must be sick, because I seen her in the onion fields with me yesterday."[6]

Religion, as Herskovits has stated, is a cultural focus for Negro peoples and a means of understanding other aspects of Negro life. The religious experiences in storefront churches serve a Durkheimian-like function in that they give strength, identity, dignity, and *raison d'être* to their members. The members are not ashamed to testify in the behalf of the Lord, and to tell what He has done for them. They tell about the "used-to's": used to gamble, used to play the numbers, used to go with other women's husbands, used to drink, etc., but now they stopped all of that since they have been converted, baptized, sanctified, and saved.

Storefront churches relieve stress and disillusionment through their organizational structure: leadership, membership, and ritual. Briefly, the minister directs and drives the membership toward a state of sanctification which helps to keep them from "hurt, harm, and danger." The membership is a warm, understanding, enthusiastic band of baptized believers. The ritual allows for both individual expression and group participation. For example, a member may not only sing in concert with others, but also, he can sing his favorite song, individually. He can pray his own prayer long and loud. A rationale may be offered for singing, shouting, howling, clapping, dancing, and playing instruments. "A lot of folks talk about getting too emotional. I wouldn't give two cents for a religion that wouldn't make me move. My God is a living God. Anything that moves can't be dead." "We believe in being free here, you come back, and feel free to enjoy yourself."[7]

There is little attempt at acculturation with the larger society. The value of education is questioned because "it won't give remission of sins," "it won't give you the Holy Ghost." "Peter, James, and John were only fishermen," "the professor [a man of learning in opposition to a man of spiritual experience] can't well the water because his well rope is too short, and the well is too deep," and "All you need to know is right here in the Bible."[8] Yet education has been considered the most acceptable means of social mobility for the Negro. The storefront church minister, rather than emphasizing values associated with social mobility, constantly preaches sin and doom in this wicked world.

In the absence of a theory and a model to explain storefront church behavior, I suggest Wallace's evolutionary scheme of the processual structure of the revitalization process as a means of understanding storefront church growth. He states:

In cases where the full course is run, this process consists of five somewhat overlapping states: 1. Steady State; 2. Period of Individual Stress; 3. Period of Cultural Distortion; 4. Period of Revitalization (in which occur the functions of mazeway reformulation, communication, organization, adaptation, cultural transformation, and routinization), and finally, 5. New Steady State.[9]

Perhaps, the Steady State, "a period of moving equilibrium. . . . [where] disorganization and stress remain within limits tolerable to most individuals," may be seen as the premigratory period in the South. The migration itself may be seen as "The period of Increased Individual Stress. . . . [when] increasing large numbers of individuals are placed under what is to them intolerable stress by the failure of the system to accommodate the satisfaction of their needs."[10] Migrants bussed and trucked to Northern farms oftimes discover the huts, cold and damp. When it rains they cannot work, cannot go into the nearest town, and have nothing to occupy their time. Wages are low, the workers are many, and food, clothes, and other commodities are higher priced than they are in the South. While Southern whites-Negro-tenant relations are paternalistic and condescending, they are also warm and personal in contrast to the instrumental, indifferent and businesslike relationships with whites in the North. Whereas in many rural areas of the South, Saturday is understood as the day Negroes go to town, shop, congregate on the corners and see their friends, many Northern villages and towns do not want Negroes in their towns and villages at all. "Anomie and disillusionment become widespread," and the period of cultural distortion begins as some migrants "attempt piecemeal and ineffectively, to restore personal equilibrium by adapting socially disfunctional expedients. Alcoholism . . . . breaches of sexual and kinship mores, hoarding, gambling for gain; 'scapegoating,' and similar behaviors."[11] This type of behavior results in low morale, low productivity, and migrants being fired, being arrested for drunkenness, and other offenses.

It is under these stresses that many migrants leave the farms heading for the larger cities in the North. Finding no jobs, poor housing, more subtle forms of discrimination than that to which they were accustomed, and few friends, those migrants who had religious home training in the South visited the nearest church. Other migrants might have visited the bars and beer joints, and then maybe find their way to the church as a final alternative.

Hylan Lewis, writing about the rural life in Kent, South Carolina, states:

Assuming that the Negro. . . . lives in a relatively "tough culture"—one marked by significant blocking of wish goals—the free-expression aspects of his religious behavior parallel the patterned indulgence in whiskey, sex and tavern behavior, and they serve something of the same function. Religious expression is a function of social and personal needs as well as tradition: its manifestations vary roughly with the indices of sophistication, status, and security."[12]

It is in this way storefront churches may be seen as revitalization movements: they are deliberate, conscious, organized efforts of migrants to create a more satisfying mode of existence by refurbishing rural religious behavior to an urban environment.

Revitalization according to Wallace has six stages: formulation of a code, communication, organization, adaptation, cultural transformation, and routinization. In terms of storefront churches, the code is the Bible: as one storefront church minister says: "All you need to know is right here in this Book."[13] The communication is the word of the Lord from the pastor: "God will look out for . . . things if the people obey. Serve the Lord," and "wait patiently upon Him, and He will bring it to pass."[14] The organization is the storefront. The adaptation is to the urban milieu.

Despite the variety of storefront holiness groups and the storefront Baptist groups, some routinization may be seen in their order of services, in the singing of hymns and other ritual aspects, and in the preaching against this wicked, unpredictable, and uncontrollable world. Thus, in the process of cultural transformation of the Negro's rural Southern heritage, there has been some routinization in ritual and values communicated in these storefront churches. Some religious groups, in the process of cultural transformation and routinization, leave their storefront buildings and become more established churches.

Thus, one minister of a church in transition from storefront to an established church, in explaining the growth of his membership, stated:

Our church was founded in 1947 on Valentine's Day. We had five members at that time. We moved from our first location, the living room of my home, to 1055 East Fayette Street. There our membership increased to nine. We were next located at 808 South McBride Street. We took in 100 members there and entered the Baptist Convention. Our church was moved next to 912 Townsend Street. We owned the property there and our membership increased to over 800. When that location became too small, we moved to the old Alacasar Theatre on Raynor and Oakwood Avenues. We stayed there until our present church was renovated. This church was completely demolished and rebuilt. We have taken in approximately 1800 members here.[15]

While many of the original members of the storefront church are still with this minister, he now leads one of the largest Negro congregations in what is becoming a new area of slum settlement for Negroes in Syracuse. Case studies of storefront churches and former storefront churches are needed. They may provide us with the answers to such questions as why some storefront churches always remain storefronts, why other storefronts pass out of existence, and why still others become organized churches.

NOTES

1. For a review of the literature on storefront churches see Ira E. Harrison's "A Selected Annotated Bibliography on Storefront Churches and Other Religious Writings," Youth Development Center, Syracuse University, Syracuse, N.Y., 1963.

2. Anthony F. C. Wallace, "Revitalization Movement," *American Anthropologist*, 58 (April 1956): 264-279.

3. B. Golden, "The Negro in Syracuse, New York," unpublished manuscript, 1937, p. 20.

4. Theodore E. Brown, "The Negro in Syracuse, New York, as Related to the Social Service Program of Dunbar Center," unpublished master's thesis, Syracuse University, 1943.

5. James Edward Blackwell, "A Comparative Study of Five Negro 'Storefront' Churches in Cleveland," unpublished master's thesis, Western Reserve University, Cleveland, 1949.

6. Statements taken from field notes.

7. *Ibid.*

8. *Ibid.*

9. Wallace, p. 268.

10. *Ibid.*, p. 269.

11. Anthony F. C. Wallace, *Culture and Personality* (New York, 1961), p. 147.

12. Hylan Lewis, *Blackways of Kent* (Chapel Hill, N.C., 1955), p. 153.

13. Statements taken from field notes.

14. Carter Godwin Woodson, *The Rural Negro* (Washington, D.C., 1930), pp. 167-168.

15. Statements taken from field notes.

22

BLACK CATHOLICS IN THE
UNITED STATES:
AN EXPLORATORY ANALYSIS

JOE R. FEAGIN

In Part III we have attempted to show the directions in which dissatisfaction with the traditional black church has been channeled—when it manifested itself in deviations within a basically religious framework. Although the alternative outlets of the various nationalistic and millenarian cults, such as the Black Muslims and Father Divine, are the best known, a significant number of black Americans have, in the century since emancipation, turned to the more formal ritual of the Roman Catholic faith. In this chapter Joe Feagin analyzes conversion trends and suggests some of the attractions Catholicism may have for the Negro disenchanted with the more traditionally favored forms of Christianity.

Analysis of the religious patterns of black Americans has usually focused on their adherence to Protestantism, particularly to the Baptist, Methodist, and Pentecostal faiths. One important and apparently growing segment of the Negro population has been neglected by scholars: black Roman Catholics. The purpose of this [essay] is to explore the limited statistical data available on black Catholics and to suggest some working hypotheses to explain the apparent upsurge of Negro conversions to Catholicism.

Reprinted from *Sociological Analysis*, 29 (Winter 1968): 186-192, by permission of the publisher.

Historical Background

From the 1700's to the 1870's there were relatively few contacts between Negroes and Catholics in the United States. Most Negroes were incarcerated in the rural South where there were relatively few Catholics.[1] In the North, on occasion, Catholic immigrant laborers found themselves competing with free black laborers for unskilled jobs in industrial areas. However this competition frequently led to mutual antagonism and even violent clashes; thus it is not surprising that Northern Negroes at an early date seem to have generalized their antagonism for Catholic laborers to the Church itself.

In the antebellum South, with only two major exceptions, Maryland and Louisiana, no areas saw extensive contacts between Negroes and the Catholic Church. Most slaveowners were Protestant; and the most successful and extensive missionary efforts among the Southern slaves before the Civil War were carried out by Baptist and Methodist proselytizers. However, some successes evidently marked the proselytizing efforts of Catholic missionaries in Maryland;[2] according to a 1785 Jesuit report to Rome there were at least 3,000 black Catholics in Maryland, doubtless most being the slaves of Catholic masters.[3] Pressures to convert were greater in southern Louisiana. In 1724 Bienville, the founder of New Orleans, issued his famous Black Code, decreeing that all slaves were to be instructed in Catholicism and baptized; similar concern for Catholicizing the slaves was manifested during the period of control. Primarily because of the efforts of Capuchin and Jesuit priests, thousands of Louisiana slaves were baptized as Catholics in this period. Migration from Louisiana and Maryland, augmented by several thousand black Catholic refugees from the Caribbean between 1790 and 1810, accounts in large measure for the presence of black Catholics in other states.

The post-Civil War upheaval, particularly in Louisiana, probably wrenched many Negro slaves from the Catholic Church, partly because of slave rejection of masters' religion, but also because of the lack of facilities for the aid and instruction of Catholic slaves in the North and West. Given this crisis, the Church gradually responded with large-scale organized efforts to convert and aid black Americans. In 1871 the Mill Hill Fathers began their work among the emancipated Negro slaves. Meeting in Baltimore in 1884, the Third Plenary Council formed the Commission for Catholic Missions among the Colored People and the Indians. Periodically ever since, the Catholic Church has reconsecrated itself to an effort both to aid Negroes and to convert them to the faith.

The Available Data

How successful have been Catholic efforts to convert Negroes? How many black Catholics were there in the nineteenth century? Has their number grown since them? Only rough, approximate answers can be given to these questions, given the uneven quality of available data. Even crude statistical estimates of the number of Negro Catholics by, for example, 1865 are difficult to find. The best guesses would seem to be the following: in Maryland, around 16,000; in Louisiana, no more than 63,000; in the entire United States, probably no more than 100,000. Given the postwar upheaval in the South, it seems likely that the number of Negro Catholics was no more than 100,000 for several decades after the war.[4]

In any case, the first fairly comprehensive census of Negro Catholics was not undertaken until 1928, and was followed by a comparable survey in 1939. As reported by Gillard, the 1928 diocesan survey counted just over 200,000 black Catholics. Given a baseline of perhaps 100,000 in the 1860's, the growth in number of black Catholics appears slow if intriguing. However by the 1939 diocesan census, the reported number of black Catholics had grown to 297,000, signaling a dramatic 50 percent gain in just over a decade.[5] It may be, however, that a portion of this increase can be attributed to more careful diocesan reports. Even more interesting is the redistribution trend evident from a comparison of the reported state statistics for 1928 and 1939. From numerous demographic studies we know that Negroes have migrated northward and westward in large numbers since World War I. Negro Catholics have also participated in this migration. According to the census reports for 1928 about three quarters of all Negro Catholics resided in Southern and border states; by 1939 the figure had dropped to 69 percent (with a larger proportion of this figure residing in the border states in 1939 than in 1928). In this same eleven-year period the proportion of Negro Catholics in Northern and Midwestern dioceses went up from 22 percent to 29 percent, while the proportion in the West hovered around 2 percent. To put it another way, by 1939 nearly half of the enumerated black Catholics in the United States, about 145,000 of them, resided outside the Deep South.[6]

Have these trends continued since 1939? Unfortunately no comprehensive national census of Negro Catholics has recently been undertaken; the best available data are the crude estimates published annually by the Commission for Catholic Missions among the Colored People and the Indians. The data for the years 1947, 1957, and 1967, summarized in Tables 1-3, were supplied to that Commission by Ordinaries receiving funds from the Commission, supplemented with data from pastors in other diocesan parishes with Negro communicants.[7] Principal areas of Negro population are represented in each of the annual Commission reports selected. However the reports do not include about half of the dioceses; most of these fall into the categories of less urban dioceses in the West or Midwest or dioceses with relatively small Negro Catholic populations. For example, most of the dioceses omitted in the 1947 report counted few Negro Catholics in the more comprehensive 1939 census. Yet these facts also suggest that the reported figures for 1947 can be construed as minimum estimates of the numbers of Negro Catholics in the various regions. Some variation in the size of the dioceses reporting occurs between 1947 and 1967 because of the splintering off of new dioceses from old ones. Since some of the newly erected dioceses, generally non-southern and less important dioceses, are apparently not included in the 1957 and 1967 reports, the reported figures for those years probably further underestimate somewhat the numbers of Negro Catholics, particularly in nonsouth areas. The usual cautions about religious statistics are certainly applicable to these data, particularly the definitional caution (Catholic figures include baptized infants), the caution that some diocesan figures are estimates not head counts, and the caution that at best only tentative conclusions should be drawn from such crude estimates.[8] Only a careful national survey could conclusively answer the questions raised here; however, in the absence of such a conclusive survey, it is of some heuristic value to examine the existing data and to suggest working hypotheses for further research.

The reported data for the years 1947, 1957, and 1967 (Table 1) suggest a continuation of the trends indicated by the 1928 and 1939 surveys, an increasing Negro Catholic population and a continuing shift in the distribution of that population to the North, Midwest, and the West over the last two decades. The reported number of Negro Catholics increased from 202,886 to 343,667 between 1928 and 1947; from 343,667 to 808,332 in 1967. Thus the number

TABLE 1

Negro Catholics by Region, 1947, 1957, 1967

Region	1947		1957		1967	
	n	Percent	n	Percent	n	Percent
Southern states	160,758	(46.8)	236,146	(41.0)	275,366	(34.1)
Border states (and D.C.)	58,892	(17.1)	106,606	(18.5)	135,185	(16.7)
Northern states	70,121	(20.4)	122,835	(21.3)	160,232	(19.8)
Midwestern states	42,121	(12.3)	76,039	(13.2)	152,868	(18.9)
Western states	11,775	(3.4)	34,299	(6.0)	84,681	(10.5)
Totals	343,667	(100.0)	575,925	(100.0)	808,332	(100.0)

Source: Commission for the Catholic Missions among the Colored People and the Indians, Annual Reports, *1948, 1958, 1968. By permission.*

of black Catholics appears to have grown systematically, although Catholics are still a relatively small percentage of the Negro population.[9] Moreover the proportion of the black Catholics in the states of the Old Confederacy went down systematically from 61 percent in 1928 to 34 percent in 1967, while the proportion outside the southern *and* border states increased from one quarter in 1928 to about one-half in 1967.[10] The impact of this redistribution, in part a reflection of migration patterns, can be seen in Southern diocesan reports to the Commission which (defensively) attribute their slow growth to their providing other sections of the country with "well educated, refined, and highly spiritual Negro Catholics."[11] It is also seen in the closing of fourteen Negro schools and seventeen churches for Negroes in the South in 1967.[12]

Paralleling these 1947 to 1967 increases in population are the reported increases in the number of churches specifically designated for Negroes (395 to 568) and of schools specifically established for Negroes (292 to 347), a majority of which are still located in the South.

The dramatic character of recent increases in the numbers of Negro Catholics can be illustrated by comparing the Negro growth rate with that of the general Catholic population (Table 2). The number of Negro Catholics seems

TABLE 2

Catholic and Negro Catholic Population Increase

Year	Negro Catholic Population[a]		Roman Catholic Population (all Ethnic Groups)[b]	
	Number	Percent Increase	Number	Percent Increase
1967	808,332	40	47,468,333	32
1957	575,925	68	36,023,977	38
1947	343,667		26,075,697	

Sources: [a]*Commission for Catholic Mission among the Colored People and the Indians,* *Annual Reports, 1948, 1958, 1968. By permission.*
[b]The Official Catholic Directory *(New York: P. J. Kenedy & Sons), 1950,* *1958, 1968 editions. By permission.*

to be growing at a faster rate than the number of all Catholics. Between 1947 and 1957 the reported Negro Catholic population jumped 68 percent, while the reported total Catholic population increased 38 percent. Although both growth rates appear to have decreased somewhat between 1957 and 1967, the Negro Catholic percentage increase was greater than the total Catholic increase. Dramatic growth seems evident from the available data. The number of Negro Catholics also seems to be growing at a faster rate than the total Negro population, a population which has been increasing 20-25 percent in each of the last few decades. However caution dictates that firm conclusions on these important issues must await a careful national survey.

Why the dramatic growth? Data in Table 23-3 point up one possible explanation. The figures in the last column of the table, based on reported data in the *Official Catholic Directory,* indicate that the portion of the Catholic population increase due to (adult) conversions has hovered around 10 percent per year over the last few decades. The comparable "conversion" percentage for Negro Catholics has declined somewhat since 1947, but still seems to be substantially higher than the total Catholic figure (33 percent vs. 9 percent). Such data point up the importance of adult conversions in the growing population. If the figures are even roughly accurate, approximately one Catholic convert in eight was a Negro in 1967, compared to one in fourteen twenty years ago.

TABLE 3

Catholic and Negro Catholic Baptisms and Conversions

Year	Negro Baptisms[a]			All Catholic Baptisms
	Infant	Adult	Percent Adult Conversions	Percent Adult Conversions[b]
1967	27,647	13,719	33.2	8.9
1957	21,519	11,374	35.0	9.9
1947	12,040	7,944	39.9	11.4

Sources: [a]*Commission for Catholic Missions among the Colored People and the Indians, Annual Reports, 1948, 1958, 1968. The numbers of Negro baptisms are minimum estimates (see note 8). By permission.*
[b]Official Catholic Directory *(New York: P. J. Kenedy & Sons), 1950, 1958, 1968 editions. By permission.*

Discussion and Conclusion: Some Working Hypotheses

In preparation for a future interview study of Negro Catholics I have combed the literature for the available statistical data presented above and for hints as to the reasons Negroes are being converted to Catholicism in increasing numbers, particularly in areas outside the traditional Catholic areas of Louisiana and Maryland.

An official Catholic explanation emphasizes the "devoted care" of pastors and their missionary "zeal in extending the Kingdom of God on earth."[13] Yet, if one grants this increased proselytizing, it is still necessary to answer other questions: Why do Negroes become Catholics? Given a near-unanimous adherence to Protestantism and an historical antagonism to the Church, why the new interest?

Several possible explanations for the attractiveness of the Church seem relevant. Two such explanations are related to the general upgrading of the Negro community and are most relevant to explaining the apparently growing number of middle-class Negroes who are joining the Church. One explanation would be that some Negroes with lower-class backgrounds, as they rise up the status ladder, feel less comfortable in lower-class Protestant churches than they did formerly. Frazier has argued that status pressures send some middle-class Negroes to Episcopalian and Presbyterian churches, or at least to more staid, higher-status Baptist and Methodist churches.[14] The Catholic Church may well provide some middle-class Negroes with an escape route from social ties with their lower-class brethren, with perhaps the first link to the Church being established through a parochial school to which they send their children.[15]

Correlated with social mobility would also be what one might term changes in religious "styles of life." Some upwardly mobile Negroes may be turning to the Catholic Church because of the services, with their emphasis on traditional ritual; such services contrast greatly with the highly emotional, less ritualistic and more social, services of many lower-class Baptist, Methodist, and Pentecostal churches. Catholic views tend to stress that the religion of Negro Protestant churches is actually "sham religion" or a kind of "refined paganism."[16] The Catholic viewpoint emphasizes its low spiritual and moral character and high "social" content. Dissatisfaction with Protestant Negro churches on these same grounds—particularly among middle-class Negroes—may well send some Negroes to the Catholic Church.

For several decades now the Catholic Church has built new schools for Negroes, North and South, and has in some cities allowed non-Catholic Negroes to send their children to regular parochial schools. Thus another plausible explanation for the increase in Negro converts may lie in the sideeffects of Catholic encouragement of non-Catholic Negroes to send their children to parochial schools. Some non-Catholic Negro parents apparently feel their children can get a better education in Catholic schools; pupil enrollments give priests a chance to enroll parents in courses on Catholic religion and morality. In some cases such enrollment is required. Reportedly such parental classes, together with other instruction calsses for Negroes, multiply converts.[17]

Yet another reason for renewed Negro interest in the Catholic Church seems to have arisen out of the civil rights struggles, especially in the last few decades. For a long time virtually the only place where Southern Negroes could attend white churches was in the Catholic parishes in southern Louisiana, as Gunnar Myrdal noted in *An American Dilemma,* although the Church at that time preferred "to have Negroes attend all-Negro churches."[18] Since the 1940's the Catholic Church in the South has often been in the vanguard in attempting to desegregate schools and colleges. Whether or not the Catholic

Church has in fact been more helpful than Protestant churches in the Negro rights cause is debatable, but the fact that Negroes perceive it this way is not. A 1966 Harris poll of Negroes revealed that a larger proportion rated Catholic priests as more helpful than harmful to the Negro rights cause (53 percent) than rated white churches, probably understood as white Protestant churches, as helpful to the cause (30 percent).[19] In the poll, ratings of Catholic priests were even more laudatory among Negroes in Northern and Western urban areas. It is these very areas that have recently seen aggressive Catholic attempts to deal with inner-city problems; and dioceses encompassing many of these urban areas also lead the list in numbers of Negro converts.[20]

Summary and Conclusion

This [essay] has presented some admittedly limited statistical evidence of an increase in the number of Negro Catholics, an increase apparently due in part to adult conversions. If the reported figures are roughly correct, Negro converts now are overrepresented among converts to Catholicism. Four possible explanations have been suggested for this phenomenon. Doubtless these explanations are not mutually exclusive; they are only presented as working hypotheses worthy of further study. If these hypotheses are substantiated by subsequent research, one might well conclude that the educational, status, ritual, and civil rights attractiveness of the American Church is a potent factor in the conversion of Negroes to the faith.

One firm conclusion that can be drawn from the available data is that a carefully conducted nationwide census of white and black Catholics, their locations and characteristics, is a necessity if we are to develop a more sophisticated understanding of the phenomena discussed [here].

NOTES

1. This historical analysis has been taken from the following sources: John T. Gillard, *Colored Catholics in the United States* (Baltimore, 1941), pp. 39-85; W. E. B. Du Bois, *Black Reconstruction* (Philadelphia, 1935), pp. 17 ff.; W. D. Weatherford, *American Churches and the Negro* (Boston, 1957), pp. 223-267.

2. See Gillard, p. 47.

3. *Ibid.*, p. 87. See C. G. Woodson, *The Education of the Negro Prior to 1861* (Washington, 1919), p. 108 *passim*.

4. Gillard, pp. 89-99.

5. *Ibid.*, p. 30. Lack of space prohibits a discussion of the smaller numbers of Negro Catholics counted in 1916-1936 Bureau of the Census surveys. Given that these surveys counted Negro Catholics only in all-Negro churches (approximately one third are in

mixed churches), Gillard's argument that they severely underestimate the number of Negro Catholics is persuasive. See *Ibid.*, pp. 107 ff.

6. *Ibid.* The years indicated are those to which the statistics are strictly relevant, insofar as this can be determined from the sources.

7. I am indebted to the Secretary of the Commission for Catholic Missions among the Colored People and the Indians for making these data available to me.

8. It should also be noted that a few parishes with Negroes did not submit reports and that in some cases the diocesan estimates apparently do not include Negroes in predominantly white churches.

9. A 1957 Census survey report, unfortunately not distinguishing between Negroes and other nonwhites, indicated that nearly 80 percent of nonwhites are affiliated with Baptist and Methodist churches, compared to substantially smaller proportions of whites. Nearly nine nonwhites in ten were Protestants compared to two in three among the general population. U.S. Bureau of the Census, *Current Population Reports,* series P-20, no. 79, 1958.

10. Data for intervening years generally bear out these patterns. 1928 percentages are based on a larger number of dioceses (reporting).

11. *Annual Report of the Secretary of the Commission for the Catholic Missions Among the Colored People and the Indians,* January 1968, p. 7.

12. *Ibid.*, p. 5.

13. *Ibid.*, p. 5. Similar comments can be found in reports of the 1940's and 1950's.

14. "Their ambiguous position in American society together with their recent rise to middle-class status are reflected in the religious behavior and attitudes of middle-class Negroes." (E. F. Frazier, *The Negro Church in America* [Liverpool, 1964], p. 79.)

15. Frazier makes a somewhat similar suggestion. (*Ibid.*, p. 80.)

16. "Winning Negro Converts," in J. A. O'Brien, ed., *Winning Converts,* rev. ed. (Notre Dame, Ind., 1957), pp. 116-129; Gillard. Fichter has observed that Catholic churches are more like large secondary associations than are typical Protestant churches. (J. H. Fichter, "American Religion and the Negro" in T. Parsons and K. Clark eds., *The Negro American,* (Boston, 1965), p. 408.

17. See *Annual Report,* p. 17; "Winning Negro Converts," p. 119.

18. Gunnar Myrdal, *An American Dilemma* (New York, 1964), 2: 870-871.

19. W. Brink and L. Harris, *Black and White* (New York, 1966-1967), pp. 234-242.

20. *Annual Report,* January, pp. 15-20.

PART IV

Black Ministers and Black Power

23

THE NEGRO CHURCH: ITS WEAKNESS, TRENDS, AND OUTLOOK

GUNNAR MYRDAL

The following selection from Gunnar Myrdal's *An American Dilemma*, in this case based heavily on a manuscript specifically prepared for the study by Guion G. Johnson and Guy B. Johnson, presents a particularly gloomy assessment of the outlook for the Negro church. Despite its potential as an instrument of power, it seemed to be following trends in the community instead of setting them as its ministry steadily declined in relative status within the Negro community. And yet, itself the product of the caste system, the Negro church is at base the black community's own and should reflect its changing concerns. How accurate were these predictions and assessments, now thirty years old? In the succeeding selections current analysts of the black ministry, the protest movements and black power (the majority of whom are themselves black) indicate some answers to these questions and pose new dilemmas as well.

Its Weakness

The Negro church is the oldest and—in membership—by far the strongest of all Negro organizations. Like the lodges, burial societies, and the great number of social clubs, the Negro church by its very existence involves a certain power consolidation. Meetings of the church officials in a denomination and church papers—read at least by most of the ministers—provide for an ideological cohesion, not only in religious matters but, to an extent, also in the common race interests. It also has some significance when, for instance, it is pointed out

Reprinted from *An American Dilemma* (New York: Harper & Row, 1944), pp. 872-878, by permission of the publisher. Copyright 1944, 1962 by Harper & Row, Publishers, Inc.

about Mr. Mordecai Johnson, the president of Howard University, that he is a
Baptist minister and has the backing of the Negro Baptist world.

Potentially, the Negro church is undoubtedly a power institution. It has the
Negro masses organized and, if the church bodies decided to do so, they could
line up the Negroes behind a program. Actually, the Negro church is, on the
whole, passive in the field of intercaste power relations. It generally provides
meeting halls and encourages church members to attend when other organizations want to influence the Negroes. But viewed as an instrument of collective
action to improve the Negroes' position in American society, the church has
been relatively inefficient and uninfluential. In the South it has not taken a
lead in attacking the caste system or even in bringing about minor reforms; in
the North it has only occasionally been a strong force for social action.

This might be deemed deplorable, but it should not be surprising. Christian
churches generally have, for the most part, conformed to the power situation
of the time and the locality. They have favored a passive acceptance of one's
worldly condition and, indeed, have seen their main function in providing
escape and consolation to the sufferers. If there is any relation at all between
the interest of a Negro church in social issues and the social status of its membership, the relation is that a church tends to be the more otherworldly the poorer
its members are and the more they are in need of concerted efforts to improve
their lot in this life. The churches where the poor white people in the South
worship are similar to the common Negro churches.[1]

Even in this respect the Negro church is an ordinary American church with
certain traits exaggerated because of caste. Of 100 sermons delivered in urban
Negro churches and analyzed by Mays and Nicholson, only twenty six touched
upon practical problems.[2] The rural Negro church makes an even poorer showing in this respect.[3] Too, the Negro church is out of touch with current social
life in the field of morals; the preaching of traditional puritanical morals has
little effect on the bulk of the Negro population, and the real moral problems
of the people are seldom considered in the church.

Practically all Negro leaders have criticized the Negro church on these points.
Booker T. Washington, for example, said:

From the nature of things, all through slavery it was life in the future world
that was emphasized in religious teaching rather than life in this world. In his
religious meetings in *ante-bellum* days the Negro was prevented from discussing
many points of practical religion which related to this world; and the white
minister, who was his spiritual guide, found it more convenient to talk about
heaven than earth, so very naturally that today in his religious meeting it is the
Negro's feelings which are worked upon mostly, and it is description of the
glories of heaven that occupy most of the time of his sermon.[4]

Ignorance, poverty, cultural isolation, and the tradition of dependence are responsible for this situation, in the same way as they are factors keeping Negroes down in other areas of life.

The frequent schisms in Negro churches weaken their institutional strength. New Negro churches and sects seldom begin because of theological divergences, but rather because a preacher wants to get a congregation,[5] because some members of a church feel that the minister is too emotional or not emotional enough, because some members feel that they have little in common with other members of the church, as well as because of outside missionary influences and division.[6] The competition between the preachers is intense and, as we said, most churches are small. There is little collaboration between the churches. Overhead expenses tend to be relatively high in the small church establishments.[7] Since, in addition, the membership of the churches is composed usually of poor people, the economic basis of most churches is precariously weak.[8]

Poverty often makes the Negro church dependent upon white benefactors. It also prevents paying such salaries[9] that ambitious young men could be tempted to educate themselves properly for the ministry.[10] In fact the idea that a preacher should have education for his task is still usually lacking, and the average preacher has not much more of it than do the members of his flock.[11] The chief prerequisite for becoming a minister in most of the denominations to which Negroes belong is traditionally not education, but a "call" which is more often the manifestation of temporary hysteria or opportunistic self-inspiration than of a deep soul-searching. There are many exceptions, of course, and they are becoming somewhat more frequent, but the preachers who come to their profession through a "call" are still numerically significant. Such preachers tend to retain the emotionalism that has traditionally been identified with the Negro's religion.

The ministry was once the chief outlet for Negro ambition. Under slavery, as we have noted, the preacher stood out as the leader and spokesman for his group. After slavery his monopoly of status in the Negro community diminished as business and professional men increased in number.[12] Increasingly status within the Negro caste is being based on education. Since there is little in the way of special attention paid to the Negro minister's education—except for a minority, practically all in the cities—he is rapidly falling in relative status. Upper- and middle-class Negroes deprecate the common uneducated Negro preacher. Initiative and leadership in matters concerning the Negro community tend to pass to this new upper class of Negro businessmen and professionals. Meanwhile, taking up preaching is still one of the few possibilities of rising for the individual without a professional training.

As a class Negro preachers are losing influence, because they are not changing as fast as the rest of the Negro community. This is now on the verge of becoming a most serious problem, endangering the future of the Negro church. As improvements in education have been rapid in the last decades, the bulk of the old Negro preachers are today below the bulk of younger generation Negroes in education. Young people have begun to look down on the old-fashioned Negro preacher.[13] Lately the problem seems to have become as serious in rural areas as in cities. It is true that city youths are better educated and more sophisticated, but so also are city ministers who occasionally make some attempt to adjust to the needs of youth.[14]

It is difficult to see how the continuing decline of the minister's prestige and leadership can be stopped. Few college students are going into the ministry.[15] The ministry is no longer a profession which attracts the brightest and most ambitious young Negroes.[16] The development under way will take a long time to manifest its complete effects. But it goes on and will spell the further decline of the Negro church as an active influence in the Negro community, if it does not begin to reform itself radically.

Trends and Outlook

The Negro church has been lagging ideologically, too. While for a long time the protest has been rising in the Negro community, the church has, on the whole, remained conservative and accommodating. Its traditions from slavery help to explain this. Its otherworldly outlook is itself an expression of political fatalism. In a city in the Deep South with a Negro population of 43,000 (Savannah), there are 90 Negro churches, 100 active preachers and another 100 "jack legs"; here where the Negro ministry with few exceptions had been discouraging a recent movement to get the Negroes registered for voting, a Negro preacher explained:

"All we preachers is supposed to do is to preach the Lord and Saviour Jesus Christ and Him Crucified, and that's all."[17]

In most Negro communities visited by the present writer the progressive Negro leaders, trying to organize the Negro community for defense, complained about the timidity and disinterest on the part of the preachers. "They talk too much about heaven and too little about down here." Regularly the explanation was given that the churches were mortgaged to influential white people and that the preacher got small handouts from employers and politicians. Without doubt the preacher's old position of the white man's trusted Negro "leader" secures small advantages not only to himself but also to his group . . . it does give him prestige in the Negro community. But as the Negro protest rises, the traditional Negro preacher alienates a growing section of the Negroes from the church.

Care must be taken, however, not to overstate the criticism against the Negro church on this point. In both the North and the South one quite often meets Negro preachers who are active in the work for protest and betterment. Progressive ministers are still exceptions, but their existence might signify a trend. There seems to be less animosity against labor unions among Negro preachers—reflecting the increase in power of the union . . . As the Negro pro test is rising, the preacher finds generally that he has to change his appeal to keep his congregation in line.

When discussing the Negro church as it is and as it might come to be, it must never be forgotten that *the Negro church fundamentally is an expression of the Negro community itself.* If the church has been otherworldly in outlook and indulged in emotional ecstasy, it is primarily because the downtrodden common Negroes have craved religious escape from poverty and other tribulations. If the preachers have been timid and pussyfooting, it is because Negroes in general have condoned such a policy and would have feared radical leaders. The rivalry and factionalism, the organizational weakness and economic dependance of the Negro church, the often faltering economic and sexual morals of the preachers and their suspicion of higher education—all this reflects life as it is lived in the subordinate caste of American Negroes.

When the Negro community changes, the church also will change. It is true that the church has not given much of a lead to reforms but has rather lagged when viewed from the advanced positions of Negro youth and Negro intellectuals. But few Christian churches have ever been, whether in America or elsewhere, the spearheads of reform. That this fundamental truth is understood— underneath all bitter criticism—is seen in the fact that Negro intellectuals are much more willing to cooperate with Negro churches than white intellectuals with white churches.[18] The Negro protest and improvement organizations cooperate with all "respectable" Negro churches. The solidarity behind the abstract church institution in the Negro community is simply amazing. The visitor finds everywhere a widespread criticism, but this is focused mainly on the preachers. Few question the church as such, its benevolent influence and its great potentialities.

The Negro church is part of the whole circular process which is moving the American Negroes onward in their struggle against caste. The increasing education of the Negro masses is either making them demand something more of their church than praise of the otherworld and emotional catharsis, or causing

them to stand aloof from the institutionalized forms of religion. Not only the
upper classes of Negroes are now critical of the shouting and noisy religious
hysteria in old-time Negro churches and new cults, but so are young people in
all classes. The issue of emotionalism is still a keen divider but the dividing
line now cuts deeper into the Negro community. In many Negro communities
perhaps the majority still cling to the old patterns and resent persons—including ministers—who will not participate with them in the display of intense
religious feeling. But, according to Mays and Nicholson, even in the rural
South the revival meetings are less successful than they used to be, the professional evangelist is beginning to disappear, and the regular sermons attempt
to be more thought-provoking.[19]

This is all part of the general process of acculturation. With considerable
lag, the Negro clergymen, too, are acquiring a better education, which is reflected in their work. Negro preachers are increasingly in competition with
professionals, businessmen, politicians, and labor union officials for local
leadership. Competition is compelling them to try to do something positive
for the Negro community. The social work programs of the relatively few
churches which have them are mainly a development of the last decade or two,
and we expect to see the trend continuing, expecially in the North. The movement to the North and to the Southern cities also tends to emanicipate the
Negro preacher from white pressure. The fact that he gets more of his prestige
from Negroes than from whites in the North is beneficial to the Negro community. These trends are making the Negro church a more efficient instrument for amelioration of the Negro's position at the same time as they are
reducing the relative importance of the church in the Negro community.

NOTES

1. "The Churches have either had nothing to say on the subjects of low wages and long
hours in the mills, or have distracted attention from economic wrongs by stressing the
calamities of individual sinfulness." (Broadus Mitchell and George S. Mitchell, *The Industrial Revolution in the South* [Baltimore, 1930], p. 144.)
2. Fifty-four others were classified as dealing with "otherworldly" topics, and the
remaining 20 were doctrinal or theological (Benjamin E. Mays and Joseph W. Nicholson,
The Negro's Church [New York: Institute of Social and Religious Research, 1933], pp.
59 and 70). Mays and Nicholson also reported, as have other students of the Negro
Church, that the sermons were characterized by poor logic, poor grammar and pronunci-
ation, and an excessive display of oratorical tricks.
3. Not only the sermons, but practically all the prayers, spirituals, and Church
school literature of the three major Negro denominations support traditional, compensatory patterns, according to Mays. (Benjamin E. Mays, *The Negro's God* [Boston, 1938],
p. 245.) Mays describes these patterns thus: "Though recognizing notable exceptions,
they are compensatory and traditional in character because they are neither developed
nor interpreted in terms of social rehabilitation. They are conducive to developing in the
Negro a complacent, laissez-faire attitude toward life. They support the view that God in

His good time and in His own way will bring about the conditions that will lead to the fulfillment of social needs. They encourage Negroes to feel that God will see to it that things work out all right; if not in this world, certainly in the world to come. They make God influential chiefly in the beyond, in preparing a home for the faithful—a home where His suffering servants will be free of the trials and tribulations which beset them on the earth." (*Ibid.*)

4. Booker T. Washington, *The Future of the American Negro* (Boston, 1899), p. 170.

5. There are plenty of Negro preachers. In 1930, Negroes constituted 9.7 percent of the population, but about 16.8 percent of all clergymen. The actual figure is probably higher than this, since some Negro preachers have other occupations, and the latter may be the ones reported to the census-taker. (*Fifteenth Census of the United States: 1930, Population,* 4: 32-33.) Many of these preachers—the so-called "jack leg" preachers—have no congregation.

6. See Mays and Nicholson, pp. 10 *et passim.*

7. On the basis of their sample study of 185 rural Negro churches and 609 urban Negro churches in 1930, Mays and Nicholson (pp. 171 and 261) report the following percentage distribution of church expenditures:

	185 Rural Churches	609 Urban Churches
Salaries	69.9	43.2
Interest and reduction of church debt	2.0	22.9
Benevolence and miscellaneous items (including insurance, rent, heat, light)	15.8	21.0
Education, missions, etc.	5.9	6.6
Repairs and upkeep	6.4	6.3
	100.0	100.0

Of the urban churches, 71.3 percent reported that their buildings were under a mortgage.

8. Negro churches usually have poor business practices. There is little secretarial help, thus there is poor accounting, and the money is sometimes just given to the minister or to a few church officers to do what they please with it. There is probably a significant amount of misappropriation of funds under this system. (See Mays and Nicholson, pp. 168-197 and 259-265, and Hortense Powdermaker, *After Freedom* [New York, 1939], p. 238.)

9. Mays and Nicholson (p. 189) reported from their 1930 sample study that 69.4 percent of Negro ministers had an annual income of less than $2,000. The average rural preacher got only $266 per church per year, but often he served several churches or had some other outside source of income.

10. According to a sample study by Woodson, "only seven-tenths of one percent of Negro high school graduates contemplate taking up the ministry, and many of those who have known to qualify themselves thus do not stay in the ministry." (Carter G. Woodson, *The Negro Professional Men and the Community* [Washington D.C., 1934], p 70)

Mays reports that there were 253 fewer students enrolled in Negro seminaries in 1939 than in 1924. Including 92 Negro students in Northern white seminaries, there were only 850 Negroes enrolled in all seminaries in 1939, and only 254 of those were college graduates. (Benjamin E. Mays, "The Negro Church in American Life," *Christendom* [Summer 1940]: 389-391.)

	Negro	White
Urban	38	80
Rural	17	47

(C. Luther Fry, *The United States Looks at Its Churches* [New York, 1930], pp. 64-66.) These figures are inflated by exaggeration in reporting and by overlooking some of the smaller churches. Mays and Nicholson(p. 302) questioned 590 urban Negro ministers and found that only 27.7 percent claimed to have graduated from college or seminary. They also reported (p. 238) that 57.5 percent of 134 rural Negro ministers had only a grammar school education or less.

In a study of 1,200 Negro ministers, Woodson found that 70 percent had no college degree. He also found that those with a degree—either in theology or in liberal arts, or both—were mostly from unaccredited colleges. (Woodson, p. 64.) When we speak of the college-trained Negro clergymen, we must keep in mind that the standards of their colleges and seminaries in the South are pitifully poor in most cases.

12. In 1930, clergymen still constituted 18.4 percent of all professionals among Negroes and only 3.4 percent among native whites. (*Fifteenth Census*, 4: 32-33.)

13. Allison Davis, "The Negro Church and Associations in the Lower South," unpublished manuscript prepared for this study (1940), pp. 120-125. Also see Willis D. Weatherford and Charles S. Johnson, *Race Relations* (New York, 1934), p. 497; and the recent studies of The American Youth Commission, expecially E. Franklin Frazier, *Negro Youth at the Crossways* (Washington, D.C., 1940), p. 133.

14. Charles S. Johnson supports, and has some evidence to prove, the position that rural Negro youth are more dissatisfied with the church than urban Negro youth. (*Growing Up in the Black Belt* [Washington, D.C., 1941] pp. 145-164.)

15. We may cite again Woodson's finding that only one percent of a sample of high school graduates expressed the intention of entering the ministry. (Carter G. Woodson, *The Negro Professional Man and the Community* [Washington, D.C., 1934].

16. In the last decade or so, there have been summer institutes established for Negro ministers—such as the one sponsored by the white Southern Methodist Episcopal Church—but relatively few Negroes participate, and even the education thus offered is completely inadequate for lack of time and money.

17. Ralph J. Bunche, "A Brief and Tentative Analysis of Negro Leadership," unpublished manuscript prepared for this study, 1940, pp. 79-80

Sterner and I once attended a Sunday evening service in a Negro Baptist church in one of the capitals of the upper South. The preacher developed the theme that nothing in this world was of any great importance: real estate, automobiles, fine clothes, learnedness, prestige, money, all this is nothing. It is not worth striving for. But an humble, peaceful heart will be remunerated in heaven. After the service we went up to the preacher for a talk. We asked him if he should not instead try to instil more worldly ambition in his poor and disadvantaged group. The preacher began to explain to us, as foreigners, that this would not do at all in the South. The role of the Negro church, he told us, was to make the poor Negroes satisfied with their lowly status. He finished by explaining: "We are the policemen of the Negroes. If we did not keep down their ambitions and divert them into religion, there would be upheaval in the South." This preacher is not typical in his philosophy of extreme accommodation or in his intellectual clarity. But it is significant that he exists.

18. On the basis of a sample study of 5,512 Negro college graduates, who were not quite representative of the total population of Negro college graduates, Charles S. Johnson, (*The Negro College Graduate* [Chapel Hill, 1938], p. 347) reports the following percentage distribution suggesting the degree of adherence to the church on the part of this group:

Not a member	5.3
Inactive member	15.1
Active member	48.1
Officer	12.5
Preacher	3.1
Not given	15.9
	100.0

19. Mays and Nicholson, pp. 102 and 139.

24

THE NEGRO MINISTRY IN PHILADELPHIA

W. E. BURGHARDT DU BOIS

THE NEGRO MINISTRY IN THE MIDDLE WEST

MONROE N. WORK and W. E. BURGHARDT DU BOIS

The following selections from the work of W. E. Burghardt Du Bois and Monroe Work indicate that perceptions of the "decline" of the Negro church and criticism of its inadequacies has a long and distinguished history. The ministers pictured here are all too often astute businessmen who nevertheless conspicuously lack those qualities that would turn them into spiritual, civic, and moral leaders of the black community. Even at this point, however, the authors are hopeful that the church might come to exist *for* the people, instead of the other way around.

The Negro Ministry in Philadelphia

The learned professions are represented among Negroes by clergymen, teachers, physicians, lawyers, and dentists, in the order named. Practically all Negroes go to their own churches, where they have, save in a very few cases, clergymen of their own race. There are not less than sixty Negro ministers in the city (possibly 100) mostly Methodists and Baptists, with three or four Presbyterians and two Episcopalians. The Presbyterian and Episcopalian clergymen are well trained and educated men in nearly every case. The ministers of the African Methodists vary; those in charge of the larger churches are all men of striking personality, with genius for leadership and organization in some lines, and in

Reprinted from *The Philadelphia Negro* (Philadelphia: Published for the University of Pennsylvania, 1899), pp. 110, 112. Reprinted from *The Negro Church*, ed. W. E. B. Du Bois (Atlanta: Atlanta University Press, 1903), pp. 83-85.

some cases, though not in all, they are well-educated men. Practically none of them are illiterate. The Baptist ministers are not on the whole so well trained as the Methodists, although some are well educated.

Taken on the average the Negro ministers of the city are good representatives of the masses of the Negroes. They are largely chosen by the masses, must cater to their tastes, and must in every way be men whom the rank and file of the race like and understand. Sometimes a strong personality, like the late Theodore Miller, will take a church and lift it to a high level; usually the minister rather follows than leads, and indicates public opinion among his people rather than forms it. The Baptist minister is the elected chairman of a pure democracy, who, if he can command a large enough following, becomes a virtual dictator; he thus has the chance to be a wise leader or a demagogue, or, as in many cases, a little of both. The Methodist minister is the appointed steward of a large corporation, of which his particular church is a small part. His success depends upon the way in which he conducts this church: his financial success, his efforts to increase church membership, and his personal popularity. The result is that the colored Methodist minister is generally a wide-awake businessman, with something of the politician in his makeup, who is sometimes an inspiring and valuable leader of men; in other cases he may develop into a loud but wily talker, who induces the mass of Negroes to put into fine church edifices money which ought to go to charity or business enterprise.

The Negro Ministry in the Middle West

There are approximately about 250 Negro churches in [Illinois] with a total membership of 15,177. The Negro population of the state was 85,078 for 1900. This gives about 22.5 percent. of Negro population of the state as members of the church. There is a large number of persons who have moved into the state that in their native homes were members of churches. These would raise the actual number of church communicants considerably, for they commune, etc., and to all intents and purposes are members of the churches where they happen to reside. These would in a census be returned as members and counted in the state where residing.

By denominations the membership is as follows: African Methodist Episcopal, 8,375; Baptist, 8,812; African Methodist Episcopal Zion, 100; Methodist Episcopal, 360; Old Time Methodist Episcopal, 100; Episcopal, 380; Presbyterian, 210; Cumberland Presbyterian, 65; Christian, 50; Catholics (not ascertained),—Adventists (estimated), 25. The total amount of church property owned in the state was about $445,000. The total expenses for 1902 were about $133,000. Of this amount about $70,000 was for pastors' salaries and about $20,000 on church debt.

The following conclusions are based on my own observations and the replies to questions sent out:

The Negro church, as a result of slavery, emphasized the emotional side of mentality and the future life. Freedom, with its changed environments and opportunities, has modified these two aspects. It is found in the study of churches of this state, that there is a decided tendency away from the emotional and the emphasizing of the future life. This is especially noticeable in both Baptist and Methodist churches, which contain the bulk of the Negro communicants. In the churches of these denominations in the city of Chicago there are only a few where the emphasis is on the emotional and the future life. There are some churches where the emphasis is placed sometimes on the emotional, the future life, and sometimes on the intellectual and this present life. There is a large number of churches in which the emphasis is almost entirely on the intellectual and the things of this life. It may be said, therefore, that in general the further the people have moved from slavery conditions the less emotional and unpractical they are religiously; the more effort there is to make religion a rule of conduct for everyday life.

Historically the Negro ministry has had three distinct stages of development and appears to be passing into a fourth stage. The minister of slavery days and early freedom, for the most part ignorant, was the leader of the people along all lines—religiously, intellectually, politically, etc. The emancipated Negro had few or no church buildings. This, with the additional fact of a large emigration to the cities, caused a demand for ministers who could build large church buildings and control large congregations. The church-building, congregation-managing minister was the result. It was not necessary that he should be intellectual or morally upright if he could meet with the demands, hence the development of this type of ministry. The need of church buildings was largely met, but almost every church had a debt upon it. There arose a demand for ministers who could raise money to pay these debts and keep the church doors from being closed. This, the third type, has more business ability than his predecessors. He is stronger intellectually and better morally. There is arising a demand for still another type of ministry, viz., the man strong intellectually and sound morally. This demand is, as yet, not very strong, mainly because there are not many churches out of debt, and the energies of the people are laregly expended in raising money to pay on church debts. It is more than probable that as the people progress in intelligence and the churches are freed from debt, thus permitting them to pay more attention to internal aspects of religion, the intellectual and moral man will become more and more the leader in the churches.

The above is not intended as a full or adequate explanation of the churches in Illinois, especially in Chicago, but rather as one of the main causes in producing the present conditions of the churches in this state.

The present conditons of the churches seems to be about as follows: they are for the most part deeply in debt. Hence the energies of the people are expended in raising money to pay interest, etc., of debt, thereby causing the emphasis to be laid on the incidentals instead of upon the essentials of the religious life. The people live for the church instead of the church existing for the people. There is not as much attention given to teaching the essentials of religion as should be, but the tendency seems to be more toward this phase as the churches are freed from debt. This is best illustrated by the institution of pastors having for their purpose the ministering to the social needs of the people. The Institutional Church, established in Chicago by the African Methodist Episcopal denomination, is the most advanced step in the direction of making the church exist for the people rather than the people for the church. Because of the financial needs and other things this church has been compelled to modify its efforts to minister to the people and lay emphasis on the incidental features.

The church appears to be occupying a somewhat less prominent place in the social life of the people than it once did, although it is yet probably the most influential factor, or one of the most influential, in their social life.

The ministry has probably improved, both intellectually and morally. It is, however, not meeting the needs of the people in the best possible manner, because there are few ministers with college and theological training, and the debt-ridden conditions of the churches call for men with ability to raise money rather than for men intellectually and morally stong.

The morals of the people are probably being raised. This is best evidenced by the widespread dissatisfaction that is found to exist among church members and the criticism of present conditions which they make: also the increasing demand for a better ministry. This criticism is: (1) one of the ministry; (a) it lacks edification; (b) it lacks morality; (c) it lacks business ability; (2) of the members; (a) of the officers of the church who are often dishonest and lacking in business ability; (b) the members lack moral sense and appreciation, i.e., the ethical standards are bad.

The church is probably losing its influence on the young people because of the scarcity of ministers able to meet the intellectual needs of the times and emphasis which the church is compelled to place on eternal things. The conditions of the churches in this state, while far from being good, are probably being improved.

1. A better type of ministry is appearing (very few).

2. The business affairs of the church are being better managed. This is notably true in Chicago.

3. The people are demanding better ministers and higher morals (demand very weak and uncertain as yet).

4. Tendency appears to be toward more honest and upright living among the members.

25

RECRUITMENT OF NEGROES
FOR THEOLOGICAL STUDIES

WALTER G. MUELDER

This discussion of the critical problems facing the Negro churches and ministers during the 1960's is by the Dean of the Boston University School of
Theology, which has provided graduate training to men such as Martin Luther
King, Jr., C. Eric Lincoln, and Joseph R. Washington, Jr. Focusing on the declining enrollment of black ministerial candidates in Methodist seminaries, Walter
Muelder's analysis suggests the variety of factors that are contributing to the
current trend. These factors include the current loss of status of the ministry
as a profession, the general disaffection of the youth with the traditional
church and their failure to be inspired to the ministry even by activist clerics,
and the diffusion of the protest movement far beyond the churches.

There has been no fundamental improvement in the situation for recruiting
Negro seminarians in the last thirty or thirty-five years. Indeed, the current
crisis would indicate a continuing deterioration. In *An American Dilemma*
Gunnar Myrdal summarized the situation about twenty five years ago and
drew on some studies that take statistics back to 1930. The United States
Census in 1910 noted 17,495 Negro clergymen which comprised 14.8 percent of all Negro professional workers. In 1930 the number increased to
25,034, or 16.8 percent of such workers. Clergymen constituted the second
largest group among Negro "professional" workers and enjoyed a complete
monopoly behind the caste wall. It was the only profession in which Negroes
had more representatives than in the general population.[1] Myrdal noted that
three possible reasons for this situation were: (1) a greater division in religious
interests than among whites, (2) the restricted opportunities in other desirable
fields, and (3) more Negro attendance at church than among whites. Insofar
as these possible reasons are valid they are positively related to the then strict

Reprinted from *Review of Religious Research*, 5 (Spring 1964): 152-156, by permission
of the author and the publisher.

caste situation, the nature and function of the Negro church, and the relative ease in terms of education with which one could become a clergyman, and have the status of a professional. There are important changes in all three of these dimensions of the situation.

An "Exaggerated American"

By 1940 it was quite apparent that the future prospects of the Negro church were dim. Myrdal[2] reported that the church was "losing out among the young people, mostly because the Negro preacher has lagged behind the rest of the Negro community and, particularly behind other professionals, in acquiring a better education." For the most part the Negro church has been an accommodative rather than a significant protest institution, though it has produced a number of outstanding protest leaders and reformers. Otherworldliness has been a mark of its religious emphases. Even in the North the Negro church has "remained a conservative institution with its interests directed upon otherworldly matters and has largely ignored the practical problems of the Negroes' fate in this world."[3] Evans Crawford's dissertation dealing with Negro Baptist churches in Chicago noted these same traits in the 1950's and the low educational state of church leadership. Myrdal has pressed the thesis that the caste system forced the Negro to become an "exaggerated American," What does this mean!

Americans generally are a religious people; Southerners are more religious than the rest of the nation, and the Negroes, perhaps, still a little more religious than the White Southerners. Negroes, on the whole, attend church probably in greater numbers than do Whites although not in greater numbers than certain White groups like the Catholics. Among Negroes, as among Whites, females attend more than males, the middle-aged and the old attend more than the youth, the uneducated attend more than the educated, the lower and middle classes more than the upper classes.[4]

Not counting Negro members in white churches, 44 percent of the Negro population were members of Negro churches, as compared to 42.4 percent of white population in white churches.

The crisis in ministerial recruitment today may reflect this "exaggerated American" phenomenon. Already by 1940 it was apparent that a marked differential between youth and age obtained. The tendency for Negro youth to abandon church is probably greater than among white youth, due in part to lack of sophistication in the Negro church, its emotionalism, puritanism, and lack of prophetic social gospel leadership. The great majority of Negroes be-

long to Baptist and Methodist churches or to small sects which have branched
from them. Upper- and middle-class Negroes tend to frown upon the old practices which still prevail in the lower classes. The split into miniature congregations has gone a long way among Negroes. This phenomenon was noted thirty
years ago by Benjamin E. Mays and J. W. Nicholson.[5] Of 185 rural churches
studied, the average membership was 145 persons of whom 50 percent were
actually contributing to financial support. In Harlem, out of 163 Negro
churches, 122 were meeting in residences or stores in 1930. These 122 churches
claimed a total membership of 14,913 or 122 each on the average.[6] Notes
Myrdal: "If there is any relation at all between the interest of a Negro church
in social issues and the social status of its membership, the relation is that a
church tends to be more otherworldly the poorer its members are and the
more they are in need of concerted efforts to improve their lot in this life."[7]
Today, in a period of social revolution, young people particularly are likely to
reject wholly an institution whose image in their experience is associated with
the past they are trying to overcome. The Negro rural church is in an even
more critical state than the urban churches.

In 1947 Harry F. Richardson[8] pointed out that, of four counties studied,
nearly half the rural ministers had no more than elementary educations. Almost three fourths had less than high school educations.

> For the minister to be beneath the youth of his parish in any important
> particular is obviously a handicap. It is one of the factors responsible for the
> lack of pastoral participation in young people's work. Certainly it jeopardizes
> the pastor's ability to lead his young people effectively.[9]

We are today suffering from the cumulative effect of the fact that in rural
areas in the 1940's only 10 percent of the Negro ministry were professionally
trained. In the deep South, Richardson estimated that only 2.8 percent of
rural Negro pastors had professional training. It is not surprising then, that
already thirty years ago Carter G. Woodson[10] found in one sample that "only
seven-tenths of one percent of Negro high school graduates contemplate taking up the ministry; and many who have been known to qualify themselves
thus do not stay in the ministry."

Crisis in the Seminaries

The situation in the seminaries has been critical for many years. In 1940 Mays
reported[11] that there were 253 fewer students enrolled in Negro seminaries in
1939 than in 1924. When 92 Negro students in Northern white seminaries were

included, there were only 850 Negroes enrolled in all seminaries in 1939, and only 254 of these were college graduates. Richardson noted that in 1944 there were sixty-one Negro students enrolled as undergraduates in sixteen Northern (white) seminaries. All of these seminaries were accredited. There were eighty-two undergraduates in the two Negro accredited seminaries. This meant that there were 143 Negro theological students in America who were receiving standardized theological instruction in 1944.

Twenty-one of the larger Negro theological schools or departments had 110 graduates in 1944, and the sixteen Northern seminaries had thirteen (13). Thus something over 123 trained Ministers were graduated from the good and poor schools in that year.[12]

In the Methodist Church the ministerial leadership picture among Negroes is not encouraging. The Central Jurisdiction has grown very slowly. Caste and segregation have left the bitter marks of oppression on the Negro portion of the church. From 1931 to 1950, according to the "Report of the Commission to Study The Central Jurisdiction" in 1956, there has been a steady and a sharp decrease in the number of full time ordained pastors in the jurisdiction. In 1931 there were 1,719; in 1950 there were only 1,262, a decrease of 457 or 27 percent. Meanwhile the accepted supply pastors increased from 316 to 569 or 80 percent. The proportion more than doubled. In other words, large proportion of the membership is being served in small churches by supply pastors. Indeed, the ministry of the Central Jurisdiction is not reproducing itself. In 1946 there were sixty-six Negro Methodist theological students in the seminaries of the nation; in 1950 there were seventy, an increase of only 6 percent, not enough to replace the annual losses or to reverse the trend in the declining number of effective pastors. The over-all picture is very critical and is not likely to improve under continuing circumstances. A study of 845 pastors from fifteen of the nineteen annual conferences of the Central Jurisdiction shows that only 155 or about 19 percent have B.D. degrees.

Another study made at Gammon Theological Seminary emphasizes the problem from several perspectives. In 1956 Prof. J. H. Graham[13] reported that there were a total of fifteen Methodist Negro seniors in eight Methodist seminaries reporting (including Gammon) out of a total of fifty-two Negro Methodists and a total of ninety-nine Negro enrollees. Reports from forty collegiate institutions for 1955-1956 showed 206 Negro preministerial students distributed as follows: Methodist institutions, 75; other church related, 59; state and private nonsectarian, 72. Of the 206 there were 60 Methodist preministerial students.

In January 1964 Dr. John O. Gross of the Board of Education of the Methodist Church released the statement that in the twelve Negro colleges of the Methodist Church there were sixty-three preministerial students. According to Dr. Shelby Rooks of the Theological Education Fund there have been fewer than a total of 300 Negro seminarians enrolled in accredited theological schools during the past five years.

A recent statistical table released by the Division of Theological Education of the General Board of Education of the Methodist Church shows the following enrollments at Gammon during the past ten years: 1953, 57; 1955, 76; 1957, 72; 1959, 94; 1961, 40; and 1963, 37. (The figure for 1959 reflects its affiliation with the Interdenominational Theological Center in Atlanta.) Although there may be some statistical compensation because of a somewhat wider dispersion of Negro B.D. students in Methodist seminaries, there is no doubt that enrollments of Negroes at that level are declining generally.

Recruitment Facts and Factors

Some of the current facts and factors that seem to be relevant to the recruitment situation may be summarized as follows:

1. The ministry, once the chief outlet for Negro ambition, is declining significantly in relative importance among professionals. It should be noted that Negro enrollments in medicine and law have also been dropping.

2. Status is increasingly based on education and educated Negroes deprecate the religion and leadership of the old-fashioned Negro church of whatever denomination.

3. Negro leadership has passed in many communities from the Negro preacher to other professional leaders and to businessmen and labor leaders.

4. Young people are particularly critical of the church and the ministry. College youth are especially critical.

5. The image of the church, provided by Southern white preachers and laymen, does not redeem the situation as Negro youth take up positions of community leadership. In many communities eleven o'clock on Sunday is still the most "Jim Crow" hour of the week.

6. In the present Negro revolution the clergy who give major leadership are identified in the minds of youth as atypical and hence do not become inspirations for choosing the ministry as some have supposed. At the same time it cannot be denied that courageous leadership by clergymen in the cause of civil rights provides a new image for some Negro youth.

7. The fact of segregation in the churches is a major factor in the situation.

8. The decline of the ministers' leadership and prestige will not be reversed in the foreseeable future because the church North and South has, with few exceptions, continued to reject inclusive brotherhood. Suburban churches reflect a marked resistance to changing housing patterns in many areas.

9. Negro protest finds major expression outside the churches.

10. The Negro church is less functional to the Negroes' social situation and possibilities than formerly. The old-fashioned Negro church is positively dysfunctional and the more up-to-date churches now divide the honors with many competing groups.

11. Long-time urbanization trends which are effective in accentuating the decline of recruitment for the ministry generally, are even more serious so far as Negro youth are concerned.

12. From an institutional point of view the economic structure of churches in the Central Jurisdiction of the Methodist Church is not such as to encourage young people to seek careers as ordained clergymen. The all-Negro denominations also lack a sound economic base in the typical local congregation. When the average local church has fewer than a hundred members it cannot support a fully educated ministry. Without suitable leadership progress is virtually impossible.

13. Radical reforms within all churches, including Negro churches, are needed before the decline noted above can be reversed. These radical reforms are lockstitched in the social fabric of America as a whole.

NOTES

1. Gunnar Mydral, *An American Dilemma* (New York, 1944), p. 321.

2. Ibid., p. 322.

3. Ibid., p. 863.

4. Ibid.

5. Benjamin E. Mays and Joseph W. Nicholson, *The Negro's Church* (New York, 1933).

6. See The Greater New York Federation of Churches, *The Negro Churches in Manhattan*, 1930, pp. 11 and 17.

7. Myrdal, p. 373.

8. Harry F. Richard, *Dark Glory* (New York, 1947), chap. 8.

9. Ibid., p. 125.

10. Carter G. Woodson, *The Negro Professional Man and the Community* (Washington, D.C., 1934), p. 80.

11. Benjamin E. Mays, "The Negro Church in American Life," *Christendom,* Summer 1940, pp. 389-391.

12. Ibid., pp. 179-180.

13. J. H. Graham, "Gammon's Recruiting Program and the Replacement Needs of the Central Jurisdiction," *The Foundation,* 46, no. 3.

26

NEGRO PREACHERS TAKE SIDES

RONALD L. JOHNSTONE

The existence of potentially militant, thisworldly leadership among the black clergy has been a thoroughly (and sometimes hotly) debated subject. But though every shade of opinion has been aired, the debaters have usually had little empirical research to support their claims. Ronald Johnstone's study of the Detroit clergy is therefore a welcome addition to the controversy. Though he has uncovered a young, highly educated militant clerical elite with disproportionate influence among the laity and traditional clergy as well, there are crucial limiting factors. Such obstacles as a lack of unity with their fellows and the heavy demands made on their time by routine church duties may seriously impair the impact of the militant black clergyman on the political action movement.

Introduction

"Come weal or woe, my status is quo." So a nameless old Negro preacher is supposed to have summarized his philosophy of making do. In so speaking he was typifying the accommodating, peace-making, don't-ripple-the-waters style of Negro preacher—one who knew he was to keep his place, encourage submission and fatalistic acquiescence on the part of his flock, and preach an otherworldly gospel. If he did his job well, he knew his choir would receive an invitation to sing spirituals in a white church or two and he could look forward to a little free coal for his church in the winter.

This is the "Uncle Tom" style of clerical leadership many Negroes have been repudiating in recent years; this is the stereotype of Negro preachers in general that the present inherits from the past 150 years. But how accurate is

Reprinted from *Review of Religious Research,* 11 (Fall 1969): 81-89, by permission of the author and the publisher.

such a description of Negro clergymen today? What are the social characteristics of Negro preachers today? Are they what they were? Are there important differences among them?

Here we have the components of an important question clamoring for
empirical data— data we shall shortly present in summary fashion. A second
question immediately follows. In brief it asks: "So what?" That is, regardless
of who and what Negro clergymen are today, of what significance is this
category of people in our contemporary changing social world? In particular,
where do they and where can they be expected to fit in the agitation and
activity called the "civil rights movement"?

However, before we make such assessments, predictions, and extrapola-
tions, we need data to give answers to the prior question of who Negro
preachers are and what characteristics and diversity they represent. In gathering data from personal interviews with a 25 percent random sample[1] of all
Negro clergymen in Detroit, it soon became highly obvious that Negro clergymen today are far from alike on most any issue one might want to name. In
fact, three distinct types emerged—militants, moderates, and traditionalists.[2]

Three Types of Negro Preachers

A *militant* says: "The black man has endured, yes suffered, about all he can
take. One of my major jobs as a minister is to help lead him out. If that causes
trouble or embarrassment for some white people, that's too bad. Action is
what we need and I must be in the forefront. My people need leadership and
prodding." Here are the Negro preachers who identify themselves as members
of inner-core planning and executing civil rights action groups—men who are
aggressive, take-charge civil rights protagonists who are not only outspoken on
the civil rights issue but are committed to action on the basis of their beliefs
and commitment. In these ranks are the Negro preachers who organized and
successfully carried through economic boycott programs against several major
retailing firms in Detroit, Philadelphia, and elsewhere. Here are the Negro
preachers who demonstrate, march, and picket.[3] Although this style and role
of the Negro preacher was not completely unknown in the past, the Negro
preachers who combined both indignation and the daring to engage in aggressive action to challenge the system were few and arose only sporadically. The
increasing numbers as well as the success of such militant preachers has become a new thing.[4]

The *moderate* is clearly distinguishable from the militant. He is inclined to
be the peacemaker, the gradualist, the treader-down-the-middle-of-the-road.

He may protest inwardly. Certainly he is well aware of conditions. He knows the plight of so many of his people. But he is more conciliatory and accom-modating than the militant as he evidences a protest that is much less audible, overt, and active than that of his militant brother. Improvement of the lot of the Negro, certainly, but carefully, quietly, slowly, without alienating the white brother—such is the moderate's philosophy.

"The most important thing as a minister is to carry out that part of my work which puts me away from all political things. I ought to do spiritual work and preach." So speaks the *traditionalist*—the Negro preacher who is passive with regard to challenges to the prevailing social order, preferring never to enter the battle arena. His attitudes and thoughts will rarely be framed in protest even to himself, nor will he join in attempts at aggressive action. Some actually are relatively unaware of problems; some have given up hope of changing prevailing conditions; most appear to be satisfied with the system since they are able to do what they want to do—make a living and preach the gospel. In any case, they are acquiescent.

Social and Religious Characteristics (Correlates) of the Three Types

As these three types have been outlined in broad strokes and as the reader can probably think of examples of each type at work in his own community, ob-vious questions arise concerning the significance of each type. Which is most representative? Is one type growing at a faster rate than the others? How much leadership potential is there from the Negro clergy ranks? Although answering such questions of significance and impact is the ultimate objective of this issue, it is exceedingly important to know more precisely who these Negro preachers are before attempting any over-all assessment. That is, who are the men in each category, and what social correlates to each type can we find? Discovering the characteristics and correlates will not only advance knowledge about a category of people on whom there has been little data available before, but it will contribute much toward answering questions of possible future impact.[5]

1. Age

The militant Negro preacher is almost certain to be a relatively young man. In Detroit, 32 percent of the militants are under forty; none of the traditionalists is this young; and only 19 percent of the moderates are under forty. On the other hand, only 25 percent of the militant preachers are over fifty-five, while 45 percent of the traditionalists and 37 percent of the moderates are fifty-five or older. Young, older, old describes the continuum of militant-moderate-traditionalist almost perfectly. Does this suggest that the degree of involvement in the civil rights movement and concern for the attendant issues among Negro clergymen is a function of age? In part, yes, but only in conjunction with other features.

2. Education

Education is another prime factor. The militant Negro preacher is clearly differentiated from his fellow clergymen in terms of the dramatically superior education he has received. Similarly, the moderate has generally attained a higher level of education than traditionalists, though significantly less than the militants. In fact, whereas over half (58 percent) of the traditionalists have no more than a high school education, none of the militants stopped there, and only 31 percent of the moderates did not go beyond high school. On the other hand, five out of every six militants have a college and/or graduate degree, with all militants having at least two years of college training. But only 16 percent of the traditionalists and 38 percent of the moderates have graduated from college.

Militants are clearly not only significantly more highly educated than the moderates and particularly the traditionalists; they have attained an education level that ranks high regardless of the standard of comparison or evaluation used. We thus see that militants are highly educated young men; traditionalists are poorly educated older men; moderates fall between on both counts.

3. Social Status Background

These preachers similarly can be differentiated on the basis of their social status background. Militants are much more likely than either moderates or traditionalists to have come from a higher family status background with fathers in the professional, proprietor, and skilled craftsmen categories. Traditionalists and moderates have fathers who were predominantly from the ranks of tenant farmers or unskilled and semiskilled laborers.

Clearly the degree of involvement in and commitment to active participation in civil rights activities on the part of Negro preachers is related very directly to their age, level of education attainment, and social status background. Although in no sense direct one-for-one causes of militance or its absence, obvious strong dispositions are evident.

But of almost equal interest and significance are other characteristics that correlate highly with militancy. Among these are theological stance, denominational affiliation, number of members attracted to one's congregation, view of the role of clergymen today, and political party affiliation.

4. Theological Stance

As might be expected from the evidence above, militants are inclined to display greater theological liberalism than their traditionalist or moderate counterparts. Nearly all militants (92 percent) but only one third of the moderates and traditionalists accept the possibility of error in scripture and reject the traditional conservative view of Biblical inspiration and inerrancy. Also, militants are significantly more likely than the others to reject the idea of the physical reality of hell.

5. Denominational Affiliation

Militants (with moderates a close second) are much more likely than their traditionalist brethren to be members of mainline Protestant denominations such as Episcopal, Congregational, Presbyterian, and Methodist churches. The traditionalists, however, are much more likely to be members of Pentecostal and more nearly sect-type religious groups. Of the traditionalists, 84 percent are either Baptist or Pentecostal; nearly half of the militants are neither Baptist nor Pentecostal.

6. Congregational Size

The size of congregations served by these Negro preachers varies considerably also. Whereas exactly two thirds of the traditionalists serve small congregations, only 17 percent of the militants serve such congregations of 200 or fewer members. At the other extreme, half the militants serve large congregations of 600 or more adult members while only 10 percent of the traditionalists and 12 percent of the moderates have large memberships in their churches. To put it even more graphically, the average number of adult members served by militants is 752. For moderates it is 308, and for traditionalists 213.

7. View of Ministry

The three types of Negro preachers also exhibit distinctive views of the ministry and their responsibilities as ministers. The militants overwhelmingly support the view that their role is as spiritual leader but equally important as leader and advocate for their people in the social, political, and economic realms. Moderates see themselves primarily as spiritual leaders but with some attendant responsibilities for their members as social beings. Traditionalists almost to a man think of their task solely as a spiritual one—preaching, converting, and leading to heaven, with of course some purely administrative responsibilities along side. These differences would be expected from our earlier definition and description of the three types. Militants, for example, are civil rights activists and planners. But it is important to know that such participation is not by accident. It follows from their concept of the ministry and their role as minister. Similarly the traditionalists' lack of participation, perhaps even lack of interest, in civil rights activity stems from an explicit rejection of such involvement as a part of their role as clergymen; "My job is to preach the Gospel."

8. Voting Behavior

With regard to political attitudes and activities we should point up two important areas in which Negro preachers differ significantly among themselves: (1) voting behavior, (2) evaluation of the effectiveness of the political process.

Although Negro voters generally have switched from a post-Civil War attachment to the Republican party to a large majority identification with the Democratic party, primarily since the appearance of Franklin D. Roosevelt, Negro clergymen do not accurately reflect such a shift. They are *not* so closely attached to the Democratic party as the Negro population generally. It is important to note, though, that the obverse does not hold. Those who do not identify as Democrats are little inclined to affiliate with the Republican party. Instead they claim the status of Independents. Our data reveal party preference as follows: Democratic (48.5 percent); Republican (13.5 percent); Independent (39 percent). However, actual voting behavior of these preachers in all major elections in Detroit (presidential, gubernatorial, and mayoralty) between 1956 and 1962 does give an edge to the Democratic side. Those voting essentially Democratic (only one crossover)—59.3 percent; those voting essentially Republican (only one crossover)—11.9 percent; those about evenly divided between Democratic and Republican candidate—27.8 percent.

Our primary interest is in comparisons among our three types of clergymen. Fully 100 percent of the militants voted a mixed pattern. Such consistency of inconsistent voting patterns is matched by only 58 percent of the moderates and 45 percent of the traditionalists. We thus have a picture of militant Negro preachers tending to assume a clearly independent stance, certainly a more independent stance than the moderates and traditionalists.

Actually, such voting behavior is consistent with the militant philosophy. The militant preacher is strongly committed to action that will lead to increased participation in and benefit from the society in which he and his people live. This requires activity in many spheres. But within each sphere, whether education, housing, jobs, legal rights, and the like, there are numerous clusters of power. As a consequence there are many foci of attack as well as many potential allies. This fact seems particularly evident in the sphere of politics. Since there are two major parties, each must be approached, pressured if possible, and played off one against the other. Strong commitment to one or the other party is interpreted by many as courting disaster through being taken for granted. And so, militants assume an independent political stance that is consistent with their general philosophy of eclecticism in choosing tactics as well as foci of attack—a point of view which says: "Work on many fronts, expecting at least a few to recede at your advance and pressure."

9. Views on Political Process

On the basis of the foregoing we might hypothesize that militants would be more likely than their moderate and traditionalist brothers to be critical of both political parties in the sense of perceiving them as not having sufficiently considered nor acted upon the problems facing Negro citizens. We find that two thirds of the militants, but only one third of the moderates and one quarter of the traditionalists, agree with the assertion that neither political party in Detroit gives a fair hearing to the demands, needs, and problems of Negro citizens. This tendency toward criticism of the political parties on the part of militants is so despite the fact, as Wilson (1960) has observed, that militants generally exhibit greater confidence in politicolegal mechanisms. Actually, our data indicate that this greater confidence generally exhibited by militants is one of the more important reasons why militant preachers are vocal in their criticism of the political parties. That is, just because the militant thinks that the political structure should and can work effectively, particularly in the sphere of civil rights, he will do his utmost in trying to make it as effective as possible. Part of his effort involves criticism and prodding.

Summary

There are many other differences among Negro clergymen that we shall not take the space to list. A sufficiently clear pattern has emerged, however,

to enable making two observations and then to proceed to some broader pro-
jections and evaluations. (1) There is clearly today no single type of Negro
preacher. Rather, there are vast and significant differences on a wide range of
features. We have capsuled the major differences into the three summarizing
types of militant, moderate, and traditionalist. (2) Some apparently highly
capable and potentially influential men are in the ranks of the Negro clergy;
these men tend to assume a militant stance insofar as civil rights are concerned.

Implications of Data for Clergy Leadership in Civil Rights Movement

Now, what does the existence of three quite clearly delimited types mean?
Particularly what can be said about the relationship of Negro clergymen to the
civil rights movement in the future? Will the ranks of Negro clergymen become a more significant reservoir of leaders for the movement? Is the stereotyped traditionalist gradually declining in number and influence?

Militants' Influence Disproportionate to Their Numbers

Only 20 percent of the Negro clergymen in Detroit are militants but over
half (nearly 53 percent) are traditionalists.[6] Already knowing the quiescent,
noninvolved, spiritually oriented character of the traditionalists, we might be
ready to conclude not only that militancy is a relatively minor and unimportant stance among Negro clergymen but also that Negro clergy ranks in
general would be a nearly blind-alley source for leaders to bring about change.
As checks on such hasty conclusions, however, several points need to be
made. First, although more in number, traditionalists are much lower in influence than the militants. We have already noted the vast differences in the
size of congregations as related to ministerial type. Although the amount of
influence a preacher has over his congregational members is almost a moot
question, the fact is that militants address and counsel with far more people
than their traditionalist and moderate counterparts. And remember that these
militants not only hold direct action civil rights views, but they also admittedly endeavor to communicate them to others. Such communication is part of
their role definition.

Relevant data show militants belong to an average of 5.4 associations and
organizations outside the strictly religious sphere, compared with an average

of only one for traditionalists. Further, three out of four militants have personally spoken with public officials about specific problems or issues; only one in three traditionalists has ever done so. What these facts suggest is that both the potential and real influence of the militants exceed their proportion in the ranks of Negro clergymen.

It is also revealing to discover that militants are much more likely deliberately to bring politics into their churches and attempt to stimulate action on the part of their parishioners. Over half of the militants but only a quarter of the traditionalsits invite or allow political candidates to address their people and use their facilities. Fully 83 percent of the militants permit campaign literature to be distributed from their churches, while only 42 percent of the traditionalists grant such permission. Further, while over half (58 percent) of the militants admittedly attempt to influence their members' votes by specifically suggesting particular candidates to them, almost none (13 percent) of the traditionalists recommend candidates by name to their members.

It was interesting and important to discover that many traditionalists seem to have a secret though somewhat intangible respect for at least some aspects of the militant stance and for militant ministers themselves. In nominating their opinion leaders, they selected militants six to one over traditionalists. They seemed to sense a need for such militancy for their people even if they did not see it as part of their task to join the militant ranks.

The Potential for Militant Influence

Our conclusion at this point is that there is more potential for militance and influence by militants among Negro clergymen than the simple proportion of militants in Negro preacher ranks would indicate. That is, we dare not dismiss the possibility of a significant contribution to and involvement in the civil rights movement by these clergymen. There would appear also to be the possibility of a spread of the militant stance among Negro preachers in the future. Witness the secret respect for militancy that can be inferred on the part of traditionalist preachers and the consensus expressed by several dozen community leaders and politicians we interviewed who said that militancy has been on the uptrend among Negro preachers during the past ten years.

The evidence seems to point to at least a *potential* contribution by Negro clergymen to civil rights agitation and progress in the days ahead. They have made some widely acknowledged contributions in the past. They spearheaded several successful economic boycotts against allegedly discriminating manufacturing and processing firms and played a successful and noticeable role in the 1961 mayoralty campaign. But what about the future? Several factors will limit their potential.

Limitations of the Potential

First, organizations of Negro ministers, whether denominational or non-denominational, are not entering the political arena to any substantial degree. They are not entering the political arena as independent organizations, but only as part of a broad community effort, and even then not all of them by any means.

Second, Negro preachers tend to remain noticeably independent entrepeneurs. Most activities directed toward affecting the political and governmental structure of the community are carried on by individual ministers acting out of personal motivation, as representatives of their local congregations, or as citizen members of various local community organizations. Thus, an individual minister may speak to a civic board or official about a personal grievance; he may come to the Housing Commission because his church is headed for demolition by the city's urban renewal program and remuneration for the church's property is not viewed as adequate; or he may be part of a local parents' group protesting segregation or overcrowding in the local high school. But in none of these instances is he representing or working with a category or group of people called "Negro preachers." In a few instances clergymen have organized a fairly large proportion of their fellow ministers behind particular efforts, but no permanent organization persists. At best they have been able to achieve "crisis" or "issue" unity that does not maintain momentum.

A third factor that tends to minimize the impact of Negro preachers beyond the walls of their churches stems from the nature and demands of their occupational role. For one thing, the time and energy required to foray significantly outside their churches are minimal. The traditional primary responsibility of these men, by definition, lies with their local congregations. The attendant activities and tasks are not only many, they are time consuming. Also, whether by default or design, many Negro preachers must assume tasks that in many white churches are handled by laymen—such functions as handling congregational business affairs and building maintenance. Nor dare we ignore the traditionally strong norm of separation of church and state in this country which may have been more deeply absorbed by the Negro than by the white churches. Although this norm of separation does not preclude clergymen from becoming politically involved, it does take strong motivation and a carefully thought-out philosophy to go counter to the familiar pattern of noninvolvement by clerics, whether Negro or white, in the sphere of politics. Another factor that tends to inhibit an active and organized moving outward of Negro preachers centers around the tendency of Negro religious groups to approach the sect end of the church-sect continuum; the sect's inherent tendency is toward withdrawal from community and political issues while focusing on spiritual and otherworldly matters.

A fourth broad factor that tends to limit the potential for civil rights leadership and activity by Negro preachers centers in their diversity and the lack of consensus among themselves. The differences along the militant-traditionalist continuum are both many and of considerable magnitude. Further, they have been almost totally unable to agree on priority problems. Even the militant preachers who are consistently similar, even alike, on so many dimensions, evidence no consensus on which one or two problems facing the Negro citizen are most crucial. Although employment rates the most frequent choice, only 32 percent could agree that it was most pressing. In fact, one traditionalist clergyman could not identify one single problem facing his people. No more than one fifth of the preachers could agree on the best general approach to solving problems facing Negro citizens.

Assessment of Leadership Potential for the Future

In short, we see in the Negro clergy as a total category or group no significant or sustaining leadership source for continuing civil rights agitation. This is not to deny that Negro preachers can still serve as a useful source of grass-roots support for programs developed by other leaders. In fact, they conceivably can serve a crucial middle-man function. There is a readiness among them to support civil rights programs and tactics once these tactics are communicated and understood.

Minimizing their leadership potential and function outside spiritual realsm also does not deny that the Negro clergy are a potential reservoir of civil rights leadership—leadership at positions above the level of the local church or neighborhood. Although this reservoir is quite small, there are Negro preachers (militants) who by desire, commitment, and training are capable of filling roles of policy-making, planning, and organizing at levels above their local congregation or denomination. They have achieved a few fairly notable successes in recent years and they have an outreach and influence disproportionate to their numbers. In all likelihood, however, they will have to be coopted by other organizations and drawn out of the local responsibilities associated with serving a neighborhood church and its band of believers if they are to make a sustained and significant impact on civil rights.

NOTES

1. The 25 percent sample comprised seventy-five ministers, fifty-nine of whom were successfully interviewed. Of the sixteen nonrespondents seven had moved to known parishes in other cities, two had moved and left no forwarding address, two were seriously ill, two had died, and three were ultimate refusals. Data from these fifty-nine clergymen provided the basis for this study.

In addition, we interviewed ten Negro clergymen who were not in our sample but were frequently mentioned as clergy leaders by the men in our sample. As an outside check on our data and conclusions as well as expanding our perspective, we interviewed forty Detroit community leaders both white and black. These were members of the Detroit Common Council and the Board of Education, the Detroit Police Department, the Urban League, the National Association for the Advancement of Colored People, the Metropolitan Church Federation, the Detroit Commission on Community Relations, Wayne State University faculty, and labor union leaders, politicians, attorneys, businessmen, and the religion editors of four Detroit newspapers.

2. Our initial categorizing device was the relationship each preacher had to a clearly militant civil rights organization composed solely of Negro clergymen in Detroit. This organization, the Negro Preachers of Detroit and Vicinity, planned and expedited several "boycotts" of major Detroit companies that were designed to bring and did bring the companies to the bargaining table with the militant preachers and ultimately increased the proportion of Negroes employed at all levels within these firms.

Three possible relationships to this organization were utilized to categorize the preachers in our sample: (1) The inner-core planners and bargainers (militants), (2) The rank and file members of the organization who supported its goals and urged members to support the boycotts (moderates), (3) Those who disclaimed membership in or even awareness of the existence of the Negro Preachers of Detroit and Vicinity organization (traditionalists). Such behavioral and action data proved highly predictive in the course of the study.

3. We conceive of militance as implying a commitment to aggressive protest against the existing social order that results in specific challenging actions

4. See Joseph R. Washington, *Black Religion* (Boston, 1964); August Meier, *Negro Thought in America, 1880-1915* (Ann Arbor, 1963); Oliver C. Cox, "Leadership among Negroes in the United States," in Alvin W. Gouldner, ed., *Studies in Leadership* (New York, 1950); James Wilson, *Negro Politics* (Glencoe, Ill., 1960); Daniel C. Thompson, *The Negro Leadership Class* (Englewood Cliffs, N.J., 1963).

5. Although scant even then, the best hard data on Negro clergymen are from studies thirty-five or more years old: Benjamin E. Mays and Joseph W. Nicholson, *The Negro's Church* (New York, 1933), and C. Luther Fry, *The U.S. Looks at Its Churches* (New York, 1930). Although Gerhard E. Lenski, *The Religious Factor* (New York, 1961) gathered data on Negro clergymen in Detroit as part of his study, relatively little information on Negro clergymen that relates directly to our study was actually reported.

6. The precise distributions in our sample were: militants 20.3 percent; moderates— 27.1 percent; traditionalists—52.6 percent.

27

THE GENIUS OF THE NEGRO CHURCH

BENJAMIN E. MAYS AND JOSEPH W. NICHOLSON

In 1933 Benjamin E. Mays and Joseph W. Nicholson published *The Negro's Church,* in which they presented a factual report, based on their research on 794 Negro congregations, on the myriad ailments of the black church. From its financial insolvency to its inability to provide sufficiently trained clergy, the Negro church seemed to be failing its members on nearly every front. But as the authors clearly recognized, the Negro's church occupied such a special place in the black community that no balance sheet or sermon content analysis could adequately explain it. The church was the Negro's own; it was his place to be free to express himself. But the black preacher was perhaps the freest man of all—from his pulpit he could speak out against all the evils corrupting Christianity in America; it was perhaps the only place from which a truly prophetic Christianity could be propagated.

The analysis reveals that the status of the Negro church is in part the result of the failure of American Christianity in the realm of race relations; that the church's program, except in rare instances, is static, nonprogressive, and fails to challenge the loyalty of many of the most critically minded Negroes; that the vast majority of its pastors are poorly trained academically, and more poorly trained theologically; that more than half of the sermons analyzed are abstract, otherworldly, and imbued with a magical conception of religion; that in the church school less than one tenth of the teachers are college graduates; that there are too many Negro churches; that the percentage of Negro churches in debt is high; that for the most part the Negro church is little concerned with juvenile delinquency and other social problems in its environment; that less than half of the reported membership can be relied upon to finance the church regularly and consistently; and that the rural church suffers most because of the instability and poverty of the rural Negroes.

Yet the authors believe that there is in the genius or the "soul" of the

Adapted from *The Negro's Church* (New York: Institute of Social and Religious Research, 1933), pp. 278, 279, 280-281, 285-286, 289-290, 291-292, by permission of the authors.

Negro church something that gives it life and vitality, that makes it stand out significantly above its buildings, creeds, rituals and doctrines, something that makes it a unique institution. . . .

The Church Is the Negro's Very Own

The church was the first community or public organization that the Negro actually owned and completely controlled. And it is possibly true to this day that the Negro church is the most thoroughly owned and controlled public institution of the race. Nothing can compare with this ownership and control except ownership of the home and possibly control of the Negro lodge. It is to be doubted whether Negro control is as complete in any other area of Negro life, except these two, as it is in the church.

A statement of this character may sound paradoxical in the light of the facts discovered in the chapter on finance, which show that 71.3 percent of the churches of this study are in debt. But churches are unique institutions, for which reason they enjoy special privileges.

Churches, unlike houses and business enterprises, are not very valuable to their creditors. Residence property, if taken from the buyer, is usually very valuable, and may return a profit. This is not true with churches. A church taken over by creditors is generally of little value to them and usually cannot be used for any other purpose. Ordinarily the financiers want the money and not the church; and they are not concerned with either the ownership or the control of the church. Another reason is the good reputation enjoyed by churches for eventually paying off their debts. Thus, for both of these reasons, indebtedness on churches generally does not involve loss of control to the creditors. . . .

Not only is this institution controlled by Negroes, but nine-tenths of the local churches are self-supporting. A few Negro churches, organically connected with white churches, churches of Negro denominations, and several Baptist churches were helped in an organized way between 1927 and 1931; but during the same period, 88.3 percent of the churches of this study received no systematic organized support from outside sources. Certainly in the majority of cases the amounts received from outside sources were so negligible that the churches would continue to exist if the outside help were entirely cut off. Even in the cases of the 11.7 percent of churches that received some organized support due to denominational connections and otherwise, there was sufficient evidence to show that control of the church was primarily in the hands of the Negro congregations.

Through and through, with or without outside help, the Negro churches of

this study are principally governed by Negroes. Many Negroes, though unable
to own homes of their own, take a peculiar pride in their churches. It gives
them a sense of ownership that can hardly exist with respect to any other
institution in the community. Since thousands do not own their homes,
they develop a loyalty and devotion to their churches that command respect
and admiration. It is characteristic of the Negro church that the Negro owns
it and that it is largely the product of his hand and brain.

Ownership and Control Provide Opportunity
for the Common Man

With races and individuals, there must be an opportunity for the development
of initiative and self-direction if real character is to be developed, and if
hidden potentialities are to be brought to the fore. Certainly the Negro
church has been the training school that has given the masses of the race
opportunity to develop.

The opportunity found in the Negro church to be recognized, and to be
"somebody," has stimulated the pride and preserved the self-respect of many
Negroes who would have been entirely beaten by life, and possibly completely submerged. Everyone wants to receive recognition and feel that he is
appreciated. The Negro church has supplied this need. A truckdriver of
average or more than ordinary qualities becomes the chairman of the deacon
board. A hotel man of some ability is the superintendent of the Sunday
church school of a rather important church. A woman who would be hardly
noticed, socially or otherwise, becomes a leading woman in the missionary
society. . . .

The Church Has Encouraged Education and Nurtured
Negro Business

Through the years, the Negro church through its ministry has encouraged
Negroes to educate themselves. The rather naïve and blind faith that many
Negro parents have had that education is a panacea for all ills came from the
Negro pastors. Mostly illiterate, and greatly lacking in formal training himself, he has continually urged the parents of his congregation to sacrifice much
in order that their children might enjoy a better day. Many a country boy or
girl would never have had the chance to attend college if the pastor of his or

her church had not urged it. Even in cases where Negro education was graciously supported by white people who were kindly and justly disposed toward the Negro, the Negro minister was often needed, and relied upon, to give sanction to and boost education. The parents did not always see the light; but the pastor insisted on it, and somehow the parents believed that the preacher knew. The existence of a large number of weak denominational schools as well as some strong ones is testimony to the fact that the Negro church has greatly encouraged education. Not only has the church urged Negroes to secure an education, but the church has nurtured and still nurtures Negro business. The great medium for the advertisement of Negro business is the church. Not only in sermons but in other ways, the authors were impressed with the way Negro pastors advise their people to help make strong Negro business such as insurance, banking, privately owned Negro enterprises and the like. . . .

A Potentially Free Ministry

It is the firm conviction of the writers that the Negro pastor is one of the freest, as well as most influential, men on the American platform today. This is due to various causes, but chief among them is the factor of the long-time prestige of the Negro minister, the respect for him and for religion; and the poverty and the financial freedom of the Negro church. . . .

Thus, one of the main theses of this chapter is that it is a part of the genius of the Negro church that it is owned by a poor race, supported by its members and, further, that this fact alone gives the Negro minister an opportunity and freedom in his church life that ministers of some racial groups might well covet. If the Negro pastor sees fit to condemn from his pulpit practices with respect to low wages, long hours, the working of children in industry, the unfair treatment of women in factories, the denying to the worker the right to organize, and the injustices of an economic system built on competition, self-interest, and profit—he is more likely not to be censured, and less likely to lose his position than his white brother who preaches in the same city. It is more than likely that no committee will wait on him advising him to go slow. No leading financier will walk out of the church threatening never to return. To the contrary, it is highly possible that the Negro minister would receive many congratulations and "Amens" from his congregation if he were to preach such a gospel.

When the Negro pastor feels the urge to preach a thoroughgoing gospel of brotherhood, applying it to the Negroes, whites, Japanese, Chinese, and other races, it is gladly received by Negro audiences. It is taken for granted that Negro ministers will courageously oppose lynching, Jim Crow law, and discrimination in the expenditure of tax money, especially as applied to schools, parks, playgrounds, hospitals, and the like.

This fellowship and freedom inherent in the Negro church should be conducive to spiritual growth of a unique kind. It furnished the foundation for the Negro church and the Negro ministry to become truly Christian and prophetic in the truest sense. The Negro church has the potentialities to become possibly the greatest spiritual force in the United States. What the Negro church does and will do with these potentialities will depend in a large measure upon the leadership as expressed in the Negro pulpit.

28

LETTER FROM BIRMINGHAM JAIL

MARTIN LUTHER KING, JR.

Benjamin Mays, whom Martin Luther King, Jr., revered as one of the great influences on his development, believed in the potentiality of the Negro ministry to mobilize the latent spiritual power of the church. Martin Luther King not only shared Dr. Mays' belief, he shaped his own ministry by it and became an "extremist" in the interest of justice and the fulfillment of the promise of equality for his people. Because of his rejection of violence and his willingness to admit white Christians to a partnership in his mission, many black leaders have scorned his approach to the problems of the black community. Nevertheless, he engaged the black institution of the church in the struggle for the social, economic, and political rights of black people as it had never before been so engaged. Militant blacks within and without the church have admitted, often grudgingly, that the barriers Dr. King smashed in his brief years of power were important ones and that his achievements will not easily be surpassed.

April 16, 1963

MY DEAR FELLOW CLERGYMEN:

While confined here in the Birmingham city jail, I came across your recent statement calling my present activities "unwise and untimely." Seldom do I pause to answer criticism of my work and ideas. If I sought to answer all the criticisms that cross my desk, my secretaries would have little time for anything other than such correspondence in the course of the day, and I would have no time for constructive work. But since I feel that you are men of genuine good will and that your criticisms are sincerely set forth, I want to try to answer your statement in what I hope will be patient and reasonable terms.

I think I should indicate why I am here in Birmingham, since you have been influenced by the view which argues against "outsiders coming in." I

Adapted from *Why We Can't Wait* (New York: Harper & Row, 1963), pp. 77-100, by permission of the publisher. Copyright 1963 by Martin Luther King, Jr.

have the honor of serving as president of the Southern Christian Leadership
Conference, an organization operating in every Southern state, with head-
quarters in Atlanta, Georgia. We have some eighty-five affiliated organizations
across the South, and one of them is the Alabama Christian Movement for
Human Rights. Frequently we share staff, educational, and financial resources
with our affiliates. Several months ago the affiliate here in Birmingham asked
us to be on call to engage in a nonviolent direct-action program if such were
deemed necesary. We readily consented, and when the hour came we lived
up to our promise. So I, along with several members of my staff, am here
because I was invited here. I am here because I have organizational ties here.

But more basically, I am in Birmingham because injustice is here. Just as
the prophets of the eighth century B.C. left their villages and carried their
"thus saith the Lord" far beyond the boundaries of their home towns, and
just as the Apostle Paul left his village of Tarsus and carried the gospel of
Jesus Christ to the far corners of the Greco-Roman world, so am I compelled
to carry the gospel of freedom beyond my own home town. Like Paul, I must
constantly respond to the Macedonian call for aid.

Moreover, I am cognizant of the interrelatedness of all communities and
states. I cannot sit idly by in Atlanta and not be concerned about what
happens in Birmingham. Injustice anywhere is a threat to justice everywhere.
We are caught in an inescapable network of mutuality, tied in a single gar-
ment of destiny. Whatever affects one directly, affects all indirectly. Never
again can we afford to live with the narrow, provincial "outside agitator" idea.
Anyone who lives inside the United States can never be considered an out-
sider anywhere within its bounds.

You deplore the demonstrations taking place in Birmingham. But your
statement, I am sorry to say, fails to express a similar concern for the conditions that brought about the demonstrations. I am sure that none of you
would want to rest content with the superficial kind of social analysis that
deals merely with effects and does not grapple with underlying causes. It is
unfortunate that demonstrations are taking place in Birmingham, but it is
even more unfortunate that the city's white power structure left the Negro
community with no alternative. . . .

You may well ask: "Why direct action? Why sit-ins, marches and so forth?
Isn't negotiation a better path?" You are quite right in calling for negotiation.
Indeed, this is the very purpose of direct action. Nonviolent direct action
seeks to create such a crisis and foster such a tension that a community which
has constantly refused to negotiate is forced to confront the issue. It seeks so
to dramatize the issue that it can no longer be ignored. My citing the creation
of tension as part of the work of the nonviolent resister may sound rather
shocking. But I must confess that I am not afraid of the word "tension." I

have earnestly opposed violent tension, but there is a type of constructive, nonviolent tension which is necessary for growth. Just as Socrates felt that it was necessary to create a tension in the mind so that individuals could rise from the bondage of myths and half-truths to the unfettered realm of creative analysis and objective appraisal, so must we see the need for nonviolent gad- flies to create the kind of tension in society that will help men rise from the dark depths of prejudice and racism to the majestic heights of understanding and brotherhood.

The purpose of our direct-action program is to create a situation so crisis packed that it will inevitably open the door to negotiation. I therefore concur with you in your call for negotiation. Too long has our beloved Southland been bogged down in a tragic effort to live in monologue rather than dialogue.

One of the basic points in your statement is that the action that I and my associates have taken in Birmingham is untimely. Some have asked: "Why didn't you give the new city administration time to act?" The only answer that I can give to this query is that the New Birmingham administration must be prodded about as much as the outgoing one, before it will act. . . .

My friends, I must say to you that we have not made a single gain in civil rights without determined legal and nonviolent pressure. Lamentably, it is an historical fact that privileged groups seldom give up their privileges volun- tarily. Individuals may see the moral light and voluntarily give up their unjust posture; but, as Reinhold Niebuhr has reminded us; groups tend to be more immoral than individuals.

We know through painful experience that freedom is never voluntarily given by the oppressor; it must be demanded by the oppressed. Frankly, I have yet to engage in a direct-action campaign that was "well timed" in the view of those who have not suffered unduly from the disease of segregation. For years now I have heard the word "Wait!" It rings in the ear of every Negro with piercing familiarity. This "Wait" has almost always meant "Never." We must come to see, with one of our distinguished jurists, that "justice too long delayed is justice denied." . . .

You express a great deal of anxiety over our willingness to break laws. This is certainly a legitimate concern. Since we so diligently urge people to obey the Supreme Court's decision of 1954 outlawing segregation in the public schools, at first glance it may seem rather paradoxical for us con- sciously to break laws. One may well ask: "How can you advocate breaking some laws and obeying others?" The answer lies in the fact that there are two types of laws: just and unjust. I would be the first to advocate obeying just laws. One has not only a legal but a moral responsibility to obey just laws. Conversely, one has a moral responsibility to disobey unjust laws. I would agree with St. Augustine that "an unjust law is no law at all." . . .

I hope you are able to see the distinction I am trying to point out. In no sense do I advocate evading or defying the law, as would the rabid segregationist. That would lead to anarchy. One who breaks an unjust law must do so openly, lovingly, and with a willingness to accept the penalty. I submit that an individual who breaks a law that conscience tells him is unjust, and who willingly accepts the penalty of imprisonment in order to arouse the conscience of the community over its injustice, is in reality expressing the highest respect for law. . . .

I must make two honest confessions to you, my Christian and Jewish brothers. First, I must confess that over the past few years I have been gravely disappointed with the white moderate. I have almost reached the regrettable conclusion that the Negro's great stumbling block in his stride toward freedom is not the White Citizen's Counciler or the Ku Klux Klanner, but the white moderate, who is more devoted to "order" than to justice; who prefers a negative peace which is the absence of tension to a positive peace which is the presence of justice; who constantly says: "I agree with you in the goal you seek, but I cannot agree with your methods of direct action"; who paternalistically believes he can set the timetable for another man's freedom; who lives by a mythical concept of time and who constantly advises the Negro to wait for a "more convenient season." Shallow understanding from people of good will is more frustrating than absolute misunderstanding from people of ill will. Lukewarm acceptance is much more bewildering than outright rejection. . . .

Oppressed people cannot remain oppressed forever. The yearning for freedom eventually manifests itself, and that is what has happened to the American Negro. Something within has reminded him of his birthright of freedom, and something without has reminded him that it can be gained. Consciously or unconsciously, he has been caught up by the *Zeitgeist,* and with his black brothers of Africa and his brown and yellow brothers of Asia, South America, and the Caribbean, the U.S. Negro is moving with a sense of great urgency toward the promised land of racial justice. If one recognizes this vital urge that has engulfed the Negro community, one should readily understand why public demonstrations are taking place. The Negro has many pent-up resentments and latent frustrations, and he must release them. So let him march; let him make prayer pilgrimages to the city hall; let him go on freedom rides— and try to understand why he must do so. If his repressed emotions are not released in nonviolent ways, they will seek expression through violence; this is not a threat but a fact of history. So I have not said to my people: "Get rid of your discontent." Rather, I have tried to say that this normal and healthy discontent can be channeled into the creative outlet of nonviolent direct action. And now this approach is being termed extremist.

But though I was initially disappointed at being categorized as an extremist, as I continued to think about the matter I gradually gained a measure of satisfaction from the label. Was not Jesus an extremist for love: "Love your enemies, bless them that curse you, do good to them that hate you, and pray for them which despitefully use you, and persecute you." Was not Amos an extremist for justice: "Let justice roll down like waters and righteousness like an over-flowing stream." Was not Paul an extremist for the Christian gospel: "I bear in my body the marks of the Lord Jesus." Was not Martin Luther an extremist: "Here I stand; I cannot do otherwise, so help me God." And John Bunyan: "I will stay in jail to the end of my days before I make a butchery of my conscience." And Abraham Lincoln: "This nation cannot survive half slave and half free." And Thomas Jefferson: "We hold these truths to be self-evident, that all men are created equal . . ." So the question is not whether we will be extremists, but what kind of extremists we will be. Will we be extremists for hate or for love? Will we be extremists for the preservation of injustice or for the extension of justice? In that dramatic scene on Calvary's hill three men were crucified. We must never forget that all three were crucified for the same crime—the crime of extremism. Two were extremists for immorality, and thus fell below their environment. The other, Jesus Christ, was an extremist for love, truth, and goodness, and thereby rose above his environment. Perhaps the South, the nation, and the world are in dire need of creative extremists. . . .

Let me take note of my other major disappointment. I have been so greatly disappointed with the white church and its leadership. Of course, there are some notable exceptions. I am not unmindful of the fact that each of you has taken some significant stands on this issue. I commend you, Reverend Stallings, for your Christian stand on this past Sunday, in welcoming Negroes to your worship service on a nonsegregated basis. I commend the Catholic leaders of this state for integrating Spring Hill College several years ago.

But despite these notable exceptions, I must honestly reiterate that I have been disappointed with the church. I do not say this as one of those negative critics who can always find something wrong with the church. I say this as a minister of the gospel, who loves the church; who was nurtured in its bosom; who has been sustained by its spiritual blessings and who will remain true to it as long as the cord of life shall lengthen. . . . In deep disappointment I have wept over the laxity of the church. But be assured that my tears have been tears of love. There can be no deep disappointment where there is not deep love. Yes, I love the church. How could I do otherwise? I am in the rather unique position of being the son, the grandson and the great-grandson of preachers. Yes, I see the church as the body of Christ. But, oh! How we have blemished and scarred that body through social neglect and through fear of being nonconformists. . . .

But the judgment of God is upon the church as never before. If today's church does not recapture the sacrificial spirit of the early church, it will lose its authenticity, forfeit the loyalty of millions, and be dismissed as an irrelevant social club with no meaning for the twentieth century. Every day I meet young people whose disappointment with the church has turned into outright disgust.

Perhaps I have once again been too optimistic. Is organized religion too inextricably bound to the status quo to save our nation and the world? Perhaps I must turn my faith to the inner spiritual church, the church within the church, as the true *ekklesia* and the hope of the world. But again I am thankful to God that some noble souls from the ranks of organized religion have broken loose from the paralyzing chains of conformity and joined us as active partners in the struggle for freedom. They have left their secure congregations and walked the streets of Albany, Georgia, with us. They have gone down the highways of the South on tortuous rides for freedom. Yes, they have gone to jail with us. Some have been dismissed from their churches, have lost the support of their bishops and fellow ministers. But they have acted in the faith that right defeated is stronger than evil triumphant. Their witness has been the spiritual salt that has preserved the true meaning of the gospel in these troubled times. They have carved a tunnel of hope through the dark mountain of disappointment.

I hope the church as a whole will meet the challenge of this decisive hour. But even if the church does not come to the aid of justice, I have no despair about the future. I have no fear about the outcome of our struggle in Birmingham, even if our motives are at present misunderstood. We will reach the goal of freedom in Birmingham and all over the nation, because the goal of America is freedom. Abused and scorned though we may be, our destiny is tied up with America's destiny. Before the pilgrims landed at Plymouth, we were here. Before the pen of Jefferson etched the majestic words of the Declaration of Independence across the pages of history, we were here. For more than two centuries our forebears labored in this country without wages; they made cotton king; they built the homes of their masters while suffering gross injustice and shameful humiliation—and yet out of a bottomless vitality they continued to thrive and develop. If the inexpressible cruelties of slavery could not stop us, the opposition we now face will surely fail. We will win our freedom because the sacred heritage of our nation and the eternal will of God are embodied in our echoing demands.

Before closing I feel impelled to mention one other point in your statement that has troubled me profoundly. You warmly commended the Birmingham police force for keeping "order" and "preventing violence." I doubt that you would have so warmly commended the police force if you had seen its dogs sinking their teeth into unarmed, nonviolent Negroes. I doubt that you would so quickly command the policemen if you were to observe their ugly and inhumane treatment of Negroes here in the city jail; if you were to watch them push and curse old Negro women and young Negro girls; if you were to see them slap and kick old Negro men and young boys; if you were to observe them, as they did on two occasions, refuse to give us food because we wanted to sing our grace together. I cannot join you in your praise of the Birmingham police department. . . .

I wish you had commended the Negro sit-inners and demonstrators of Birmingham for their sublime courage, their willingness to suffer and their amazing discipline in the midst of great provocation. One day the South will recognize its real heroes. They will be the James Merediths, with the noble sense of purpose that enables them to face jeering and hostile mobs, and with the agonizing loneliness that characterizes the life of the pioneer. They will be old, oppressed, battered Negro women, symbolized in a seventy-two-year-old woman in Montgomery, Alabama, who rose up with a sense of dignity and with her people decided not to ride segregated buses, and who responded with ungrammatical profundity to one who inquired about her weariness: "My feets is tired, but my soul is at rest." They will be the young high school and college students, the young ministers of the gospel and a host of their elders, courageously and nonviolently sitting in at lunch counters and willingly going to jail for conscience sake. One day the South will know that when these disinherited children of God sat down at lunch counters, they were in reality standing up for what is best in the American dream and for the most sacred values in our Judeo-Christian heritage, thereby bringing our nation back to those great wells of democracy which were dug deep by the founding fathers in their formulation of the Constitution and the Declaration of Independence.

NOTE

This response to a published statement by eight fellow clergymen from Alabama (Bishop C. C. J. Carpenter, Bishop Joseph A. Durick, Rabbi Hilton L. Grafman, Bishop Paul Hardin, Bishop Holan B. Harmon, the Reverend George M. Murray, the Reverend Edward V. Ramage. and the Reverend Earl Stallings) was composed under somewhat constricting circumstances. Begun on the margins of the newspaper in which the statement appeared while I was in jail, the letter was continued on scraps of writing paper supplied by a friendly Negro trusty, and concluded on a pad my attorneys were eventually permitted to leave me. Although the text remains in substance unaltered, I have indulged in the author's prerogative of polishing it for publication.

29

BLACK POLITICS

JOSEPH R. WASHINGTON, JR.

There was a time during the early 1960's when Joseph Washington, Jr. argued, in his controversial *Black Religion* (Boston: Beacon Press, 1964), that it was "the responsibility of all Negro congregations which exist essentially because of racial ties to go out of business." But the optimistic period of the civil rights movement is history now, and Dr. Washington has given his thought on the Negro church a searching reexamination. The old Negro church as mere haven is doomed, but the new black church, which will rise phoenix-like from its ashes, will reaffirm it as a "movement for freedom and equality." As a political force at the crucial local level, the church, which has the loyalty of the masses, may be able to provide the cohesiveness necessary for the realization of the ultimate goal—the revolution of the white preconsciousness. The black church, by injecting religion into politics, can mold a unity that will not disintegrate in the face of immediate political or economic gains, but will hold firm until social equality, the fundamental birthright of black Americans, has been acknowledged.

The institutional center of the Negro community is the Negro church. The riots in the Northern and urban communities cannot be understood as sanctioned by the Negro church or stemming from its agitation. As the dominant social institution of the community, the Negro church condones in no way the destructive violence which erupts in the warring madness of a Los Angeles, Chicago, or Springfield in the summers, as in other cities of our past and future. The Negro church continues to be for the present the heart of the Negro community in the South where riots do not occur as in the North, partly because the vicious segregation of the South has provided the Negro there with the opportunity of owning businesses in particular and property in general so that the Negro underdog has a stake in even a segregated economy. This outcome of a thoroughly segregated society augurs well for

Reprinted from *The Politics of God* (Boston: Beacon Press, 1967), pp. 207-227, by permission of the author. Copyright 1967 by Joseph R. Washington, Jr.

the future of Negro-white relations in the South together with the thus far largely southern-based civil rights movement which demonstrates the insufficiency of economic well being for the privileged few who have functioned in the past, consciously or not, to keep the majority of Negroes in tow.

These dilemmas of Negro-white segregation and class separations within the Negro community have resulted in the migration to the North of the lower-class Negro at the bottom of the heap who has the least stake in the society, seeking in the North the opportunity denied in the South. While the South has permitted Negroes to advance economically within the Negro community, the process has been ingeniously selective and promotes the survival of the fittest. The North has not condoned a dual system, preferring to operate on the basis of including exceptional Negroes into restricted areas of its economy, a process which has allowed a fewer number of Negroes to advance in business and the ownership of property than in the South. Since there is not a sufficient number of Negro businessmen in the South to include the lower-class masses they act as inhibitors and are of sufficient strength to aid the in-migration of the masses to the North. The even less numerical strength of Negro businesses in the North results in an absence of control of the Negro masses, providing the possibility for the only outlet of a frustrated mass in riotous destruction.

Negroes are of sufficient numbers in the North and whites of sufficient deference to the democratic creed to prevent the return of Negroes to the South or a segregated southern pattern in the North. The only way out of the ghetto is that of full inclusion into society. The question is since whites will not rapidly move in this direction by their own initiative, how can the pace be quickened? Presently, despite their adoration of property, whites are even more concerned to preserve preference for whites and willing to take chances on the destruction of property they so dearly love—presumably on the basis that there is enough financial power in the economy to rebuild the destruction of property, whereas the inclusion of Negroes fully into the society is irreversible. In the long run, barricading Negroes in ghettos will not prove an adequate deterrent, but, as the Los Angeles riots of August 1965 revealed, they provide a postponement of the inevitable which is less of a sacrifice than equality. This is the antireason of whites which is no more to be condoned than the emotive response of Negroes through riots. To rob a people for three generations of full economic equality, which not only means poverty at the lowest levels but an equally weighted poverty at the highest levels of becoming big businessmen and at the middle level of becoming middle-class businessmen—to so rob a people for so long and then attempt to compensate by emergency measures of poverty programs is the height of preconscious irrationality. It is equally a preconscious irrationality to give men a taste of the goods of society and deny them full measure or allow them to be full partners in the society. Obviously, the Negro male is not allowed to compete equally in business with the white male because the Negro male is not accepted equally and therefore cannot gain the natural clientele of the general public. With the availability of lower-class jobs rapidly receding, these situations tend toward the disintegration of the Negro family and the desperation for material goods, which takes the form of rerobbing what has been robbed. Negroes engaged in riotous vandalism may not be comparable to Robin Hood, but neither is their status, for a Robin Hood could be accepted in the larger society from which he chose dissent as Negroes cannot now be in this society. People tend to respond irrationally if they are treated irrationally. The new technique of rationally formed rights and equal opportunity programs are based upon the preservation of the irrational white preconsciousness, which is the real objective of riotous irrationality.

Heretofore, the function of the Negro church has been that of a haven. In effect it has served as a cut-rate social outlet, selling itself for quantity rather than quality, offering cheap white medicine in colored doses of several hours of relief for a week-long headache. Without the Negro church's false offering of second-class status—a substitute for first-class equality—there would have erupted more riots on a larger scale in more communities. Let us prevent their irrational occurrences in future summers by better means than that of hiring more police to protect the status quo. The 1965 and 1966 Los Angeles riots might well serve notice that the old technique of the Negro church at the heart of the community is no longer strong enough to combat disadvan-tages, weakened as it is by strengthened desired for real freedom with and for equality. In the absence of freedom with equality, material goods gained in any way possible and the gratification of destruction is the next best thing. Indeed, the time is short for the Negro church as the heart of the community. There is no question about its demise. What is at stake is the terms on which it will cease and desist as a Negro qua Negro institution of courage, power, wealth, and strength with meaning.

The history of histrionic black politics in churches can no longer be tolerated by the Negro church unless it desires to abdicate its opportunity for creative responsibility in providing the Negro a base in each community for a means to bring about the permanent power and wealth momentarily felt in a riotous war. The one value of the Los Angeles riot worth nurturing beyond the inextinguishable reality of powerlessness and poverty is the actual power of the Negro community. Nearly $250 million in destruction resulted from the negative concertedness of Los Angeles Negroes in 1965–1966. Would not the amount of power and wealth generated through a Negro com-munity in concert toward positive goals—sustained, strategically concentrated, and with a permanent, community-based political machine—would it not be greater than that of a riot?

The responsibility of the Negro church in the process is inseparable from the opportunity through its engagement of the Negro masses. It has the task of neither controlling riots for the well being of the white ownership of property nor of providing a means of escape from suffering via the route of religious services which culminate in the ineffective if spirited "waiting for Godot." The spiritual outpouring of the masses may well be needed for a long time to come and moreover may be instrumentally effective if this spirit in churches becomes, like the spirit in the civil rights movement protests, a source of strength—this time for political action beyond protest.

To be quite candid, Negro churches may not be the imperative required to gain the political power increasingly sought by other Negro organizations; but one thing is clear—a perceptive Negro church can hardly miss the truth that insofar as these other organizations are effective, the need for the Negro church will decrease proportionately. It is also clear that if the Negro church releases its hold on the Negro masses in return for the support of existing power structures that in the long run cannot but bring the personalities and institutions power and health which now exist only because both take advantage of the disadvantaged—the process will be speeded up immeasurably. Herein lies the opportunity of the Negro church in black politics which is also its responsibility for the Negro masses. The Negro church began as a movement for freedom and equality and although it has slipped into the ameliorative role of a sociocultural institution, it is not yet clear that it cannot reaffirm its original function, especially in view of its present dysfunction with respect to the substantive issues which confront its people. In truth, there is no other live option.

If this option is to be a living one, the leadership of Negro churches will have to be led indigenously, no outside Negro institutions of social uplift will be able to bring this about. Some ideas may have to change among the presidents and staff of the two national Baptist conventions, as well as bishops and officers of the several Methodist Episcopal churches—no less the less populous Negro ecclesiastical institutions. If the imagination is lacking to envision the present need of Negro churches for religious and even sacramental support for the political unity of its masses, the desperation of the masses may fill the leadership gap. It would not be too much to ask of Martin Luther King, Jr. to spend his energies in reshaping the intent and content of directions within and among the national Negro ecclesiastical leadership which affects the local churches. This would be no substitute for direct action in local communities. Confrontation of both institutionally based Negro church leadership and the masses is necessary for the indispensable changes called for in objectives if not methods. It should not be surprising to find, were such a radical move undertaken, the real leadership and motivation within the masses themselves and therefore the greatest possibility for realization of the mass-based Negro church. A pincer movement within the Negro church would ultimately result in the destruction of the Negro church based on the present nonvoluntary, Negro-white ghettos. Yet, a pincer movement would be based upon the constructive task of releasing the masses and their leadership from barriers to their involvement in the process of change, without which involvement there can be no change. The value of this pincer movement outweighs all of the blood, sweat, and tears it demands. For the Negro mass is amassed at the bottom of society and nowhere is their presence identifiable more regularly than in the Negro church. It cannot be reiterated too often or too strongly that despite the frustrations, the white community will move no faster than the Negro community forces it to move through power, which is potentially within the Negro church—though by no means exclusively.

As an institution, the Negro church has long ago lost the respect and support of secular leadership organizations and leaders in the Negro community, despite the fact that a number of Negro churches support the NAACP. Negro ministers who join in a movement such as the Southern Christian Leadership Council demonstratively withdraw from the institutional Negro church. Clearly, the way in which King has used the Negro church in detachment from it has not only won respect from Negro leadership outside the church but clearly illuminated the untapped power potential in this community center. If Negro ministers and the masses can be directed to engage in political power, their objective will not be to elicit the respect of intellectuals, though this would be an inevitable outcome. In any case, despite the antipathy between nonecclesiastical Negro leadership organizations and the Negro church, or for that matter the failure of the Negro church to be true to its inception resulting in the increasing number of other organizations, these organizations need all the support they can get to organize the masses into a powerful political force for change. The support of Negro churches would be most welcome.

The moral and theological bases for Negro churches' involvement in politics [are] not . . . in conflict with or contradiction to the function of the church. Together with the moral requirement to meet the needs of Negroes through a positive acceptance of the masses and their capacity to engage in the challenge of change, the theoretical, theological, moral, and political groundwork is unmistakable.

Given this theological and theoretical basis for moral action and change, the next step is to gain the moral commitment to responsibility. This calls for skill and knowledge for redirection within the institutional Negro church. Whatever tactics are used for this purpose (e.g., appeal to tradition, conscience, suffering—disclosure of sham through shame, opportunity for advancement of parishioners lost—education), "pragma" rather than dogma must be the rule.

Beyond the moral situation, a radical theological perspective, and an institutional commitment, a practical method is required. This practical method the Negro church cannot provide. It can indulge in practical politics wholeheartedly out of experience in ecclesiastical politics which have been less moral than these times require and certainly more exclusive and circumscribed. There is a sense in which the Negro church may lose face in practical community politics insofar as it works in concert with other organizations. This loss of prestige can be turned into face-saving through several significant functions the Negro church is in a position to contribute, First, the Negro church is the most natural means for the regular gathering of the largest number of Negroes in the community. To contribute the people in concert is its primary task in the new demand and opportunity of black politics. Second, the Negro church, aware of its role in the process of fundamental social change, can bring to bear upon white preconsciousness its contradiction of the Biblical faith through relentless efforts in social integration of churches and communities. The position must be that of the impossibility of a church's being Christian without the demonstrated presence of Negroes and whites which requires the removal of discrimination in housing, which is possible only with equality of income, which cannot be gained without equality of social acceptance. In any planned effort within the Negro community for a direct attack upon social inequality there will be an ample number of Negroes to carry forth the main burden of politics through cohesion of Negroes in Negro churches. Third, real commitment of the Negro church in politics will earn it the right of its inheritance, the populous center of the Negro masses instrumental in the cooperation of all Negro organizations for the advancement of the people. This cooperation through political union would not interfere with the different functions of the various organizations (e.g., NAACP—litigation; Urban League—economic opportunity; Student Nonviolent Coordinating Committee—youth development; CORE—enlistment of nonchurch-based masses; churches—cohesiveness of church-based masses), but would mean a united political front.

Thus, in the new politics, of necessity and moral rightness, a real function of the Negro church would include mass cohesion on a broad base to provide a center for the mass-centered and issue-oriented politics of independence. The clearest model for such political unity is in the Mississippi Freedom Democratic Party (MFDP) which not only uniquely demonstrates the power

lessness of black politics South and North, so far, but the real possibility
therein were it supported fully by the institutional Negro church.

What is now needed (and the Negro church must support if it is to be
responsible to its oppressed masses, who are not needed in a society of abundance and therefore are passed off as "drags") is the real organization of the
community. Although the Negro church has been the titular head of the
Negro community, it has not engaged in its mobilization for power; rather,
it has done little more than open its doors through which the masses have
flocked with little if any nurturing. Thus the Negro church has not been
involved in community mobilization and is without the essential skills and
techniques for this fundamental operation.

Indeed, none of the old-line Negro organizations is in position to provide
more than support in this area of community mobilization and even the
more recently developed SCLC is at best equipped for short-term organization of a select community for the more emotional force of protest. The
Negro church and other Negro organizations which are committed to the
Negro masses will need to learn mobilization through cooperation with other
movements.

A good beginning for community organization would be to utilize the
techniques of Saul Alinsky and his Industrial Areas Foundation. Alinsky,
well-portrayed in Charles Silberman's *Crisis in Black and White*,[1] is the highly
respected and paid community organizer, well known for his strategy of mass
jujitsu in Chicago's TWO (The Woodlawn Organization). The IAF has branched
out into many communities where mobilization has taken place as often outside formal social structures (in low-income neighborhood house meetings
for example) as within structures calling upon IAF consultation or direct
involvement. Alinsky is a firm believer in grass-roots democracy via the
masses, insisting that theory be tested by its pragmatic value rather than
building a theory which is then taken untried to the field. While he does not
respond favorably to ecclesiastical institutions as such, he works well with
and for religious community organizations which request his leadership and
may for this reason praise churches extraordinarily on occasion:

> The biggest change I've seen in the twenty years or so that I've been
> involved in social action is in the role the churches are playing. Back in the
> 1930's an organizer might expect to get some help from the CIO or from a
> few progressive AFL unions. There wasn't a church in sight. But today they
> have really moved into the social arena, the political arena. They have taken
> over the position organized labor had a generation ago. They are the big
> dominant force in civil rights.[2]

It may be necessary to wait for Alinsky's forthcoming book on the subject to learn of his "rules for revolution." But the Negro church, and the other Negro community organizations with which it must cooperate if the Negro community is to turn its potential into political power, can learn now from Alinsky how to build "a strong, disciplined, vital organization which will maintain its form and force over an extended period of time."[3] Alinsky aptly criticizes the civil rights movement for relying on the single issue of civil rights instead of building community-based organizations on many issues including "housing, jobs, schools, consumer prices, representation and power at the decision making centers, health, crime, and every other aspect of life that affects the welfare and future of the local people and their children."[4] The art of organization is the alliance of groups with varying interests which can be supported in agreed upon priorities while working for common objectives of the total community.

Such development of a community into an organization depends upon concrete and immediately realizable goals. Stemming from these successes is the unity necessary for the middle-range and long-range goals of more abstraction. To build such an organization in community after community requires sophistication, manpower, money, stamina, intelligence, experience, and compromise. These never are in abundance in any community with commitment to the grubbiness of politics. A beginning in the large urban communities can be seen with the IAF, the Northern Student Movement, Students for a Democratic Society, and the Student Nonviolent Committee. These groups are a good beginning, but they are not enough, leaving as they do too many communities without organization and those with organization without enough cohesiveness upon which to ground astuteness.

This process could be more effective if Negro churches would sponsor leadership schools throughout the country directed by Saul Alinsky and his teams of organizers, as well as other proven groups, to which ministers and laymen would be sent for the express purposes of learning the tactics of organizing a community. To learn how to project grievances into public issues instead of riots is the key to Alinsky's success, which needs to be mastered and extended into a formidable political power.

Community organization is basic, but its purpose must be for practical black politics. In the South the MFDP has shown the way without community organization on the strength of not being represented. This experience of the MFDP is insufficient in the North, and even now in the South with the voting rights bill. Together with community organization there must come an awareness on the part of the masses not only of their frustrations but of their power to turn these defeats into gain, perhaps even with the "ace" of riots as the ultimate threat, comparable to the wildcat strike in the labor movement. Since it takes more than leadership to organize a community and to build the community into a political power, it is a question as to how the Negro masses can gain the awareness and commitment needed now. While in cooperation with other groups in community organization for black politics, what the churches can provide is the drumming into the Negro masses of their sorry plight in such a fashion and with such consistency as has previously been the case in making the masses feel better than they are or providing the suggestion of future reward. If such a constant confrontation with their unfortunate lot were combined with the opportunity to translate their frustrations into ways of securing the necessary transformations of society, the cruelty involved might not bring immediate compensation via solution of social problems but it would aid in the realization of the plight of the Negro masses, which is the precondition of community organization for political power on a nationwide scale.

When the trust in ministers and churches is taken into consideration, along with the deference of religion, there is a force for black politics which does not require a political ideology to be acquired by the Negro masses. What is needed are ministers and laymen who can be trusted and will instruct the fellowship in the realities of sophisticated city politics in unsophisticated ways. Most of all the masses require inspiration to create the only power for real change—their collectivity in mutual trust against the preconsciousness of white middle-class society which favors a few Negroes in order not to accept masses. To make the transition from social centers through community organizations to political power structures does not mean an independent political party detached from the Democratic or Republican party. It does mean an independent political movement within the parties, an alignment of the ghettos for a viable political movement. The rallying cry of the pulpit must be that this is a racist society, inciting not to riot but to political concert for purposes of changing the local power structures in each community and therefore the economic forces which respond positively to legislative changes, in lieu of root changes required to eliminate the profound social evils.

Direct engagement of the Negro church in politics will result not only in a broad base but the much needed injection into the movement of black politics the hope based upon the Kingdom of God which cannot be shaken by despair. Despair is the inevitable result of hope based upon human beings and institutions. Based on the brotherhood of man demand, black politics will be informed by a faith more sustaining, if not more instrumental, than an ideology. Ideologies do not necessarily lose their ground for hope; they are more often than not illusions of grandeur. Faith in the demand of the brotherhood of man permits the alignment with all groups seeking the equality of the Negro. Such faith deploys political bickerings via the commitment to the Kingdom of God that requires all human groups to work together toward its requirement and seeks its spirit in realignments beyond every crushing defeat. It is this faith the Negro church can offer instead of ideology—better still, a faith against which to evaluate ideology and with which to inform it.

If the Negro church will enter the arena of black politics as an institution in each community, whether by leadership from the top or coercion from the bottom, it will together with other groups in large measure determine whether the Negro will remain half slave and half free. It is a serious question: Can the Negro be deghettoized within a democracy or must he remain a victim of ghetto? If the latter, it means that the United States will be following the pattern of South Africa, and in this event it is only a matter of time: thus, the imperative of the Negro church reasserting its role. Whether or not time has run out and it is not now possible to bring about the fundamental social change needed for the Negro to be equal is not now certain. It is certain that if the Negro church does not assume an active and cooperative role in the guidance of the masses toward a designed destiny, the immense task of mass reaffiliation in other groups may be too costly and too long for the realization of the democratic creed.

We are now beset by the alternatives of political power: to shape the political and economic confluences of the North and thus of the South toward equality *or* spontaneous riots which lead to a police state. The history of America attests to the vigorous role of religious institutions in mobilizing immigrant people for strength in union. In 800 A.D., Charlemagne turned to the church for the political unification of the empire. The "suffering servant" people of Israel did not differentiate between the community of faith and the community of politics. More than any other institution, the Negro church has the ear of the Negro masses. It is the masses which set the pace for the Negro group by their sheer dominance. The exceptional Negro is feared neither in the white North or the white South. It is the black horde which whites fear, and in keeping back this vast majority they inevitably deny full equality to all Negroes. The last chance for the Negro to be accepted lies in the arena of politics dominated by the masses. The last chance for the Negro church to be effective lies in its exercise of influence to form with other groups a mass political base. The last chance for a democratic America lies in effective black politics, lacking which violence will pour forth from Negroes and they will be overwhelmed by a greater violence and there will result a police state with "justice and freedom" for neither whites nor blacks.

If the future of Negro-white relations depends upon the Negro's gaining power via politics, black politics cannot be concerned with power for power's sake. Political power for blacks means a voice in the decisions of the com-

munity and the opportunity for negotiations with the white power structure
for the good of the community. There is no community good if it is not
good for the Negro, add there is no good for the Negro which is not good for
the community. The present emphasis in human relations, which the swing
toward politics clearly manifests, is upon changing behavior. To change
behavior and therefore social structures, it is generally assumed by social
scientists, eventuates in the change of attitudes. It is not a question of
changing either white attitudes or white behavior but both. It is an illusion
to assume that when whites are forced to sit down with Negroes and negotiate
their attitudes will change toward the Negro, who will be seen as an equal,
just as the illusion once was dominant that attitudes must be changed to bring
about a change in behavior. Of course, there is a difference between civil
rights negotiating from pressure and power politics as the basis for negotiations. Politics is the way of democracy. But politics does not change human
nature. Nothing would be more foolish than for Negroes to expect from
concerted power a sudden change in behavior and attitudes. Power can change
social structure, but not the human beings who are structured in social
groups. Only through political power will Negroes increasingly share in the
economy, but this is not to be equated with equality. The real value of black
politics is in providing the Negro with a new image based upon real power
which will allow him to take the offensive in both the change of social
structures and social living. This is evident in the Negro middle class, marked
as it is by the same unacceptability as the lower class. Without the result of
social equality, the gains of political and economic equality are of no ultimate value. Today, the immediate objective must be political unity of
Negroes, the means to economic well-being. About this there is no question.
The long-range goal of social equality may not be possible in a racist society
dominated by white preconsciousness. Yet, the Negro will be as frustrated
tomorrow as he is today if he aims for political and economic power and
assumes that in gaining both he gains social equality. He must ultimately aim
for nothing less than social equality, at which he must work with the same
vigor as political and economic power.

The Negro church in its engagement in politics for blacks must turn to
those with expertise in community organization, economics, and politics. In
attracting and gaining the allegiance of the masses of Negroes, the Negro
church is responsible to and for the masses. No less than instilling in the
masses a fervor for politics equal to religious fervor, the Negro church must
also make them aware that ideologies, methods, strategies, and planning,
though absolutely essential, are not absolutes. They are the necessary tools of
democracy. The Negro church must be a school in the democratic process
and one of its first lessons should be to make clear that economic and political

power can be achieved and earned, while social equality is a birthright which
can neither be achieved nor earned, though it may be denied. It is because
the Negro has been denied his birthright, social equality, that he does not
have political and economic equality. The reverse is simply not true. Only a
change in Negro-white group relations will bring about social equality. To
place confidence in political and economic power as the means to social
equality is but to be taken in by a more sophisticated and updated interpretation of the old line that when Negroes prove themselves they will be accepted.
Many Negroes have proved themselves according to any objective standard—
none has been accepted.

In this next stage of Negro-white group relations, the Negro church must
challenge the even now dominant mood which offers the motivation of
political and economic equality. This mood takes the tack that the Negro must
develop a class consciousness among the masses, which is tantamount to an
ideological warfare between Negroes and Negroes as well as between Negroes
and whites. The Negro church cannot avoid fellowship with those who take
this line and should not for they are often the source of tactical astuteness.
The Negro church in working with ideologists must work with the Negro
masses, reminding them that all Negroes suffer from segregation discrimination and this is motivation enough to engage in community politics for
blacks. The Negro cannot become a tool for those who wish a radical reconstruction of economics via an independently based Negro political movement.
To become so would not result in the gaining of the birthright the Negro has
been denied. If the present democratic system and free enterprise system are
flexible enough and sufficiently responsive to power for the well-being of
most whites, the fact that there are poor whites and Negroes may mean
changes occur too slowly, not that the necessary changes cannot occur within
the system. The poverty-stricken white and the poverty-stricken Negro do
not share the same plight. That the Negro has a movement going for him
which other poverty-stricken groups do not have is a fact. It does not follow
from this he should become a foil for those who wish to eliminate poverty by
the militancy of the Negro. The movement of the Negro will aid this democracy and this economy to improve the lot of its own people and the people
of the world. But this is not what motivates the Negro; the history of the
Negro church is a singular reminder of this fact. What motivates the Negro is
that he is an outcast and therefore his objective is to radically change, not
simply reconstruct or reform or renew, the fundamental value of white preconsciousness. It is not certain whether this change is possible until every
method within the limits of democracy has been tried. The remaining method
to be tried is the mixing of what so many have been taught to avoid: religion
and politics. In the past they have been tried separately by Negroes, a key

difference from whites. Their value is in the power which comes from a people working in concert. Nothing less than the tangible rewards of religion in politics is sufficiently cohesive for the Negro to unite for the long, long attack upon white preconsciousness. If in the process there are transformations of traditional operational procedures, and some Negroes receive exceptional opportunities, or all Negroes are raised economically along with their white brethren—these are but nourishments for the substantive task.

The solution to Negro-white group conflicts is not lacking because knowledge is unavailable. There is more than enough information. The conflicts persist because of a conflict of interests and opinions within and between white power structures and Negro groups. Thus, the function of the Negro church in black politics is to bring about unity among Negroes whereby the disagreements as to how social equality can be achieved will be subordinated to the unity for its achievement. A unified Negro body in each community can affect even more the daily and long range decision-making processes of local governments than those at the national level. In the domestic sphere, national policies reflect the conflicts of interests at the local level. Each community in urban America is governed by the process of politics, the varying ideas, opinions and interests. Both elected politicians and appointed bureaucrats engage in politics. The engagement of the Negro church in politics would not be for group power politics alone—to which elected politicians are peculiarly sensitive. It would be an engagement for the purposes of establishing an image or presence which affects administrative decisions. Politicians respond to overt pressure of groups, particularly at election time. Administrators or bureaucrats are subject to politics in their decisions more out of concern for effective implementation than for favors or a mutual exchange.

The unity of blacks in politics means that the Negro church is concerned equally for the politics of politicians and the politics of administrators. Administrative decision-makers are influenced not only at the time of decision making but prior to this in what is to form the content of decisions. What is allowable in the thinking stage, the planning board stage, the proposal stage is a matter of politics—that which is allowable or determined either by voting bloc power or special interest groups. The unity of the Negro through the church means not only the pressure of voting bloc power but the presence of a special interest group. The advantage of black politics is a united front on both political bases, a counterweight to conflicting white ideas and interests with respect to the inclusion or exclusion of the Negro special interest in each decision of the community. The Negro has to be concerned about all community interests. The plus factor of white politics is the special interest of the Negro group for the neglected dimension of social equality. Toward this total concern the Negro church can contribute the solidarity of the masses which will not sell out for mere economic or political growth where this jeopardizes the opportunity for social equality, or merely postpones consideration of social equality.

In capitalizing upon the role of politics the Negro will need to disavow bickering and cherish conflict. The fundamental principle to be advocated is that the special self-interest of the Negro for social equality and all of its subsequent economic benefits is in the public interest. The fact that the Negro is not a social equal is a political reality. The Negro must be determined to change this political fact of inequality. To do so requires the control of conflicting political interests and modes of achievement within the Negro community whereby the Negro group becomes a moral force of revolutionary significance. Thus, the added role of the Negro church is not only to pay lip service to the principle that the masses can make decisions for themselves, but also to provide this possibility through not allowing black politics to become so machine-like as to make the machine a higher priority than the people. Such vital concern for the masses requires the Negro church to be a permanent political organization, voluntary through and through. What the Negro church has that any political group requires for maintenance of strength is prestige for masses, their involvement in an organization of congenial people who are committed to increasing the good of their fellowship and the community. These are the natural strengths of the Negro church and imperatives for nonecclesiastical as well as ecclesiastical politics.

With this strength the Negro church can function as a mediator with other Negro organizations, forming a cooperative which initiates programs for the pressing immediate and long-range needs of the Negro. To be effective as a mediator does not mean the Negro church needs to be the initiator of political programs, it can give or withhold its sanction and therefore exercise enormous influence—particularly with its hold on the masses. Its positive role is in building personal ties of support through building up a strong family bond so that there is a sense of personal commitment to the well-being of relations. Beyond the strengthening of personal and family ties among the masses, the Negro church has a responsibility of engaging the middle- and upper-middle-class Negroes whose destiny vis-à-vis equality is tied to the breakthrough of the masses.

It is a formidable task, unifying Negroes despite the numerical urban strength and the visible gap between their hopes and deferred attainments. An unprecedented maturity is essential to develop a singularity and prevent schisms through the push and pull of those militants who demand black politics be reform politics, machine politics, independent or nonpartisan politics, or politics of alliances. While unity of the Negro is basic everywhere, the tactics must reflect the peculiarities of each community, each issue, and each stage in the over-all objective. What is necessary in each situation is not a matter of knowledge or general principles, it is a matter of experience and intuition. There are a small but sufficient number of Negro and white citizens able and willing to provide the necessary resources for effective political action, given the unification and commitment of Negroes.

It is true that family disorganization, the economic instability of the male, limited education and skills are marks of the masses which are the extraordinary heritage of the Negro, compounding his desire for security above his sense of community. The basic securities of adequate education and attractive employment and homes must be provided. Yet the achievements of these fundamental conditions will not automatically yield loyalty to the Negro family and community. The heritage of second-class citizenship, which results in both destructive frustrations of the male Negro lashing out and apathy, can be countered only by a sense of common unity that transcends individual and family disorganization. This the Black Muslims have taught us. The evolutionary process of providing the Negro male job status and family loyalty need not be a deterrent to a revolutionary Negro group unity. The alienation of the Negro male and the atomization of the Negro family we will have with us for decades, however many emergency measures are unleashed to upgrade employment. The disunity of the Negro community need not follow.

To the extent the Negro community continues to be divided it will be so because an historically divisive Negro church, seeking first personal and then institutional loyalty, fails to meet the opportunity of emphasizing its unitive powers for the larger interest of the total people. In such an event, the Negro church at the center of the masses who are the Negro community will be an unredeemable imbalance of immorality, decadence, selfishness, irrelevance, irresponsibility, and unmitigated corruption. It will then earn its despise and hasten its demise.

The opportunity of the Negro church to which the masses has given blind allegiance is to unify them wherein lies the real possibility for overcoming the influence of the destructive elements within the Negro community as well as outside of it. The emergence of political orientations within an increasing number of civil rights movements are possessed with either the position that the Negro masses must become class conscious and thus oppose blacks and whites of the middle class or that the Negro masses must be siphoned off into the middle class in the hopes that a small number of Negroes remaining in the masses will not be detrimental to an expanding middle class. The Negro church cannot become a party to any divisiveness. It knows that all Negroes are in the same situation of statuslessness, a condition that cannot be corrected by disunity but *may* be through unity. The fact that some Negroes enjoy more economic rewards than others does not mean they have a monopoly on courage, community interests, and the willingness to improve their lot and those of their children where the opportunity is clear. Though tagged as the group interested in welfare as opposed to middle class interest in status, it was the lower-class Negro who braved, for the most part, the lines of jeering whites in the desegregation of schools. At bottom all Negroes desire economic security, but the absence of equal economic gains is as inevitable in the Negro community as in the white community. Clearly, various economic levels do not necessitate division of the Negro group, given a good and even high rate of living for those at the lower levels. It is clear that the small middle-class Negro group is dependent upon the rise in opportunity of the lower-class Negroes. The further up the economic scale the masses rise, the middle class rises proportionately further. A dedicated Negro church will give itself for the unity of the masses not only as a basis for their improvement but as a basis for the unity of all Negroes. For a unified, militant, and skillful lower class is the necessary condition to bind all Negroes together.

The singularity of the Negro masses would form an attractive body which the middle-class Negro need no longer fear. Having overcome *internal* hatred, all Negroes could then accept the hatred expressed by whites and make political use of this hatred. In the drive for social equality, hatred is a necessary basis for Negro-white relationships, and though it is neither inevitable nor an acceptable basis, it is a concrete one to be affirmed. Hatred is not idealistic, it is realistic and therefore pragmatic. Since the white community is based upon an irrational presupposition, the rational use of irrationality may prove the most permanent basis for a relationship, which is after all the essence of politics.

Social equality may elude the Negro as surely as equality of economic well being between Negroes. The function of the Negro church is not to be deluded by but increase the broad base of political unity to unite the Negro through economic well-being and prevent him from being satisfied. It is the voice of the Negro church which must be heard loud and clear. Whether or not the Negro can win or be given his birthright, his primary motivation must be not to allow whites to have any security in their birthright until *all* groups have their right. The task of the Negro is not to change the minds and hearts of dominant whites. The task is to change their world. They must seek first the Kingdom of God and then all else will be added. This is not only black politics, it is good politics, it is the demand of the Kingdom of God—the rudimentary principles and practices of the politics of God.

NOTES

1. Charles Siberman, *Crisis in Black and White* (New York, 1964).

2. Saul Alinsky, "A Professional Radical Moves in on Rochester," *Harper's,* July 1965, p. 52.

3. *Ibid.*

4. *Ibid.*

30

BLACK POWER

NATIONAL COMMITTEE OF NEGRO CHURCHMEN

In the following statement the National Committee of Negro (now Black) Churchmen clearly assert their determination to rechannel the Negro church into a politically involved institution of the social gospel. Black-white relations in America have been characterized by too much black conscience and an equal surfeit of white power. Setting themselves the task of the essential reformation of the black church, they are no less demanding of others. It is the responsibility of American leaders to see that equality in the law is carried into real life, of white clergymen to understand the necessity of black power, of black citizens to understand that power can come only through unity and to recognize even now the necessity of reconciliation with whites, and of the mass media to continue to wield their power for the revelation of truth.

We, an informal group of Negro churchmen in America, are deeply disturbed about the crisis brought upon our country by historic distortions of important human realities in the controversy about "black power." What we see shining through the variety of rhetoric is not anything new but the same old problem of power and race which has faced our beloved country since 1619.

We realize that neither the term "power" nor the term "Christian conscience" is an easy matter to talk about, especially in the context of race relations in America. The fundamental distortion facing us in the controversy about "black power" is rooted in a gross imbalance of power and conscience between Negroes and white Americans. It is this distortion, mainly, which is responsible for the widespread, though often inarticulate, assumption that white people are justified in getting what they want through the use of power, but that Negro Americans must, either by nature or by circumstances, make their appeal only through conscience. As a result, the power of white men and the conscience of black men have both been corrupted. The power of

Reprinted from *The New York Times*, July 31, 1966, by permission of the National Committee of Negro Churchmen.

white men is corrupted because it meets little meaningful resistance from
Negroes to temper it and keep white men from aping God. The conscience
of black men is corrupted because, having no power to implement the
demands of conscience, the concern for justice is transmuted into a distorted form of love, which, in the absence of justice, becomes chaotic self-
surrender. Powerlessness breeds a race of beggars. We are faced now with a
situation where conscienceless power meets powerless conscience, threatening the very foundations of our nation.

Therefore, we are impelled by conscience to address at least four groups
of people in areas where clarification of the controversy is of the most urgent
necessity. We do not claim to present the final word. It is our hope, however,
to communicate meanings from our experience regarding power and certain
elements of conscience to help interpret more adequately the dilemma in
which we are all involved.

To the Leaders of America: Power and Freedom

It is of critical importance that the leaders of this nation listen also to a voice
which says that the principal source of the threat to our nation comes neither
from the riots erupting in our big cities, nor from the disagreements among
the leaders of the civil rights movement, nor even from mere raising of the
cry for "black power." These events, we believe, are but the expression of
the judgment of God upon our nation for its failure to use its abundant
resources to serve the real well-being of people, at home and abroad.

We give our full support to all civil rights leaders as they seek for basically
American goals, for we are not convinced that their mutual reinforcement
of one another in the past is bound to end in the future. We would hope that
the public power of our nation will be used to strengthen the civil rights
movement and not to manipulate or further fracture it.

We deplore the overt violence of riots, but we believe it is more important
to focus on the real sources of these eruptions. These sources may be abetted
inside the ghetto, but their basic causes lie in the silent and covert violence
which white middle-class America inflicts upon the victims of the inner city.
The hidden, smooth and often smiling decisions of American leaders which
tie a white noose of suburbia around the necks, and which pin the backs of
the masses of Negroes against the steaming ghetto walls—without jobs in a
booming economy; with dilapidated and segregated educational systems in
the full view of unenforced laws against it; in short: the failure of American
leaders to use American power to create equal opportunity *in life* as well as

in law–this is the real problem and not the anguished cry for "black power."

From the point of view of the Christian faith, there is nothing necessarily wrong with concern for power. At the heart of the Protestant reformation is the belief that ultimate power belongs to God alone and that men become most inhuman when concentrations of power lead to the conviction–overt or covert–that any nation, race or organization can rival God in this regard. At issue in the relations between whites and Negroes in America is the problem of inequality of power. Out of this imbalance grows the disrespect of white men for the Negro personality and community, and the disrespect of Negroes for themselves. This is a fundamental root of human injustice in America. In one sense, the concept of "black power" reminds us of the need for the possibility of authentic democracy in America.

We do *not* agree with those who say that we must cease expressing concern for the acquisition of power lest we endanger the "gains" already made by the civil rights movement. The fact of the matter is, there have been few substantive gains since about 1950 in this area. The gap has constantly widened between the incomes of nonwhites relative to the whites. Since the Supreme Court decision of 1954, de facto segregation in every major city in our land has increased rather than decreased. Since the middle of the 1950's unemployment among Negroes has gone up rather than down while unemployment has decreased in the white community.

While there has been some progress in some areas for equality for Negroes, this progress has been limited mainly to middle-class Negroes who represent only a small minority of the larger Negro community.

These are the hard facts that we must all face together. Therefore, we must not take the position that we can continue in the same old paths.

When American leaders decide to serve the real welfare of people instead of war and destruction; when American leaders are forced to make the rebuilding of our cities first priority on the nation's agenda; when American leaders are forced by the American people to quit misusing and abusing American power; then will the cry for "black power" become inaudible, for the framework in which all power in America operates would include the power and experience of black men as well as those of white men. In that way, the fear of the power of each group would be removed. America is our beloved homeland. But, America is not God. Only God can do everything. America and the other nations of the world must decide which among a number of alternatives they will choose.

To White Churchmen: Power and Love

As black men who were long ago forced out of the white church to create
and to wield "black power," we fail to understand the emotional quality of
the outcry of some clergy against the use of the term today. It is not enough
to answer that "integration" is the solution. For it is precisely the nature of
the operation of power under some forms of integration which is being challenged. The Negro church was created as a result of the refusal to submit to
the indignities of a false kind of "integration" in which all power was in the
hands of white people. A more equal sharing of power is precisely what is
required as the precondition of authentic human interaction. We understand
the growing demand of Negro and white youth for a more honest kind of
integration: one which increases rather than decreases the capacity of the
disinherited to participate with power in all of the structures of our common
life. Without this capacity to *participate with power*—i.e., to have some
organized political and economic strength to really influence people with
whom one interacts—integration is not meaningful. For the issue is not one
of racial balance but of honest interracial interaction.

For this kind of interaction to take place, all people need power, whether
black or white. We regard as sheer hypocrisy or as a blind and dangerous
illusion the view that opposes love to power. Love should be a controlling
element in power, but what love opposes is precisely the misuse and abuse
of power, not power itself. So long as white churchmen continue to moral-
ize and misinterpret Christian love, so long will justice continue to be sub-
verted in this land.

To Negro Citizens: Power and Justice

Both the anguished cry for "black power" and the confused emotional
response to it can be understood if the whole controversy is put in the context of American history. Especially must we understand the irony involved
in the pride of Americans regarding their ability to act as individuals on the
one hand, and their tendency to act as members of ethnic groups on the
other hand. In the tensions of this part of our history is revealed both the
tragedy and the hope of human redemption in America.

America has asked its Negro citizens to fight for opportunity *as individuals*
whereas at certain points in our history what we have needed most has been

opportunity for the whole group, not just for selected and approved Negroes. Thus in 1863, the slaves were made legally free, as individuals, but the real question regarding personal and group power to maintain that freedom was pushed aside. Power at that time for a mainly rural people meant land and tools to work the land. In the words of Thaddeus Stevens, power meant "forty acres and a mule." But this power was not made available to the slaves and we see the results today in the pushing of a landless peasantry off the farms into big cities where they come in search mainly of the power to be free. What they find are only the formalities of unenforced legal freedom. So we must ask, "What is the nature of the power which we seek and need today?" Power today is essentially organizational power. It is not a thing lying about in the streets to be fought over. It is a thing which, in some measure, already belongs to Negroes and which must be developed by Negroes in relationship with the great resources of this nation.

Getting power necessarily involves reconciliation. We must first be reconciled to ourselves lest we fail to recognize the resources we already have and upon which we can build. We must be reconciled to ourselves as persons and to ourselves as an historical group. This means we must find our way to a new self-image in which we can feel a normal sense of pride in self, including our variety of skin color and the manifold textures of our hair. As long as we are filled with hatred for ourselves we will be unable to respect others.

At the same time, if we are seriously concerned about power then we must build upon that which we already have. "Black power" is already present to some extent in the Negro church, in Negro fraternities and sororities, in our professional associations, and in the opportunities afforded to Negroes who make decisions in some of the integrated organizations of our society.

We understand the reasons by which these limited forms of "black power" have been rejected by some of our people. Too often the Negro church has stirred its members away from the reign of God in *this world* to a distorted and complacent view of *an otherworldly* conception of God's power. We commit ourselves as churchmen to make more meaningful in the life of our institution our conviction that Jesus Christ reigns in the "here" and "now" as well as in the future he brings in upon us. We shall, therefore, use more of the resources of our churches in working for human justice in the places of social change and upheaval where our Master is already at work.

At the same time, we would urge that Negro social and professional organizations develop new roles for engaging the problem of equal opportunity and put less time into the frivolity of idle chatter and social waste.

We must not apologize for the existence of this form of group power, for we have been oppressed as a group, not as individuals. We will not find our way out of that oppression until both we and America accept the need for Negro Americans as well as for Jews, Italians, Poles, and white Anglo-Saxon Protestants, among others, to have and to wield group power.

However, if power is sought merely as an end in itself, it tends to turn upon those who seek it. Negroes need power in order to participate more effectively at all levels of the life of our nation. We are glad that none of those civil rights leaders who have asked for "black power" have suggested that it means a new form of isolationism or a foolish effort at domination. But we must be clear about why we need to be reconciled with the white majority. It is *not* because we are only one tenth of the population in America; for we do not need to be reminded of the awesome power wielded by the 90 percent majority. We see and feel that power every day in the destructions heaped upon our families and upon the nation's cities. We do not need to be threatened by such cold and heartless statements. For we are men, not children, and we are growing out of our fear of that power, which can hardly hurt us any more in the future than it does in the present or has in the past. Moreover, those bare figures conceal the potential political strength which is ours if we organize properly in the big cities and establish effective alliances.

Neither must we rest our concern for reconciliation with our white brothers on the fear that failure to do so would damage gains already made by the civil rights movement. If those gains are in fact real, they will withstand the claims of our people for power and justice, not just for a few select Negroes here and there, but for the masses of our citizens. We must rather rest our concern for reconciliation on the firm ground that we and all other Americans *are* one. Our history and destiny are indissolubly linked. If the future is to belong to any of us, it must be prepared for all of us whatever our racial or religious background. For in the final analysis, we are *persons* and the power of all groups must be wielded to make visible our common humanity.

The future of America will belong to neither white nor black unless all Americans work together at the task of rebuilding our cities. We must organize not only among ourselves but with other groups in order that we can, together, gain power sufficient to change this nation's sense of what is *now* important and what must be done *now*. We must work with the remainder of the nation to organize whole cities for the task of making the rebuilding of our cities first priority in the use of our resources. This is more important who gets to the moon first or the war in Vietnam.

To accomplish this task we cannot expend our energies in spastic or ill-tempered explosions without meaningful goals. We must move from the politics of philanthropy to the politics of metropolitan development for equal opportunity. We must relate all groups of the city together in new ways in order that the truth of our cities might be laid bare and in order that, together, we can lay claim to the great resources of our nation to make truth more human.

To the Mass Media: Power and Truth

The ability or inability of all people in America to understand the upheavals of our day depends greatly on the way power and truth operate in the mass media. During the Southern demonstrations for civil rights, you men of the communications industry performed an invaluable service for the entire country by revealing plainly to our ears and eyes, the ugly truth of a brutalizing system of overt discrimination and segregation. Many of you were mauled and injured, and it took courage for you to stick with the task. You were instruments of change and not merely purveyors of unrelated facts. You were able to do this by dint of personal courage and by reason of the power of national news agencies which supported you.

Today, however, your task and ours is more difficult. The truth that needs revealing today is not so clear-cut in its outlines, nor is there a national consensus to help you form relevant points of view. Therefore, nothing is now more important than that you look for a variety of sources of truth in order that the limited perspectives of all of us might be corrected. Just as you related to a broad spectrum of people in Mississippi instead of relying only on police records and establishment figures, so must you operate in New York City, Chicago, and Cleveland.

The power to support you in this endeavor *is present* in our country. It must be searched out. We desire to use our limited influence to help relate you to the variety of experience in the Negro community so that limited controversies are not blown up into the final truth about us. The fate of this country is, to no small extent, dependent upon how you interpret the crises upon us, so that human truth is disclosed and human needs are met.

SIGNATORIES

Bishop John D. Bright, Sr., AME Church, First Episcopal District, Philadelphia, Pennsylvania
The Rev. John Bryan, Connecticut Council of Churches, Hartford, Connecticut
Suffragan Bishop John M. Burgess, The Episcopal Church, Boston, Massachusetts
The Rev. W. Sterling Cary, Grace Congregational Church, New York, N.Y.
The Rev. Charles E. Cobb, St. John Church (UCC), Springfield, Mass.

The Rev. Caesar D. Coleman, Christian Methodist Episcopal Church, Memphis, Tennessee

The Rev. Joseph C. Coles, Williams Institutional C.M.E. Church, New York, New York

The Rev. George A. Crawley, Jr., St. Paul Baptist Church, Baltimore, Maryland

The Rev. O. Herbert Edwards, Trinity Baptist Church, Baltimore, Md.

The Rev. Bryant George, United Presbyterian Church in the U.S.A., New York, New York

Bishop Charles F. Golden, The Methodist Church, Nashville, Tenn.

The Rev. Quinland R. Gordon, The Episcopal Church, New York, N.Y.

The Rev. James Hargett, Church of Christian Fellowship, U.C.C., Los Angeles, Calif.

The Rev. Edler Hawkins, St. Augustine Presbyterian Church, New York, New York

The Rev. Reginald Hawkins, United Presbyterian Church, Charlotte, North Carolina

Dr. Anna Arnold Hedgeman, Commission on Religion and Race, National Council of Churches, New York, New York

The Rev. R. E. Hood, Gary, Indiana

The Rev. H. R. Hughes, Bethel A.M.E. Church, New York, N.Y.

The Rev. Kenneth Hughes, St. Bartholomew's Episcopal Church, Cambridge, Massachusetts

The Rev. Donald G. Jacobs, St. James A.M.E. Church, Cleveland, Ohio

The Rev. J. L. Joiner, Emanuel A.M.E. Church, New York, New York

The Rev. Arthur A. Jones, Metropolitan A.M.E. Church, Philadelphia, Pennsylvania

The Rev. Stanley King, Sabathini Baptist Church, Minneapolis, Minn.

The Rev. Earl Wesley Lawson, Emanuel Baptist Church, Malden, Mass.

The Rev. David Licorish, Abyssinian Baptist Church, New York, N.Y.

The Rev. Arthur B. Mack, St. Thomas A.M.E.Z. Church, Haverstraw, N.Y.

The Rev. James W. Mack, South United Church of Christ, Chicago, Ill.

The Rev. O. Clay Maxwell, Jr., Baptist Ministers Conference of New York City and Vicinity, New York, New York

The Rev. Leon Modeste, The Episcopal Church, New York, N.Y.

Bishop Noah W. Moore, Jr., The Methodist Church, Southwestern Area, Houston, Texas

The Rev. David Nickerson, Episcopal Society for Cultural and Racial Unity, Atlanta, Georgia

The Rev. LeRoy Patrick, Bethesda United Presbyterian Church, Pittsburgh, Pennsylvania

The Rev. Benjamin F. Payton, Commission on Religion and Race, National Council of Churches, New York, New York

The Rev. Isaiah P. Pogue, St. Mark's Presbyterian Church, Cleveland, Ohio

The Rev. Sandy F. Ray, Empire Baptist State Convention, Brooklyn, N.Y.

Bishop Herbert B. Shaw, Presiding Bishop, Third Episcopal District, A.M.E.Z. Church, Wilmington, N.C.

The Rev. Stephen P. Spottswood, Commission on Race and Cultural Relations, Detroit Council of Churches, Detroit, Michigan

The Rev. Henri A. Stines, Church of the Atonement, Washington, D.C.

Bishop James S. Thomas, Resident Bishop, Iowa Area, The Methodist Church, Des Moines, Iowa

The Rev. V. Simpson Turner, Mt. Carmel Baptist Church, Brooklyn, N.Y.

The Rev. Edgar Ward, Grace Presbyterian Church, Chicago, Ill.

The Rev. Paul M. Washington, Church of the Advocate, Philadelphia, Pa.

The Rev. Frank L. Williams, Methodist Church, Baltimore, Maryland

The Rev. John W. Williams, St. Stephen's Baptist Church, Kansas City, Mo.

The Rev. Gayraud Wilmore, United Presbyterian Church U.S.A., New York, N.Y.

The Rev. M. L. Wilson, Covenant Baptist Church, New York, New York

The Rev. Robert H. Wilson, Corresponding Secretary, National Baptist Convention of America, Dallas, Texas

The Rev. Nathan Wright, Episcopal Diocese of Newark, Newark, N.J.

(Organizational affiliation given for identification purposes only.)

31

THE CASE FOR A NEW
BLACK CHURCH STYLE

GAYRAUD S. WILMORE, JR.

When he issued this call for a revolution in black and white church relations,
Dr. Wilmore was Chairman of the Division of Church and Race, Board of
National Missions, The United Presbyterian Church in the U. S. A. From
his vantage point in the bureaucratic hierarchy of a prominent white Protestant denomination, Wilmore has perceived, in aggravated form, the problem
of black congregations in white denominations, and ultimately, in white
society. Before the black church can rescue Christianity for people of any
color, it is going to have to liberate its "whitenized" self, a process requiring
an immersion in black culture and the ideology of black power. There may
still be a role for the white denomination in service to the ghetto community
under the guidance of black leaders, but not before it has truly purged itself
of its ingrained racism.

It became clear that black power could not be understood or interpreted
by white churches and white churchmen on the march between Memphis
and Jackson in the summer of 1966. Nor was it possible to correct the distortions of what had happened, as perceptions and explanations became confused both inside the movement itself and outside. That task, as far as the
churches were concerned, had to be performed by Negro churchmen who
were close enough to the national scene to have a panoramic view, who had
been deeply enough involved with Dr. King and the civil rights movement to
have won their right to speak boldly, and who were black enough to challenge,
without deep feelings of guilt and betrayal, the white brethren who were
beginning to show signs of reconciling with the great mass of white liberal
opinion and backlash *against* black power.

Something else was even more obvious by the summer of 1966. The fa-

Reprinted from *Church in Metropolis*, 18 (Fall 1968): 18-22, by permission of the
author and the publisher.

mous slogan which the Federal Council of Churches had adopted in the late 1930's—"A non-segregated church in a non-segregated society" had become totally bankrupt as an expression of church action in the race field. The banner of a nonsegregated society begged too many burning questions to be unfurled as a brave pronouncement of where we were and where we thought we were going. Was it not of the very nature of the church in the United States that it is and always has been segregated by race and class? Was there any indication that the majority of either white or black Christians wanted it differently?

Was there any reasonable expectation that churches could be desegregated before widespread desegregation occurred in housing, public schools, and in the informal and associational structures of American society? Finally, should black Christians permit themselves to be integrated within overwhelmingly white church structures without the freedom to develop and maintain their own leadership echelons and without determinative power concerning the effect on their lives?

The Need for New Styles of Black-White Relationships

Sobered by the failure of the old civil rights movement in the North—and made wiser by the interracial confrontations which have occurred over the last several months, we approach the problem of reconciling black and white within the one church of Christ from a different direction. Black churchmen in predominantly white denominations know well that the real question is not whether these churches can become truly integrated on Sunday morning, but whether, in the next twenty-five to fifty years, these churches will have any meaningful contact with black people at all! If that question can be answered affirmatively we must inquire how that contact will contribute to the dignity and humanity of both black and white people in a time of revolutionary change.

It is not merely segregation or integration which are at stake today. It is rather the question of the viability of the Christian church in the United States—and perhaps in Western civilization. It is the question of whether or not this church can any longer encompass within it the masses of nonwhite persons, who make up the majority of the peoples of the earth, without undergoing radical changes in its understanding of its purpose in the world vis-à-vis robbed, subjugated, and excluded peoples, without dismantling its organizational structures for mission and without bringing to an end its basic conformity to European theological traditions and Anglo-Saxon styles of life and structures of value. The church cannot proceed through this period of crisis as a viable and relevant institution without a radical change in its spiritual and physical relationship to black Christians—most of whom are in all black churches—and to the black community as a whole.

Historical Christian Racism

Looking back to the seventeenth and eighteenth centuries we are amazed by the ease with which American Christians used the institution of religion to protect a double standard of human justice which suited their economic self-interest. No amount of scholarly research and eloquence by white church historians about the "deep sympathy and solicitude" the Christian slaveholder had for his slaves, or about the zeal with which the major denominations threw themselves into the task of evangelizing the slave population after the revolution, can make us forget that the churches themselves excluded the black man from the very freedoms which they justified for white men on the basis of Christian faith.

Therein lies the core of moral corruption in the American churches today and the kernel of American racism.

The original attitude of the churches found it expedient to separate love and justice where black people were concerned and that attitude prevailed in the end. What Lincoln might have said was that the war was a test to determine whether this nation or any nation, conceived in liberty and dedicated to the proposition that all men are created equal, could extend those same ideas to black men as well as to white men and still endure. That test has not yet been determinatively made, for what was guaranteed to the freedman in the amendments to the Constitution and the early civil rights laws, have never been satisfactorily delivered and the nation still endures half slave and half free. We still face the test!

Likewise, church integration has always been a one-way street. Everything black was subordinate and inferior and would have to be given up for everything white. The white church, in its accommodation to white middle-class society, attempted to make over the black man and his church in its own image and to force the black community into the mold of the white society to which the white church had always been in bondage and which it conceived to be the nearest thing on earth to the Kingdom of God in Heaven.

The Black Church Development

The black churches which split off from the white Methodist and Baptist denominations in the latter part of the eighteenth and early nineteenth century borrowed heavily from the white churches which had first evangelized them and ordained their clergy. However, these black churches were able to develop their own styles of life and their own institutions. An authentic black culture and religion were germinated. Whatever may be said of the deficiencies or excesses of their preaching and brand of churchmanship, they were the preeminent expression of the yearning for freedom and dignity by a people who had been introduced to a religion, but excluded from all but the most demeaning aspects of the cultural mold of that religion.

On the other hand, the black churches which remained a part of the main line white denominations were excluded from participation in the main line culture. They were obliged to substitute whatever they held of their own for a system of white cultural and religious values. Thus a system developed in the black church and community that could only be a poor facsimile of the "real" thing—a second-class culture for second-class Christians.

Despite the fact that the white denominations have made a lasting contribution to these churches and to their communities by establishing hundreds of churches, schools, and colleges throughout the nation (and especially in the South), it must nevertheless be conceded that as long as these institutions remain under white control—they remain unable to interpenetrate the white cultural accretion with a distinctive black ingredient as a viable component of the American ethos. At best, they were the objects of a benevolent paternalism and either atrophied or were smothered to death in the avid embrace of the Great White Father and the Great White Mother. At worst, they were hostages thrown over the walls of the white churches to keep at bay the wolves of a guilty conscience and a national embarrassment. In such a situation it was inevitable that a kind of cynicism would develop on both sides, and that one day these whitenized black Christians would say, "There ain't nothing Charley can do for me but lay his money on the line and move on. That's the name of the game we've been playing with one another and if he's satisfied with it, so am I!"

Whitenized Black Churches Today

The problem of the whitenized black churches today is how to recover their own self-respect by demythologizing the white cultural bag through which the faith was transmitted to them and in which they have curled themselves up so comfortably. In so doing they may discover that the essence of the Christian faith not only transcends ultimately the ethnocentric culture of the white man, but that of the black man as well; that this Christ, in whom there is neither Jew nor Greek, bond nor free, male nor female, is also neither black nor white.

Indeed, in liberating itself from the mythology of white Christianity and standing over against the suburban captivity of the white church, the whitenized black churches may be able to illuminate a theme from the left wing of the Protestant Reformation that the American experience has increasingly made opaque. Namely, that while the church is not permitted to create its own culture alongside the secular, it does stand in a dialectical relationship to culture—more often in opposition than accommodation—its most severe critic and reformer rather than its champion and celebrant.

Black Power and Dignity

This possibility rests upon what may at first appear to be a contradictory position, but is in fact a necessary concession to the perverted reality of the black man's religious situation in America. Before the whitenized black churches can immerse themselves in ecumenical Protestantism in the United States and perform their critical and reformatory role in relationship to the total culture, these churches must immerse themselves in a black ecumenicity and in a black culture, both of which they have repudiated in the past, but for which they, nevertheless, have a peculiar responsibility.

Is this to say that the Christian faith as viewed through the black power movement is but yet another expression of an ethnocentric religion of culture? To this question we must today give a qualified affirmative answer. Qualified, because what we are seeking in the posture of black religion is temporary and transitional—a way of correcting the errors of the past and preparing the ground for the future. But we must insist that if the Christian church is to become a dynamic influence in the black community, which will continue to be beleaguered by white racism, it must become not only a religi-

ous institution, but a community organization. It must develop and embrace
an ideology of black power not only as a defense against the racism of the
white church and white culture, but as a necessary alternative to the cynical,
materialistic youth in its flight from the dehumanizing effects of a spurious
white Christian culture. Is it any wonder that black Christians are resisting
easy and unexamined black and white relationships?

A Word to Our White Brothers

This is a hard saying that will not be readily accepted by our white Christian
brethren. But the time has come when we, who have accepted from their
hands a religion devoid of an ethic relevant to our real situation and a culture
in which we were never permitted to participate on equal terms, must stand
back from them to reassess our relationship to our own people and to the
hostile society to which the white church continues in servile accommodation and for whose sake white Christians have betrayed us—their black
brothers in Jesus Christ. We must stand back and be in a strategic exodus
from this unequal engagement, this degrading, debilitating embrace, until we
have recovered our own sense of identity, our true relationship to the people
we serve, and until the white church is ready to enter into that partnership
in life and mission which is able to renew the whole church of Christ.

The National Committee of Negro Churchmen at the meeting of their
board of directors on April 5, 1968, took action to declare the following to
the white religious establishment.

We believe it would be a tragic mistake for predominately white denominations to choose to by-pass this institution in an effort to relate to and invest
in the urban ghettoes. The Black church has a physical presence and a con-
stituency already organized in these communities. It is available as a means
by which the whole Christian community can deal substantively and effectively with the urban crisis, the sickness of body and spirit which we see in
the metropolitan centers of America today.

We, therefore, call upon the white churches and churchmen to take with
utmost seriousness the black church as the only, though imperfect, link with
inner city life for the mission of the church and we insist that the mission
structure of the national denominations must identify with and be led by the
black churches if their efforts are to have either credibility or reality.

We, therefore, call upon the white churches and churchmen to re-appraise
their strategies and expenditures so that the rich potential of the black
churches can be fulfilled with the excellent by-products of mutual respect,
comradeship and ecumenical development resulting therefrom.

In the light of the above considerations and recommendations and in order

to prepare black churches to better serve the communities in which they exist
the National Committee of Negro Churchmen commits itself to the development of a new and creative style of black churchmenship which will emphasize its distinctive task and opportunity. There are four interrelated dimensions
for this new style of mission.

1. The renewal and enhancement of the black church in terms of its
   liturgical life, its theological interpretation, its understanding of its
   mission to itself, to the white church and to the nation.
2. The development of the black church, not only as a religious fellowship,
   but as a community organization, in the technical sense of that term,
   which uses its resources, influence and manpower to address the problems of estrangement, resignation and powerlessness in the political,
   cultural and economic life of the black community.
3. The projection of a new quality of church life which would equip and
   strengthen the church as custodian and interpreter of that cultural
   heritage which is rooted in the peculiar experience of black people in
   the United States and the faith that has sustained them for over two
   centuries on these shores.
4. The contribution of the black church, out of its experience of suffering
   and the yearning for freedom, of that quality of faith, hope and love
   which can activate, empower, renew and unite the whole Church of
   Christ.

Only under these conditions can we remain in these predominately white
denominations and maintain our connections to, much less our integrity in,
a revolutionary black community, where God is bringing to naught the things
which are and bringing into existence the things which do not exist. Unless
black churchmen and black institutions within these historic denominations
redefine their role in the black community in such terms as these, there is
no sense in talking at all about the task of predominantly white denominations in relation to the black community.

The evangelistic task and the renewal and unity of these two aspects, one
black and the other white, of American Christianity, can be considered in
the light of three possibilities.

Consultation on Church Union

First, the Consultation on Church Union (COCU) may be able, within the
next ten years, to unite in one church, on a precisely calculated basis of
equality, the predominantly white and the predominantly black denominations. Despite the apparent openness of the white denominations and the fact
that the three largest black Methodist bodies have remained in the consulta-

tion, this seems to be an unlikely possibility for the foreseeable future. Even
if the three Methodist churches were to come into the union, the black
Baptist and Pentecostal groups would be outside, and they contain such
large numbers of Negroes that the interracial character of American Protestantism would be only slightly more discernible than it is today.

Indeed, one must ask if the success of COCU, even if all of the major
black churches participated in the union, would affect the de facto segregation of the American churches in any real sense? Without limiting the power
of the Holy Spirit, it is difficult to imagine that within the present century
we will see a sufficient distribution of the black population throughout the
nation and a sufficient diminution of color prejudice to integrate existing
and new local congregations to such an extent as to have more than a small
proportion of blacks and whites worshiping together on Sunday morning.
We should no longer delude ourselves if we are going to get about the real
business of evangelism.

But even more important in the present climate of black awareness is
the necessity of black churches dealing with their own disunity and irrelevance
in the ghetto. In view of the new role that the younger clergy are discovering
in relation to the black power movement, it is improbable that they will be
easily persuaded to turn time and attention from the mobilization of black
people for community action to prepare their people for delicate ecumenical
encounters with white churches and the interminable red tape of church
union.

One thing is certainly clear as one studies the COCU reports, unless the
Consultation is more willing to dialogue on the thorny issues of race and face
more forthrightly the psychological, theological, and structural problems of
authentic church integration in an increasingly polarized and racist society,
there is even less hope that black churchmen will do more than go along for
the ride until the white brethren get the message that evidently has not been
communicated up to now. White supremacy is dead!

The White Church Role

A second possibility emerges for the predominant white denominations in
the present crisis. It is to release their most competent black urban pastors
to study the total resources and characteristics of each black congregation in
terms of its revolutionary function in the black community, and to recommend whatever radical reallocation of national and judicatory resources
should go into these churches to cast them into a new posture and relation-

ship to the black community. It would be highly desirable for some black ecumenical mechanism to be created in neighborhoods or sectors of the metropolitan area that would serve as a conduit, an indirect means and strategy for channeling large sums, with no strings attached, from national and regional sources to local communities. IFCO, of course, is already involved in some such intermediate operation between sources of church funds and ghetto communities. Its basic purpose and scope, however, as well as its resources, are not elaborate enough to serve the objectives envisioned in this model. What is called for is a large-scale, multimillion dollar mission enterprise of black cluster ministries, lay apostolates, experimental ministries and ecumenical task forces in black communities, all oriented toward church community organization and militant political and economic action programs undergirded by a black theological and cultural renaissance.

The question is whether we can now design and finance this new secular mission in the black community, recruit and train both its lay and clerical leadership across denominational lines, and project it onto the vortex of the black revolution in such dramatic ways as to attract and serve not only the black poor, but also the increasingly alienated black youth, the new Afro-American student generation, and the emerging middle class.

A New Relationship

A third possibility exists in the proposals that have been put forth for the predominantly white Protestant denominations to stop worrying about organic union among themselves and rapprochement with Roman Catholicism and begin to enter, on an unprecedented scale, into ecumenical relations in life and work with the five great all-black denominations and about twenty-four smaller churches that comprise more than 90 percent of all black Protestants in the United States.

This is not a suggestion that black and white denominations simply exchange fraternal greetings and enroll each other's prestigious churchmen at church conventions. What is meant is that the white denominations begin to do joint planning for a total mission to the emerging megalopolises or regional cities with the black denominations. Actually given the mission structure of many of these black churches it may mean joint planning and strategy execution between key black congregations and key white congregations and white urban mission structures.

The inequality of financial and material wealth among these entities could be neutralized to some extent if the white denominations learn to accept from black hands what God has given and when black churches learn that black religion has something to give to the whole church of Christ. White churches may give money. Black churches which are not affluent may give contributions in kind for the development and execution of various kinds of non-residential and urban fringe ministries beamed to the middle classes, joint missionary education and teacher-training projects, joint liturgical study and renewal and new concepts in seminary education, recruitment, and placement. The possibilities for black-white cooperation, short of organic union, are myriad, even given the present mood, if the black churches and churchmen are given a little respect—in the profound sense that word has taken on in the "soul community."

It is perhaps too obvious to mention that in joint mission strategy planning and action such groups as the denominational black caucuses, the emerging geographical black caucuses and the National Committee of Negro Churchmen should be consulted and utilized to the fullest extent.

The three possibilities for the evangelistic advance of predominantly white churches upon territory now occupied by black congregations—whether of the white or of the historic black denominations—depend finally not upon money or real estate or equipment. Their success depends upon the determination of the white churches to attack the racism within their ranks and institutional structures with the same vigor and holy zeal with which they threw themselves into missionary activity among people of color in the South following Emancipation and in Asia and Africa in the ninteenth century.

Perhaps it will take even more effort than this in the struggle against the systemic racism and the covert racist presuppositions and myths of the white churches. But there are no real possibilities for mission in the black community, joint or otherwise, until the white church establishment begins to use church law to deal with racism among its members, to force compliance with official policy and pronouncement and to desegregate every aspect of church life—beginning with the bureaucratic structures where decision-making power lies, running through the mission agencies, educational institutions, and local churches, and continuing in decisions about questions of qualifications, recruitment, training, and creating new opportunities of meaning and worth for black leadership.

In a world that God made for all to enjoy and live in to the full, some men have taken more of their share of the power which makes the good life possible. In their dehumanization of other men they make faith in a just God impossible. The church that is engaged in the business of evangelism comes into this situation with power, speaks the word of judgment and performs the act of mercy which reveals unmistakably that the God whom it serves is the one of whom Mary said:

He has shown strength with his arm, he has scattered the proud in the imagination of their hearts, he has put down the mighty from their thrones, and exalted those of low degree; he has filled the hungry with good things, and the rich he has sent empty away.[1]

NOTE

1. Luke 1:51-53.

32

THE BLACK CHURCH AND BLACK POWER

JAMES H. CONE

Gayraud Wilmore, Jr. emphasized a period of black ethnocentrism as a necessary—but ideally temporary—stage in the drive toward a new ecumenical Christianity. In this selection James Cone radiates so little hope that the black church can fully revolutionize itself that he hesitates to look beyond the black power phase. Cone believes that the black church confronted the agonizing implications of enslavement to a "Christian" people in the era before the Civil War. But in the era after emancipation, it saved its buildings and members, but lost its soul and joined the white church in its apostasy. The black church does at least have a heritage of suffering and obedience, which gives it a decided advantage over its white counterpart in carrying out the radical mission of Christ on earth. Still, only by embracing a black theology can the church become a living force in the black community.

> The progress of emanicipation ... is ... certain: It is certain because that God who has made of one blood all nations of men, and who is said to be no respector of persons, has so decreed. ... Did I believe that it would always continue, and that man to the end of time would be permitted with impunity to usurp the same undue authority over his fellows, I would ... ridicule the religion of the Saviour of the world. ... I would consider my bible as a book of false and delusive fables, and commit it to flame; Nay, I would still go further: I would at once confess myself an atheist, and deny the existence of a holy God.
> THE REV. NATHANIEL PAUL, July 5, 1827

The black church was born in slavery. Its existence symbolizes a people who were completely stripped of their African heritage as they were enslaved by the "Christian" white man. The white master forbade the slave from any

Reprinted from *Black Theology and Black Power* (New York: Seabury Press, 1969), pp. 91-115, by permission of the publisher.

remembrance of his homeland. The mobility created by the slave trade, the destruction of the family, and the prohibition of African languages served to destroy the social cohesion of the African slaves. The slave was a *no-thing* in the eyes of the master, who did everything possible to instill this sense of nothingness in the mentality of the slave. The slave was rewarded and punished according to his adherence to the view of himself defined exclusively by the master.

The black man was shackled in a hostile white world without any power to make the white man recognize him as a person. He had to devise means of survival. This accounts for the slave's preoccupation with death. Death was a compelling and ever-present reality for the slave "because of the cheapness with which his life was regarded. The slave was a tool, a thing, a utility, a commodity, but he was not a person. He was faced constantly with the imminent threat of death, of which the terrible overseer was the symbol; and the awareness that he (the slave) was only chattel property, and dramatization."[1]

> *Death is gwinter lay his cold icy hands on me, Lord.*
> *Death is gwinter lay his cold icy hands on me, Lord.*
> *One mornin' I was walkin' alone*
> *I heard a voice and I saw no man*
> *Said go in peace and sin no more,*
> *Yo' sins fo'given an' yo' soul set free.*
> *One of dese mornin's it won't be long,*
> *Yo'll look fo' me an' I'll be gone.*

The black church was the creation of a black people whose daily existence was an encounter with the overwhelming and brutalizing reality of white power. For the slaves it was the sole source of personal identity and the sense of community. Though slaves had no social, economic, or political ties as a people, they had one humiliating factor in common—serfdom! The whole of their being was engulfed in a system intent on their annihilation as persons. Their responses to this overwhelming fact of their existence ranged from suicide to outright rebellion. But few slaves committed suicide. Most refused to accept the white master's definition of black humanity and rebelled with every ounce of humanity in them. The black church became the home base for revolution. Some slaves even rebelled to the point of taking up arms against the white world. Others used the church as a means of transporting the slaves to less hostile territory. Northern independent black churches were "'stations' in the 'underground railroad'; at which an escaping slave could get means either to become established in the North or to go to Canada."[2] Most used the church as a platform for announcing *freedom* and *equality*.

The black churchman did not accept white interpretations of Christianity, which suggested the gospel was concerned with freedom of the soul and not the body. While it is true that most of the spirituals are otherworldly and compensatory in character and that many black preachers pointed to a "land flowing with milk and honey," this fact must be viewed in the light of the ever-present dehumanizing reality of white power. It is because whites completely destroyed their hopes in this world that blacks sang "I's So Glad Trouble Don't Last Always" and "I Know de Udder Worl' Is Not Like Dis." A large majority of black slaves refused to believe that God was irrelevant, but, as they looked at this life, he appeared not to care. Therefore, in order to cling to hope, the average black slave had to look forward to another reality beyond time and space.

It should be emphasized, however, that even the slaves who looked forward to a new life in heaven did not accept the view of the white preacher that God ordained slavery for them. White power may have persuaded some to be passive and accept the present reality of serfdom; but generally when slaves sang of heaven, it was because they realized the futility of rebellion and not because they accepted slavery.

Sometimes it is forgotten that not all of the spirituals are otherworldly and compensatory. Some are protesting and rebellious in character. Comparing their own enslavement with Israelite bondage in Egypt, they sang "Go Down, Moses." The approach may be subtle, but it is clear:

> *When Israel was in Egypt's land,*
> *Let my people go:*
> *Oppressed so hard they could not stand,*
> *Let my people go:*
> *Go down, Moses, 'way down in Egypt's land;*
> *Tell old pharaoh – Let my people go.*

Even more militant was "Oh, Freedom!" The black slave knew that to fight for freedom is to do the work of God. For him death was preferable to life if the latter must be in slavery. Consequently, he sang: "Oh, freedom! Oh freedom! Oh freedom o-ver me! an' be-fo' I'd be a slave, I'd be buried in my grave, and go home to my Lord an' be free."

Other spirituals which revealed the slave's determination to relate Christianity to a life of freedom in this world are: "I'm Going To Lay Down My Life for My Lord," "Lord, Want To be a Christian in My Heart," "I'm A-going To Do All I Can for My Lord," and "I Want To Live So God Can Use Me." There is no suggestion here that Christianity is merely private, isolated, and unrelated to the conditions of this life. Christianity has to do with fighting with God against the evils of this life. One does not sit and wait on God to do all the fighting, but joins him in the fight against slavery. Therefore, they sang, comparing themselves with Joshua, "Joshua Fit de Battle of Jericho.

The Black Church before the Civil War

The birth of the independent black churches and the teaching of the free
black preachers show clearly that Christianity and earthly freedom were
inseparable for the black man. The black church was born in protest. In this
sense, it is the precursor of black power. Unlike the white church, its reality
stemmed from the eschatological recognition that freedom and equality are
at the essence of humanity, and thus segregation and slavery are diametrically
opposed to Christianity. Freedom and equality made up the central theme
of the black church; the protest and action were the early marks of its unique-
ness, as the black man fought for freedom. White missionaries sought to
extol the virtues of the next world, but blacks were more concerned about
their freedom in this world. Ironically it was the black man's deep concern
for freedom and equality which led him to accept Christianity. He saw that
the white master's religion was the best way to freedom.

There are independent black churches today because black people refuse
to accept the white master's view of the Christian faith. As early as 1787
Richard Allen and his followers walked out of St. George's Methodist
Episcopal Church at Philadelphia because they refused to obey the dictates
of white superiority. Allen describes the experiences in this manner:

We had not been long upon our knees before I heard considerable scuffling
and low talking. I raised my head up and saw one of the trustees, H— M—,
having hold of the Reverend Absalom Jones, pulling him up off his knees,
and saying, "You must get up—you must not kneel here." Mr. Jones replied,
"Wait until prayer is over." Mr. H— M— said, "No, you must get up now,
or I will call for aid and force you away." Mr. Jones said, "Wait until prayer
is over, and I will trouble you no more." With that he beckoned to one of
the other trustees, Mr. L— S— to come to his assistance. He came, and
went to William White to pull him up. By this time prayer was over, and we
all went out of the Church in a body, and they were no more plagued with
us in the Church. . . . My dear Lord was with us, and we were filled with
fresh vigor to get a house erected to worship God in.[3]

The organization of the African Methodist Episcopal Church followed soon
after.

Sometimes white Northern churchmen want to distinguish their attitudes
toward blacks from those of their Southern brethren, suggesting that their
doors have always been opened to blacks. The doors may have been opened,
but only if blacks accepted their assigned places by whites. Northerners
should be reminded that existence of all black independent churches among

"freemen" is due exclusively to black refusal to accept the racism deeply embedded in the structure of white churches. Like Southerners, white Northern churchmen did not regard blacks as equals and therefore regulated the affairs of church life in the interest of white superiority. The Richard Allen episode is one example of what blacks did throughout the North. By freeing themselves from white control, blacks were able to worship God in the true spirit of the gospel, independent of the claims of white supremacy. The black church became the only sphere of black experience that was free of white power. For this reason the black church became the center for emphasis on freedom and equality. As Mays and Nicholson say: "Relatively early the church, and particularly the independent Negro church, furnished the one and only organized field in which the slave's suppressed emotions could be released, and the opportunities for him to develop his own leadership."[4]

Some black preachers, like the Rev. Highland Garnet, even urged outright rebellion against the evils of white power. He knew that appeals to "love" or "good will" would have little effect on minds warped by their own high estimation of themselves. Therefore, he taught that the spirit of liberty is a gift from God, and God thus endows the slave with the zeal to break the chains of slavery. In an address, to be sent to slaves, in 1848, at Buffalo, New York, he said:

If . . . a band of Christians should attempt to enslave a race of heathen men, and to entail slavery upon them and to keep them in heathenism in the midst of Christianity, the God of heaven would smile upon every effort which the injured might make to disenthrall themselves. Brethren, it is as wrong for your lordly oppressors to keep you in slavery as it was for the man-thief to steal our ancestors from the coast of Africa. You should therefore now use the same manner of resistance as would have been just in our ancestors when the bloody foot-prints of the first remorseless soul-thief were placed upon the shores of our fatherland. The humblest peasant is as free in the sight of God as the proudest monarch that every swayed a sceptre. Liberty is a spirit sent from God and, like its great Author, is no respecter of persons. Brethren, the time has come when you must act for yourselves. It is an old and true saying that, "If hereditary bondmen would be free, they must themselves strike the blow."[5]

Nat Turner, a Baptist preacher and a slave, not only urged rebellion against white slaveowners, but became an ardent leader of the most successful slave revolt. He felt commissioned by God to lead slaves into a new age of freedom. In 1831, he and his group killed sixty whites in twenty-four hours before they were overpowered by state and federal troops.

While most black preachers did not take part in revolts, few failed to see that God hated slavery. For the Rev. Nathaniel Paul, God *had* to hate it, and to the point of being actively involved in its elimination. "Did I believe that it [slavery] would always continue . . . I would at once confess myself an atheist, and deny the existence of a holy God."[6] God must be against slavery, and not merely passively against it, but actively fighting to destroy it. It was impossible to believe in God and at the same time accept slavery as ordained by him.

Most black preachers were thus in a state of existential absurdity. They could not understand why God even permitted slavery. Like the Biblical Job, they knew that whatever their sins or the sins of their forefathers, they did not justify slavery. The punishment did not fit the crime. Furthermore, they knew that their white oppressors were no more righteous than they. It was this contradiction which led Nathaniel Paul to ask:

> Tell me, ye mighty waters, why did ye sustain the ponderous load of misery? Or speak, ye winds, and say why it was that ye executed your office to waft them onward to the still more dismal state; and ye proud waves, why did you refuse to lend your aid and to have overwhelmed them with your billows? Then should they have slept sweetly in the bosom of the great deep, and so have been hid from sorrow. And, oh thou immaculate God, be not angry with us, while we come into thy sanctuary, and make the bold inquiry in this thy holy temple, why it was that thou didst look on with calm indifference of an unconcerned spectator, when thy holy law was violated, thy divine authority despised and a portion of thine own creatures reduced to a state of mere vassalage and misery?[7]

These words sound like a Job or a Habakkuk questioning the righteousness of God. Slavery is contradictory to the character of God; it is absurd to affirm the love of God and watch men brutalized by the whips of white power. God must answer, if he expects the black man to be his servant. Therefore, Nathaniel Paul can only affirm his faith in God in view of his assurance that God hates slavery and that his righteousness prevails over evil.

> Hark! While he answers from on high: hear Him proclaiming from the skies—Be still, and know that I am God! Clouds and darkness are around about me; yet righteousness and judgment are the habitation of my throne. I do my will and pleasure in the heavens above, and in the earth beneath; it is my sovereign prerogative to bring good out of evil, and cause the wrath of man to praise me, and the remainder of that wrath I will restrain.[8]

We can easily see that his view of the God of Christianity is closely tied to the present reality of this world. There is no suggestion here that the gospel is unrelated to this life. God cannot be God, a God worthy of worship and praise, and also ordain or even permit slavery. To think otherwise is to deny reality. How can we affirm his existence and believe that he permits slavery? It was this contradiction which disturbed the very "soul" of the black preachers. Belief in God was not easy for them. It was an awesome experience, burdened with responsibility. Daniel A. Payne, an A.M.E. bishop (elected in 1852) put it this way:

> Sometimes it seemed as though some wild beast had plunged his fangs into my heart, and was squeezing out its life-blood. Then I began to question the existence of God, and to say: "If he does exist, is he just? If so, why does he suffer one race to oppress and enslave another, to rob them by unrighteous enactments of rights, which they hold most dear and sacred?" Sometimes I wished for the lawmakers what Nero wished—"that the Romans had but one neck." I would be the man to sever the head from its shoulders. Again said I: "Is there no God?"[9]

This agonizing experience over God's existence makes the twentieth-century death-of-God theology seem like child's play. There is something ironical about affirming God's death in view of one's identity with a cultural structure which enslaves. If the affirmation of God's death grows out of one's identity with suffering, then it is understandable, perhaps necessary. But if it arises out of one's identity with an advancing technological secular society which ignores the reality of God and the humanity of man, then it appears to be the height of human pride. This is the most disturbing fact in relation to recent developments in American white theology. Most American white Protestants who sense an identity with the death-of-God movement in Protestant theology take their cue from Dietrich Bonhoeffer. It was Bonhoeffer who said:

> Honesty demands that we recognize that we live in a world as if there were no God. And this is just what we do recognize—before God! God himself drives us to this realization. God makes us know that we must live as men who can get along without Him. The God who is with us is the God who forsakes us (Mk. 15:34)! We stand continually in the presence of the God who makes us live in the world without the God-hypothesis.[10]

From this and other similar quotations, some theologians have concluded that Bonhoeffer inaugurated a new age, an age of no-God. But what most white Protestant professors of theology overlook is that these are the words of a prisoner, a man who encountered the evils of Nazism and was killed in the encounter. Do whites really have the right to affirm God's death when they have actually enslaved men in God's name? It would seem that unless whites are willing to endure the pain of oppression, they cannot authentically speak of God. Relevant theology can only arise when it is unreservedly identified with the suffering of the oppressed.

It was the black preacher's unqualified identification with the black slave which created his doubts about God's existence. Similarly, it is understandable when many black power people shun the religion of Christianity and view God as meaningless in the black revolution. It may even be necessary, in light of white prostitution of the faith. But the black preachers during slavery did not think it necessary. They were assured that God was alive and that he was working in history against the evils of slavery. It was this assurance of which Payne spoke.

> But then there came into my mind those solemn words: "with God one day is as a thousand years and a thousand years as one day. Trust in him, and he will bring slavery and all its outrages to an end." These words from the spirit world acted on my troubled soul like water on a burning fire, and my aching heart was soothed and relieved from its burden of woes.[11]

This peace of which Payne speaks is not an easy peace. It is a restless peace; it is a peace that makes him fight against human slavery, despite the odds. In a speech, delivered June 1839 at the Franckean Synod, he said:

> I am opposed to slavery, not because it enslaves the black man, but because it enslaves *man.* And were all the slaveholders in this land men of color, and the slaves white men, I would be as thorough and uncompromising an abolitionist as I now am; for whatever and whenever I may see a being in the form of a man, enslaved by his fellowman, without respect to his complexion, I shall lift my voice to plead his cause, against all the claims of his proud oppressor; and I shall do it not merely from the sympathy which man feels towards suffering man, but because *God, the living God,* whom I dare not disobey, has commanded me to open my mouth for the dumb, and to plead the cause of the oppressed.[12]

I am not unaware that many slaves accepted their condition as slaves because of the fear of white power. We may even assume that some black ministers preached that Christianity was unrelated to earthly freedom. We have already observed that most of the spirituals are not protest songs, but a means of making a psychological adjustment to the existence of serfdom. For this reason, white slavemasters believed that Christianity made the slave a better slave. In the South there were few independent black churches. Most slaves worshipped with their masters or in their own church closely supervised by "reliable" white persons. Most writers refer to church among the slaves as the "invisible institution."

It is important to note that white masters urged the slaves to worship with them and usually prohibited independent black churches. The reason is clear. The black Northern independents carried the message of freedom and equality

to the Southern black slave, causing alarm among the white masters. "The
religious congregations in the towns and the fellowship in the fields were the
home base for Negro liberators, who not only preached freedom but pro-
voked insurrections."[13] After the Nat Turner revolt, whites began to set up
stricter laws to govern the behavior of the slaves. Whites realized that the
black man could not be trusted to remain obedient, subservient to the will
of the master, if the former was permitted to hear the gospel of the black
independents or black slaves inspired with the spirit of freedom. Therefore,
in order to ensure that the master's dominance over the slave would not be
preempted by a higher will, the master prevented all instruction in religion
except by authorized white persons.

In an effort to dissipate the slave's passionate desire for freedom, white
missionaries sought to interpret the meaning of Christianity in the light of a
futuristic eschatology, trying to convince the slave that the Christian gospel
was concerned with pietistic moralities in this life as a means of gaining
eternal life upon death. Thus Christianity was supposed to be concerned with
the other world, what Nietzsche called "the illusion of worlds-behind-the-
scene." But the black churches refused to accept an interpretation of Christianity which was unrelated to social change. They knew that though
Christianity is eschatological, it must be related to the suffering of black
men now. Though the black preacher looked to the future and spoke of it
in heavenly terms, it was because of his vision into the future that he could
never reconcile himself to the present evil of slavery. To look toward the
future is to grasp the truth of God, and to grasp the truth of God is to
become intolerant of untruth.

The German theologian Jürgen Moltmann has surprisingly caught the spirit
of the black slave preachers. To hope in Christ means that there is "not only a
consolation in suffering, but also the *protest of divine* promise against suffering."[14] The Christian must be assured that God is fighting against it. God
must be the enemy of all those who in "sloth" put up with evil. Hope, then,
as seen in the minds of the slave preachers, is not patience but impatience,
not calmness but protest. As Moltmann says: "Those who hope in Christ can
no longer put up with reality as it is, but begin to suffer under it, to contradict it: . . . Peace with God means conflict with the world."[15] If there is no
vision of the future, we can easily reconcile ourselves with the *present*—the
evil, the suffering and death. That Payne, Garnet, Paul, and others could not
keep quiet in the face of the injustice of slavery rests not on their faith in
man, but on God who in Christ promised wholeness. That is why they made
the black church a disturbance in society.

The white missionaries sought to interpret hope in a way that made it unrelated to the present. They taught the slave that to hope means to look to heaven for a reward for being obedient to the master on earth. It meant accepting his present deplorable lot as a slave. With this view, Christian hope not only cheats the slave of the meaning of the present; it cheats God—the present reality of God and his involvement in the world on behalf of man. "As long as hope does not change the thought and action of men" in the present, it is meaningless.[16]

It would seem that black preachers before the Civil War were wiser than they have been pictured. They emphasized in word and deed the very point which is Moltmann's central thesis. On the one hand, the concept of hope is central in the preaching of black ministers. They taught their people to look to the future, to visualize a new day. And the spirituals bear testimony to their concern for the future. On the other hand, their concern for the future did not relieve them of their responsibility for the present. Instead, it enhanced it. Through the hope which arises in Jesus, the present became intolerable. They could no longer reconcile slavery and Christianity. They heard the promise, and the promise was "incongruous with the reality around them, as they" groped "in hope towards the promised new future. The result was not the religious sanctification of the present, but a break-away from the present towards the future."[17]

Benjamin Mays and Joseph Washington have shown that for the pre-Civil War black preacher, Christianity was inextricably related to social justice in this world.[18] Washington called this concern "folk religion" and placed it outside the main stream of Christian tradition.[19] But the heretics were not the slave preachers, but white missionaries who sought to use Christianity as an instrument for enslavement. Like the early Christians who saw the difference between "law" (Judaism) and "gospel" (Christ), the black slave preachers saw that slavery and Christianity were as different as white and black. This recognition made the early black churches the center of protest against the system of slavery. It is true, as Washington suggests, that the slave preachers were virtually theologically illiterate, and even to this day few blacks have made any substantial contribution to white theology. But literacy was never a precondition to religious insight. As Hordern says, Jesus did not say, "Blessed are the brilliant," but, "Blessed are the pure in heart for they shall see God."

It was, rather, white Christianity in America that was born in heresy. Its very coming to be was an attempt to reconcile the impossible—slavery and Christianity. And the existence of the black churches is a visible reminder of its apostasy. The black church is the only church in America which remained recognizably Christian during pre-Civil War days. Its stand on freedom and equality through word and action is true to the spirit of Christ.

The Post-Civil War Black Church

The Southern "invisible institution" among blacks became visible in a host of new black churches, united in spirit to the already existing black independents. The founding of a church was one of the ways blacks expressed their new freedom. According to Mays and Nicholson, "the freedom which the Negro felt in this period is best revealed by the fact that of the 333 rural and urban churches of this study which originated then, 231, or 69 percent came into existence through the initiative of individuals and groups."[20]

It is important to point out that the new organizations were sometimes directly related to expulsions from white churches. Here it becomes clear that white masters "accepted" black slaves in their churches as a means of keeping the black man regulated as a slave. There was no mutual relationship between equals. Therefore, when whites saw that it was no longer economically advantageous to worship with blacks, they put blacks out of their church as a matter of course. Some whites were gentle in the process, giving the blacks a plot of ground or occasionally a building for a place of worship. (That was a small price for 250 years of slavery!)

It is a credit to the humanity of black people that they recognized their presence in white services as an adjunct of slavery. Therefore, many of them left before being expelled. For this reason, we may describe the black churches during this period as a place of retreat from the dehumanizing forces of white power. It was one place in which the blacks were "safe" from the new racist structures that replaced slavery. The black church gradually became an instrument of escape instead of, as formerly, an instrument of protest.

Following the Civil War black leaders were recruited from the churches to serve in public capacities previously closed to black people. But the end of reconstruction meant the end of black involvement in state politics. The new Jim Crow structure had devastating effects comparable to slavery. In slavery one knows what the odds are and what is needed to destroy the power of the enemy. But in a society which pronounces a man free but makes him behave as a slave, all of the strength and will power is sapped from the would-be rebel. The structures of evil are camouflaged, the enemy is elusive, and the victim is trained to accept the values of the oppressor. The "second-class citizen" is told that his oppression is due to his ignorance and his mental inferiority. At this point the oppressed is duped into believing that if only he were like the oppressor, he would no longer be ridiculed. A crash program of self-help is then devised to bridge the gap between the educated and the ignorant. This is largely the role of the black churches, the Booker T. Washingtons in the area of religion.

The black church thus lost its zeal for freedom in the midst of the new structures of white power. The rise of segregation and discrimination in the post-Civil War period softened its drive for equality. The black minister remained the spokesman for the black people, but, "faced by insurmountable obstacles, he succumbed to the cajolery and bribery of the white power structure and became its foil."[21] The passion for freedom was replaced with innocuous homilies against drinking, dancing, and smoking; and injustices in the present were minimized in favor of a kingdom beyond this world. Black churches adopted, for the most part, the theology of the white missionaries and taught blacks to forget the present and look to the future. Some black ministers even urged blacks to adopt the morality of white society entirely, suggesting that entrance into the kingdom of heaven is dependent on obedience to the laws of white society. A jail sentence or a fine meant that a person was immoral, subject often to churchly probation and sometimes to expulsion. Other ministers said that suffering in this life was necessary for the next life. Undue concern about white injustice was thus a sign of a loss of faith, a failure to realize that patience and long-suffering were more pertinent to final judgment than zeal for present justice. "Seek first the Kingdom of God and its righteousness and all these other things will be added unto you." This meant endurance now, liberty later.

The black minister thus became a most devoted "Uncle Tom," the transmitter of white wishes, the admonisher of obedience to the caste system. He was the liaison man between the white power structure and the oppressed blacks, serving the dual function of assuring whites that all is well in the black community, dampening the spirit of freedom among his people. More than any other one person in the black community, the black minister perpetuated the white system of black dehumanization.

The National Association for the Advancement of Colored People and the Urban League (and later the Congress of Racial Equality, the Southern Christian Leadership Conference, and the Student Nonviolent Coordinating Committee) were created because of the failure of the black church to plead the cause of black people in white society. Just as the black church is a visible reminder of the apostasy of the white church, the current civil rights protest organizations are visible manifestations of the apostasy of the black church. Forgetting their reason for existing, the black churches became, as Washington appropriately describes, "amusement centers," "arenas for power politics," and an "organ for recognition, leadership, and worship." They became perversions of the gospel of Christ and places for accommodating the oppressed plight of black people.

It was not long before the black people themselves began to recognize the failure of the black church and its ministers to speak to the needs of black people. During the Great Depression the terms of censure were characteristically blunt. St. Clair Drake and Horace R. Cayton report these criticisms of black ministers:

> Blood-suckers! . . . they'll take the food out of your mouth and make you think they are doing you a favor.

> You take these preachers . . . they're living like kings–got great big Packard automobiles and ten or twelve suits and a bunch of sisters putting food in their pantry. Do you call that religion? Naw! It ain't nothing but a bunch of damn monkey foolishness.[22]

Church members were almost as critical, as shown by three separate comments.

> I'm a church member. I believe churches are still useful. But like everything else, there is a lot of racketeering going on in the church.

> Ministers are not as conscientious as they used to be. They are money-mad nowadays. All they want is the almighty dollar and that is all they talk about.

> The preachers want to line their pockets with gold. They are supposed to be the leaders of the people, but they are fake leaders.[23]

In all fairness to the black church and its leaders, it should be pointed out that the apostasy of the black church is partly understandable. If they had not supported the caste system of segregation and discrimination, they would have placed their lives and the lives of their people in danger. They would have been lynched and their churches burned. Thus, by cooperating with the system, they protected their lives and the lives of their people from the menacing threat of white racism. But this is not an excuse for their lack of obedience to Christ. It merely explains it.

But the real sin of the black church and its leaders is that they even convinced themselves that they were doing the right thing by advocating obedience to white oppression as a means of entering at death the future age of heavenly bliss. The black church identified white words with God's word and convinced its people that by listening in faithful obedience to the "great white father" they would surely enter the "pearly gates." Thus the creativity of the black church which characterized the pre-Civil War period is missing after the war.

To add to this error, the black ministers received personal favors from white society. Their churches were left alone. As long as blacks preached "about heaven and told Negroes to be honest and obedient, and that by and by God would straighten things out,"[24] whites supported black churches by loaning them money to build new structures. Churches could get enormous loans and gifts from white businessmen when no other group could. Whites found that it was a good investment for the maintenance of the caste system, despite the fact that church property is useless from an economic perspective if the black people fail to repay. And the black ministers served them well. They kept the status quo intact and assured Mr. Charlie that black people were appreciative of his generosity toward the black community.

Even in the north the black church failed to maintain its freedom from white controls. The criticisms cited from Drake and Cayton on the black church were made by people from Chicago. Like Southern black ministers, they too emphasized white moralities as a means of entrance in God's future kingdom. Few black Northern churches joined the oppressed blacks by challenging the existing white power structure.[25] Generally, they pursued worldly matters with the major emphasis on the "almighty dollar" for personal use.

We may conclude that except in rare instances, the black churches in the post-Civil War period have been no more Christian than their white counterparts. The rare instances refer chiefly to the recent work of a few black ministers in the nonviolent movement, with the late Martin Luther King, Jr., as their leader. At least during its early stages this movement was a return to the spirit of the pre-Civil War black preachers with the emphasis being on freedom and equality in the present political structure. King saw clearly the meaning of the gospel with its social implications and sought to instill its true spirit in the hearts and minds of black and white in this land. He was a man endowed with the charisma of God; he was a prophet in our own time. And like no other black or white American he could set black people's hearts on fire with the gospel of freedom in Christ which would make them willing to give all for the cause of black humanity. Like the prophets of old, he had a dream, a dream grounded not in the hopes of white America but in God. Nor did the dream of the future relieve him of responsibilities in the present; instead, it made him fight unto death in order to make his dream a reality.

It may appear that white America made his dream into a nightmare by setting the climate for his assassination and later memorializing his name with meaningless pieties. But his dream was grounded in God, not man. It was this realization that caused him to say the night before his death: "I've been on the mountain top." Like Moses he did not see the promised land but retained the unshakable certainty that God's righteousness will triumph.

Because of King's work we are now in the beginning stages of real confrontation between black and white Americans. He may not have endorsed the concept of black power, but its existence is a result of his work. Black power advocates are men who were inspired by his zeal for freedom, and black power is their attempt to make his dream a reality. If the black church organizations want to remain faithful to the New Testament gospel and to the great tradition of the pre-Civil War black church, they must relinquish their stake in the status quo and the values in white society by identifying exclusively with black power. Black power is the only hope of the black church in America.

Some black ministers are beginning to catch the spirit of black power and are seeking to embrace it. A case in point is the group of some 250 black Methodists who met in Cincinnati in February, 1968, in order to assess their place in the United Methodist Church and their role in the black revolution. In "The Black Paper," they began with a confession:

> We, a group of black Methodists in America, are deeply disturbed about the crisis of racism in America. We are equally concerned about the failure of a number of black people, including black Methodists, to respond appropriately to the roots and forces of racism and the current Black Revolution.
>
> We, as black Methodists, must first respond in a state of confession because it is only as we confront ourselves that we are able to deal with the evils and forces which seek to deny our humanity.
>
> We confess our failure to be reconciled with ourselves as black men. We have too often denied our blackness (hair texture, color and other God-given physical characteristics) rather than embrace it in all its black beauty.
>
> We confess that we have not always been relevant in service and ministry to our black brothers, and in so doing we have alienated ourselves from many of them.
>
> We confess that we have not always been honest with ourselves and with our white brothers. We have not encountered them with truth but often with deception. We have not said in bold language and forceful action that, "You have used 'white power' in and outside of the church to keep us in a subordinate position." We have failed to tell our white brothers "like it is!" Instead, we have told our white brothers what we *thought* they would like to hear.
>
> We confess that we have not become significantly involved in the Black Revolution because, for the most part, white men have defined it as "bad"; for the other part, we have been too comfortable in our "little world," and too pleased with our lot as second-class citizens and second-class members of The Methodist Church.
>
> We confess that we have accepted too long the philosophy of racism. This has created a relationship in which white people have always defined the "terms," and, in fact, defined when and how black people would exist.
>
> We confess that we have accepted a "false kind of integration" in which all power remained in the hands of white men.[26]

They not only confessed but emphasized that the embracing of black power is the only meaningful response "to racism in America and racism in

The United Methodist Church." They said: "It [black power] is a call for us
to respond to God's action in history which is to make and keep human life
human."[27] The black Methodists went on to outline a beginning program for
black and white churches interested in making a relevant response to the
black power revolution.

Another sign of hope in black churches occurred when several leaders of
many denominations issued a statement on "black power" in 1966.[28] While
they failed to endorse the concept of black power as a working concept,[29]
as did the "Black Methodists for Church Renewal," they did stress the fact
that white racism is the basic reason for black unrest in America. And they
also recognized that "powerlessness breeds a race of beggars."

But we must warn our black churchmen that there are dangers in making
confessions and writing papers. It is so easy to think that a careful, rational
articulation of the problem means that the oppressor will concede and cease
his work of dehumanization. But the evaluation of the problem is merely the
first step in problem-solving. The black church must be willing to proceed
with a concentrated attack on the evils of racism. It also must realize that
the war is not over because one battle is won. The fight against injustice is
never over until all men, regardless of physical characteristics, are recognized
and treated as human beings. When that happens, we can be certain that
God's kingdom has come on earth.

It seems that some black churchmen are beginning to realize the importance of backing one's resolutions with relevant action. It was heartwarming
to hear that the "Black Methodists for Church Renewal" walked out of the
Methodist General Conference at the moment of the communion celebrating
the new United Methodist Church, in order to witness to the brokenness of
the Methodist community. But one must be willing to do more than leave
during communion. A more forceful confrontation is evidently necessary. It
may be that black Methodists and their brothers elsewhere will need to confront churches with what is required to destroy ecclesiastical racism and be
prepared to withdraw unless their demands are met. It is time for the church
to be relevant by joining Christ in the black revolution. Unless the black
church is prepared to respond to Christ's command of obedience by becoming one with the unwanted, then it, like its white counterpart, is useless as a
vehicle for divine reconciliation.

Some may think these criticisms are too harsh and fail to point to the
basic value of the black church in the black community. Some black churchmen may want to argue that the church, because it is owned by blacks, is
important in giving many black people a sense of "somebodyness" in a hostile
white world. It is the black church which bestows a sense of worth on many
"common" blacks because the barriers encountered in society as a whole dis-

appeared in the church. Therefore, the church provides an opportunity for the common man (maid, truckdriver, etc.) to explore his abilities. For this reason, it is not uncommon to find the educator and the laborer on the same church board, and often the latter is the chairman. The black church provides an opportunity for self-expression, a freedom to relax, and release from the daily grind of white racism. Is this not enough to warrant the existence of the black church?

It may warrant its existence but not in Christ. The existence of *the* church is grounded exclusively in Christ. And in twentieth-century America, *Christ means black power!* It is certainly the case that the major institutional black churches have not caught the spirit of black power. They have, for the most part, strayed from their calling, seeking instead to pattern their life after white models. The divinely appointed task of proclaiming freedom and equality was abandoned in the ungodly pursuit of whiteness. Joseph Washington puts it graphically: "Heretofore, the function of the Negro Church has been that of a haven. In effect it has served as a cut-rate outlet, selling itself for quantity rather than quality, offering cheap white medicine in colored doses of several hours of relief for a week-long headache."[30] The only hope for the black church is to repent by seeking the true mission of Christ in the world.

It is clear that there are creative possibilities in the black church which seem to be absent in its white counterpart. The black church has a heritage of radical involvement in the world. This past is a symbol of what is actually needed in the present. The white American church has no history of obedience; and without it, it is unlikely that it will ever know what radical obedience to Christ means. Since it is identified with the structure of power, it will always be possible for it to hedge and qualify its obedience to Christ. Also, being white in soul and mind, the white church must make a "special" effort in order to identify with the suffering of the oppressed, an effort which is almost inevitably distorted into plantation charity. To follow the line of least resistance means that it cannot be for Christ. It seems that the major white church institutions have followed that course so long that the probability is slight that they can free themselves from the structures of power in this society.

The black church, on the other hand, by virtue of being black, is automatically a part of the unwanted. It knows the meaning of rejection because it was rejected. All the black church has to do is to accept its role as the sufferer and begin to follow the natural course of being black. In so doing, it may not only redeem itself through God's spirit, but the white church as well. The black church, then, is probably the only hope for renewal or, more appropriately, revolution in organized Christianity. It alone has attempted to be recognizably Christian in a hostile environment. It alone, being victimized by color, has championed the cause of the oppressed black people. Black church-men are in a position to reaffirm this heritage, accepting the meaning of blackness in a white society and incorporating it into the language and work of the gospel. Speaking a true language of black liberation, the black church must teach that, in a white world bent on dehumanizing black people, Christian love means giving no ground to the enemy, but relentlessly insisting on one's dignity as a person. Love is not passive, but active. It is revolutionary in that it seeks to meet the needs of the neighbor amid crumbling structures of society. It is revolutionary because love may mean joining a violent rebel-lion.

The black church must ask about its function amid the rebellion of black people in America. Where does it stand? If it is to be relevant, it must no longer admonish its people to be "nice" to white society. It cannot condemn the rioters. It must make an unqualified identification with the "looters" and "rioters," recognizing that this stance leads to condemnation by the state as law-breakers. There is no place for "nice Negroes" who are so distorted by white values that they regard laws as more sacred than human life. There is no place for those who deplore black violence and overlook the daily violence of whites. There is no place for blacks who want to be "safe," for Christ did not promise security but suffering.

The pre-Civil War black ministers had no trouble breaking the law when they saw human life at stake. It was beside the question whether slavery was lawful. The question was, Is it consistent with the gospel? If not, they must fight it until death. It was this realization which inspired Martin Luther King to engage in his program of civil disobedience.

So far, the black church has remained conspicuously silent, continuing its business as usual. The holding of conferences, the election of bishops, the fund-raising drive for a new building or air-conditioner seem to be more important than the blacks who are shot because they want to be men. The black church, though spatially located in the community of the oppressed, has not responded to the needs of its people. It has, rather, drained the com-munity, seeking to be more and more like the white church. Its ministers have condemned the helpless and have mimicked the values of whites. For this reason most black power people bypass the churches as irrelevant to their objectives.

Today we enter a new era, the era of black power. It is an age of rebellion and revolution. Blacks are no longer prepared to turn the other cheek; instead, they are turning the gun. Blacks are dying in the streets at the hands of hired gunmen of the state because they refuse to respond to white oppression. This is an era when many blacks would rather die than be slaves. Now the question is: What do the black churches have to say about this? It is time for the black churches to change their style and join the suffering of the black masses, proclaiming the gospel of the black Christ. Whether they will do this is not clear now. What is clear is that they are poised at the moment of irrevocable decision, between costly obedience and confirmed apostasy.

It is hard to know whether to laugh or weep as the churches make bargains with the principalities and powers: prayers on public occasions, tax exemptions, shying away from vital issues, exhortations to private goodness, promotion of gutless "spirituality," institutional self-glorification—they are all knotted together in a monstrous ungodly tangle that spells death to black humanity. There is, of course, a difference between white churches and black churches. But the similarities are striking. Both have marked out their places as havens of retreat, the one to cover the guilt of the oppressors, the other to daub the wounds of the oppressed. Neither is notably identified with the tearing-healing power of Christ. Neither is a fit instrument of revolution.

In such a situation the idea of "renewal" seems futile. Renewal suggests that there is a core of healthy, truthful substance under all the dirt and rust. But dirt can grind away a delicate mechanism, and rust can consume rather than merely cover. The white church in America, though occasionally speaking well and even more rarely acting well, generally has been and is the embodiment of what is wrong with the society. It is racism in ecclesiastical robes. It lives and breathes bigotry. The black church embodies a response to racism at the level of sheer survival at the price of freedom and dignity. Both have taken the road marked "the good life," avoiding the call to discipleship, which is the call to suffering and death. For this reason, renewal in any ordinary sense seems out of the question.

NOTES

1. Howard Thurman, *The Negro Spiritual Speaks of Life and Death* (New York, 1947), pp. 13-14.

2. Gunnar Myrdal, *The American Dilemma* (New York, 1944), p. 860.

3. Richard Allen, *The Life, Experience, and Gospel Labors of the Right Reverend Richard Allen* (Philadelphia, 1887), p. 5.

4. Benjamin E. Mays and Joseph W. Nicholson, *The Negro's Church* (New York, 1933), p. 3.

5. Quoted in Benjamin E. Mays, *The Negro's God* (Boston, 1938), p. 46.

6. Quoted in *ibid.*, p. 42.

7. *Ibid.*, pp. 43-44.

8. *Ibid.*, p. 44.

9. *Ibid.*, p. 49.

10. Quoted in Paul M. Van Buren, *The Secular Meaning of the Gospel* (New York, 1963). See also Bonhoeffer, *Letters and Papers from Prison*, trans. R. Fuller, Frank Clarke, and others, rev. ed. (New York, 1967), p. 188.

11. Quoted in Mays, p. 49.

12."Bishop Daniel Alexander Payne's Protestation of American Slavery," *Journal of Negro History*, 52 (1967): 60

13. Joseph R. Washington, Jr., *Black Religion* (Boston, 1964), p. 202.

14. Jürgen Moltmann, *Theology of Hope,* trans. J. W. Leitch (New York, 1967), p. 21. There is a remarkable correlation between Moltmann's viewpoint on Christian hope and the perspective of the slave preachers.

15. *Ibid.*

16. *Ibid.*, p. 33.

17. *Ibid.*, p. 100. Moltmann is here describing the role of the promise of God in the life of Israel, a description that seems strikingly appropriate to the situation of black people.

18. Mays and Nicholson, *Negro's Church;* Washington, *Black Religion.*

19. It is interesting to note that Washington seems to have reversed his perspective in his more recent *Politics of God* (Joseph R. Washington, Jr. *The Politics of God* [Boston, 1967]), where black folk religion is described as authentic Christianity and black people are described as God's chosen people.

20. Mays and Nicholson, p. 30.

21. Washington, *Black Religion*, p. 35.

22. St. Clair Drake and Horace R. Cayton, *Black Metropolis*, vol. 2 (New York, 1962), p. 420.

23. *Ibid.*

24. Mays and Nicholson, p. 7.

25. One important exception was the Abyssinian Baptist Church and its minister, Adam Clayton Powell, Jr. During the early 1940's he recognized the meaning of the gospel and its perversion by white churches. "The great wedge that keeps America split is the hypocrisy of the Christian Church. The fundamental postulate of Christianity is equality and brotherhood. We have perverted this glorious doctrine to exclude interracial love. Religion has lost its ethical integrity and there, its moral dynamic" (*Marching Blacks: An Interpretative History of the Rise of the Black Common Man* [New York, 1945], p. 95).

26. "Findings of Black Methodists for Church Renewal," Service Center of the Board of Missions, United Methodist Church, (Cincinnati, 1968), pp. 3-4.

27. *Ibid.*, pp. 4-5.

28. "A Statement by the National Committee of Negro Churchmen," *The New York Times,* July 31, 1966.

29. This failure is probably due to the early confusion regarding the meaning of the term.

30. Washington, *Politics of God*, p. 209.

33

COMING IN OUT
OF THE WILDERNESS

ALBERT B. CLEAGE, JR.

During the past several years—certainly since the death of Martin Luther King, Jr.—there has been a heightened demand (among those who believe in the black church and care about its survival) for a new religion of black power which can provide unity and a sense of direction to the black community. From his pulpit in the Shrine of the Black Madonna, the Reverend Cleage, Jr. is preaching a radical Christianity of black power. He is gathering about him a new elite, a committed black congregation that can develop the racial consciousness and faith in the black nation which is black power. When the people have built their nation in a white society—then only will they be ready to enter the Promised Land.

> And your children shall be shepherds in the wilderness . . . and shall suffer for your faithlessness. . . . *NUMBERS 14:33*

Our text is from the Book of Numbers, the 14th chapter, 33rd verse. We are dealing with a critical period in the life of the nation Israel. Having fled from captivity in Egypt, the nation Israel was trying to enter the promised land. They believed that the land had been promised to them by God. God had led them out of captivity and bondage in Egypt and across the desert wilderness. Now they had to decide whether or not they dared enter the land which had been given to them by God. Last week we dealt with the text, "Let us go back into Egypt," and the fear of the people and their reluctance to make the necessary sacrifices.

Our text reads, "And your children shall be shepherds in the wilderness . . . and shall suffer for your faithlessness." This has to do with the relations which

Reprinted from *The Black Messiah* (New York: Sheed and Ward, Inc., 1968), pp. 266-278, by permission of the publisher. Copyright 1968 by Sheed and Ward, Inc.

each generation has with the generations which have gone before. It is said again in the Bible in different words, "The fathers have eaten sour grapes and the children's teeth are set on edge." We hand down intangible things as well as property to our children. Here in the Book of Numbers, the nation Israel has demonstrated its fear. They have murmured against God, they have murmured against Moses. They have lacked the courage to do the things necessary to secure their freedom. And so their children are to be punished for their faithlessness. Their children are to be shepherds in the wilderness.

If we were to describe the black man's life in America today, we could certainly call ourselves shepherds in the wilderness, propertyless, wandering nomads, going from place to place, dependent upon chance, upon circumstance, without a real place to call home. Shepherds in the wilderness.

To be a shepherd in a rich and fertile land is one thing, but to be a shepherd in a wilderness is quite another. And so God is saying to Israel, "You haven't measured up to the demands that were placed upon you. You were created in the image of God. You were supposed to stand up and be a man. You didn't have the courage, and now you are to be punished. I am sending you back into the wilderness because you lack the courage to do the things necessary to enter into the promised land. And your children will suffer for your faithlessness. You could have fought your way in, if you had had the courage. But you were faithless. And so your children will be shepherds in the wilderness." And God told them that everyone over the age of twenty would have to die before Israel could enter into the promised land, because they bore the mark of slavery. Fear, self-hatred, and self-contempt had been built into them, and they were too old to root it out. So God sent them off to wander in the wilderness for another forty years. Only when those who bore the mark of slavery had died could their children have another chance to fight their way into the promise land.

It is easy for us to take this as just a Bible story recounting the faithlessness of Israel, the fears of Israel, the lack of courage of Israel, and God's punishment. But it is not so easy to recognize the faithlessness of black people here in this country for the past 400 years, and how God could say to us today, in the same way, that our children will be shepherds in the wilderness and will suffer because of our lack of courage. You can ask "When were we ever faithless? We've been oppressed, we've been downtrodden. We've been deprived." And that is true. But the people who accept oppression, who permit themselves to be downtrodden, those people are faithless because God did not make men to be oppressed and to be downtrodden. And many times a man faces the choice between living as a slave and dying as a man. And when we choose to live as slaves, we are faithless and our children will be shepherds in the wilderness.

Sometimes we forget our history. I have a little book which I read from time to time. It is called *One Hundred Years of Lynchings.*[1] Everywhere in America today we hear talk of the necessity for firm government action to end violence in the streets. White lawmakers tell us that it may be necessary to suspend the Constitution to permit police officers to stop and search anybody. Legislators are greatly upset because of crime in the inner cities and the constant danger of riots, and they suggest that mayors be given the power to declare martial law. Combine the right of any mayor to call martial law with the sophisticated weapons that city police are now purchasing, and we have a very dangerous situation which will permit a mayor to call martial law and have police gun down defenseless black citizens with deadly Stoner rifles. White folks say that this is necessary to fight crime in the streets.

I would like to suggest that crime in the streets didn't just start in Watts two years ago. Crime in the streets is not something new in these United States. Crime in the streets is part of the American tradition. It is part of the American way of life. Why, all of a sudden, are people concerned about crime in the street? I give you *One Hundred Years of Lynchings* with the detailed account of 5,000 lynchings in the United States. Not every lynching is included, certainly, because most lynchings were not even reported. Another black man just disappeared. These were just the ones that were written up in the newspapers. You can see the names in the back of the book, page after page after page.

The names of black men and women who were lynched in the United States—you can hardly read them because the print is so small, but you can read the stories which have been reprinted from newspaper accounts. Crime in the streets all over these United States, year after year, in every community! This is a part of American life. This is our history. This is our tradition. This is what we have lived with. The book opens with a recent account. Houston, Texas. "Four masked youths hung a Negro man from a tree by his heels last night and carved two series of KKK's into his chest and stomach after beating him with chains, allegedly in reprisal for recent city demonstrations by Negro students at Texas Southern University." And that wasn't so long ago. Well, that was just one. Maybe you think, "Must have been something wrong with him or they wouldn't have done it."

Here's another one way back in 1880. First Negro at West Point knifed by fellow cadets. Fellow cadets. They are getting ready to be officers in our armies. "West Point, New York, April 15, James Webster Smith, the first colored cadet in the history of West Point was recently taken from his bed, gagged, bound and severely beaten, and then his ears were slit. He said that he cannot identify his assailants, and the other cadets claimed that he did it himself." Crime in the streets. November 22, 1895, "Texans Lynch Wrong

Negro." It didn't make any difference, they went out and got "the right one"
and lynched him too. Crime in the streets.

You bear with me just a minute. "Sam Hock Burned at the Stake. Negro
who was thought to have murdered Alfred Cranford's wife was burned at the
stake one mile and a quarter from Newland, Sunday afternoon, July 23, at
2:30 o'clock. Fully 2,000 people surrounded a small sapling to which he was
fastened and watched the flames eat away his flesh, saw his body mutilated
by knives, and witnessed the contortions of his body in his extreme agony."
This was a black man. Could have been related to any one of you. Two
counties, Campbell and Cowitta, were directly involved in the crime. White
people throughout the entire state "waited with impatience for the moment
when the Negro would pay the penalty for his sinister deed. Everybody waited
for the moment when they were going to lynch him. Such suffering had seldom been witnessed. And through it all the Negro uttered hardly a cry.
Those who witnessed the affair saw the Negro meet his death and saw him
tortured before the flames with unfeigned satisfaction." Crime in the street.

Two thousand people from two counties came together, and publicly
lynched this black man. No masks, no concealments. Crime in the streets.
For sickening sights, harrowing details, and blood curdling incidents, the
burning of Hock is unsurpassed by any occurrence ever heard of in the history of Georgia. He was never identified as the person who participated in
the crime. "Negro Burned Alive in Florida. Second Negro Then Hanged."
Crime in the streets. You go through the book and it makes you sick to the
stomach. You begin to wonder what kind of people these white people are.
You don't know anything about crime in the streets until you go back and
read what white folks have done to black people in this country. You have
to bear all of this in mind just to keep "crime in the streets" in its proper
perspective.

The thing that is amazing to us now is that we permitted it to be done. We were
there. We could have defended these black men who were being tortured and
lynched. But each one of us was an individual. We were taking care of our pre-
cious black skins. There is one story that is enough to make you cry. A white mob
was chasing this very young black boy who had nothing to do with a crime.
He ran to his father's house. And his father ordered him away. "Go away. I
can't help you. If I do, they'll get me too." Can you think of anything more
symbolic of individualism? His own son. "Get away from my house. Hide out
there in the woods and swamps until the dogs find you. I don't want them to
get me, too."

"Your children shall be shepherds in the wilderness and shall suffer for
your faithlessness." For more than 100 years we permitted this kind of thing
to happen. That was our faithlessness. We let it happen! They could go into

the middle of a black community and take a black man out and lynch him.
They would often round up black people from miles around, and make them
watch. That was our faithlessness. And that is what God is talking about. Our
children shall be shepherds in the wilderness *and shall suffer for our faithlessness.*

Now we look around and ask "How did black folks ever get like this?" Why
are we always fighting one another? Why don't we trust each other? Why
aren't we organized? Just think back, for more than 100 years we betrayed
each other daily because we were afraid. We let the white man kill and rape
our brothers and sisters. It is a wonder that we have enough sanity left in
this generation to begin the building of the black nation. We have so much
to forget. It is a wonder that even today we can say, "Fear is gone."

Some of you say, "If God is just he ought to make it possible for us to go
into the promised land right away. We have suffered enough." God cannot
wipe out our weakness and faithlessness to each other. We must make amends
for more than one hundred years. For every moment of cowardice, when our
grandfathers hid under their beds while black men died, there has to be a
moment of courage before we can dare think about entering a promised land.
For every moment when our sons came to us and we turned aside because
we were afraid, we must now go out to meet them wherever they are. For
every moment of cowardice there must be a moment of courage. For every
moment of individualism, there must be a moment of togetherness. We can't
enter the promised land like this. There's too much blood on us. We still
carry the mark of slavery. Each time we stood and watched and did nothing,
it wasn't just the black man being lynched who died. The manhood and soul
of every black man who could resisted and didn't, died at the same time.

Until we make amends, we are not fit for a promised land. Don't ask,
"When is the Kingdom coming?" Ask, "What can I do to wipe out 100 years
of self-hatred, cowardice, and betrayal? What can I do now in my lifetime to
wipe out those years of which I am ashamed, those years in which I was
afraid to defend my brothers and sisters? What can I do?" Don't ask, "Is the
promised land at hand, and do they have the red carpet out for us to march
in?" The red carpet is already there. It is the blood of our mothers, our
fathers, and our grandfathers.

Our children shall be shepherds in the wilderness and shall suffer for our
faithlessness. Our faithlessness has been our individualism, our fear, our self-
hatred, the years when we did nothing. One hundred years of lynchings. It is
a horrible recital. And remember that for every case recounted, there must be
100 or even 1,000 whose stories were never told. But we were there.

Shepherds in the wilderness, not ready for the promised land. What do we
do as we wander in the wilderness? That is the problem that confronts us

today. What do we do today as we wander in the wilderness to which we have been condemned by our own faithlessness? How do we prepare ourselves and our children to end our exile? Today our basic task consists of bringing together a nation, bringing together black men, women, and children with courage, who believe in themselves and who love each other. This means that we must conquer individualism. We must realize that our strength, our power, our hope, everything that we dream of, lies in our coming together. We will wander in the wilderness until we find a way to unite as one people.

We must build a program. It is not enough just to come together, however delightful that may be, or to say "black is beautiful" however wonderful that may be. However warm the feeling may be, upon the basis of that feeling we must build a program. It is easy to take the first steps, to begin to understand that you are somebody, that the white man has been lying to you for 400 years, to look back at history and to understand what the black man has gone through, to rediscover the black man's culture, his glorious heritage, and to realize that we must unite if we are to change conditions by escaping from our powerlessness. But even then we don't really know what to do. How do we build "a nation within a nation," a black nation in the middle of the white man's world? That is the basic problem which must be solved. How do we build a black nation, with economic power, with political power, and with control over our educational institutions, and our police department? How do we take that kind of power? That is the problem. And we will wander in the wilderness until we solve it. We will wander in the wilderness until we learn who we are, how to unite and rise above individualism, and how to program for power.

No one is going to do it for us. There is no blueprint in the white man's book to tell black people how to struggle for power. Most of the things that you read in his books are designed to keep you from discovering how to struggle for either power, freedom, or justice. We must do it for ourselves. But we are easily confused. We say unity must be the main thing because we have been separated so long. We know that all these things couldn't have happened to us if we had been together. We look about us and we realize that almost everything that has happened to us couldn't have happened if we had been together. If we were together, we could very easily control the city of Detroit. If we were together, we could own businesses everywhere. We wouldn't be trying to get one little coop supermarket open, we would be opening them in every section of the city.

But unity is not enough if that unity must be secured by sacrificing the things we believe. This is going to be one of our big problems. Everybody is going to be demanding unity on any basis. "Why don't we get together?" And white folks are going to use it to embarrass us whenever possible, screaming

"Why don't you black folks get together?", until we begin to feel self-con-
scious about not agreeing with every black halfwit who makes a suggestion.
You know how it is everytime you go somewhere now, you get into an
argument. I don't care whether you go out to dinner, or on a date, or to a
club meeting or a card party, or even on the job. Wherever you go, you find
yourself the center of controversy. Perhaps you'd like to suggest that if we
could just soften what we're talking a little bit, we could get unity faster.
That's a great temptation.

But that lowest-common-denominator kind of unity is not the kind we're
looking for. We want to bring all black people together because all black
people believe in something together. Until we share a common faith we can't
have unity. It's not enough to say "Well, come on in. You don't believe in
anything but we'd like to have you anyway just because you're black." We
have more than 1,000 members in the Shrine of the Black Madonna. We
have more than 1,000 members who believe in the nation. Suppose we
brought in 1,500 more who didn't believe in anything. They'd just look
around and say, "That's a booming thing over there. Let's join." And so
1,500 more would come in and pretty soon we wouldn't have a black nation
any more but just a whole mass of black people who don't believe in anything.

True, we would then have 2,500 members, but would we be any stronger?
No, we would be weaker. Because then on every issue we would have to
deal with individualistic black people who don't believe in anything, who
are not committed to anything. At every step we would be held back by
people who do not have any idea of the movement, of what we are trying to
do. They could not participate in a black revolution which they do not
understand. Our strength lies in bringing people into the nation who understand and believe, and in training and developing ourselves as quickly and as
completely as possible. We do not want people who still bear the mark of
slavery in the organizations of which we are a part. We are growing in strength
because we are together in a sense that black people are not together anywhere else in the world.

Now we are moving into the complex and difficult area of building black
power through carefully designed programs of struggle and development. If
we were not together in understanding and commitment, programming would
be impossible. We would have a meeting, we'd start talking about what we're
going to do, and we would have a million different ideas. Agreement would
be impossible. There would be people arguing "Let's not do anything controversial. Let's not make the white man mad. Let's not get out on a limb.
Let's not take any chances." Then we wouldn't be a black nation with discipline, program, and leadership anymore. We would be just another black

church trying to get by from Sunday to Sunday. We believe in the doctrine
of black power as a religious concept revealed to us, as God's chosen people,
in the Old Testament and in the teachings of Jesus.

We are trying to build a black unity that stems from a concept of self-
determination for black people. We have a basic analysis of the world in
which we live. Black people must have black pride. They they must come
together in terms of black unity, and black consciousness, because this is the
basis of black power. And only Black power can make possible self-determination because all of life is a power struggle. If you don't believe that, then you
are not ready for the black nation. You belong out in the wilderness. We
can't go into a promised land with people who don't accept the doctrine of
self-determination—a doctrine which we deduce from the fact that we were
created in the image of God.

We also believe in the doctrine of accountability, which reflects the
teachings of Jesus regarding the responsibilities of love within the nation.
Every black man, woman, and child must feel that he or she is accountable to
the black nation. Even in school a child must feel accountable to the black
nation. If a teacher trying to teach a class is acting a fool (and a whole lot of
them are), a black child must feel the same sense of responsibility that you
would feel on your job if someone was doing something harmful to the black
nation. That black child must tell the teacher, "I am sorry but we can't have
that in this room."

I am not asking black children to be impertinent. The child must say we
can't have that, and when the teacher asks why, the child must be ready to
tell the teacher why. "We can't have that in this room for a variety of reasons.
First, you are teaching us self-contempt and we are through with that. We
do not care to have you giving us symbols of white supremacy and white
superiority." He must be able to explain it to the teacher because most
teachers do not understand and many of our children do understand. They
must be able to defend what they believe in terms of self-determination. And
if it becomes necessary, they must be ready to go to the principal and explain
"I have a backward teacher who is using the wrong books, saying the wrong
things and I don't like it." Then the principal will call the parents. And if you
are an old handkerchief-head parent, you will go to school and say, "Johnny,
I told you to do what the teacher said. Why are you up here causing trouble?"
But if you have any sense and you are in the Nation, you'll go to school and
tell the teacher that "What Johnny said is absolutely correct. I support Johnny
100 percent. Are you going to take care of it here or must we go elsewhere?"

Sometimes we don't think that our children ought to get involved, but
they must. That's where they learn. And when your child is talking to other
children, your child has to know how to argue just like you argue with old

folks. Because if we are going to be a nation, we must understand what we're doing, and your children must understand. All day long out in the street they are being indoctrinated to accept the American dictum, "a nigger ain't nothing." Your child must be able to refute that position, because we have a lot of black kids who think that that is a smart analysis of the racial situation. And if your child can't answer it, he will believe it.

We have to come to the place where building a black nation takes on real meaning in our daily lives, where we know what we stand for, where we can defend it, speak for it, and fight for it if need be. And so, as we go about building the nation, we must understand the kind of unity we're trying to build. We're trying to educate black people everywhere. Perhaps that is an arrogant thing to say. But that's what we are trying to do. And don't think that because a man has a Ph.D., he doesn't need you to educate him. You can go to a learned meeting where only professional black people are holding forth, and most black high school age young people could educate them because all of their basic assumptions are wrong. The same thing is even more true of educated white people.

We're trying to educate black people and we're trying to bring them into the black nation. We're trying to create a black unity that's built on understanding and commitment. I know many black people who understand but are not willing to be committed. Because it's in their self-interest not to be committed. They can make more money not committed than they can committed. Sometimes you wonder how you can argue with a person day after day and always come out where he has lost the argument, only to find him the next day with the same stupid arguments all built up again. He has a reason. His problem is not one of logic, but of self-interest. Look at his total situation. Maybe he's bucking for a promotion. He has some little thing that is separating him from the unity of the black nation.

You have to teach people so that they will understand, but you have to realize also that many black people are not ready because they have commitments on the other side. They're working for the white man. The man is paying them well. A black man told me recently, "I can't afford to get in things. I live good; I've got all I want. And the man takes care of me. I can't afford a black revolution." Then he added, "When you all get the revolution over and you can afford me, then you come get me." I told him, "Don't worry, we'll come and get you all right."

Our basic task is bringing black people together and building a nation. This church is the hub of the emerging black nation. From it we go out in all directions to educate, to set up action centers, to do the things that must be done. I know some of you who have joined during the last few months are impatient to be doing something. You are going through a period of really trying to understand what the nation is all about. During the next three months you will be assigned. We are opening centers all over the city and we are going to need people working in each center. We can't expect everybody in the black community to come in here on Sunday morning. So we are planning centers for the east side, the northwest side, southwest Detroit, Inkster, Royal Oak Township, and Pontiac. In each one we will need fifteen to twenty people working. I know that the transition from listening and talking to working is a difficult one, and some of you all would much rather say "Amen" than be assigned to some district to work with people you never have seen before. But they are our black brothers and sisters and someone must talk to them. We are going to build one black community, one black nation, all stemming from the hub which is at the Shrine of the Black Madonna. That's the only way we can come in out of the wilderness. We are preparing for tomorrow. If we cannot enter into the promised land, we can at least build the institutions that are necessary so that our children can enter in, with courage and knowledge. Our children will not be shepherds in the wilderness because of our faithlessness.

Heavenly Father, we thank thee for strength as we undertake to build a nation, to educate our people, to build black consciousness, black pride, black unity, and black power, that we may obtain self-determination. We thank thee and we understand that these tasks which we undertake for ourselves are thy will. We do these things in thy name, and in the name of the son, the black Messiah, Jesus. Help us and bind us together. Give us the commitment necessary to do the things which must be done. All this we ask in his name. Amen.

NOTE

1. R. Ginzberg, *One Hundred Years of Lynchings* (New York, 1962).

Index

abolitionists: and Christianity, 151, 339; and slave church, 35-36, 71

adaptive phrase of revitalization movements, 235-237, 244

African Baptist Church, 71

African Episcopal Church of St. Thomas, 50

African heritage: attitude of black Americans toward, 166; attitudes of slaveowners toward, 335-336; and black church, 21, 33, 40-41; of black Jews, 203-204

Africanisms in black church, 43-48, 58-59, 60-61, 167-170, 172, 173*n*

African Methodist Episcopal Church, 19-20, 34, 42, 147, 338

African Methodist Episcopal Zion Church, 20, 21, 42, 147

Africans, *see* slaves

afterlife, 151; and Father Divine cult, 191-192; and protest, 157-158; and slave religion, 56; *see also* otherworldliness

age(s): of church board members, 105-106; determined by Father Divine cult, 179; and militancy, 155-156, 156*t*, 277-278; and religiosity, 103-106, 155-156, 156*t*; *see also* black youth, older people, rural youth

Alabama Christian Movement for Human Rights, 293

Alinsky, Saul, 305-306

Allen, Richard, 20, 49-50, 339

anti-Semitism: and black Jews, 208*n*-209*n*; and black militants, 25-26

Armageddon, 215-216, 230, 237

assimilation: black church as barrier to, 134-135; and Black Muslims, 222; and gospel singing, 136-137; and new black middle class, 137-141; and riots, 300-301; and role of black church, 308

associational involvement: as measure of group involvement, 7; and social class, 127-218

Association for Black Seminarians, 23, 24

auxiliaries, 112-113, 115

Baldwin, James, 24, 151

baptism(s): and African heritage, 46-48; and black religion, 168; and conversion of slaves, 59, 247; of white and black Catholics compared, 251*t*

Baptist church: antislavery sentiment of, 55; attendance of blacks and whites compared in, 8; auxiliaries in, 113; black converts to, 31, 59; of blacks and whites compared, 45; in Chicago, 267; clash between old and new in, 104-106; and communion, 108; funeral services of, 109; origins in slavery, 33; reasons for black membership in, 46-48, 168; and revivalism, 6

behavior codes, *see* moral standards, morality, religious bans

Benezet, Anthony, 50, 51

Bible: in black churches, 103; and Black Muslims, 215-216; in militant sermons, 355-356; and protest, 154

Birmingham, Alabama, 292-298

black bishops, 32, 148

black business, 133, 138; and black church, 87, 289-290; in North and South compared, 300

Black Catholic Clergy Caucus, 23, 25

black Catholics, 34, 147; data on, 248-251; historical background of, 247; increase in numbers of, 250*t*, 251-253; in lower classes, 142*n*; in new black middle class, 140-141; by region, 249*t*

black caucuses, 23-25, 27

Black Caucus of the Unitarian-Universalist Association, 23

black church: and African heritage, 21,

integration: *(cont'd)*
  effects of, 131-133; of white church,
  338-339
intellectuals: attitude toward black
  church, 146, 264*n*; and Black Muslims,
  235, 237
Interfaith City-Wide Coordinating Committee against Poverty, 26

Jehovah's Witnesses, 153, 154, 247
Jews: and black militants, 25-26; relations
  with black Jews, 199; strength of
  communal bonds of, 7; *see also* anti-
  Semitism, black Jews, Commandment
  Keepers cult
Johnson, Mordecai, 257-258
Jones, Absalom, 49-50
Jones, Charles Colcock, 56-57

Kent study of differential religious behavior, 106-113, 243-244; auxiliaries
  in, 112-113; and church attendance,
  100-102; and meaning of religion, 102-
  106; and money-raising activities, 114-
  116; and prayer bands 110-111; and
  relationship of religiosity to needs, 117
King, Dr. Martin Luther. Jr., 8, 144, 153,
  158, 302; and black church, 302-303,
  348; death of, 17. 18, 21; and Gandhi's
  philosophy, 137; letter to clergymen
  from, 292-298; and Malcolm X, 236;
  and protest tradition of Baptist church,
  20
Krueger, E. T., 6, 9
Ku Klux Klan, 214-215, 295, 357

labor unions, black members of, 134, 167
laws: against slaves and free blacks officiating at funerals, 70-71; attitude of
  black ministers toward, 352; and nonviolent action, 294-295
leaders, of America. 317-318; black clergy
  as, 283-285; of black community, 259,
  273; of Black Muslims, 212, 229, 235;
  political responsibility of, 302-303; of
  protest movement, 212; recruitment in
  black churches, 71-72, 345
Lenski, Gerhard, 6-7
Lewis, Hylan. 243-244
liturgical churches, ritual elements of,
  122-122*t*
liturgy, classification of churches by use
  of, 121, 122*t*, 123*t*, 124*t*, 125*t*
Louis X, 231

Louisiana, black Catholics in, 247, 248
lower-class blacks: associational life of,
  128; and Black Muslims, 219-220, 229,
  230; contacts with white community,
  132; and gospel singing, 135-137; and
  role of black church, 143-144
Lyell, Charles, 68, 71
lynchings, 215, 357, 359

magic, 6, 60; and Father Divine, 186
Magnolia myth, 213-214
Malcolm X, 226, 228, 229, 230, 235,
  237. 239*n*
marriage, attitude of Father Divine cult
  toward, 171, 180
Maryland, black Catholics in, 247, 248
mass media, tasks of, 322
Matthew, Rabbi Wentworth Arthur, 195*ff*
May, Benjamin E., 83, 84, 88, 164, 165,
  167, 258. 271-272, 339, 344
"mazeway" concept, 227, 232, 237
membership in black churches, 82, 89*n*;
  in Black Muslims, 228; by denominations in Philadelphia, 266; dual, 141;
  in Father Divine cult, 186-188, 191;
  in Harlem, 147; in Kent, 101-102, 107;
  maintenance of, 78; of new black
  middle class, 140-141; by sex, 106*t*;
  of slaves, 69; social reasons for, 90*n*;
  in South, 32
Methodist Church: in Chicago, 267; and
  Consultation on Church Union, 330-
  331; and conversion of slaves, 31, 59;
  origins in slavery, 33; recruitment of
  seminary students by, 272-273; relation to slave church, 33-34; and revivalism, 6; and segregation, 149
Messenger, the, *see* Elijah Muhammad
messianic stage of revitalization movement, 227, 232
MFDP, *see* Mississippi Freedom Democratic Party
middle-class black Americans, 27-28; attitude toward black ministers, 269; and
  Catholic Church, 252; membership in
  Father Divine cult, 192; new, *see* new
  middle class; relations with Negro
  masses. 314; and religious bans, 86;
  upper- and lower- compared, 127
migration to North, 214-215; causes of,
  300; and rise of storefront churches,
  241-242
militancy: of Black Muslims, 228-229;
  definition of, 286*n*; and social and